The 'Lucy Poems':
A Case Study in Literary Knowledge

MARK JONES

The 'Lucy Poems': A Case Study in Literary Knowledge

UNIVERSITY OF TORONTO PRESS
Toronto Buffalo London

Toronto Buffalo London
Printed in Canada

ISBN 0-8020-0434-2

Printed on acid-free paper

Canadian Cataloguing in Publication Data

Jones, Mark, 1957–
The Lucy poems : a case study in literary knowledge

Includes bibliographical references and index.
ISBN 0-8020-0434-2

1. Wordsworth, William, 1770–1850 – Criticism and interpretation – History. 2. Wordsworth, William, 1770–1850. Lyrical ballads. I. Title.

PR5887.3.J65 1995 821′.7 C95-930345-6

University of Toronto Press
acknowledges the financial assistance to its publishing program of the Canada Council and the Ontario Arts Council.

This book has been published with the help of a grant from the Canadian Federation for the Humanities, using funds provided by the Social Sciences and Humanities Research Council of Canada.

This book is lovingly dedicated
to Lucile Irene Jones
and to the memory of Jack Kullman Jones,
extraordinary parents.

Contents

Preface

Since this book focuses on what we know as Wordsworth's 'Lucy Poems,' I stress at the outset that it is not primarily a study of William Wordsworth. It is a study of reading, editing, and criticism amid the rise of the institutional study of English literature *since* Wordsworth. The 'Lucy Poems' never existed as such in Wordsworth's day, but were invented by Victorian critics and editors shortly after his death. The text Wordsworth created is more complicated and less consistent than one would guess from the group of five lyrics now found in class-room anthologies and selections: 'Strange fits of passion have I known,' 'She dwelt among the untrodden ways,' 'I travelled among unknown men,' 'Three years she grew in sun and shower,' and 'A slumber did my spirit seal.'[1] To create this lyric group or 'sequence,' editors have had to gather poems the artist dispersed, to rule out several border-cases (e.g., 'Lucy Gray,' 'Among all lovely things,' 'Louisa'), and to rule an important one in: 'A slumber,' though it makes no mention of 'Lucy,' has become the best known 'Lucy Poem' of any. That the 'Lucy Poems' are an editorial fiction might not be front-page news in a small town on a slow day; indeed, since the grouping has been deconstructed before, this should not be news at all.[2] But the apparent frivolousness of this fiction makes one curious about its reasons, and particularly about the reasons for its persistence within an institution that does know better and that has repudiated, as mystifications, so many of its other inheritances from nineteenth-century criticism. This study not only examines the formation and persistence of the 'Lucy Poems' grouping, but uses it as a case to illustrate, sometimes to arraign, the modern literature institution's will to knowledge. I argue, in brief, that the Victorian 'Lucy Poems' grouping originated as a simplification of an intolerably indeterminate text and that it has been perpetuated because, in facilitating interpretation, it has also served to legitimate 'English' as a 'discipline' capable of producing 'knowledge.' Since this may seem like a lot to hang on such a tiny 'case,' I hasten to make two clarifications. First, the extrapolation of large conclusions from small evidence is not entirely my own, but is a prominent feature of the 'case' I investigate: it belongs to the many theorists who use one or more of the 'Lucy Poems' to 'exemplify,' 'illustrate,' or 'prove' their interpretive theories and, by extension, literature's interpretability. Second, this study's conclusions are based not on the tiny case of the 'Lucy Poems,' but rather on a broad range of critical and editorial practice surrounding those poems. The poems are my focus, not my evidence.

In other words, this is a case study not of the 'Lucy Poems' but of their institutional management. In this sense, Wordsworth's role is incidental: I suppose that a study of the reception of Coleridge's 'conversation poems' or of Keats's 1819 odes might come to similar conclusions. Yet in some ways the 'Lucy Poems' provide an especially appropriate and revealing case. Not only are they manageable in size, not only is their critical history eventful, but as part of the 1800 *Lyrical Ballads*, they participate in a historic 'experiment' in literary reception. Wordsworth calls the *Lyrical Ballads* 'experiments' in both his 1798 'Advertisement' and his 1800 'Preface.' The Preface questions the notion that authors lie under a 'formal engagement' to 'gratify' readers' expectations, and by implication it substitutes a model of reception involving authorial provocations and a rather free reader-response.[3] Individually indeterminate because of specific 'simplicities' of diction and syntax, and indeterminate en masse because of the uncertainty of their intertextual relations, the lyrics (and the specific arrangements) from which the 'Lucy Poems' group has been created might best be understood as an experiment in the provocation-response model envisioned by the 'Preface,' and as having, in a sense, invited all the editorial and interpretive efforts this study investigates. But the predominant nature of this interpretive effort is, I don't know how ironically, to repress consciousness of the indeterminacies that provoke it. My first chapter is therefore necessarily about Wordsworth in that it seeks to recover the indeterminacy of that initial textual situation. It is a preliminary attempt to de-simplify and de-interpret the poems so that the historical accretions of interpretation may become visible.[4]

The rest of this study traces the editorial and critical response to the indeterminacy of these poems. Since Barbara Herrnstein Smith isolated 'closure' as a formal feature, romanticists have often observed that romantic texts are less 'closed' than others, meaning especially that they are more difficult, more resistant to conclusive interpretation.[5] I tend to share this view, especially in thinking that such resistance is one thing that makes the history of the 'Lucy Poems' interesting. Yet such generalizations about closure often treat it wholly as an objective textual function by omitting the factor of the reader. Despite the existence of 'interpretive communities,' readers do vary, so that a text which one reader finds closed, another will find open. In tracing the history of such a small corpus as the 'Lucy Poems,' the real closure-variation between interpreters becomes obvious as a recurring tension between individuals (or communities) that can and those that cannot tolerate indeterminacy. Chapters 2 to 5, chronological but not entirely sequential, explore versions of this polarization.[6]

As chapter 2 shows, mainstream Victorian critics typically cite the 'Lucy Poems' to illustrate moral or biographical arguments, a purpose that dictates unambiguous appropriations of 'meaning.' In close parallel, Victorian editors effaced important elements of textual uncertainty to define the 'Lucy Poems,' including 'A slumber,' as a 'sequence,' and thus bent lyric to the more popular and consensual conventions and comprehensions of narrative form. Chapter 3 explores Victorian parody and allusion as counter-culture to these authoritative modes of criticism. Though modern scholarship tends to view parody as a disguised form of commentary, a survey of 'Lucy Poems' parodies suggests that the best of them, such as Samuel Butler's mock-reading of 'She dwelt,' shun commentary and indeed seem designed to mimic, not other texts, but their commentators. If parody is, as some claim, a form of criticism, I argue that it is an anti-authoritative, anti-definitive form; the very antagonism between it and authoritative interpretation makes it, like the 'Lucy Poems' themselves, useful for illustrating the repressive simplifications of the interpretive regime. I show how interpreters, theorists, and anthologists have collaboratively contained and trivialized parody since the Victorian period, especially in representing it as a genre, and contend that we therefore read the real parody of this period not in the anthologies of verse-parody but in nominally non-parodic forms – in mere poetry and (as Mikhail Bakhtin would suggest) in novelistic allusion. Thus, among the strongest nineteenth-century 'parodies' of the 'Lucy Poems' are Mary Shelley's *The Last Man* and Herman Melville's *Pierre; or, the Ambiguities* – intertexts that magnify rather than resolve the poems' indeterminacies.

Chapters 4 and 5 explore similar polarizations in two series of modern commentaries. Tracing the ways in which the institution's desire for disciplinary status has affected actual interpretive practice, chapter 4 explores a long and active debate over the general determinacy and actual meaning of 'A slumber.' E.D. Hirsch, Jr, initiated this debate in 1960 by using readings of 'A slumber' to illustrate the possibility of 'objective interpretation,' and he has since been answered by theorist-critics who would seem to represent a broad range of the theoretical spectrum, from objectivism (Monroe Beardsley) to subjectivism (Norman Holland). Yet even those who seem most opposed to Hirsch's objectivism join him in his claims to 'knowledge' and 'discipline'; and in the interest of these claims all disputants, even those who stress indeterminacy in theory, minimize in practice the real obstacles to deciphering 'A slumber.' Thus, ironically, despite all its insuperable difficulties, 'A slumber' has been constructed as a set-piece for illustrating interpretability; nothing, I suggest, could be more revealing about the depth of the institution's will to knowledge or about the devious rhetoric of this knowledge's production.

Chapter 5 turns from meta-disciplinary argumentation to look more closely at the actual meanings attributed to the 'Lucy Poems' in the twentieth century. The chief determinant of interpretive changes has inevitably, I argue, been the shift in our presuppositions about the nature of 'nature' and about what Wordsworth himself understood by that concept. While the Victorians spoke optimistically of Lucy's education by nature, rarely even acknowledging her death at the end of 'Three years,' it has been impossible for interpreters since about 1930 to overlook her death or to assume or accept the benignity of Wordsworthian nature. A reconception of Wordsworthian nature is reflected both in transcendental symbolist readings, which suppose that material nature and even incarnate human existence are for Wordsworth mere 'signposts' to the infinite (the tradition of A.C. Bradley and David Ferry), and in new-allegorist readings, which suppose that 'nature' is an effect of linguistic *différance* (the tradition of Paul de Man). Both of these traditions read Lucy as mere signifier and deny her the status of a loved human and a woman in the interest of producing conclusive interpretations. They may be contrasted, I argue, with more dialectical readings (a tradition exemplified by Geoffrey Hartman) that posit Wordsworth's double valuation of nature, and likewise of Lucy, as both being and meaning. Such readings not only seek to re-humanize the poetry in response to symbolist and allegorical abstraction; they also imply the insufficiency of any single valuation, thus leaving the interpretive process radically open. In some degree they emulate Wordsworth's own stereoptical mode of reading – 'A Spirit, yet a Woman too!' – acknowledging both the necessity of interpretation as process and its insufficiency as product. It remains to say only that this study endorses intertextual and dialectical interpretive modes for their wisdom *about* interpretation, which lies partly in knowing what knowledge an interpreter must not claim.

This study began with a suggestion by Karl Kroeber for something handier. A very different version was filed as my doctoral dissertation at Columbia University in 1988. Kroeber's explicit guidance has always been generous in every sense of the word, but still greater has been his contribution by example, both as scholar and as teacher. Notwithstanding the pitfalls on which this study dwells, I have never doubted, thanks to him, that the study of literature may, at its best, deserve its place among both the disciplines and the humanities.

This study is indebted also to those who examined its ancestor the dissertation, Carl Woodring, Otis Fellows, John Middendorf, and Michael Riffaterre; to generous good advice from G. Thomas Tanselle; and to a sustaining circle of friends and characters at Columbia, particularly Mike Neth, Steve Jones, and Jay Williams. Mark Langlet has been a brilliant friend and advisor in matters of literary theory and criticism. Several friends and colleagues at Queen's, Maggie Berg, Bert Hamilton, Elizabeth Hanson, Fred Lock, Peter Sabor, and Paul Stevens, have generously given advice, information, or criticism on parts. Tilottama Rajan and Jack Stillinger both gave their valuable time to read a longer version of the whole, much to the advantage and shortening of the present one. Sincere thanks to all of these, as well as to Kerry McSweeney, Les Monkman, Mark Reed, and Mel Wiebe for advice and support along the way.

Further back and farther away, this book is indebted as well to John Cooper, Greg Goekjian, and the late James Hart and James Lill, all of Portland State University. To students of literature, who are too frequently also the students of debt, it may not seem strange to see so small a property mortgaged to so many. In any case, this book owes everything all over again to my family, especially to my mother and father, and to my endlessly generous brother Don. And yet again to my wife Patricia Rae, who, while teaching and pursuing her own research, still managed to play that tough double role of critic, muse, and critic. So be it when we shall grow old.

I am grateful to the reference and inter-library loan departments at the Columbia University Libraries and to the librarians of Cornell University, the British Museum, the Bodleian at Oxford, and the Beinecke Rare Book and Manuscript Library at Yale. I am grateful too for financial assistance in the form of a President's Fellowship from Columbia University, a Richard M. Weaver Fellowship from the Intercollegiate Studies Institute, an Advisory Research Council grant from Queen's University, and a grant in aid of publication from the Canadian Federation of the Humanities.

A portion of chapter 2, section 2, has appeared in *boundary 2* 18 (1991), and a version of a portion of chapter 3 is forthcoming in *Representations*. I wish to thank the editors for permission to reprint.

Texts and Abbreviations

Full bibliographical information appears in the Works Cited list at the end of this volume. Except where otherwise specified, I cite the latest texts of Wordsworth's poems from *The Poetical Works*, ed. Ernest de Selincourt and Helen Darbishire (abbreviated *PW*), and from the Norton *Prelude*. Editions of the five lyrics usually grouped as the 'Lucy Poems' appear in an Appendix to this volume, and these are used throughout, save that in quoting critics I have reproduced their quotations.

Prose refers to *The Prose Works of William Wordsworth*, ed. W.J.B. Owen and Jane Worthington Smyser, and 'Owen' to *Wordsworth's Literary Criticism*, ed. W.J.B. Owen, which is cited only for the 1805 version of the Preface to *Lyrical Ballads*. *Letters* refers to *The Letters of William and Dorothy Wordsworth* or, as context makes clear, to the *Collected Letters of Samuel Taylor Coleridge*. Other short forms are as follows:

BL Samuel Taylor Coleridge, *Biographia Literaria*
CEY Mark Reed, *Wordsworth: Chronology of the Early Years, 1770–1799*
CMY Mark Reed, *Wordsworth: Chronology of the Middle Years, 1800–1815*
DI Mikhail Bakhtin, *The Dialogic Imagination*
RR *The Romantics Reviewed*, ed. Donald Reiman
WP Geoffrey Hartman, *Wordsworth's Poetry, 1787–1814*
TT *The Three Trials of William Hone* (three separately paginated pamphlets)

The 'Lucy Poems'

In an obscure corner of a Country Church-yard I once espied, half-overgrown with Hemlock and Nettles, a very small Stone laid upon the ground, bearing nothing more than the name of the Deceased with the date of birth and death, importing that it was an Infant which had been born one day and died the following. I know not how far the Reader may be in sympathy with me, but more awful thoughts of rights conferred, of hopes awakened, of remembrances stealing away or vanishing were imparted to my mind by that Inscription there before my eyes than by any other that it has ever been my lot to meet with upon a Tomb-stone.

Wordsworth, 'Essays upon Epitaphs' III (*Prose* 2:93)

Even so unambiguous an object as a plain colour, it has been found, can arouse in different persons and in the same person at different times extremely different states of mind. From this result it may seem no illegitimate step to conclude that highly complex objects, such as pictures, will arouse a still greater variety of responses, a conclusion very awkward for any theory of criticism. ... But just here a crucial point arises. There seems to be good reason to suppose that the more simple the object contemplated the more varied the responses will be which can be expected from it. For it is difficult, perhaps impossible, to contemplate a comparatively simple object by itself. Inevitably it is taken by the contemplator into some context, and made part of some larger whole. ... A single word by itself, let us say 'night,' will raise almost as many different thoughts and feelings as there are persons who hear it. The range of variety with a single word is very little restricted. But put it into a sentence and the variation is narrowed; put it into the context of a whole passage, and it is still further fixed; and let it occur in such an intricate whole as a poem and the responses of competent readers may have a similarity which only its occurrence in such a whole can secure.

I.A. Richards, *Principles of Literary Criticism* 4–5

1 'Mysterious Silence': The 'Lucy Poems' as Provocations

Poetics and interpretation are often considered antithetical: as an account of a literature's construction, its provenance, purposes, and strategies, a poetics may appear to have a neutral, descriptive status that an interpretation cannot have. But in critical practice, accounts of poetics are generally preliminary to interpretation, guiding and justifying certain kinds of approach to a literature; moreover, they are necessarily based on interpretation. To 'describe' a poetics is to prescribe a hermeneutics; conversely, it is strategic for a hermeneutics (or even for a particular interpretation) to present itself as a descriptive poetics.[1] The argument of this chapter, that a provocation poetics underlies the 'Lucy Poems,' is not hermeneutically innocent: in attributing the radical obscurity of these poems to a specific artistic design, I *read* this obscurity as a device to provoke the constructive activity of readers. But while the 'poetics' I propose here is admittedly a reading, it is meant to be a minimal one, its purpose being merely to highlight and explain the history of interpretive activity these texts have elicited.

For any study of interpretation seems to demand that one first distinguish it from what it interprets; but how can one appeal to the poems themselves rather than to one's own interpretations? In the spirit of Fredric Jameson's comment that 'only another, stronger interpretation can overthrow ... an interpretation already in place' (*Political Unconscious* 13), I suggest that only through counter-interpretations can one know where interpretations have been. But rather than offer a 'stronger interpretation,' a provocation poetics of the 'Lucy Poems,' which accounts for them while emphasizing how much they do *not* reveal, may serve as a strategically minimal counter-interpretation: minimal enough to reveal interpretive accretions, interpretive enough to justify or make sense of these accretions – that is, as interpolations that are 'called-for.'

The initial problem of precipitating interpretations 'already in place' is more considerable than it would seem if we regarded interpretation as a distinct activity that was always declared or that was confined to scholarly journals. But it is interpretation's nature to attribute itself to the interpreted; the most enduring readings are the least visible as such. To use Wolfgang Iser's model of texts with provocative 'gaps' (*The Implied Reader* 34, 38, 40), reading not only fills such gaps, but in so doing conceals both their existence and its own, paradoxically clarifying the text by obscuring the very features that demand clarification. In the case of the 'Lucy Poems,' the most basic inventions of the interpreters, such as the grouping itself and the reference of 'A slumber' to Lucy, have thus come to be more or less 'obvious' features of the text itself. The starkest aspect of this paradox lies in the dismissal of Wordsworth's quasi-ordering of these poems in favour of more definite 'Lucy Poems' groupings. Wordsworth's odd ordering both requires interpretation and gives more freedom to do so than is comfortable; yet precisely to justify more restrictive editions, critics have rejected Wordsworth's ordering as a dictatorial intrusion of his editorial (rather than authorial) intention. Thus not only is the uncertainty of the text reduced, but it is reduced by a fiction that it never existed. The new groupings, meanwhile, guide and constrict interpretive activity under the guise of removing Wordsworth's interpretive impositions and returning to the text itself.

A central provocative feature of the lyrics that came to be considered as the 'Lucy Poems' is the silence of their author, both within them and about them. Romantic and Victorian critics frequently remark the poems' reticence, though they disagree whether it is a virtue. In 1851, someone praises 'the deep but subdued and *silent* fervour' of 'She dwelt' (the favourite of early readers).[2] Another admirer writing in 1849 praises stanza 3:

> That is true pathos. We are moved to our soul's centre by sorrow expressed as that is; for, without periphrasis or wordy anguish, without circumlocution of officious and obtrusive, and therefore, artificial grief; the mourner gives sorrow words. ... But he does it in words as few as may be: how intense their beauty! (Parson 294)

Equally enthusiastic is John Wilson's comment of ten years earlier:

> ... how powerfully pathetic! ... Of the conclusion, it may perhaps be said, that

it represents the sorrows of bereavement in the only way in which this can perfectly be done, by suggesting to the reader's mind the strength of their influence, from the impossibility of attempting to express them. (Wilson, *Essays* 3:328)

These comments on 'She dwelt' are true in some measure of all five 'Lucy Poems.' 'The difference to me!' is terse – at least one parodist observes that it goes unspoken whether 'the difference' is for better or worse.[3] The other poems are still less explicit. 'Three years,' remarking the present 'quiet' of nature and the 'memory of what has been, / And never more will be,' merely suggests the 'difference to me'; 'I travelled' does not actually state that Lucy is absent; and 'A slumber' and 'Strange fits' are curtailed on the suggestion of death.[4]

If the early commentators praise the poems' reserve for its evocation of pathos, the silence they emphasize explains other effects as well. The scepticism of Thomas Powell, writing in 1831 as 'Pierce Pungent,' makes this clearer than positive judgments can:

Although ['A slumber'] stands by itself, and is without title prefixed, yet we are to know, from the penetration of Mr. Wordsworth's admirers, that it is a sequel to the other deep poems that precede it, and is about one Lucy, who is dead. From the table of contents, however, we are informed by the author that it is about 'A Slumber;' for this is the actual title which he has condescended to give it, to put us out of pain as to what it is about. (563)[5]

Powell is right to emphasize, in his sarcastic way, the difficulty in distinguishing a minimalist text from its most generous readings. Lacking even a title, the poem is miserly with information, and Powell may be justified in suspecting that it gets credit from 'Mr. Wordsworth's admirers' for being deeper than it is. Even today it remains uncertain whether 'A slumber' is a 'Lucy Poem' and consequently 'what it is about.' How can it be profound if we don't know what it says? But while Powell specifies the usual obstacles to understanding this poem, his negative judgment of it could not be more singular. Readers who continue to debate the meaning of 'A slumber' never question its greatness, and that value judgment may be more due to the spareness Powell ridicules than in spite of it.

This fundamental obscurity underlying a rich critical tradition is an important feature of all the 'Lucy Poems.' Even the silence surrounding them is mysterious. David Simpson remarks on the unusual 'wealth of information' that generally characterizes Wordsworth studies: 'we hardly ever find ourselves reading Wordsworth as we read, for example Shakespeare, about whose biography so little is known' ('Public Virtues' 171). In this respect the 'Lucy Poems' are an exception. Most were written during Wordsworth's residence in Goslar, Germany, in the winter of 1798–9, but this period is among the thinner places in our knowledge of his activities. The usual contemporary sources – letters, journals, memoirs, and notes – offer almost nothing. Wordsworth's one reference to poems 'about Lucy,' dating from 1809 when he was pondering a new poetical ordering, fails to say which poems he would have included under this umbrella (*Letters* 2:335). Even the notes he dictated to Isabella Fenwick in 1841, which comment generously on the biographical background, literary sources, and purposes of many poems, including several written in Germany, fall almost silent when it comes to the 'Lucy Poems.' Of 'Three years,' Wordsworth comments: '1799. Composed in the Hartz Forest.' The note for 'Strange fits,' 'She dwelt,' and 'I travelled' reads: 'These three poems were written in Germany, 1799.' For 'A slumber' there is no note at all (Grosart 3:23, 39).[6]

There are many poems for which Wordsworth provided no notes, but his silence on the 'Lucy Poems' has been a source of wonder; indeed, it has probably been more significant for vigilant readers than anything that might have been stated explicitly. As Thomas De Quincey notes in 1839,

> he always preserved a mysterious silence on the subject of that 'Lucy,' repeatedly alluded to or apostrophized in his poems, and I have heard, from gossiping people about Hawkshead, some snatches of tragical story, which, after all, might be an idle semi-fable, improved out of slight materials.[7]

It is not known whether De Quincey questioned Wordsworth about Lucy without success, or whether he refers merely to the general silence which all readers experience. Since the men were in close communication for years, the former is possible, and if Wordsworth made Lucy a *personal* secret, the popular assumption that he was concealing biography may be correct. But not all silences are 'mysterious,' and it is equally possible that the 'mysterious silence' surrounding Lucy has artistic, and specifically heuristic, motivations.[8]

1. The 'Lucy Poems'? Wordsworth's Quasi-Grouping

It has long been settled among editors and critics, with few exceptions, that the 'Lucy Poems' consist of 'Strange fits,' 'She dwelt,' 'I travelled,' 'Three years,' and 'A slumber' – most commonly in that order. So well established is this grouping in the public mind that some anthologies even present the five lyrics as numbered sections of a larger super-poem.[9] But so explicit and definite a grouping was never made in authorial editions or described by Wordsworth. Apparently an invention of Victorian criticism, the 'Lucy' group was first suggested, however dimly, in Powell's essay of 1831, and first explicitly proposed by Margaret Oliphant in 1871. Though Palgrave's *Golden Treasury* (1861) had printed all except 'Strange fits' together, the grouping as it exists today was not seen in print until Matthew Arnold's influential selection of Wordsworth's poems appeared in 1879. The actual genesis of the grouping is explored in the next chapter; here I wish only to examine Wordsworth's non-grouping of these poems in relation to his general poetical arrangements to show that, while the 'Lucy' grouping is not authorial, it is not entirely a freak of criticism either. Though in editions such as Arnold's the grouping undeniably falsifies Wordsworth's text, the association of these poems in interpretation is a foreseeable consequence of Wordsworth's practice, and might even be construed as fulfilling his purpose.

In repeatedly suggesting or announcing the death of a beloved woman – yet so nebulously that we may think her a child rather than a woman (and John D. Rea thinks she is a he, Hartley Coleridge) – Wordsworth could hardly have failed to see that he was authoring a mystery. His peculiar ways of arranging the poems seem calculated to aggravate this mystery. To return to the poem that bewildered Powell, 'A slumber' does not name Lucy, yet it uses the pronoun 'she' three times. Considered alone, the poem may seem to describe a mystical trance, 'she' being taken to refer to the speaker's 'spirit' of line 1. Yet following poems on Lucy, as it always did – 'She dwelt' in *Lyrical Ballads*, and 'Three years' thereafter – the poem may seem to refer to her. Asking which is the real poem is like asking what a chameleon's natural colour is. Critics have argued persuasively for either reading, but the fundamental question is why Wordsworth placed the poem as he did if he intended the former reading or why he did not refer it more definitely to Lucy if he intended the latter. Why is it not placed between two 'Lucy Poems,' or why is Lucy not named at least in a title, as Powell seems to wonder? The issue is similar with the entire grouping: if Wordsworth meant for the poems to be amalgamated, why did he not group them himself? And if not, why did he repeatedly refer in them to Lucy, and associate them all with one another at various times?

One answer is that Wordsworth tossed the poems off and thereafter disregarded them. Frederika Beatty suggests that Wordsworth 'regarded these lyrics lightly' because his first recorded mention of any of them, in a letter to Coleridge, calls 'She dwelt' and 'Strange fits' 'two or three little Rhyme poems which I hope will amuse you' (Beatty 44; *Letters* 1:236). Mary Moorman (1:422) dismisses that remark as a self-defensive depreciation of the lyrics: Coleridge hoped Wordsworth was writing *The Recluse.* But the comment itself may not be so disparaging as it sounds. Wordsworth regarded pleasure as the immediate aim of poetry, and in any case he is describing inferior early versions that might more fairly be called 'little Rhyme poems.'[10] On the whole it is hard to be convinced that Wordsworth could long neglect poems so highly praised by contemporaries including Dorothy Wordsworth, Coleridge, Lamb, and Crabb Robinson, and singled out for notice in a positive review (see chapter 2, sections 2–3).

More specifically, the care that Wordsworth took in revising each poem and in arranging and rearranging his corpus makes it seem unlikely that he overlooked the grouping that has seemed so natural to Arnold and subsequent editors.[11] Indeed, his second thoughts about the placement of 'I travelled' and 'A slumber' suggest that he considered but rejected such a grouping. In a letter of [29] April 1801, he transcribed 'I travelled' (the only 'Lucy Poem' not in the 1800 volume) for Mary Wordsworth as 'a short poem to be read after "She dwelt among"' (*Letters* 1:333). Mary accordingly wrote the poem in after 'She dwelt' in a copy of *Lyrical Ballads* (1800) presented to Isabella Addison in 1802 (now at St John's College, Cambridge).[12] This presents the tentative order: 'Strange fits,' 'She dwelt,' 'I travelled,' 'A slumber,' and (separated by nineteen poems) 'Three years.' Ernest de Selincourt takes the letter to Mary as proof that 'I travelled' was 'written shortly before' the letter was sent, and thus as explaining 'its absence from the 1800 vol[ume]s.'[13] But it should not be inferred that Wordsworth would have placed it in *Lyrical Ballads* if he could, for two more editions appeared in 1802 and 1805, and 'I travelled' still did not appear until *Poems, in Two Volumes* (1807), where it followed 'Among all lovely things my Love had been.'

At one point, apparently, 'I travelled' was intended for the 1802 volume and then deliberately cancelled; this cancellation is significant not just for this poem, but for the 'Lucy' grouping as a whole. There is a tradition, though without hard evidence, that

Wordsworth sent the MS of this poem to the printer of 1802, instructing him to insert it on the page following 'A slumber did my spirit seal.' A pen however is run through the MS – which is in W[ordsworth]'s own hand.

These are the words of a note by J. Dykes Campbell from about 1868, as quoted by Jared Curtis, who finds 'no reason' to doubt them ('A Note' 197–8; see also Butler and Green xxxv, 820). (The manuscript in question was among the Longman manuscripts purchased by Yale University in 1934, but it was lost shortly before Yale's purchase.) The significance of such a placement of 'I travelled' was noted in 1904, when Lane Cooper objected to Walter Raleigh's *Wordsworth* (1903) that 'A slumber' is not a 'Lucy Poem,' and an unidentified respondent (presumably Raleigh) countered:

That ['A slumber'] was meant to form one of the 'Lucy' group we have no doubt whatsoever. Another member of the group – 'I travelled ... ' – was written in 1802; and in his instructions to the printer of the 'Lyrical Ballads,' vol. ii., second edition, published in that year, Wordsworth directs that 'I travelled ... ' is to follow 'A slumber ... ' (Cooper, 'Raleigh's' 17)

That is, in the 1802 edition 'A slumber' would not just have followed poems naming Lucy but would have been sandwiched between them, literally and graphically included. This account confirms Campbell's description of the lost manuscript, yet that the manuscript was cancelled prevents its carrying any weight as a sign of final intention. In any case 'A slumber' was never surrounded by poems mentioning Lucy in later editions. What these accounts do suggest is that Wordsworth's final ordering of the poems – and in particular his highly ambiguous placement of 'A slumber' *after* rather than *among* poems on Lucy – is not inadvertent but deliberate. And yet he still placed the poems in a way that suggested the grouping he did not create.

In some respects the modern canon of 'Lucy Poems' appears extremely arbitrary. While 'A slumber' (the most popular with modern critics) does not even mention Lucy, two poems that do mention Lucy (or *a* Lucy) – 'Lucy Gray' and 'Among all lovely things my Love had been' – are almost universally excluded. Moreover, these pieces first appeared with now-canonical 'Lucy Poems': 'Lucy Gray' appeared in the second volume of *Lyrical Ballads* (1800), and 'Among all lovely things' immediately preceded 'I travelled' in *Poems, in Two Volumes* (1807). Periodical attempts by critics to alter the canon suggest how select the current grouping is. A few have tried to disengage the problematic 'A slumber.'[14] But more common are attempted additions. In a work of 1911, Eric Robertson prints an ingeniously 'eviscerate[d]' 'Lucy Gray' (i.e., without stanzas 4–14) to show its affinity with 'the true "Lucy" group' (151). By 1918, others wish to add 'Surprised by joy' (Baker 437). The more ambitious G.M. Harper proposes not only 'Among all lovely things' and the shortened 'Lucy Gray,' but also "Tis said, that some have died for love,' 'Louisa,' 'To a Young Lady' ('Dear Child of Nature'), and part of 'The Two April Mornings' (128–31). Rendel Harris (8–9) suggests 'She was a Phantom of delight,' Ernest de Selincourt pronounces it 'highly probable that ['Alcaeus to Sappho'] is a poem that [Wordsworth] had rejected from the series of poems to Lucy' (*PW* 2:531; compare *CEY* 257n57 and Butler and Green 457), and John Jones argues in 1954 that 'Lucy Gray' and 'The Danish Boy,' both 'also written in Germany, ... ought to be included' (71–3). Other pieces have been noted, not specifically for inclusion in the canon, but for striking similarities in theme or language: a draft of 'Nutting' in which a Lucy is addressed;[15] the sonnet 'Written in Very Early Youth' ('Calm is all nature as a resting wheel'), which in some ways anticipates 'A slumber' (Fry 156); and the much later 'Presentiments' (1830), sometimes compared with 'Strange fits' (Durrant, *Wordsworth* 146–7).

The development of a 'Lucy Poems' canon has been accompanied, in short, by the growth of a 'Lucy Poems' apocrypha, and these border–'Lucy Poems' help to clarify the canon's criteria. 'Louisa' is perhaps the most likely of the poems proposed. With 'I travelled,' it was tentatively slated for *Lyrical Ballads* (1802) but withheld until 1807; and it was thereafter printed in 'Poems Founded on the Affections' immediately preceding 'Strange fits,' 'She dwelt,' and 'I travelled.' In rhyme and metre it resembles not these poems but 'Three years,' to which it also bears deeper similarities:

> I met Louisa in the shade,
> And, having seen that lovely Maid,
> Why should I fear to say
> That, nymph-like, she is fleet and strong,
> And down the rocks can leap along
> Like rivulets in May? ('Louisa,' lines 1–6; *PW* 2:28)

> 'She shall be sportive as the fawn
> That wild with glee across the lawn
> Or up the mountain springs;

And hers shall be the breathing balm,
And hers the silence and the calm
Of mute insensate things.' ('Three years,' lines 13–18)

'Louisa' seems a strong candidate, and may even form a sort of bridge between Wordsworth's two clusters of 'Lucy Poems.' Its placement and the echo of 'Lucy' in 'Louisa' not only solicit comparison, but suggest that there is no clear demarcation between poems about Lucy and poems not about Lucy. Ultimately, one may feel that 'Louisa' is merely a borderer, that the mere similarity of Louisa's name epitomizes the mere similarity of this poem to the others. But like the other apocrypha it makes one aware of how readers have had to select the 'Lucy' canon from a larger poetic continuum.[16]

One can generalize from the established canon that a true 'Lucy Poem' is an untitled lyrical ballad that either mentions Lucy or is always placed with another poem that does, that either explicitly mentions her death or is susceptible of such a reading, and that is spoken by Lucy's lover. Though Lucy is clearly beloved, she is so obliquely described that one can hardly tell whether she is lover or child. This definition excludes both 'Lucy Gray' and 'Among all lovely things,' and indeed all the apocrypha.

It may appear that, as a mere generalization from the canon itself, this definition can neither justify nor explain the canon. Most obviously, the effort to accommodate 'A slumber' – clearly the most problematic member of the grouping – imposes certain obliquities on the generic description. But the definition does suggest two reasons why the 'Lucy' canon has, for all its seeming arbitrariness, resisted the efforts of its reformers. The first is the grouping's semi-legitimacy. It is just possible to rationalize it as quasi-authorial: that 'A slumber' followed 'She dwelt' in *Lyrical Ballads*, and 'Three years' thereafter, not only suggests a strong link between 'A slumber' and poems naming Lucy, but also provides a faint connection (if more than the name 'Lucy' be needed) between 'Three years' and the others. No such intentions can be invoked for, say, 'Surprised by joy.' Second, this definition contains the historical principle of exclusion for superficially similar poems: as stated by Poe, 'the death ... of a beautiful woman is, unquestionably, the most poetical topic in the world – and equally is it beyond doubt that the lips best suited for such a topic are those of a bereaved lover.'[17] The 'Lucy' canon was shaped largely by the sentimental susceptibility of Poe's contemporaries (and successors), for whom it mattered less that a 'Lucy Poem' name Lucy than that its heroine be dead. If poems such as 'Among all lovely things' and 'Louisa' treated deaths, they would likely be considered 'Lucy Poems' despite other difficulties. 'Louisa' is ruled out less by the difference in name than by the suggestion that it still may be possible to

> sit beneath the walls
> Of some old cave, or mossy nook,
> When up she winds along the brook
> To hunt the waterfalls. (lines 15–18)

'Dear Child of Nature' is ruled out not by its omission of Lucy's name but by its grandmotherly envisionment of its addressee: 'old age serene and bright, / And lovely as a Lapland night, / Shall lead thee to thy grave' (lines 16–18). It would be hard to overstate the importance of this second rationale for the canon, since it points to interpretation's teleological aspect and even to its artistic bent: editors and interpreters work not only from certain givens, but also toward certain results.

It can therefore be said that the 'Lucy' canon reflects the vagaries of editors and critics, though that is not the whole truth. Quarried as it is out of the larger range of poems, the grouping is something like a species in natural science: it reflects a culture's way of seeing, but we can only assume that it also reflects some objective similarities among its members. This is not to justify Arnold's editorial grouping of the poems or to suggest that Wordsworth, had he grouped them, would have included these five and no others. The point is rather that Wordsworth invited readers to make their own connections and that they made them. The important question, finally, is not whether a given grouping is right, but what the readerly activity invited by Wordsworth's text can reveal about the functions of both provocation and response.

Uncertainty is what makes the 'Lucy Poems' interesting, though editorial groupings work to obliterate uncertainty. For instance, as modern critics have found, it is precisely the proximity of 'A slumber' together with its failure to mention Lucy that makes it so compelling as a 'Lucy Poem.' If this study slants disproportionately toward this tiny lyric – especially as we consider modern criticism – it is because, by occupying the margins of the grouping, it lies at the centre of the problem. Its liminal status – both what attracts most readers and what most readings would resolve – is in many ways the emblem of the 'Lucy Poems' problem.

In insisting that 'A slumber' straddles the fence, I am doing my best to de-interpret or describe its situation: it is and is not a 'Lucy Poem.' This is both an admission of my own uncertainty and a claim for the poem's dual or ambiguous status, and in the latter sense my description escapes interpretive commitment no more than do the other readings I hope to measure against it. But while there is no escaping this situation, counter-interpretation can at least highlight areas of uncertainty and of presumption that have gone largely unacknowledged; if it does not attain to a descriptive certainty itself, counter-interpretation can at least reveal the uncertainties of statements that might otherwise be taken as descriptive. De Quincey and others assume that Wordsworth's 'mysterious silence' is biographically motivated, and I suggest that it is artistically motivated instead. This is a de-interpretation only in that, as a re-interpretation, it reveals the interpretive status both of De Quincey's suspicion and of itself, as rival interpretations. I see no final way to choose between such readings. We have no hard evidence that Wordsworth's reticence constitutes a material suppression (Annette Vallon, so far as we know, never sat 'Beside an English fire'), but we can always continue to read 'Lucy' as 'Annette' or 'Dorothy' merely by translating any resistant textual features according to a consistent logic of suppression and displacement. By positing artistic purposes for Wordsworth's silence, my interpretation resituates De Quincey's referential speculations as the effects of Wordsworth's art rather than its causes. But my hope is not to determine that the chicken came before the egg; on the contrary, it is to recall that this situation (like many others in these poems) is an indeterminate one. The specific intention behind Wordsworth's 'mysterious silence' may be irrecoverable, but it is also, happily, less important than its provocative effect.

2. Poetic Dishabille: The Art of Disorder in Wordsworth's Corpus

> ... among the best writers it is by means of hyperbaton that imitation approaches the effects of nature. For art is perfect when it seems to be nature ...

> This verse is dedicate to Nature's self,
> And things that teach as Nature teaches ...

> Wordsworth's poetry, when he is at his best, is inevitable, as inevitable as Nature herself. It might seem that Nature not only gave

> him the matter for his poem, but wrote his poem for him. He has no style.
>
> To write without style, to write unseen, would be, at once, to reduce visibility and vulnerability, or to be purposive without purpose.[18]

If Wordsworth considered but refrained from grouping the 'Lucy Poems,' one may suppose that his purpose was to ensure that his readers would make the connections. Paradoxical as it sounds, this seems more plausible once one considers the improbable ordering he imposed on his corpus. For the most part this ordering has been misunderstood, therefore disliked, and therefore discarded – a state of affairs intimately related to the editorial creation of definite 'Lucy Poems' groupings.

The most helpful historical account of Wordsworth's ordering is given by James Scoggins, who distinguishes between the *classification* of poems and their *arrangement* within each class; in what follows I preserve this distinction and use *ordering* to refer to overall organization. Wordsworth's arrangement of his poems, which Scoggins calls 'the more useful feature of [his] system' (56), has raised no controversy. There is generally a chronological progress within each category, and poems with obvious affinities or similarities, as well as veritable 'companion pieces,' are usually found together: 'Expostulation and Reply,' 'The Tables Turned,' and 'Lines Written in Early Spring'; the poems naming Matthew; 'The Waterfall and the Eglantine' and 'The Oak and the Broom'; 'To the Small Celandine' and 'To the Same Flower'; 'Beggars' and 'Sequel to the Foregoing.' Poems of similar quality or theme are also arranged together. The 'Poems of the Imagination' category begins, impressively: 'There was a Boy,' 'To the Cuckoo,' 'A Night-Piece,' 'Airey-Force Valley,' 'Yew-Trees,' 'Nutting,' 'The Simplon Pass,' and 'She was a Phantom of delight.' The 'Lucy Poems' and 'Yarrow Poems' are the only groupings avoided by Wordsworth that have seemed 'natural' to most of his readers.[19]

The obstacle for both editors and critics has been Wordsworth's less intuitive classification of his works.[20] Scoggins points out that the earliest orderings, especially in *Lyrical Ballads*, stressed arrangement, but even *Lyrical Ballads* presents in small the main features and difficulties of the later classification. The title itself is a classification that confuses more than it clarifies. John Stoddart's review of the 1800 edition objects: 'what Ballads are not *Lyrical*? Besides, [the volumes include] many compositions in blank verse, not at all Lyrical' (*RR* 134). Carl Woodring observes: 'The term seems self-contradictory if we think of ballads as narratives to be sung and of lyrics as simple, subjective, non-narrative songs'; yet the full title of 1798, *Lyrical Ballads, with a Few Other Poems,* seems to imply 'that the term "lyrical ballads" had a meaning clear enough to distinguish certain poems in the volume from others not of that kind' (*Wordsworth* 24). As these comments (and the disagreement between them) reveal, even this isolated instance of Wordsworth's cross-typing forces the re-examination of our categories. Wordsworth's second volume (1800) only compounds such difficulties: though it presents a series of 'Poems on the Naming of Places' numbered I–V, the volume begins with 'Hart-Leap Well' and 'The Brothers,' and ends with 'Michael,' all of which also recount the namings of places. 'Michael,' which immediately follows the series but is not numbered as part of it, begins with a reference to 'Green-head Gill' that makes one half expect an explanation and thus focuses the question of the poem's exclusion from the series.[21] In 1815, when Wordsworth first began collecting his published poems, he made a fuller 'system' of his ambiguous classifications,[22] explaining that

> poems, apparently miscellaneous, may with propriety be arranged either with reference to the powers of mind *predominant* in the production of them; or to the mould in which they are cast; or, lastly, to the subjects to which they relate. (*Prose* 3:28)

The general complaint of readers is that Wordsworth appears to forget his use of 'either' in this statement, and employs all three methods together.[23]

But we should not dismiss Wordsworth's categories for being unsystematic or overly systematic without considering that they are anti-systematic. Shaftesbury's sentiment that '[t]he most ingenious way of becoming foolish is by a system' (1:189) was not alien to the romantics; after the Preface to *Lyrical Ballads,* Wordsworth was regularly accused of ruining his natural gifts by adherence to 'system.'[24] But he was usually no friend to system himself,[25]and in his peculiar classification one may at least suspect an implicit critique of the usual systems of pigeon-holing that diminish particularity and prevent more 'natural' or unprejudiced reading. Discussing natural history, Michel Foucault observes that taxonomy entails the effort, not to look 'harder and more closely' at the object, but rather 'to restrict deliberately the area of its experience.'[26] In terms of literary taxonomy, to type a work is to dictate both the means and the limits of one's reading. Wordsworth's taxonomy is not dissimilar to that of Borges' 'Chinese encyclopaedia,' which classes animals as '(a) belonging to the Emperor, (b) embalmed, (c) tame, (d) sucking pigs,' and so on (Foucault, *Order* xv). Foucault cites this 'Chinese' taxonomy to suggest that the presuppositions and operations of any taxonomic system are essentially arbitrary and idiosyncratic, even when shared by an entire age or culture.[27] Wordsworth's presentation of 'Poems *of the Imagination*,' 'Poems referring *to the Period of Childhood*,' and 'Miscellaneous *Sonnets*' as apparently parallel categories serves the same role of making idiosyncrasy visible. It is, in effect, parodic, undermining rather than encouraging the habit of reading according to conventional expectations.[28]

Wordsworth remarked in his Preface of 1815 that 'for him who reads with reflection, the arrangement [i.e., ordering] will serve as a commentary unostentatiously directing his attention to my purposes' (*Prose* 3:28) – an odd remark, considering that his categories are undeniably, and I would argue designedly, difficult to use in interpretation. Because there are three criteria for classing poems, there is no necessary relation between many poems and their rubrics; most 'belong' in more than one category. It is therefore unhelpful to attempt, as Scoggins does, sorting poems that belong in a class from those that do not, and as Gene Ruoff suggests, it is a dubious method that makes 'the category of a poem justify a particular interpretation of it' ('Another' 360). Indeed, Wordsworth moved some poems from class to class. While the 'Lucy Poems' are classed in the 'Poems Founded on the Affections' and 'Poems of the Imagination,' Ruoff cites manuscript evidence that Wordsworth considered placing 'A slumber,' 'I travelled,' and 'She dwelt' under 'Epitaphs and Elegiac Pieces.'[29] Can we conclude that 'A slumber' is elegiac, and therefore about a person? Does the decision not to place it there indicate that it is not elegiac? That the 'Lucy Poems' fall under two separate headings is no assurance that they are 'about' different things. It shows only that Wordsworth wished to separate them, which might as easily have been a matter of arrangement.

Though I have so far used these terms interchangeably, Wordsworth's categories are more precisely provocative than heuristic: they provoke questioning and reflection (and, as it turns out, rejection) rather than cuing specific interpretations. If we attended more fully to their provocative effects and to Wordsworth's enduring commitment to them, we would be less apt to complain, as Richard Bourke has recently done, that by '1802 Wordsworth's original interest in the empowerment of his readership was slackening' (178). Historically, the heuristic view of the categories has been important as a pretext for getting rid of them. The 'disintegrators' present them (partly, it is true, on the strength of Wordsworth's own remark) as an elaborate system of authorial comment by a poet who has lost his poetic gift and become his own reader. On the principle that authors' interpretations have no privilege, it follows that Wordsworth's 'interpretive' ordering can be discarded or disregarded with good conscience. To justify his own chronological edition, John Hayden remarks that 'Wordsworth could be a great poet without being a great editor' (1:25). Likewise distinguishing the poet from the 'editor' Wordsworth, Judith Herman complains that the latter tried to advertise neglected poems by reclassing them, but that 'the compromises' are 'too much in favor of the editor who manages to salvage poems only by devaluing them' (87). Even though Ruoff warns against the pitfalls of hypothesizing 'two Wordsworths,' the authorial classification leads him to distinguish in the same essay between Wordsworth poet and Wordsworth critic:

> [T]he first task of systematic criticism is classification and organization. ... [Wordsworth] is offering nothing less than to perform the critic's first task for him by staking out the major tendencies of his work and suggesting interrelationships among them.

Ruoff argues that 'Wordsworth's Wordsworth deserves as much attention as, say, Coleridge's or Arnold's or Hartman's' ('Critical' 77). But even allowing for his understatement, Ruoff grants too much to the disintegrators in characterizing Wordsworth's ordering as one editorial act among others. To take Wordsworth's disposition of his corpus as an extra-textual matter is to make it discretionary and put it on its merits. But on this conception Wordsworth's bizarre ordering is bound to lose for the simple reason that we have prejudiced the question: we are already assuming what Wordsworth's ordering questions, both the separability of poetry and ordering, and the criterion of convenience. Arnold's pioneering selection (1879) exemplifies this assumption. Arnold finds Wordsworth's classification 'ingenious but far-fetched,' and therefore selects and rearranges the poems while advertising that 'I have not ventured on detaching portions of poems, or on giving any piece otherwise than as Wordsworth himself gave it' (9:43, 54). What he forgets is that Wordsworth repeatedly presents his own poems as both wholes in themselves and parts of a larger poetic whole.[30]

Non-authorial orderings thus involve a curious duplicity: by presenting the authorial ordering as a merely interpretive accretion, they justify themselves as anti-interpretive, thus pretending to preserve or even liberate the text while actually stripping it of its most radical ambiguity. But the main ulterior motivation for such efforts is convenience. As Walter Pater claims in 1874,

> Of all poets equally great, [Wordsworth] would gain most by a skilfully made anthology. ... [T]he mixture in his work, as it actually stands, is so perplexed, that one fears to miss the least promising composition even, lest some precious morsel should be lying hidden within ... (40–1)[31]

Matthew Arnold's selection of 1879 solved the problem announced in its preface, that Wordsworth's voluminous 'inferior work ... obstruct[s] our approach to' the 'first-rate work' (Arnold 9:42); thus, as Pater acknowledged (43n), it fulfilled Pater's wish. But both men clearly assume the criterion that Wordsworth's ordering challenges. In stripping the poems of their ambiguous status as both wholes and members, their orderings are undeniably more convenient, and yet convenience and art are two different things.

Just as Wordsworth's mixed classes undermine taxonomic impulses, the contiguity of poem and poem undermines conceptions of objective poetic wholes. Though many readers today know of an independent series called the 'Matthew Poems,' in Wordsworth these poems are parts of a continuum, numbers X, XI, and XII of 'Poems of Sentiment and Reflection.' By not declaring whether he intends a definite group, Wordsworth problematizes habitual critical assumptions.[32] To consider the poems either way, alone or together, must be our decision. Supposing we decide to group them, we must still decide which to include; whatever 'whole' we consider is therefore partly our own creation. Since this freedom to amalgamate and divide has the effect of putting in doubt the objective existence of texts, and conversely of foregrounding the reader, it is more freedom than most readers want. Hence the popularity of editorially imposed orderings, which impose boundaries: a reordered text has by necessity reconceived each poem as an unambiguous unit, whether as an independent piece or as a member of a definite group. The text becomes, to use Coleridge's phrase, a 'heap of little things.' And in reducing the poems to singular status, such disintegrations restore to us both the use of our habitual interpretive assumptions and our unselfconsciousness regarding them.

Wordsworth's ordering has virtues as well as inconveniences, but the virtues reside mostly *within* the inconvenience. One is the tendency to baffle prejudice by confronting one with poems one otherwise tries to avoid. Editions that exclude 'Airey-force Valley' or set it among poems of 1835 are likely to prejudice readers against it as a product of Wordsworth's later years. But encountering it between 'A Night-Piece' (1798) and 'Yew Trees' (1803), where Wordsworth put it, one is more likely to have to judge it anew, giving it the attention that alone can prove that it deserves attention. For as Wordsworth says of a poet, 'you must love him, ere to you / He will seem worthy of your love' ('A Poet's Epitaph,' lines 43–44). Pater makes an excellent case for the Wordsworthian inconvenience, even while arguing for convenience:

> This constant suggestion of an absolute duality between higher and lower moods, and the work done in them, stimulating one always to look below the surface, makes the reading of Wordsworth an excellent sort of training towards the things of art and poetry. It begets ... a habit of reading between the lines. ... [Wordsworth] meets us with the promise that he has much, and something very peculiar, to give us, if we will follow a certain difficult way ...
>
> But although the necessity of selecting these precious morsels for oneself is an opportunity for the exercise of Wordsworth's peculiar influence, and induces a kind of just criticism and true estimate of it, yet the purely literary product would have been more excellent, had the writer himself purged away that alien element. (41–42)

We might seriously consider, what Pater seems to reject, that Wordsworth's design is oriented less toward a 'purely literary product' that readers might comfortably praise on authority than toward the exercise and process of reading, especially between the lines (see Arac).

Yet any defence of Wordsworth's ordering as artistic and intrinsic, rather than interpretive and extrinsic, must come to terms with his own presentation of it as 'a commentary unostentatiously directing [the Reader's] attention to my purposes.' While this seems to admit to an interpretive function, it is important to note that Wordsworth speaks of 'purpose' rather than 'intention.'[33] As a general principle, I accept the position of Wimsatt and Beardsley that an author's statement of intention (or intended meaning) for a particular text cannot be binding (see chapter 4 below). On the other hand, it remains useful to heed the more general purposes of authors – that books be read rather than used for door stops, that they be read in a certain order and not from back to front, that they be taken allegorically or realistically, as truth or as fiction, and so on. This is a matter not of accepting the statements of an authority mechanically or on principle, but of taking guidance. In fact, we generally infer such purposes rather than have them dictated to us, and alter our inferences according to our success.

Though Wordsworth generally prefers a liberating concept of 'purpose' to the more confining concept of intention, he still gets taken as an intentionalist. Walter J. Ong, confronting Wordsworth's statement that each poem has a 'purpose,' demands: 'But is this not a *deus ex machina* or perhaps even the intentional fallacy, promulgated by author rather than critic?' (260). But the passage Ong cites quite explicitly rules out such specific intentions:

> ... each of [these poems] has a worthy *purpose*. Not that I mean to say, that I always began to write with a distinct purpose formally conceived; but I believe that my habits of meditation have so formed my feelings, as that my descriptions of such objects as strongly excite those feelings, will be found to carry along with them a *purpose*. (Preface to *Lyrical Ballads*, Owen 72)

The apparent paradox of unintended purpose is really an evasion of what we now call authorial intention.[34] Wordsworth appears as dubious as anyone about the value of an author's specific intention and the possibility of discovering it, though he speaks of his own work. He downplays intention even more powerfully in his *Letter to a Friend of Robert Burns* (1816), speaking of Burns's 'Tam o' Shanter': 'I pity him who cannot perceive that, in all this, though there was no moral purpose, there is a moral effect' (*Prose* 3:124). At issue is not only a procedural insight into the difficulty of discovering authorial designs, but a literary model featuring a radical inconsequence between design and effect, writing and reading.

In his statement about his own purposes, Wordsworth assures us that they are there without saying what they are or how to find them. So far from imposing his own sense of the poetry's meaning, this statement invites inferential activity in a dearth of clues. It is a performative rather than constative statement:[35] it supplies potentially inventive readers with the necessary supposition that speculated meanings are not merely projected but discovered. Thus it sets the scene for a kind of reading that might be called invention-as-discovery. This scene is remarkably similar to the scenes of reading *in* Wordsworth: for Wordsworth's own preferred objects of interpretation, whether natural or muted human objects, are both purposive (which facilitates the supposition of discovery) and non-linguistic (which rules out simple transmission of messages and gives scope to inference). This parallel between reading *in* Wordsworth and the reading *of* Wordsworth reflects his desire

> that a work of mine,
> Proceeding from the depth of untaught things,
> Enduring and creative, might become
> A power like one of Nature's. (1805 *Prelude* 12:309–12)

If we take this to mean that his work should be, not merely as powerful as Nature's, but similar in its working, this statement is not unusual in Wordsworth.[36] As nature is to him, so, as he conceived them, his works might be to their readers.

To read Wordsworth as he 'reads' the faces of his mountains, clouds, and solitaries would be to engage, not with providence, but with a supposition of providence. Though Wordsworth speaks of nature in providential terms, all his encounters leave one in doubt whether the purposes ascribed to nature are its own or the projections of its zealous interpreter. The simplest examples may be the passages on the 'ministry of fear' from the first book of the *Prelude*, but 'Resolution and Independence' provides the paradigmatic lines:

> Now, whether it were by peculiar grace,
> A leading from above, a something given ... (lines 50–1)

The poetic tactic in these lines goes beyond even that of the usual Wordsworthian 'surmise' made famous by Geoffrey Hartman (*WP* 8–13): the speaker never states the alternative to the 'whether' clause, but leaves it to be inferred. The alternative, apparently, is not important unless a reader happens to supply it. Even if this speaker's experience is not 'really' one of prevenient grace, the reading of the experience is the important thing; it may be either the suspicion of grace or grace itself that finally sustains the 'independen[t]' seeker. The same structure holds in a reader's supposition of Wordsworth's 'purpose': since he assures us only that there is a purpose, and leaves *what* purpose to our supposition, the purposes we suppose originate wholly with neither author nor reader. His declarations of 'purpose' do not announce his own providence of meaning, but constitute a providential fiction within which readers provide for themselves.

The ministry of Wordsworthian nature differs radically from traditional views of providence in that its suppositional quality is foregrounded; and the difference between the ministry of 'purpose' in Wordsworth's poetry and more traditional views of literary transmission replicates this difference. This is not to say that Wordsworth's texts are the first in which readers half invent the meaning they discover. But it is to say that Wordsworth breaks with the traditional *view of* authorship and readership, in which author provides and reader receives, correctly or incorrectly. And such a change of models will itself effect changes in texts, fostering different attitudes to and uses of them. Whether or not it reflects Milton's views, the authorship metaphor in *Paradise Lost* exemplifies an authoritarian model of writing and its relation to a theology of providence. While Milton's God argues in book 3 that there is not 'Providence absolute' in his cosmos, only 'foreknowledge,' his sleight becomes apparent in the authorship figure: Adam and Eve, he says, are 'Authors to themselves in all / Both what they judge and what they choose' (3:123–4). The enjambed transition from 'all' to 'both' reduces Adam and Eve from authorship to readership. God is the only true author, for He defines the alternatives (with Me or against Me) between which Adam and Eve merely 'choose,' rightly or wrongly. So far from being 'authors,' they are, as this word suggests, readers on the most straitened model. Indeed, the resourceful, 'self-tempted, self-depraved' Satan, who had to create the 'against Me' alternative before it could be chosen, is the only true co-author in this cosmos, and he represents presumption.

In contrast, Wordsworth envisions a true collaboration between nature and its readers, for while his nature is always assumed to be purposive, its purposes are too obscure to issue in 'right' and 'wrong' readings; they are virtually whatever a good reader construes them to be – a 'good' reader being anyone who construes them in uplifting or 'chearful' ways. Similarly, Wordsworth accepts the creativity of literary readers far more than was hitherto common. Samuel Johnson was well aware of such creativity:

> There is nothing in the art of versifying so much exposed to the power of imagination as the accommodation of the sound to the sense, or the representation of particular images, by the flow of the verse in which they are expressed. Every student has innumerable passages, in which he, and perhaps he alone, discovers such resemblances ...

It is scarcely to be doubted, that on many occasions we make the musick which we imagine ourselves to hear; that we modulate the poem by our own disposition, and ascribe to the numbers the effects of the sense. (*The Rambler* nos. 92, 94 [Johnson 122, 136])

But Johnson notes the reader's part with anxiety: the text is 'exposed' to our vagaries. Wordsworth may respond to Johnson directly, but in any case he shows more largesse in such matters:

I require nothing more than an animated or impassioned recitation, adapted to the subject. Poems, however humble in their kind, if they be good in that kind, cannot read themselves; the law of long syllable and short must not be so inflexible, – the letter of metre must not be so impassive to the spirit of versification, – as to deprive the Reader of all voluntary power to modulate, in subordination to the sense, the music of the poem; – in the same manner as his mind is left at liberty, and even summoned, to act upon its thoughts and images. (Preface, 1815, *Prose* 3:29–30)

Just as Wordsworth replaces the provident God with an uncertain 'ministry' of nature whose purposes are not certainly its own, so in his literary theory he replaces precise and authorially coded intentions with the more nebulous 'purposes' that receptive and reflective (passive yet active) readers must 'discover.' Whereas in Sidney and other pre-romantic theorists the aptest model for the poet was God, Wordsworth plays Nature.

We may be sceptical, of course, of a claim to 'teach as Nature teaches,' whether it is made by or for Wordsworth. My point is not to naturalize Wordsworth's artificial product, but merely to observe that the natural scene of reading served him as a model for regarding the literary one, especially in its foregrounding of the reader's suppositional activity. If this model enabled Wordsworth to shun the authoritarian or intentionalist stance, this may indeed be less a matter of humility or generosity than of anxiety. To attribute meaning to the reader is, among other things, to refuse the traditional responsibility of the author. Traditionally, as Harold Bloom remarks, the fear of conscious and absolute creativity is a fear of presumption:

Poetry whose hidden subject is the anxiety of influence [which for Bloom includes all poetry, at least since the Enlightenment] is naturally of a Protestant temper, for the Protestant God always seems to isolate His children in the terrible double bind of two great injunctions: 'Be like Me' and 'Do not presume to be too like Me.'

The fear of godhood is pragmatically a fear of poetic strength ... (*Anxiety* 152)

With or without the theological model, presumption always remains an anxiety for writers. Within a theology such anxieties can be defused by the posture of inspiration, which resubordinates creativity, but Wordsworth's playing of Nature and his reliance on the reader's participation constitutes a more radical evasion. Yet even as a posture or idealization, playing Nature has effects. Negatively, the 'natural' posture can be a powerful ideological imposition: Arnold's statement that Wordsworth's 'best' writing is 'as inevitable as Nature,' that 'He has no style' (9:52), reflects Arnold's own blindness to ideology wherever he agrees with Wordsworth.[37] More positively, a naturalism consisting in inexplicit purposiveness may delimit ideological impositions upon the reader by 'summon[ing]' the reader to impose her own inferences. The history of the 'Lucy Poems' shows that Wordsworth's lack of specificity with regard to the grouping as well as in the poems themselves has succeeded in sharing out responsibility, in making accomplices of his readers. But we must be alert to the other side of this dynamic also, which is the tendency of readers to refuse or return this responsibility, especially by casting Wordsworth as an intentionalist.

Wordsworth emulates Wordsworthian Nature as much in his ordering as in the individual poems. So far from being an authorial intrusion on readers' freedom of interpretation, his ordering serves to free and stimulate readers. For on the one hand it appears purposeful, and is claimed to be so; but on the other, as we have seen, it has a chaotic surface making its purpose hard to divine, especially with regard to specific poems. The 1815 Preface speaks of 'poems, apparently miscellaneous,' and remarks that

I should have preferred to scatter the contents of these volumes at random, if I had been persuaded that, by the plan adopted, any thing material would be taken from the natural effect of the pieces, individually, on the mind of the unreflecting Reader. (*Prose* 3:28)

Concern for the 'natural effect of the pieces' results in curious alternatives: either the very elaborate and artificial ordering Wordsworth in fact used, or a random one. Averill provides a useful view of the ordering when he notes Wordsworth's 'desire that his life's random product seem like a legitimate whole' ('Shape' 388). Such seeming can depend as much on the perceiver as on the ordering itself, and Wordsworth appears to have trusted to perception. His 'whole' is produced not by an elaborate and definite ordering but by a naturalistic structure comprising a superficial disorder and a pretence of purpose, or a promise of 'real' order beneath the surface, that encourages the invention-as-discovery of pattern. It is significant in this context that when Wordsworth explicitly condemns random orderings in 1826, he makes it clear that what he fears for is the arrangement, not the categorization:

> Miscellaneous poems ought not to be jumbled together at *random* – were this done with mine the passage from one to another would often be insupportably offensive; but in my judgement the only thing of much importance in arrangement is that one poem should shade off happily into another ... (*Letters* 4:440)

Shortly thereafter, he also condemns chronological orderings as essentially egotistical – 'except where determined by the course of public events; or if the subject be merely personal' (*Letters* 4:444). Such an ordering would make his lyrics retrace 'the growth of [the] poet's mind,' as *The Prelude* did already (an effect presented in justification by some chronological editions).[38] But it would be egotistical in the deeper sense of being more arbitrary than the order Wordsworth used. To order the poems chronologically *would* be a post-poetic act, an editorial operation of questionable authority.

I have represented Wordsworth's more poetic ordering of his poems as provocative and liberal, indeed as giving the reader more freedom than may be comfortable. But the one thing it appears to disallow is precisely what has been done with the 'Lucy Poems' in Arnold's selection and thereafter: the grouping of poems Wordsworth separated, and the definition of groupings he left unclear. If we cannot simply assume a unified intention behind poems that are contiguous in Wordsworth's ordering, we can more safely assume a purpose behind his dividing similar poems. But more than this, I would argue that an intentionalist editing of Wordsworth still makes sense though intentionalist interpretation does not.

If, as I have argued, Wordsworth's purpose is to provoke interpretation, this purpose is both fulfilled and circumvented in editions printing the 'Lucy Poems' as a definite grouping or as a single poem. The association of different poems and their appreciation as parts of larger wholes lies within this purpose; but editorial groupings, intervening between Wordsworth's text and his subsequent readers, impose a spuriously definite intention on the poems and in good measure prevent those readers from associating the poems in their own way. Thus it is one thing to group the 'Lucy Poems' in interpretation, and quite another in an edition. No one could object to interpreting the 'Lucy Poems' *as* a group, provided we recall that it is a point of interpretation; problems of intentionality arise only when a reader, influenced by the critical and editorial tradition, assumes the grouping as self-evident.

If we cease to regard Wordsworth's ordering as a merely interpretive or editorial act on his part, it becomes the more authoritative and sacrosanct, since it must be regarded at the level of other strictly textual questions. Indeed, in failing to respect this ordering as textual, defenders of the 'Lucy Poems' grouping show a certain confusion. They invariably rely on clues provided by Wordsworth's ordering to justify an ordering he never sanctioned. When all five 'Lucy Poems' are grouped, 'A slumber' is usually included with the others on the grounds that it always followed a poem naming Lucy in authorial editions. But if the poet's intention in ordering his poems is not to be respected, how can we, in forming our own arrangements, appeal to the proximity in which he placed these two poems?[39]

Final authorial intention has been accepted as a guiding principle with far less demur for editors than for interpreters, and for good reasons.[40] For one, it is easier to determine what an author meant *to* put on paper than what was meant *by* it; for another, strict adherence to authorial intention in editing is not likely to conflict with the establishment of relevance, as it may in interpretation. Editing is not mechanical, of course; one must often judge what an author meant in order to infer what he or she meant to put on paper. But in general the intentionalist editor need not pretend to follow the workings of an author's mind as closely as does an intentionalist interpreter. We can tell that Wordsworth intended to include certain poems in 'Poems of the Imagination' without concerning ourselves with what, precisely, he intended by 'Imagination.' For this reason, I think editors can appeal to Wordsworth's textual intention without being accused of an intentionalist fallacy. Indeed, strictly following Wordsworth's intention in the textual sense is the best way to protect ourselves, as readers, from the pre-interpretations imposed by editors' intentions.

3. The Lyrics Apart: The Toils of Simplicity

> The extreme simplicity which some persons have objected to in Mr Wordsworth's poetry, is to be found only in the subject and the style: the sentiments are subtle and profound. ... His poems bear a distant resemblance to some of Rembrandt's landscapes, who ... out of the stump of an old tree, a break in the sky, and a bit of water, could produce an effect almost miraculous.

> 'But she is in her grave, – and oh
> The difference to *me*!'

> 'Well now, are those lines really by Mr. Wordsworth? I declare they are very pretty. But do you not think, that, "oh, the difference to *me*!" is a little bit too simple?' Not in the least. Would you have liked the verse better had it been, (if the rhyme permitted,) 'What pangs my bosom rend?' The simplicity of the expression matters little if it fulfils the purpose of the author; and it is of no consequence how common the words may be, if they are only the surface to a mine of thought. The great object of poetry is, to suggest more than she expresses, and especially at the close of a strain, she is fortunate if she can leave food for reflection. ...[41]

Interpretation hates silence much as nature hates a vacuum – it rushes in to fill it. Not only does it clarify the indefinite and simplify the polyvalent, but it frequently conceals the extensiveness of the originary difficulties and thus of its own operation. Nothing is more commonplace, for instance, than the admission that 'A slumber did my spirit seal' is ambiguous, but such a 'description,' which too often implies that the poem might mean two things, already leaps over and conceals interpretive difficulties far greater than the single dilemma it acknowledges (or imposes). Though it is, in a sense, the legitimate business of interpretation to obliterate silences and obscurities, its ostensive decisions about obvious cruxes are frequently less important than are its veiled denials of more extensive preliminary difficulties. Hence, as I have argued, the necessity of beginning a study of interpretation with a de-interpretive effort, even though that effort itself be unavoidably interpretive. I have tried to show that the editorial definition of Wordsworth's poems as singular and detachable wholes, which facilitates the 'Lucy Poems' grouping, constitutes a massive interpretive simplification that is, nevertheless, virtually never presented as such. This refusal to self-identify has made it durable. The analogous interpretive move concerning the individual poems is the fiction of Wordsworth's 'simplicity.'

'No single word in Wordsworth is more complex than "simple,"' says Gene Ruoff ('Critical' 80); this is equally true of Wordsworth criticism. Wordsworth's reviewers used the term extensively, both to praise and to condemn. 'We infinitely prefer the simplicity, even of the most unadorned tale in this volume, to all the meretricious frippery of the *Darwinian* taste,' writes a reviewer (perhaps Francis Wrangham) of the first *Lyrical Ballads*. Others, such as Francis Jeffrey, complain frequently of the 'affectation of great simplicity.'[42] One obvious objection to this term is that, like many 'descriptive' terms, it can circularly validate itself in interpretation: the assumption that a work is simple will promote simple reading. Perhaps the first to deplore this assumption, Coleridge hoped his analysis of Wordsworth in the *Biographia* would 'remove'

> the strange mistake so slightly grounded, yet so widely and industriously propagated, of Mr. Wordsworth's turn for SIMPLICITY! I am not half as much irritated by hearing his enemies abuse him for vulgarity of style, subject, and conception; as I am disgusted with the gilded side of the same meaning, as displayed by some affected admirers with whom he is, forsooth, a *sweet, simple poet!* (*BL* 2:158)

But it is still not uncommon to see the 'Lucy Poems,' and especially 'A slumber,' described as 'so straightforward,' 'so intensely simple and human,' even as their greatest difficulties go unexamined.[43]

For the most part, however, modern critics have begun to find, with Elizabeth Drew, that Wordsworth's 'simplicity is deceptive' (132), and to use the word with irony. F.R. Leavis comments on 'A slumber':

> the emotional power is generated between juxtaposed opposites. It is generated between the two stanzas, or between the states represented by the two stanzas: 'she was, she is not' – the statement seems almost as bare and simple as that. But the statement is concrete, and once the reading has been completed the whole poem is seen to be a complex organization, charged with a subtle life. (54)

David Perkins notes that the poems are in tone 'deceptively casual. They can easily be read in too shallow a way' (*Wordsworth* 193). A more recent commentator has even sought to explain 'the apparent power and complexity of "A slumber"' (Hall 169). 'Simplicity' so readily gives way to its opposite in discussions of these poems that one may suspect a hidden identity between them. David Simpson's observation that Wordsworth 'creates mystery and stimulates self-consciousness through simplicity, through the use of language in its minimal state' (*Irony and Authority* 62; see also 63, 150) helps clarify the ambiguity of 'simplicity': poems that are exceedingly simple textually – in their vocabulary, in their avoidance of complex grammatical constructions, in the speaker's failure to expand on his feelings – generate complexity in interpretation. Wordsworth's simplicity can be as Coleridge says, 'so slightly grounded, yet so widely and industriously propagated,' only because in the textual sense the notion is very well grounded. That is what makes 'simplicity' so powerful as an interpretive fiction: it is easy to move from convincing accounts of the poems' simplicities to simplifications of their possible meanings. The following counter-interpretations attempt to reveal the interpretive difficulties both generated by the real simplicity of the 'Lucy Poems' and hidden by the myth of their simplicity. My point is, of course, less to argue that the interpretations of these poems are false, than to show how pervasive and necessary they are, how extensively these poems demand the creativity of their readers.

The most extreme case of this equivocal 'simplicity' is 'A slumber.' Brevity, if nothing else, makes it appear simple, while its liminality in the grouping gives it a special complexity in interpretation. The main stem of existing critical dispute is the uncertainty whether the poem refers to Lucy and to her death; for now I shall simply operate within the assumption that it does, and return to this question later. Most commentary that makes this assumption has centred on the poem's second stanza; most disputed has been the significance of its last line, 'With rocks, and stones, and trees.'[44] But this too I leave for later discussion, for stanza 1 is far more difficult to construe, line 1 most difficult of all, and these are the difficulties least often acknowledged.

Grammatically, either 'A slumber' or 'my spirit' might be the subject of line 1, though the former is almost universally assumed.[45] Within this assumption, it is far from plain what 'seal' means, though it is seldom queried.[46] Interpreters can apparently do without a precise denotation, and concern themselves instead with whether its connotations are positive or sinister. But without positing some denotation for 'seal,' it is difficult to understand the first line. Three or four of the many definitions and usages listed in the *OED* appear plausible in this context. To 'seal' (*v.*[1]) may be to 'fasten, fix immoveably' (definition 9b) or to close (def. 8); the latter sense may have either positive overtones of healing, as in 'to close up (a wound) with a covering' (def. 8b) – as Geoffrey Hartman sometimes takes it (*WP* 159; *Saving* 148) – or more negative overtones, as in to 'enclose, shut up within impenetrable barriers' (def. 11) – as Michael Cooke suggests (60). We must also consider more figurative uses of 'seal,' as in '*to seal* (a person's) *lips*, to bind or constrain to silence or secrecy; *to seal* (a person's) *eyes* or *ears*, to render blind or deaf' (def. 6b). Among Wordsworth's usages (Lane Cooper's concordance lists only six other uses of the verb and four of the noun), at least two may be relevant. In *The Excursion*, the Solitary describes his wife's reaction to losing the second of their two children: she remained 'Calm as a frozen lake,'

as if in her,
Who, to the lowest region of the soul,
Had been erewhile unsettled and disturbed,
This second visitation had no power
To shake; but only to bind up and seal;
And to establish thankfulness of heart
In Heaven's determinations, ever just.
(*Excursion* 3:650–8; *PW* 5:98–9)

The similarity of this passage to the 'Lucy' reading of 'A slumber' may appear to justify Hartman's association of 'sealing' with 'healing.' But here the bereavement is the agent of the sealing, while in 'A slumber' it appears to follow the sealing of the spirit. And another use of 'seal' apparently contradicts these healing overtones: at the end of act 4 of *The Borderers*, Eldred describes the blind Herbert, whom he has left dying on the ground: 'He will never open them [his eyes] more; even when he spoke to me, he kept them firmly sealed as if he had been blind' (lines 1976–7). Thus Wordsworth's other uses of 'seal' establish a range of possible connotation rather than determining a single connotation.

The latter passage does, however, suggest a denotation for 'seal' in 'A slumber.' The *OED* notes that 'In *to seal the eyes*, this verb is not always distinguishable from the figurative use of SEEL' ('Seal,' v^1, def. 6b):

to close the eyes of (a hawk or other bird) by stitching up the eyelids with a thread tied behind the head; chiefly used as part of the taming process in falconry. ... *transf.* To close (a person's eyes). (*OED* 'Seel,' *v*)[47]

In *The Borderers*, 'seal' is both literal and figurative: Herbert is already blind, but he is hoodwinked by Marmaduke just as Marmaduke is by Oswald. Similarly, if the line 'A slumber did my spirit seal' describes a hood-winking, it implies the figure of bird or eye for the speaker's 'spirit,' and thus describes a blinding of the spirit far more precisely than is usually noted.[48]

A very different sense of 'seal,' made more plausible by the word's conjunction with 'spirit,' is 'to mark election,' as in Revelation:

> And I saw another angel ascending from the east, having the seal of the living God: and he cried with a loud voice to the four angels, to whom it was given to hurt the earth and the sea.
>
> Saying, Hurt not the earth, neither the sea, nor the trees, till we have sealed the servants of our God in their foreheads. (Rev. 7: 2–3)

James Boulger offers a similar usage from Calvin's *Institutes*: 'that alone is true faith which the Spirit of God seals in our hearts' (Boulger 395). Boulger does not offer an entire reading of the poem in keeping with this usage of 'seal,' but he suggests that its 'religious or spiritual overtones' will 'disallow a purely naturalistic reading' (396). The naturalist reader may simply deny that Calvin's sense of 'seal' applies to this poem. But it is remarkable that this sense may make possible a Christian reading of a poem that has so often been seen as either naturalistic or pantheistic.[49]

This and Wordsworth's other uses of 'seal' are more suggestive, then, than conclusive. E.D. Hirsch argues that interpreters must be aware of an author's peculiar vocabulary and habits of usage, but while he believes this will help determine the author's probable meaning (*Validity* 214–15, 222), it proves more useful for multiplying possible meanings. At this stage we may take 'seal' at will as suggesting healing, entrapment, blinding or deception, or spiritual election – in keeping, of course, with other decisions and with what the other features of the text allow. The difficulty is the greater in that the meaning of 'slumber' and even 'spirit' are likewise open to construction. What would a 'slumber' be that could 'seal' one's 'spirit'? With its uneasy interrelation of uncertain terms, the line is a riddle, but it does not necessarily have a 'solution.' That is undoubtedly why it is so often glossed as a whole rather than construed from its elements, and then treated as though perfectly plain: as one critic writes, '"A slumber did my spirit seal" is an image; it means obviously that his awareness of death was sealed off from his consciousness' (Jackson 153).[50]

Line 2, 'I had no human fears,' is simple in appearance, but it presents similar difficulties. We might ask what the fears are of, but Cleanth Brooks raises a more intriguing question – who they are for ('Irony' 735–6). Brooks admits that this ambiguity may not be conscious on Wordsworth's part, but at any rate it is overdetermined: not only by the want of a 'for' phrase modifying 'fears,' but also by the ambiguity of the word that does modify 'fears,' 'human.' The interpreter's conception of 'human,' though it may be unconsciously imported, will have considerable weight in any reading of the poem: for if 'human' is *merely* human, the phrase implies 'no fears for myself'; if 'human' is 'humane' or super-animal, it implies 'no fears for her.' '[N]o human fears' may also imply a distinction between human and non-human senses of time. Compare Burns, 'To a Mouse':

> Still, thou art blest, compar'd wi' *me*!
> The *present* only toucheth thee:
> But Och! I *backward* cast my e'e,
> On prospects drear!
> An' *forward*, tho' I canna *see*,
> I *guess* an' *fear*! (lines 43–8; Burns 102)

Given the poem's openings into the time before and time after, such a sense of 'no human fears' may be more relevant than the other.

And yet what does it matter? Whatever 'human fears' are, the speaker denies that he had them. Lines 2 and 3 both make one ponder precisely what is being ruled out of the poem. Much ingenuity has been spent on the 'thing' of 'she seemed a thing,' though 'seemed' suggests that this is what she was *not*. In 'that could not feel / The touch of earthly years,' the pleonastic 'earthly years' evokes the apparently irrelevant question what *un*earthly years could be. This question is not entirely irrelevant, however. For the structure of this statement is like that of line 2 – NEGATIVE + ADJECTIVE + NOUN: both lines seem calculated to create an uncertainty whether the adjective or the noun is being negated. By reading NEGATIVE (ADJECTIVE + NOUN) – 'no fears' and 'no years' – we arrive at the relatively simple reading. Yet the NEGATIVE (ADJECTIVE) + NOUN reading – 'no *human* fears' and '[no] *earthly* years' – remains possible. This derivation of unearthly suggestions from earthly vocabulary affords a good illustration of Wordsworth's purpose in *Lyrical Ballads*, as Coleridge describes it: 'to give the charm of novelty to things of every day, and to excite a feeling analogous to the supernatural' (*BL* 2:7). Also as Wordsworth describes it: to use 'a certain colouring of imagination, whereby ordinary things should be presented to the mind in an unusual way' (Preface, Owen 71). In both statements, the significance of remaining with 'ordinary things' is that the poem depends on the reader, not merely on the writer, to estrange their everyday appearance. Since emotions directed toward the supernatural are usually characterized by wonder or suspicion, the supernaturalism of 'no earthly years' (like that of 'whether' in 'Resolution and Independence') is far more effective than one that is simply stipulated. But it depends on readings that unpack 'simplicity' rather than disambiguate complexity; it is a part of our reading *process*, and tends to be repressed by decisive interpretations that aim at *a* meaning.

An interpreter who has surpassed or suppressed these difficulties encounters a second (and for these poems highly characteristic) area of difficulty. The speaker does not say 'Because I had no human fears,' or 'Therefore,' 'Though,' 'That is,' 'And,' 'Still,' 'But,' or 'When I had no human fears.' Since no conjunction is used, any of these might be understood. Since each has very different implications, this lack of connective presents an even greater problem than the others. As Frances Ferguson has remarked of another instance of Wordsworth's asyndeton, 'One hardly knows whether to describe these lines as containing too little or too much' (71). One may turn to punctuation for guidance, but it presents problems too, for the first edition uses a comma (which favours the readings 'that is' or 'and'), while later editions use a semicolon (which favours the 'still' or 'but' or even the 'therefore' reading). Even the appeal to punctuation assumes a previous judgment about texts.

The problem of disconnection appears also at the end of line 2. This line is punctuated in all the authorial editions with an end-colon, which may divide the stanza in two much as the poem itself is halved. But then what are the temporal and causal connections between the first two lines and the last? Are lines 3–4 a restatement of 1–2, as J. Hillis Miller has supposed? ('On Edge' 103).[51] That view might provide a purchase on lines 1–2, if only we understood 3–4. But though the poem is frequently taken as divided between simple past (stanza 1) and present (stanza 2), it is also possible that stanza 1 itself marks separate stages in a temporal or causal progress – that is, the colon that Miller implicitly reads as 'that is,' might also be read as either 'therefore' (progression) or 'because' (regression). It seems to me that the pause after 'seal' is even stronger than the colon after 'fears,' since the especial strangeness of line 1 sets it off from the rest. Line 1 may describe the bereavement (the 'slumber' being taken as someone else's slumber, that is, as the speaker's discovery of death, on the analogy of the 'seal' passage of *The Excursion*), lines 3–4 the period *before* the bereavement, and stanza 2 the ever-present of the 'slumber' adumbrated in line 1. In contrast to the common reading in which stanza 1 describes the speaker's luxuriant or enchanted state before the death, and stanza 2 his rude awakening,[52] this reading would telescope awakening and 'slumber,' making the poem describe nothing beyond the severe shock resulting from a loved one's death – a reading supported by the flat, matter-of-fact tone of stanza 2.[53] As a variant of this reading, lines 2–4 may describe the speaker's immediate reaction to the death (lines 3–4 may describe the corpse), his self-reminder, not uncommon in bereavement, that the dead need not be pitied because indeed they *cannot* 'feel / The touch of earthly years' that for the bereaved continue to unfold.

I do not present these readings – or rather outlines – as more attractive or more compelling than the usual, but merely as plausible; my purpose is only to point out how much the poem makes the reader invent. The very ease and subtlety with which we 'half-create' this poem tends to make us oblivious to the extent of our own activity. What has long been regarded as a simple or a merely ambiguous poem (Is it about Lucy or not? Does he love her or wish to escape her? Is she dead, or living in nature? Is he bitter or accepting?) is a fragile simplification of a far more extensively polysemous text. One cannot read it without making more questionable assumptions than there are lines.

We might pursue these questions further, but other elements of verbal ambiguity – especially the reference of 'she' – will arise as we consider the criticism. At this point at least two other kinds of ambiguity and assumption are raised by the juxtaposition of stanzas 1 and 2. It is customary to contrast the stanzas in terms of verb tense, time past and time present, but there is a more disturbing contrast between the subjectivity and obscurity of stanza 1 and the objectivity and clarity of stanza 2. These perfectly correlative contrasts suggest that the speaker is surer in speaking for her than for himself. If such sudden lucidity regarding the 'other' raises suspicions, the ground of *our* uncertainty and assumption has shifted from grammar to the psychology of the speaker – to the motives and status of his statement. The apparently assured and definite statement that 'She neither hears nor sees' could not be more lucid grammatically, but it remains unclear, especially after the obscurity of stanza 1, what the clarity itself signifies. Is the statement descriptive, self-reassuring, insistent? The claim about *her* insensibility might well displace the speaker's own 'slumber' and thus guard against guilt feelings (similarly, 'A slumber did my spirit seal' might be 'I shut her out' with a displacement of agency, just as 'wayward thoughts will slide / Into a lover's head' might be 'I thought bad things'). In any case, the speaker's own inability to see her has become an assurance of her inability to see him (compare 'I travelled,' line 16).[54] A need for reassurance of her death need not be entirely dark psychologically; it might be viewed as a need for the awkward comfort of certainty. But as these considerations can merely suggest, so long as we are interpreting human speech we are involved in the necessity of positing not only grammatical meanings but also mental attitudes and strategies, which implies a range of possibilities far more extensive than the 'literary' options of ironic and dramatic modes (though the difficulties entailed by these should not be underestimated). Nor is this a decision one can evade by disclaiming interest in psychoanalytic criticism; every reading of these poems supposes a psychology.

This poem's abrupt transition from obscurity to lucidity also suggests the importance of another major ground of supposition: our linguistic model. One always resorts to grammar when it becomes available, yet the obscurity of stanza 1 pushes interpreters to the obvious option of 'reading' it dramatically rather than grammatically. This is a resource within language, not a step outside of it, but it does entail a shift in specific models. As John Danby suggests in connection with the last lines of 'She dwelt,'

> At maybe the most primitive level words are under-agents often to pre-verbal things. They can be merely phatic expressions indicating joy, pain, sadness, *etc.*, and unless we recognize the situations which literally ex-press the noises the expressions so-called will be meaningless. Some good poetry (Schiller might say it was the voice of 'nature') comes near to a simplicity of this sort. ... Language in these cases, as with the emotional scream, is the under-agent of situation. The words call out from an implied dramatic setting. The situation implied – and our response to what it means – the words as such have little control over. (18)

We may be reluctant to assume that poetry uses language in such ways precisely because this assumption would rule out the usual means by which we discover and 'prove' certain meanings in the text. But texts that baffle our accustomed grammatical approach even more than 'She dwelt' does may force us to read much as Danby suggests. In a variant of the concept of 'blockage' used by formalist and reader-response theorists, Michael Riffaterre identifies 'ungrammaticality,' in the sense of 'deviant grammar or lexicon (for instance, contradictory details),' as a basic resource of poetical language (*Semiotics* 1–2). Ungrammaticalities test readers' resourcefulness, and they are therefore useful also for foregrounding the resourcefulness and the specifically linguistic assumptions that underlie all reading. Because 'A slumber' is not even consistently 'ungrammatical' but makes its readers shift from ground to ground, it makes such assumptions particularly visible. Even stanza 1 is not simply or definitely ungrammatical, but puts us in doubt of grammar.

Rhetorical tropes are local and strategic 'ungrammaticalities,' in Riffaterre's sense; to make sense of them we are forced outside grammar.[55] Sometimes, as in cruder forms of irony, all that is entailed may be a minor detour to a secondary rule: perhaps sarcasm might be decoded through a simple rule of reversal. But in most cases there appears to be no simple rule to which we can appeal, no decoding procedure. However 'simple' in reputation, the 'Lucy Poems' frequently resort to strategies of the latter sort, especially to paradox and oxymoron. In 'She dwelt,' for instance, it has been observed that lines 3–4 are contradictory, that 'untrodden ways' is oxymoronic, and that the images of stanza 2 are inconsistent.[56] These disorders are the poem's most obvious appeals to our own sense-making faculties, and it is, conversely, in our construal of such features that the ingenuity of our reading is most evident. But for this very reason, the readings of such passages can also reveal how much interpreters deny their own creativity and attribute their own simplifications to the text. Exploring the relations between metaphor and paradox, Cleanth Brooks considers the star and violet images in 'She dwelt,' stanza 2, as 'simple metaphors,' in opposition to the complex and paradoxical conceits of Elizabethan poetry. To reconcile the inconsistency between the violet and star, Brooks suggests that in these 'comparisons' the world's view of Lucy is contrasted with the speaker's: 'Though Lucy, to the great world, is as obscure as the violet, to her lover she is as fair as Venus' ('Metaphor' 319). This contrast thus forecasts the personal emphasis of the poem's conclusion, 'The difference to me!' Brooks comments: 'Wordsworth has (in this instance, wisely, I think) not spelled it out, but forced the reader to make the interpretation for himself and thus involve his own imagination' (319). My own argument follows Brooks closely on this point, but in calling these disconnected images 'comparisons' and predicating them of Lucy, Brooks overlooks an even more elementary instance of the poet's failure to 'spell it out.' Wordsworth's grammatical simplicity requires more of Brooks in this reading than Brooks, in making this point, is willing to admit.

According to Brooks, eliciting such reader involvement is what good poetry does – but only to a point. A poem fails if, like Pound's four-word poem 'Palimpsest,' it leaves too much to the reader. The reader then 'has, for all practical purposes, to write the poem, and ... there is no way to tell that one reader's interpretation realizes the poem any better than another's' (320). Evidently, then, Brooks believes his explanation for the contrast between the 'comparisons' in 'She dwelt,' though not stated in the poem and necessarily 'imagined' by himself, is nevertheless really implicit in the poem so that his reading is correct in some final way. He makes exceptionally good sense of the poem, but he cannot have it both ways. If he accepts his own principle that the poem must not leave so much open that we cannot adjudicate between readings, there is a self-deception in his failure to note that he has grammatically completed the stanza. To acknowledge the extent of his creativity would be to acknowledge the indefensibility of his reading against others and thus to condemn not just this reading but also (by his standards) this poem. If this is true of 'She dwelt,' how much truer of 'A slumber' – yet Brooks proceeds on the same page to praise 'A slumber' (as 'another of the Lucy poems'), and returns later to criticize poems lacking 'fixities and definites' (324).[57] We will explore this type of argument more fully in connection with Hirsch. Here the crucial point is the paradoxical result of Wordsworth's grammatical 'simplicity': precisely because the requisite filling-in is so elementary, even an extremely analytical critic is inclined to overlook it. Brooks takes 'fixities and definites' for granted even while fixing and making definite, so that a poem requiring simplification gets represented as a 'simple' one.

'Strange fits,' often viewed as the most straightforward of these lyrics, also provokes inquiry through contradictions while frustrating definitive resolution through a radically disjunctive, or 'simple,' style. The initial problem is lexical: what are these 'fits of passion,' and how are they 'strange'? Since 'strange' often means *not* known, the statement 'Strange fits of passion have I known' may perplex a reader much as 'untrodden ways' perplexed F.W. Bateson – especially since the perfect tense of 'known' suggests recurrence. But if we attempt to resolve this contradiction by examining the 'fits of passion,' the succeeding lines are inconclusive, for it is not even certain that the poem describes a fit of passion. As in 'A slumber,' the problem is an ambiguous connective:

Strange fits of passion have I known:
And I will dare to tell,
But in the Lover's ear alone,
What once to me befel.

'And I will dare to tell' makes a compound statement rather than a complex one; it is simpler grammatically than 'which I will dare to tell,' but the latter would be simpler to interpret. We cannot be sure whether he refers to one thing in his past (the fit, which once befell him) or to two things (the fit, and what befell him). The latter may seem unlikely at first, but the 'fit' might be the cause or effect of his adventure; indeed, the difficulty in accepting what follows as a 'fit of passion' seems to favour this view.[58]

Even if the 'strange fits' were identified with 'what once to me befel,' to take stanzas 2–6 as describing 'what once to me befel' entails a further assumption. For he has just said that he would tell this 'in the Lover's ear alone.' If we assume that the poem narrates 'what ... befel,' is it spoken in a Lover's ear? If not, is line 3 an unmeaning expression, or do we infer that the speaker, like 'The Thorn''s retired sea-captain, cannot keep a secret? To take the poem as spoken in a 'Lover's ear' is to infer either a dramatic setting or that all readers are lovers. And while that is not nonsensical, it puts a special strain on the claim for strangeness in line 1.

'I travelled' also appears to be one of the more explicit 'Lucy Poems' – which may be why it has been least read. And yet here, too, what is most obvious – that Lucy has died – is an effect of our own artful resolution of contradictions: that one can be 'among' men who are 'unknown' and that one can love without knowing that one loves; that the self-same statement (lines 15–16) should imply both that Lucy is what endears England to the speaker and that she is gone. These are paradoxes of memory and belated appreciation, and they turn on the question of what it is to *know*, as the two uses of this word in the first stanza indicate. To say 'I travelled among unknown men' is one way of saying you did not care for them. But the speaker promises to stay because he did not know how he loved England until he left; and if that is how the heart works, how can he be sure he will not discover that he misses the 'unknown men' and 'lands beyond the sea,' now that he has left *them*? Moreover, if love is discovered in the absence of the loved one, won't it be allayed or at least obscured by her presence? This is, presumably, why he left in the first place. The phrase 'The joy of my desire' seems to defuse these suspicions by telescoping the anxiety of desire with the pleasure of satisfaction; 'Among thy mountains' puts the speaker at England's breast. Where desire and fulfilment can coincide, fidelity seems peculiarly possible. Yet 'The joy of my desire' is itself a past-tense statement of desire for a life no longer lived; and indeed, since the speaker had left England's mountains, it appears to be a retrospective idealization. The speaker's strange uncertainty in 'I *seem* / To love thee more and more' – which estranges him from himself – is therefore appropriate but probably understated. Because of fulfilment's power to cancel desire, it is, ultimately, Lucy's *non*-existence that ensures the endearment of the closely associated England.

It is generally assumed, as I've just done, that the poem is uttered after the death of Lucy, though the final lines raise a problem much like the negative adjectives of 'A slumber.' As Margaret Drabble has noted, the last line

> could possibly mean that Lucy is dead, and that she does not now survey any green fields at all – or it could merely mean that the last time Lucy looked at a field, it was, since she lives in England, an English one. The first of these meanings seems to be too big for the words, the second too little – the real meaning seems to lie, impossibly enough from a logical viewpoint, somewhere between the two. (66)

This problem goes to the heart of the 'Lucy' grouping, since it is really the explicit statements of 'She dwelt' and 'Three years' that make the death of Lucy a plausible inference in 'I travelled.' But equally significant is the appeal in Drabble's reasoning to something like balance or decorum. If the closing vagueness elicits our completion of the poem's meaning, it also elicits a sort of artistry: the question is not just 'Is it plausible?' but 'Is it fitting?' Interpretation involves a will not only to make sense, but to make the 'best' sense possible. Notwithstanding Drabble's feeling that death would be 'too much,' however, this aesthetic consideration (the same one that helped shape the 'Lucy' canon) pushes most readers toward the assumption that Lucy is dead. To assume that she is not dead, but simply gazing at something besides fields, as Drabble suggests, makes the last line seem overwrought and bathetic; it also makes the displacement of focus in the speaker's love-declaration, from Lucy to England, less explicable and fitting. Moreover, it rules out the macabre logic by which the poem's dialectic of desire-in-absence and not-in-presence is resolved: were Lucy living, we would still have reason to suspect that the traveller might tire of England/ Lucy. What dictates Lucy's death here may be nothing more than the readerly desire for poetic closure.

The poem seems to describe, in short, the love (and loss) of woman leading to the love of nature – or, as the majority of the commentary has it, to the love of country, to patriotism.[59] For 'England' presents a major ambiguity – land or state? A patriotic reading might make the sublimation of sexual love more socially satisfactory, but it also seems further beyond the boundaries of the poem. As Alfred Cobban writes,

> In a well-known verse of one of the Lucy poems is reflected the awakening in [Wordsworth's] heart of patriotic sentiment, which was destined in time to fill and more than fill the void left by the collapse of republican enthusiasm. By now, moreover, the British Government, even the irrepressible Dundas, were as heartily sick of the war as was the people. Pitt resigned. ... (142)

Politically aware as Wordsworth was, it may be difficult to see how Dundas and Pitt belong in a poem whose imagery of England is mountains, fields, and Lucy. But this doubt has no more to do with problems of Cobban's specific reading than with the psychological and linguistic assumptions of our own. While this passage is admittedly not the finest example, politicizing interpretation of this basic type has had more powerful advocates and theorists since the time of Cobban's writing. On the premise that the political-historical has been repressed, sublimated, or otherwise written *out* of the poem, it may be reasonable to read it back *in* through what Marjorie Levinson calls 'a theory of negative allegory,' or by taking 'the signified [as] indicated by an identifiably absented signifier.'[60] If such a policy of reading silences seems paradoxical, the procedure itself is not dissimilar to interpretation as we have seen it elsewhere: it is occasioned by silences, it 'reveals' these as quite the opposite, as forms of repression/expression, and it proceeds to unfold them. Granting that not every silence is pregnant and that assumptions of repression can therefore be more or less warranted, such a procedure is no more objectionable than it is unusual. What seems to me remarkable in new-historicist rewriting is primarily that its procedure has recently been made so public; it has been objected to less because it constitutes a new hermeneutic departure than because its practitioners have made a policy of declaring their practice. While I for one find Cobban's political 'I travelled' uncompelling, to complain that his politics are imposed or imported may be to miss the point that whichever reading we give 'England' will involve some (re-)importation of putatively banished meaning. And the poem's own silence is such that our choice of import may have more to do with how we have contextualized it than with the poem itself. Cobban's patriotic reading gains authority from its context in a reading of Wordsworth's contemporaneous political attitudes; a reading of 'England' as landscape will gain authority from a 'Lucy Poems' context.

The interpretive history of 'Three years' offers the best example of the variability of 'Lucy Poems' interpretations within a certain range of shared assumptions. Nineteenth-century readers stressed Nature's care for Lucy. Coleridge called the poem 'Nature's Lady' in 1800 (*Letters* 1:632), and Palgrave's *Golden Treasury* titled it 'The Education of Nature' (180); to judge from the criticism of the period, there was no ironic intent in these re-titlings. In his popular lecture 'Of Queen's Gardens' (1865), to illustrate the purposes and ideals of women's education, Ruskin read his audience the poem's first four stanzas, declaring that they 'point you to the source, and describe to you, in a few syllables, the completion of womanly beauty' (*Sesame and Lilies* 101).[61] Needless to ask why Ruskin did not quote stanza 7; but this omission, far from being peculiar to Ruskin, is all but universal in nineteenth- and early twentieth-century commentaries, in which Arnold's belief that Wordsworth viewed nature as a nourisher and moral restorative prevailed.[62] Today, on the other hand, no one seems capable of reading the poem without stressing stanza 7 and finding macabre undertones. As Scoggins puts it, 'this conclusion and the sequel poem ['A slumber'] cannot but make us wonder that the inevitable result of Nature's influence is death' (112). The shift occurred with H.W. Garrod's 1929 essay on 'Wordsworth's Lucy.' Garrod quotes stanza 7, and remarks:

> It is this last stanza that I have never understood. 'Thus Nature spake', making high promises; and 'The work was done' – the glory of these promises, we must suppose, was fulfilled. But to what end or meaning? Lucy's race was run. She died. Was it *that* work which Nature schemed to do? 'The work was done', and Lucy died? Is that what Wordsworth means to say? Or does he mean to say that 'the work was done', the perfect woman planned was made – *and yet* Lucy died? (82–3)

Garrod concludes that 'between Lucy's perfection in Nature and her death there is, for Wordsworth, really no tragic antithesis at all.' Since Garrod there have been disagreements whether an implicit 'but' or (as he has it) an 'and so' marks the transition to stanza 7, but it has never again been possible simply to ignore the end of the poem.[63]

The modern discovery of a seventh stanza to 'Three years' makes the strength of ideological supposition in Victorian reading particularly obvious to us, though it was, naturally, invisible to them. Ruskin's appropriation of 'Three years' to illustrate 'woman's true place and power' (99) – in the Home – occurs, once it is printed, in a book

> chiefly written for young people belonging to the upper, or undistressed middle, classes; who may be supposed to have choice of the objects and command of the industries of their life. It assumes that many of them will be called to occupy responsible positions in the world, and that they have leisure, in preparation for these, to play tennis, or to read Plato.
>
> Therefore also – that they have Plato to read if they choose, with lawns on which they may run, and woods in which they may muse. It supposes their father's library to be open to them ... (Ruskin 12)

Envisioning his privileged young audience 'with lawns on which they may run, and woods,' Ruskin seems to model them on the Lucy of 'Three years,' even as his reading of Lucy's education in 'Three years' models itself on this vision of their tutelage by a benevolent patriarchy. As this extreme ideological closure shows, Ruskin's reading is informed not merely by a literary Victorian prejudice of Wordsworthian nature's benevolence, for through this prejudice it reflects also the values of Victorian patriarchy: an implicit faith in the benevolence and efficacy of governance, and an implicit acceptance of the existing social relations as proper and natural. The resulting circularity – Patriarchy informs the reading of Wordsworthian nature (as benevolence), which informs the reading of 'Three years,' which reinforces Patriarchy (as Nature) – is a paradigm of interpretation's power to co-opt authority (Wordsworth) for ideology (Patriarchy). In this context 'Wordsworthian Nature' is not just Wordsworth's view of Nature, but Wordsworth's view, as represented by the Victorians, *as* Nature. Ruskin's (by modern standards) extraordinary view of 'Three years' as exemplifying the education that makes a woman 'wise, not for self-development, but for self-renunciation: wise, not that she may set herself above her husband, but that she may never fail from his side' (100), co-opts Nature when it co-opts Wordsworth. 'Observe, it is "Nature" who is speaking throughout,' he notes (101n). Ethel Wheeler, using the poem to illustrate 'Great Men's Visions of Womanhood' in 1898, explicitly naturalizes 'Wordsworth's Vision':

'Wordsworth's vision of womanhood is abstracted directly from Nature at the fountain-head. ... [his] healing and renewing power is as great as that of Nature's self' (270). But if such claims reveal the power of readings to naturalize ideology, they are themselves more wielded-by than wielding. The force of this ideology is not just to give all readings before Garrod a common slant, but literally to blind them all to the same issue – 'She died.' What cannot be made sense of within the paradigm is very simply not seen.

In Garrod the strain to understand ('I have never understood') is the strain of recognition, but to modern eyes it has been increasingly obvious that Lucy dies in stanza 7. So far from justifying confidence in our own perspicuity, however, the spectacle of the Victorians' blindness should make us conscious of ideological channelling in all reading – no doubt we wear similar blinders of our own. Our ability to recognize Lucy's death at all is largely contingent on our ability to assimilate it as irony, and thus (whether we find it an 'unmeaning' or cosmic irony or more specifically a result of too much governance) as a critique of patriarchy. And this ability participates in and depends on historically specific attitudes: on a modern (post-war) distrust of patriarchy; on an increasingly ironic understanding of Wordsworth and Wordsworthian nature; and on an increasingly secular view of nature generally.[64] Today, one might easily defend an ironic or anti-patriarchal reading of 'Three years' as typically Wordsworthian and even substantiate it with analogous texts,[65] but this shows no more than a widespread change in the habits and assumptions used in reading Wordsworth. The appropriate question may be whether we can *not* read the death in 'Three years.'

What Garrod discovered at the end of 'Three years' is not just Lucy's death, but the problem of its ambiguous relation to Nature's tutelage – like many of the ambiguities in 'A slumber,' an issue of a simple and uncertain connective. 'No adversative particle suggests that, between the "work" that was "done" and the death of Lucy, there is any opposition of idea or feeling,' he remarks (83). Does Lucy's death mean that a benevolent Nature has failed, that a malignant Nature has succeeded, that Nature is indifferent, or that its benevolence surpasses understanding? This seemingly irreducible problem has been as much the centre of commentary since Garrod as the tacit omission of stanza 7 was before; it might therefore stand as pre-interpretive, as a matter of description. But as the very fact that it had to be 'discovered' suggests, even this basic ambiguity is 'obvious' to us only as nature's benevolence was 'obvious' to the Victorians – as a function of our own reading. It is not an objective feature of the text, but is already contingent on a habit of reading that takes Lucy's death as an unfortunate epilogue to the story of 'Nature's education,' especially as its result.

To illustrate this point, I offer here a counter-interpretation showing that Lucy's death may be the *occasion* of Nature's interruption rather than its unexpected result. Though Garrod asks why Lucy 'grew in sun and shower' for 'Three years,' then declares that it does not bother him, he overlooks a less trivial problem concerning these years: the poem's contradictory depictions of nature and Nature. 'Three years she grew in sun and shower, / Then Nature said ... ' Personified 'Nature' states an intention to foster a Lucy who is already, like a flower, being fostered by a realistic nature. The conflict may escape notice, since what the interruptive Nature announces for Lucy is reminiscent both of 'sun and shower' and of Wordsworthian nature elsewhere.[66] But not only does the personification seem to conflict with Wordsworth's declared avoidance of personification in the Preface to *Lyrical Ballads* (Owen 74), in the poem itself it conflicts with the realistic nature in its intentionality: while 'Nature' is full of providential intentions, 'sun and shower' makes no promises at all. Thus, while the poem has been read as recounting a rivalry between the speaker and Nature for Lucy, it also presents a rivalry between two visions of nature.[67] One way to resolve the duality of these visions is to explain one as the speaker's representation of nature as it exists in itself, the other as it '*seem[s]* to exist to the *senses*, and to the *passions*' (*Prose* 3:63) – so that the speaking Nature is passion's version of the 'calm, and quiet' nature. In the Preface, Wordsworth admits that personifications 'are, indeed, a figure of speech occasionally prompted by passion,' and that he has 'made use of them as such,' though he 'reject[s] them as a mechanical device of style' (Owen 74). In this light, the poem's providential Nature is not supernatural in itself, but is the supernaturalization projected by passion.[68] And in this light, though it comes as a surprise on a first reading, Lucy's death is actually the poem's point of departure, the event that engenders the passion that colours the speaker's vision of nature. It is only at the end that, 'all passion spent,' the speaker returns to the everyday perception of nature, 'This heath, this calm, and quiet scene.' So far from being unconsolatory, the poem becomes, on this reading, an elegy – but one in which the consolation, the coming-to-terms with Lucy's death, inhabits the redescription of Lucy's life and death – as apotheosis. Carl Woodring was first to read 'Three years' as elegy: 'But how soon, the poet thinks and says, Lucy "left to me This heath, this calm, and quiet scene.'' ' The inferred 'But' reflects Garrod's perception of a closing ambiguity and decides, crucially, on the 'adversative': Woodring reads the poem as 'deepen[ing] a dramatic fantasy toward cosmic irony' (*Wordsworth* 46). But if, as I have suggested, Lucy's death is the occasion rather than the issue of the personified Nature, the question of the final stanza's relation to the rest of the poem does not arise, and an ironic reading is out of the question.

This reading is hardly 'verified,' proved 'most correct,' or made 'valid' by the appeal to Wordsworth's statements about personification – a point to which we must return in connection with Hirsch. Moreover, it merely presents new ambiguities, one might even say contradictions, that are, it seems to me, undecidable. Woodring cites the poem's debt to the lines in *Paradise Lost* on the field of Enna, 'where *Proserpin* gath'ring flow'rs / Herself a fairer Flow'r by gloomy *Dis* / Was gather'd' (4:269–71), observing the highly traditional nature of the poem's consolation. 'Lucy was a flower both nourished and gathered by Nature, with the implication of ancient myth that the gods take the most beautiful for themselves' (46). In the second of his 'Essays upon Epitaphs' Wordsworth himself cites a Christianized version of this conceit – which he paraphrases, 'God took her, who was my delight, from this earth to bring her nearer to himself' – and calls it 'reasonable and affecting' (*Prose* 2:73). As even these examples show, this conventional consolation – generically, 'Lucy was too good to live' – is assimilable to different creeds; and the irresolvable question of 'Three years,' implicit in the ambiguity of 'Nature,' is which creed its consolation refers to. On the one hand this vision of Lucy's death may strike one as apotheosis, as firmly in the pagan tradition cited by Woodring; on the other, the very God-like intentionality of this 'Nature' draws it closer to the Christianized conceit cited by Wordsworth.

Certain other features of the poem reinforce this duplicity: for one, the suspiciously Christian substance of 'Grace' is to be discovered 'Even in the motions of the Storm'; for another, there is the convertibility of these lines from stanza 2:

> 'The Girl, in rock and plain,
> In earth and heaven, in glade and bower,
> Shall feel an overseeing power
> To kindle or restrain.'

At first it appears to be Lucy, and only later the 'overseeing power,' that is to be 'in rock and plain, / In earth and heaven, in glade and bower.' The fleeting suggestion that Lucy is to be in both 'earth and heaven' (which should, incidentally, prevent her death from being a total surprise) hardly proves that the speaker sees her glorification in Christian terms; but it at least tempers the two other possible readings of the passage, the naturalistic reading (Lucy 'in rock and plain') and the pantheistic one (the 'overseeing power' in 'rock and plain').[69] Much in the same way, we found, the word 'seal' may temper the naturalistic and pantheistic readings of 'A slumber.'

My counter-interpretations have attempted to recover complexities, and in several cases to show how Wordsworth's complexity is generated by 'simple' vocabulary and syntax, while his 'simplicity' is generated by the sleights and oversights of reading. It can no doubt be objected, not that I have complicated, but that I myself have simplified the poems in the process, for to focus on certain ambiguities it is usually necessary to neglect others. Critics who have disputed the significance of 'trees' in 'A slumber,' and who have reasoned minutely about that poem's last two lines, have generally consolidated the contexts. But even the most cautious reader cannot be conscious of all reading assumptions. It is not just that acknowledging inhibits; the assumptions are too many.

To call these poems ambiguous is therefore a gross if comforting understatement. No doubt that is true of most literary texts, but the 'Lucy Poems' appear unusually polysemous. They can be (and have been) read as sentimental or ironic, optimistic or pessimistic, naturalistic or pantheistic, loving or murderous, as celebrating nature's care or as lamenting its indifference. I have traced this flexibility in part to the language of the individual poems, and in part to the oddities of Wordsworth's ordering. But it also owes something to the oddity of the unauthorial 'Lucy Poems' grouping. Precisely because it was *not* formulated by Wordsworth, this grouping is almost infinitely variable. Critics sometimes consider the poems singly, sometimes take two, three, or four; a systematic consideration of all five together is relatively rare.[70] This variability has interpretive effects, since 'A slumber' will take on different emphases and meanings considered alone or coupled with different 'Lucy Poems.' The uneasiness with Wordsworth's textual intention, even the conviction that it is wrong, allows one to create new wholes (ruling out the poems that do not fit the pattern one has in mind) with a clear conscience. But though this involves a violation in one sense, the violation itself is specifically responsive to Wordsworth's own poetics. One does not invent new poetical wholes by taking two or three of Shakespeare's or Sidney's sonnets or two or three *In Memoriam* lyrics, for the simple reason that one cannot maintain the fiction of the validity of such groupings.[71]

We do not need to go so far as to call the 'Lucy Poems' indeterminate. Practically speaking, it means little to speak of the 'determinacy' or 'indeterminacy' of texts themselves. As 'A slumber' suggests, meaning can always be 'determined' where readers are determined. But I could agree with Hirsch that the 'Lucy Poems' are 'determinate' in meaning if he would only stand by this definition of the term:

> Ambiguity or, for that matter, vagueness is not the same as indeterminateness. ... To say that verbal meaning is determinate is not to exclude complexities of meaning but only to insist that a text's meaning is what it is and not a hundred other things. Taken in this sense, a vague or ambiguous text is just as determinate as a logical proposition; it means what it means and nothing else. This is true even if one argues that a text could display shifting emphases like those magic squares which first seem to jut out and then to jut in. With texts of this character (if any exist), one need only say that the emphases shift and must not, therefore, be construed statically. Any static construction would simply be wrong. (*Validity* 230)

If it has been difficult to say what the 'Lucy Poems' mean in themselves, or even how they work, it may be because their 'determinacy' is of this Protean or 'magic square' variety. But we may now proceed to consider more fully what they have seemed to different eyes.

2 Reading against Uncertainty: Nineteenth-Century Closures

A record of change is not history without some scheme of development (including, of course, adverse development or decline); in this sense history is indissociable from narrative. But to seek such development in an 'evolution' or 'progress' of 'Lucy Poems' criticism is to broach problems that have dogged literary history from its beginnings. René Wellek states that literary history arose as a discipline in the later eighteenth century, H.R. Jauss that it has been in 'steady decline' for the past 150 years.[1] The explanation for such an inglorious career is evident in the term itself: since letters epitomize the necessity of reading, and thus of questioning whether we know the object or only our reading of it, literary objects remind historiography in an unusually stark manner that its foundations are interpretive.[2] Any effort to historicize a genre such as dramatic monologue or a mode such as allegory must first read particular texts either as instances of the kind or as alien to it. But if the fact that literature exists as it is read embarrasses literary history, history of criticism may need a double indulgence. So far from judging historical criticisms against a stable primary text, it confronts an unstable relation between two layers, 'primary' and 'secondary,' both of which exist as they are read. In so far as the criticism's very purpose is to alter our view of its object, this difficulty is compounded: to take a common situation, when one critic elaborates the insights of another, this makes it more difficult to appreciate the performance of the first, for critic B may have subtly altered my perception both of critic A's performance and of the 'primary' text by which it is presumably to be measured. Since I myself do not perceive the 'primary' text neutrally, but am in fact critic C, I must also be wary of positing my reading as a standard that historical readers more or less approximate. Can the 'development' of interpretation mean anything but its development toward my own? Ruling this out, can it mean anything but a succession of changes?

The first extant commentary on any of the 'Lucy Poems' other than by William and Dorothy Wordsworth illustrates these difficulties. While still in Germany, Coleridge received news of his son Berkeley's death from Thomas Poole, and in his reply of 6 April 1799, he passes directly from his musings on the evanescence of life to Wordsworth's 'A slumber':

> But I cannot truly say that I grieve – I am perplexed – I am sad – and a little thing, a very trifle would make me weep; but for the death of the Baby I have *not* wept! – Oh! this strange, strange, strange Scene-shifter, Death! that giddies one with insecurity, & so unsubstantiates the living Things that one has grasped and handled! – / Some months ago Wordsworth transmitted to me a most sublime Epitaph / whether it had any reality, I cannot say. – Most probably, in some gloomier moment he had fancied the moment in which his Sister might die. (*Letters* 1:479)[3]

Coleridge then writes the poem out under the title 'Epitaph'[4] and takes up other matters when he resumes his letter two days later. We don't know how much of this reflects Coleridge's creativity, for we don't have the letter in which Wordsworth originally sent him the poem; but nowhere on record did Wordsworth ever title the poem 'Epitaph' or refer to it as one.[5] What is most striking about Coleridge's commentary – the connection between the poem and Dorothy's 'fancied' death – is presented as supposition. The 'fancy' might derive from 'Strange fits,' for William and Dorothy had sent Coleridge a version including the variant: 'Strange are the fancies that will slide / Into a lover's head' (*Letters* 1:238). But not only does 'Strange fits' remain of uncertain relevance to 'A slumber,' Coleridge was quite capable of supplying such 'fancies' independently; indeed, the 'fancies' of 'Strange fits' may as easily be indebted to Coleridge's own 'Sonnet, Composed on a Journey Homeward' (1796), on the birth of Hartley:

> O my sweet baby! when I reach my door,
> If heavy looks should tell me thou art dead,
> (As sometimes, through excess of hope, I fear)
> I think that I should struggle to believe
> Thou wert a spirit ... (lines 7–11; *Poetical Works* 154)[6]

The coherence of Coleridge's reading of 'A slumber' with his own mental habits and with his state of mind at the time of writing gives some idea of the inventiveness of his reading, but it is anyone's guess where his invention begins and ends. We might guess better if we had read Wordsworth before Coleridge, but the very success of his reading makes that unlikely even for those who do not read Coleridge.

The 'progress' from Coleridge's association of 'A slumber' with Dorothy's 'fancied' death to similar readings of our own period is equally problematic. Coleridge's letter was first published in the Heinemann edition of 1895. Yet in the mid-1950s, when F.W. Bateson suggested that Lucy's death was Wordsworth's symbolic solution to his and Dorothy's discovery that they were falling in love, he was met with surprise and hostility.[7] Richard Matlack gave the thesis a more cynical turn in 1978: so far from fearing family romance, Matlack argues, Wordsworth in Goslar longed to join Coleridge in Göttingen, which Dorothy, in various ways, made impossible. '[H]e both needed and resented her,' and 'the Lucy lyrics began to form as an outlet for Wordsworth's ambivalence and frustration' (51). I find no record that readers found Matlack's thesis as startling as Bateson's; but, as 'Wordsworth's Lucy Poems in Psychobiographical Context,' it was judged sufficiently current to appear in *PMLA* 178 years after Coleridge first identified Lucy with Dorothy. My point is not that Matlack's essay is redundant, merely that its 'development' evidently cannot be gauged as can developments in technology. We cannot fairly gauge this as progress without knowing where Bateson and Matlack borrow from Coleridge and where they surpass him, and here the question is not simply whether they say what Coleridge said, but whether he said what they say.

Evidently Bateson and Matlack (both of whom quote Coleridge) and the contemporary Wordsworth specialists did not think so. With a will, one can argue even now that Coleridge's commentary is innocent of murderous implications: it might mean simply that Wordsworth feared Dorothy's death. But the phrase 'he had *fancied* the moment' has macabre possibilities. If we assume that the sense of 'desired' was implicit and generally available before being developed by Bateson and Matlack, their originality consists largely in attributing a *simply* murderous impulse to the poem, in short in disambiguating Coleridge's commentary; thus Coleridge seems not only to anticipate them, but to do so with a richer reading that both includes and exceeds theirs. The question is whether we would have found this meaning in Coleridge before. Likewise, though Bateson and Matlack use Freudian terminology unavailable to Coleridge, not only might his 'some gloomier moment' be taken to describe a psychic state such as they describe; the popular triumph of a Freudian psychology makes it more and more difficult not to understand such comments in its terms – and as Freud said, 'The poets and philosophers before me discovered the unconscious' (Trilling 32). Developments in our cultural assumptions will unavoidably affect our reading of Coleridge even where we are unconscious of it: in building on our precursors we may also pay an inadvertent tribute by which they prove to anticipate us, after all, in everything. But if the tribute runs both ways, to distinguish the building-on from the borrowing-from is very hard. History of criticism may either purchase a semblance of progress by 'historically' restricting Coleridge's statement to pre-Freudian meanings – thus stripping it of its modern resonances – or it may admit these at the cost of minimizing criticism's progress in close to two centuries since. But in either case it constructs itself on constructions.

1. Criticism in Contexts

These difficulties in plotting a triumphal progress of criticism ending at our own door do not invalidate history of criticism so much as they point it toward its more proper and interesting objects. The predominant object of the present study is the development of criticism not in any teleological sense, but in a reactive and admittedly relative one: not criticism's development-toward (e.g., clarification), but its development-out-of (e.g., disagreement). Criticism generally foregrounds the relation between the critic and the text ostensibly received or clarified, but less obvious contextual determinants and ulterior ends may be equally important. Rather than commit itself to criticism's own ideal and ostensive functions, history of criticism can profitably dwell on these complicating factors and purposes, thus plotting, rather than 'progress' from period to period, the tensions – between ostensive and covert purposes, between 'intrinsic' and 'extrinsic' factors – within given periods. With historical change in these conditions, these tensions also change: for instance, Victorian criticism of the 'Lucy Poems' is, in general, overtly interpretive and anti-analytical, while recent work tends to be more overtly analytical and anti-interpretive. But there is little warrant for regarding such changes as marking progress in our knowledge of the texts or of their meanings rather than shifts in criticism's conditions and ulterior aims.

To consider criticism among these complicating factors and purposes is, of course, to consider it in a socio-political context. But just as it includes virtually everything, this term means virtually nothing until the context is more concretely specified. Fredric Jameson calls such specific contexts the 'concentric frameworks' or 'horizons' of cultural interpretation, and though he specifies three such frameworks for the purpose of his own study, what both his terms imply is that one's choice of 'horizon' is to some extent arbitrary, depending on the aims of one's analysis.[8] As explained by Gadamer, from whom Jameson borrows the concept, '[a] horizon is not a rigid frontier' (216): 'The historical movement of human life consists in the fact that it is never utterly bound to any one standpoint, and hence can never have a truly closed horizon' (271). I take the denial of the 'closed horizon' to mean, among other things, that no consideration of an object within a specific horizon can claim to be exhaustive, since the object always also inhabits more intrinsic and more extrinsic horizons. Thus, if concreteness demands the specification of our analytical horizon, fairness demands that we recognize the arbitrariness and incompleteness of any analysis, no matter how searching, within this horizon.

I stress this arbitrariness because modern studies have overwhelmingly favoured what Peter Uwe Hohendahl calls *The Institution of Criticism* (1982) as the proper context for describing what Terry Eagleton calls *The Function of Criticism* (1984), and in so far as this horizon is considered exhaustive it tends to produce reductive characterizations which are, in fact, aptly reflected by Eagleton's nominative singular. The cover of my paperback edition shows 'Function' circled in red, graphically suggesting how an emphatic singularity of function is produced by circumscription; the severity of Eagleton's analysis comes from his reducing criticism's plural functions to its function *within* its institution, whether the partisanship of the eighteenth- and nineteenth-century Reviews or modern academic criticism's 'establish[ment of] its professional legitimacy' (*Function* 38–40, 57). It would be wrong, of course, to neglect criticism's institutional aims, especially in a period which saw – again in Eagleton's phrase – 'The Rise of English.' Such analyses are valuable as correctives to criticism's own self-representations – as in 'humanism' and 'disinterestedness.'[9] Still, such analyses can hardly exhaust the plural functions of criticism. In fact, the institutional enclosure criticized by Eagleton is not simply an objective event in the self-development of literary study, as he represents it (*Function* 56–7, 65), but is partly an illusion of his analytical focus. Reducing the multifarious 'socio-political context' to the institutional context makes systematic socio-political analysis feasible, even simple, but as a conceptual containment of far more complex affiliations it may also inadvertently perpetuate the illusion of neutrality it sets out to explode:

> modern criticism [Eagleton argues] was born of a struggle against the absolutist state. It has ended up, in effect, as a handful of individuals reviewing each other's books. ... Today, apart from its marginal role in reproducing the dominant social relations through the academies, it is almost entirely bereft of such a *raison d'être*. It engages at no significant point with any substantive social interest, and as a form of discourse is almost entirely self-validating and self-perpetuating. (*Function* 107–8)

In a similar analysis putting Eagleton himself in the institutional margin, Edward Said envisions the academy as a closed system of 'three thousand critics reading each other,' and denigrates modern academic criticism as 'marginal' and 'noninterfer[ing]' (10, 28–9).[10] These depressing portraits grant with a vengeance the political neutrality criticism occasionally claims for itself; but such strategic contempt may also entail a dangerous misrepresentation. In both Eagleton and Said, the closed horizon of the institution facilitates an analysis admitting criticism to be political *within* its institution, political in the most petty sense, while dismissing ulterior political functions, including that of the institution itself. For instance, to call 'reproducing the dominant social relations' a 'marginal role' is to confuse a specific and by definition powerful political program with the imaginary apolitical, and thus to affirm the illusion that most empowers such a program in the first place.

This is not to propose that we read the criticism of Wordsworth's 'Lucy Poems' directly in the context of international politics, even if that context should not be dismissed out of hand. What W.J.T. Mitchell calls 'the politics of interpretation' emerges concretely only if we closely consider more *intrinsic* contexts than the institutional one. Not just the politics but the 'point' of criticism as an intellectual activity has everything to do with its bearings this and that side of the institutional horizon; what makes the vision of 'three thousand critics reading each other' depressing is its programmatic suppression of these bearings. The typical Sunday Supplement attack on deconstruction or 'political correctness' employs its external venue to the same abstractive effect: it cites numbers, names names, and lists titles rather than engage the specific arguments it dismisses. Yet the external venue (specifically, the perch on the outer institutional walls) appears to be essential to 'literary anti-professionalism' even when that anti-professionalism is, as Stanley Fish remarks, 'a feature of the profession itself.'[11] When Eagleton finds it 'hard to believe that, in a nuclear age, the publication of yet another study of Robert Herrick is justifiable' (*Function* 108), his unreading dismissal depends directly on the closed horizon of the institution, since that is all that determines Herrick as canonical, 'literary,' and frivolous. It is, of course, the rhetorical and corrective point of such arguments to pay 'more attention to how teachers ... *profess* than to what they *say* about culture or about the role of literature' – as Richard Ohmann describes his own method (27). But criticism is not just institutionally determined; it is overdetermined. A competent description of its functions and development must heed also its more immediate conditions and more specific arguments, what critics *say*.

The period of 'Lucy Poems' criticism sees the 'Rise of English' as a modern institution, but it also sees the rise of 'theory' and considerable changes in the specific practices of criticism. Rather than view the latter developments as simple functions of the former, I think all three must be viewed as cognate functions of and in broader social developments, particularly the rise of 'the common reader' and democratization in general. Coleridge's infamous remarks of 1817 on these events are useful reminders of the anxieties they involved for the learned classes:

> among the other odd burs and kecksies, the misgrowth of our luxuriant activity, we have now a READING PUBLIC – as strange a phrase, methinks, as ever forced a splenetic smile on the staid countenance of Meditation; and yet no fiction! For our Readers have, in good truth, multiplied exceedingly, and have waxed proud ...

The reading public is, as Coleridge jokes in a footnote, 'voonders above voonders,' like a learned pig or a reading fly; and it calls for a proper system of 'national education' to bring it under control (*Lay Sermons* 36–40).[12] With more heterogeneous readers reading, the 'Lucy Poems' criticism inevitably evolves among similar anxieties concerning the plurality of interpretations and the consequent uncertainty of learned opinion. And to these anxieties the institution of English and literary theory both stand as countervailing educational projects. The function of practical criticism that stands out as most important in this context, and which my own analyses therefore privilege, is *persuasion*: that by which one's reading is urged upon others, by which 'wrong' readings are rejected, by which both readings and procedures are standardized, by which perspectival difference is collapsed, by which the very possibility of diversity is contained. The persuasive function necessarily radiates across criticism's concentric cultural horizons: if it appears most concretely within specific literary-critical disputes (is 'A slumber' ironic or pantheistic? are appeals to authorial intention relevant?), it appears most generally, within the institution and beyond, as a form of social indoctrination.

Institutional factors are most visible in the earliest 'Lucy Poems' criticism, if only because the institutions of this period are strangest to us. I therefore turn to this commentary to consider the extent of these factors' relevance before considering subsequent commentary in relation to the modern anxiety of difference. The earliest surviving 'Lucy Poems' criticism derives entirely from what appear, to a modern viewpoint, special contexts: the overtly political Reviews and the letters and memoranda of Wordsworth's family and friends. Much of what seems strangest in this criticism – that it is predominantly judgmental; that it presumes meanings rather than interpret overtly; that it is usually so brief – is easily explained by reference to the strange institutional setting. But beyond these superficial matters, I think the institution explains little directly, and that the modern liberal institution can explain even less than can the more constrictive institutions of most romantic criticism, the Reviews.

Most of the earliest criticism of the 'Lucy Poems' is indeed so brief that we can view all of it (so far as I know) from Reviews and letters up to 1835, before venturing any observations. John Stoddart's review of *Lyrical Ballads* (1801) calls 'Strange fits' and 'She dwelt' 'the most singular specimens of unpretending, yet irresistible pathos,' compares them favourably with Burns in point of 'artlessness,' says 'they have a secret connection,' and reprints them entire. An anonymous review of *Poems, in Two Volumes* belittles 'Among all lovely things' as 'the very climax and *ne plus ultra* of absurdity,' and continues: 'Another string of flat lines about Lucy ['I travelled'] is succeeded by an ode to Duty ...'[13] Francis Jeffrey's review of George Crabbe (1808) contrasts Crabbe, who 'exhibits the common people of England pretty much as they are,' with 'Mr Wordsworth and his associates,' who 'show us something that mere observation never yet suggested to anyone' (133). Jeffrey cites 'Strange fits' as an instance of this eccentricity:

> Love, and the fantasies of lovers, have afforded an ample theme to poets of all

ages. Mr Wordsworth, however, has thought fit to compose a piece, illustrating this copious subject by one single thought. A lover trots away to see his mistress one fine evening, staring all the way at the moon: when he comes to her door,

> 'O mercy! to myself I cried,
> If Lucy should be dead!'

And there the poem ends! (136)

There Jeffrey's commentary on Lucy ends as well. In 1815 a reviewer of Wordsworth's collected poems writes of 'Three years,' *in toto*, 'One of these poems (which has no title, but might have been called *Lucy* or *the Darling*) has more of the character of Shenstone's productions than any of the rest. The following are the first and last verses ...'[14]

In the letters of the Wordsworth circle, Coleridge's remarks to Poole on 'A slumber' (discussed above) are unusual in offering anything like an interpretation. In another letter of 1800 he says, 'I would rather have written Ruth, and Nature's Lady than a million such poems [as his own "Christabel"]' (*Letters* 1:632). The only other extant comment by Coleridge occurs in the *Biographia* (1817), where 'Three years' is cited as an instance of 'the perfect truth of nature in [Wordsworth's] images and descriptions' (2:148–9). Dorothy, in sending early versions off to Coleridge, declares that 'Strange fits' 'is a favorite of mine – i.e., of me Dorothy.'[15] Charles Lamb lists 'the Song of Lucy' among '[w]hat most please me' in a letter of 30 January 1801 thanking Wordsworth for a copy of *Lyrical Ballads* (*Letters of Charles and Mary Anne Lamb* 265–6); presumably he means 'She dwelt,' which was titled 'Song' in 1800 and which Lamb copied for Thomas Manning two weeks later. As he tells Manning (15 February 1801),

> Writing to *you*, I may say, that the 2d vol. has no such pieces as the 3 I enumerated. – It is full of original thinking and an observing mind, but it does not often make you laugh or cry. – It too artfully aims at simplicity of expression. And you sometimes doubt if simplicity be not a cover for Poverty. The best Piece in it I will send you, being *short* – I have grievously offended my friends in the North by declaring my undue preference. But I need not fear you –
>
> [the text of 'She dwelt']
>
> This is choice and genuine, and so are many more. But one does not like to have 'em ramm'd down one's throat – 'Pray take it – its very good – let me help you – eat faster.' – . – . (273–4)

Lamb makes a show of being more frank with Manning, but he had forthrightly informed Wordsworth of the same judgments: 'I do not *feel* any poem in [volume 2] so forcibly as the Ancient Marinere, the Mad mother, and the Lines at Tintern Abbey in the *first*' (266). His complaint to Wordsworth regarding 'The Old Cumberland Beggar,' that its 'instructions' are too prominent and 'dont slide into the mind of the reader' (265), may make an oblique reference to 'Strange fits.' In a letter to Dorothy, 2 March 1801, John Wordsworth quotes Stoddart's positive notice of 'Strange fits' and 'She dwelt' (99). And if we may believe a letter of Benjamin Bailey from 1849, Keats found 'the simplicity of the last line' of 'She dwelt' 'to be the most perfect pathos' (Rollins 2:276). The award for minimalist commentary must go to William Blake, who, sometime around 1826, apparently put X's by the titles of 'Lucy Gray,' 'Strange fits,' and 'Louisa' in the contents page of Wordsworth's *Poems* (1815) (665).

Aside from fact that there is, as yet, barely any suggestion of the modern 'Lucy Poems' grouping (Stoddart's mention of 'a secret connection' refers to two poems which were, after all, contiguous in his edition), this body of criticism raises two important considerations.

First, while the 'institutional' context is essential for explaining the general shape and similarity of this criticism, especially its brevity, it cannot specifically explain how and why one commentary differs from another. The romantic Reviews were generally conceived of as communal organs of taste; as Hazlitt says in the essay 'On Criticism' (1822), 'There must be *tasters* for the public' (8:215). John O. Hayden observes that 'the reviewers thought their critical function was to influence both the writer and the reader. Duty to the writer was more often mentioned; frequently the poet was to be set straight on certain errors of content or form' (*The Romantic Reviewers* 243–4). This judgmental and selective conception of the critic's function (which applies to most epistolary criticism as well) may explain the criticism's overtly judgmental character, but cannot begin to explain the judgments themselves. An institution like the Reviews might best be considered as a *forum* that visibly *forms* criticism, but more or less externally and without wholly determining it. We can see this better by contrast with the early criticism I have excluded from the lists above, a journal entry by Henry Crabb Robinson (1816) and two passages from more extended essays by John Wilson (1829) and Thomas Powell (1831). The more liberal venue of these commentaries facilitates a criticism more diverse in function and more similar to that of recent periods – a criticism that not only passes judgments, but also lingers to interpret, and even to analyse preliminary complexities such as the distinction between the poem itself and its reading. Thomas Powell, as we have seen, challenges positive judgments of 'A slumber' by implying that its profundity is actually projected by Wordsworth's admirers. Similarly, but more sympathetically, Wilson points to the evocative function of 'simplicity' in 'She dwelt,' asserting that '[t]he great object of poetry is, to suggest more than she expresses' (*Essays* 1:314). Of 'A slumber,' he remarks:

> Here, how much is said in little – how many themes for reflection are suggested! That form, which the imaginative colouring of real passion had invested with immortality, is now no more than the inanimate productions of nature. Once the living vehicle of the soul, and almost identified with it, in the wondrous motions of eye and lip, it is now immoveable and impassive as the solid rocks! It is a subject too painful to dwell upon. (*Essays* 1:318)

This anticipates modern commentaries not only in perceiving an absolute division between past and present, life and death, but also in stressing the phenomenological complexity of this division: it is not purely a contrast between the heroine's life and death, but also between the speaker's love and grief, or between imaginative reading (the 'colouring of real passion') and disillusioned witness. Henry Crabb Robinson, discussing 'She dwelt,' similarly dwells on the reading *within* it. For him, the poem shows

> the powerful effect of the loss of a very obscure object upon one tenderly attached to it – the opposition between the apparent strength of the passion and the insignificance of the object is delightfully conceived ... (1:191)

If the judgmental function is still evident in these commentaries, it is not their predominant function; indeed, the greater emphasis on subjectivity, on the *readers* of and in the poems, inevitably perplexes this function. Though the overt political stance of *Blackwood's Edinburgh Magazine*, in which Wilson's commentary first appears, is 'ultra-Tory' (Hayden 62), and though Crabb Robinson is politically conservative as well, the transition from the judgmental, concise, and tonally objective criticism of the Reviews to the reflective, relaxed, and more subjective forms of criticism in the magazine or personal journal epitomizes the liberalization of 'the institution of criticism' since the romantic period. Most obviously, but not insignificantly, a relaxation of spatial constraint results in an expatiating criticism; Wilson's essay on Wordsworth runs to 120 pages. Within the liberalized institution there is less consensus regarding the function of criticism and, what is much the same, more freedom of comment. It is true, on the one hand, that this 'freedom' is still scarcely absolute, and on the other that it is, itself, an important 'institutional' consideration.[16] Nevertheless, the more freedom of comment the institution permits, the less useful it is in explaining what is done within that freedom.

The second consideration raised by these commentaries is partisanship or 'bias.' The source of bias to be most suspected in early 'Lucy Poems' criticism is personal and familial, so much of it issues from intimates (even inmates) or acquaintances: Dorothy Wordsworth, Coleridge, Stoddart, Lamb, Crabb Robinson, Wilson, Keats, De Quincey. This is true of early Wordsworth criticism in general: add Hazlitt, Southey, Barron Field, Arnold, and Aubrey de Vere. Yet bias of this sort is probably not worth belabouring. Not only are the causes for bias obvious, hence easy to allow for, but most of this criticism remains surprisingly disinterested by the usual standards. Friends like Southey, Lamb, Wilson, and Sara Hutchinson were not always the kindest of critics, while others like Hazlitt, Coleridge, Keats, and De Quincey continued to write enthusiastically of the poet even when estranged from the man.

The early commentary's other partisan commitments are less obvious to modern eyes and ultimately less extricable from a 'purely literary' assessment.[17] In so far as we tend not to read the 'Lucy Poems' as political pieces, we are inclined to miss political factors in their reception. It is therefore important to recall that they *may* be read politically: 'The difference to me!' has strong individualistic overtones; 'I travelled' may be read as a tale of dissent, voluntary exile, remorse, and repatriation; 'Three years' may be taken as pro- or anti-patriarchal.[18] Wordsworth's earliest readers often understood what we see as simply aesthetic innovation in political terms, as 'revolution,' and reacted accordingly.[19] Moreover, with its claims to innovation, the 1800 Preface provided a quasi-political context for poems that might have otherwise seemed apolitical even to Wordsworth's contemporaries; the most hostile reviews of *Poems, in Two Volumes* (1807) took the poems as products of the revolutionary 'system' formulated seven years earlier.[20] De Quincey argues that Wordsworth's early unpopularity began in the experimental claims in the 1798 'Advertisement' and in the Preface's polemics. 'Nothing more injudicious was ever done by man,' he says of the Preface, but after applying its statements to the diction of earlier poets, he demands: 'what is it that you are proposing to change? What room for a revolution?' ('On Wordsworth's Poetry' 545–6). The originality of *Lyrical Ballads* remains an item of dispute precisely because it is an issue less of poems revolutionary in themselves than of Wordsworth's manipulation of his audience to expect and therefore 'discover' novelty.[21] It remains a task to define both innovation and politics in this poetry precisely because they are often not *in* the poetry but in the way it was presented. This makes the politics of Wordsworth's reception difficult to reckon.

Nevertheless, the early 'Lucy Poems' commentary serves well to illustrate the fallacy of Arnold's influential exposé of partisan commitment as 'the bane of criticism' (3:270–1). Bias, personal or political, does not necessarily vitiate criticism, and 'considering the source' likewise does little to explain a criticism away. Crabb Robinson's reading of 'She dwelt' as an 'opposition between the apparent strength of the [speaker's] passion and the insignificance of the object' may seem monstrously chauvinist to many of today's readers. In calling Lucy 'a very obscure *object*,' an 'it,' Crabb Robinson seems to expose primarily himself, especially in the assumptions that translate otherness (whether gender, class, or city/country difference) as thingness, 'obscurity' as 'insignificance.' Yet his reading does reflect the text also; whether or not we can endorse it, it replicates in usefully exaggerated fashion the poem's own 'egotistical sublime,' its tendency to devalue the 'object' qua object even while sublimating it within the subject: 'The difference to me!' The same holds for more hostile commentaries, as Thomas Powell and Francis Jeffrey illustrate. Powell's 'pungent' discussion of 'A slumber' apparently targets the bardolatry of the 'Wordsworthians,' but it illuminates the poem and the dynamics of its reception far more than do other criticisms that appear less predisposed. Jeffrey's stage-wonder before 'Strange fits' – 'And there the poem ends!' – no doubt serves his peculiar, long-standing grudge against Wordsworth. But if only in registering a contemporary's sense of novelty, it is also more revealing than the judicious approvals of Dorothy Wordsworth, Lamb, and others; it is, as a later critic says, 'an unintentionally good criticism' (Augustus Jack 98n). If these cases suggest that bias and even spleen cannot in themselves invalidate criticism, subsequent developments will show still more clearly the justice of Geoffrey Hartman's remark that '[n]ot our subjectivity is to be feared but our over-reaction to it' (*Beyond* xi). Criticism's modern ailment has proved to be, not bias, but the bias against bias.

2. 'Lucy Poems' Criticism and the Anxiety of Uncertainty

The 'Lucy Poems' criticism, from 1800 to the present, occupies the period of what Paul de Man terms the 'crisis of criticism.' The crisis arrives, he says, because 'the observation and interpretation of others is always also a means of leading to the observation of the self,' and because this inward turn appears to undermine the outward observations that initiate it.[22] For de Man, the 'link' between criticism and crisis is thus an essential one; but it may also be explained historically, for the secular reading community since the eighteenth century has increasingly reflected upon its own activity while also seeking to minimize the subjective and differential aspects of reading. The criticism of the 'Lucy Poems' has grown up in the midst of this reflectivity, and inevitably carries its mark. Moreover, as unusually indeterminate texts, the 'Lucy Poems' seem calculated to aggravate the 'crisis of criticism.' Their historical treatment can therefore be used to illuminate this crisis and vice versa.

The complex of self-consciousness and anti-self-consciousness afflicts romantic poetry and modern criticism alike, and in both cases the 'crisis' might be traced both to developments in Enlightenment philosophy and aesthetics and to the historical extension of readership to a fuller range of social classes.[23] A brilliant remark by Friedrich Schlegel seems to observe the affliction as it spreads: 'Everyone's view of poetry is true and good as far as that view itself is poetry. But since one's poetry is limited, just because it is one's own, so one's view of poetry must of necessity be limited' (54). By Schlegel's time both limitations were already familiar metacritical topoi, and the limitations of criticism had long begun to be addressed by the emergence of literary 'theory' in its specifically modern guise as a prophylaxis against subjectivity.[24] Most obviously, perhaps, the eighteenth century saw the rise of the essay format now so familiar in literary theory, the two-part, problem-solution essay which opens with a notice of readerly differences (surveys of idiosyncratic readings, lists of absurd or conflicting evaluations) and ends with a containment or cure of the spectre (recommendations for standards and methods, exhortations to generosity, formulations of reason). Representatives of this *pseudocritica epidemica* tradition include Pope's 'Essay on Criticism' (1711), Johnson's ninety-third *Rambler* essay (5 February 1751), Hume's essay 'Of the Standard of Taste' (1757), and (later, but characteristic) Hazlitt's 'Of Criticism' (1821). Prominent modern instances would include I.A. Richards' *Practical Criticism* (1929) (see note 12 above), William Empson's *Seven Types of Ambiguity* (1930), which proliferates ambiguities only to recommend an intentionalist hermeneutics by which to control them (241–3), and E.D. Hirsch's *Validity in Interpretation* (1967), where the opening move is reduced to a few complaints about creeping relativism (e.g., vii–ix, 212–13) and closural theory reigns supreme. But as the very persistence of such projects suggests, the subjectivity problem has been stronger than its containments. Pope's couplet, 'Tis with our judgments as our watches, none / Go just alike, yet each believes his own' (9–10), is stronger than are his ensuing calls for deference to nature and rules (68–140), his exhortation to 'gen'rous converse' (641), or his assimilation of perspectival difference to sickness: 'all looks yellow to the jaundiced eye' (559). The fretting of Johnson, Hazlitt, and Arnold over the prevalence of 'political criticism' (Hazlitt 8:220) has likewise been more persuasive than their proposed cures, 'common sense' and 'disinterestedness.' Just as Descartes has come to stand for the very scepticism he sought to contain, these projects are better evidence of our doubts than of our assurances.

Wordsworth's wry note to Coleridge regarding the reception of *Lyrical Ballads* typifies the 'crisis of criticism' in 1801, but also since then:

For Coleridges entertainment I send the following harmonies of criticism –

Nutting Mr C. Wordsworth worth its weight in gold	Nutting Mr Stoddart can make neither head nor tail of it.
Joanna Mr John Wordsworth the finest poem of its length you have written	Joanna Mr Stoddart takes the description of the echoes as a thing regularly and permanently believed of course can make nothing of the poem.
Poet's Epitaph Mr Charles Lamb the latter part eminently good and your own.	Poet's Epitaph Mr Stoddart the latter part I dont like, it is very ill written.
Cumberland Beggar Mr John Wordsworth Indeed every body seems	Mr Charles Lamb The instructions too direct You

delighted with Cumberland
Beggar.

Idiot Boy
Mr John Wordsworth
To a Lady friend of mine I
gave the 2 vol: they were
both new to her. The idiot
Boy of all the poems her
delight; could talk of no
thing else.
But here comes the Waggon!

seem to presume your readers are
stupid &c. &c.

Idiot Boy
Mr Stoddart
Thrown into a *fit* almost
with disgust, cannot *possibly*
read it.

(*Letters* 1:319–21)

These 'harmonies' anticipate I.A. Richards' 'protocols,' but Wordsworth's open formulation, omitting (for whatever reason) the usual efforts to reconcile or explain his readers' differences, suggests more graphically the recalcitrance of criticism's crisis in a period when more readers have less in common.

What is missing at the end of Wordsworth's protocols is, of course, the usual corrective recourse to 'theory.' But the anxiety of difference does not only produce 'theory'; it also affects critical practice. In considering the criticism of the 'Lucy Poems,' I assume that there is no pure 'response' to the poems themselves, uncrossed by response to the 'crisis' of criticism itself. Just as romantic poetry ranges between two polarized responses to subjectivity, celebration and denial, modern criticism ranges between the 'creative' and 'objective' poles.[25] In plotting 'Lucy Poems' criticism on this scale, I seek to show the ways in which practical criticism has both registered and been inflected by anxieties of difference.

It may be necessary to stress that 'creative criticism' is not just an extreme response to discontents in contemporary criticism, or merely a sport of wit in Wilde's 'The Critic as Artist' (1890), but also a romantic response to the suspicion that there is no objective criticism – a playful yet fundamentally serious response, reformulating a perceived necessity as a virtue.[26] In pronouncing that one's view of poetry is itself poetry, Schlegel effectively presents 'creative criticism' as both problem and solution.[27] But an exponent closer to home is John Wilson. In 1817, Wilson wrote a savage attack on Wordsworth's *Letter to a Friend of Robert Burns* (1816) in *Blackwood's Edinburgh Magazine*, then a eulogistic defence and then another attack – all of which appear to be written with conviction. On the surface, this presents a case of inconsistency more frightening than Wordsworth's tabulated 'harmonies of criticism,' since it all issues from one man in the span of a few months.[28] Even at its most 'responsible,' Wilson's criticism can seem whimsical: a single essay can attack the closing of 'Strange fits' – '"Oh, mercy!" to myself I cried, / "If Lucy should be dead!"' – for 'vulgarity of diction' (*Critical* 1:239), then comment on 'She dwelt':

> 'But she is in her grave, – and oh / The difference to me!'. ... The simplicity of the expression matters little if it fulfils the purpose of the author; and it is of no consequence how common the words may be, if they are only the surface to a mine of thought. (314)

The same comment could be applied as well to the former poem; the difference in Wilson's judgments seems to reflect primarily his own moods. His treatment of Wordsworth's *Letter* has understandably been read as yellow journalism, even as schizophrenia.[29] But if his practice is suspect by conventional standards, it may constitute a challenge to those standards, not just a lapse from them. J.H. Alexander presents the efforts of Wilson and other *Blackwood's* writers as early experiments in 'creative criticism' specifically targeting the 'objective' criticism of the *Edinburgh Review*. '*Maga* made a point of admitting the validity of differing attitudes,' Alexander notes; '[t]he reader is encouraged, as in Romantic poetry, to make his own connections, and ... the irony is also educative' (61, 63). Though this may appear a wildly generous reading of Wilson, Alexander makes a persuasive case for it. Wilson wrote in 1818: 'Scarcely one syllable of truth – that is, of knowledge – has ever appeared in the Edinburgh Review on the general principles of Wordsworth's poetry' (quoted by Strout, 'John Wilson' 390n). And one of the *Blackwood's* group, possibly Wilson himself, describes Wilson's practice as parodically immersing objectivist postures within a perspectivist process: 'by doing all that [the *Edinburgh Review*] could do in one Number, and then undoing it in the next,' Wilson 'convinced the Brutum Pecus that 'tis all quackery and humbug' (quoted by Alexander 61).

Wilson may exemplify 'creative criticism' at the lunatic fringe, but this concern with truth, knowledge, and humbug suggests that his practice is not merely capricious: motivated by a hyper-consciousness of perspective, his practice parodically accentuates it to bring the high authoritarian ground of more objectivist criticism in question. Is it possible that this hyper-consciousness should afflict only a few Schlegels and Wilsons? I think it may be presumed that *all* modern criticism worth speaking of, even the objectivist practice that Wilson opposes, responds to the same doubts, and perhaps never more so than when it seems to forget them. One merit of this presumption is that it may deepen our understanding of objectivist critical practices. It is easy to regard the objectivism of mainstream nineteenth-century criticism as a sort of naïveté, but it is only one side of a polarized field, and we cannot appreciate it fairly until we appreciate it whole, including the anxieties and alternative practices to which it responds. The rest of this chapter examines the nineteenth century's grouping and narratization of the 'Lucy Poems' as an effort to objectify and fix literary meanings and judgments. But on the other hand lie the unfixing and self-undermining efforts of nineteenth-century 'creative criticism,' parody and allusion, which are treated in chapter 4. To understand either of these movements it is important to bear in mind that they are not chance gestures in Victorian criticism but antithetical responses to a common problematics.

3. Gathering Lucy

> ... the sad friends of Truth, such as durst appear, imitating the carefull search that *Isis* made for the mangl'd body of *Osiris*, went up and down gathering up limb by limb still as they could find them.
>
> John Milton, *Areopagitica* (*Prose* 317)

The nineteenth century's most decisive interpretive accomplishment with the 'Lucy Poems' was to gather them as such. Hugh Sykes Davies offered a critical history of this grouping in 1965; I follow his account more or less passively before offering qualifications, since it is lucid and insightful and not often cited. Indeed, the scholarly community's strange and extensive neglect of Sykes Davies' arguments against the 'Lucy Poems' grouping seems to reflect its continuing need for the grouping: what cannot be refuted can still be ignored.[30]

Sykes Davies notes that Wordsworth's 'simplicity' in arranging his poems 'suggested ... a kind of duplicity' to some, and he cites De Quincey's insinuation (1839) that the poems veiled something material: 'he always preserved a mysterious silence on the subject of that "Lucy."'[31] As Sykes Davies observes,

> Here is the 'Lucy' problem in embryo, but with its main features already distinct: the supposition that the poems containing her name must form a group

linked by concern for a particular young woman, and the speculation as to who she might have been in reality. (147)

Noting that De Quincey dropped the comment on Lucy when he reprinted his essay on Wordsworth in 1854, Sykes Davies suggests that such speculation was generally laid aside out of 'tact' until after Wordsworth's death (147–8). Thenceforth, he asserts, the Lucy grouping was the work of 'anthologists and editors,' particularly Francis Turner Palgrave and Matthew Arnold (148). In sequence, Palgrave's *Golden Treasury* (1861) collected 'She dwelt' (titled 'The Lost Love'), 'I travelled,' 'Three years' (titled 'The Education of Nature'), and 'A slumber'; Arnold's slender selection, *Poems of Wordsworth* (1879), printed 'Strange fits,' 'Three years,' 'She dwelt,' 'A slumber,' and 'I travelled.'[32] Sykes Davies points out the significance of Arnold's ordering:

There, for the first time, the four poems which have ever since made up the 'Lucy group' were printed together, and 'A slumber' was firmly sandwiched between the last two, so that there was no chance of its acquiring any independent life of its own. (148)

Both Palgrave's and Arnold's books were popular and must have been influential in establishing the 'Lucy Poems'' sequentiality, if not their sequence. Reviewing Arnold's selection in 1880, Aubrey de Vere defends the assertion that Wordsworth 'has written love poems' by citing 'the five associated with the name of Lucy.' He identifies, as first to fourth in the sequence (thus altering Arnold's order), 'Strange fits,' 'I travelled,' 'Three years,' and 'a retrospect,' 'She dwelt.' 'The last,' he continues,

is a dirge, which those who confound the passionate with the exclamatory will do well to pass by, but which to others will appear in its stern brevity and absolute hopelessness, the tragic rising to the terrible – [quoting 'A slumber did my spirit seal' *in toto*].

That these poems are love poems is certain: whether they were founded on reality, the poet has left unrecorded. We derive on this subject no information from the invaluable notes signed I.F., and written at Wordsworth's dictation ...

No one was less disposed than Wordsworth to minister to that vulgar curiosity which in these days respects no sanctuary. ... He was confidential on subjects respecting which others have nothing to confide; but confidences such as those in which some poets have been profuse would have been against his instincts. ('The Genius' 13–15)

Sykes Davies aptly remarks:

> It is, of its kind, a splendid passage, exemplary of the amenity with which a scholar who was also a gentleman, and a minor poet to boot, could make the very best of a non-existent case. The tone is so tactfully respectful of the 'sanctuary' of the poet's private life that the trespass upon it almost escapes unnoticed; the air of 'he would an'if he could' is so gently pressed, and so well introduced by the candid admission that there was no firm evidence anywhere as to the reality of 'Lucy' – the very fact that Wordsworth had revealed nothing is made to look like a proof that he had plenty to reveal, had it not been 'against his instincts'. And 'A slumber' is so deftly included among the poems 'associated with the name of Lucy' that it seems quite churlish to point out that the name does not in fact occur in it. This is indeed the way to create literary myths; and this was indeed the way in which this one was created. (149–50)

De Vere's biographical innuendo, perhaps even more than Arnold's edition, sparked interest in the grouping. Sykes Davies notes that two studies of Wordsworth published the following year (1881) repeat 'de Vere's legend.' Indeed, F.W.H. Myers, though Sykes Davies does not quote him, outdoes de Vere in respectful innuendo:

> And here [in Goslar] it was that the memory of some emotion prompted the lines on *Lucy*. Of the history of that emotion he has told us nothing; I forbear, therefore, to inquire concerning it, or even to speculate. That it was to the poet's honour, I do not doubt; but who ever learned such secrets rightly? or who should wish to learn? It is best to leave the sanctuary of all hearts inviolate, and to respect the reserve not only of the living but of the dead. Of these poems, almost alone, Wordsworth in his autobiographical notes has said nothing whatever. One of them he suppressed for years, and printed only in a later volume. One can, indeed, well imagine that there may be poems which a man may be willing to give to the world only in the hope that their pathos will be, as it were, protected by its own intensity, and that those who are worthiest to comprehend will be least disposed to discuss them. (34)

As Myers' supposition of 'reserve' shows, the interpretation of silence as suppression is central not just to the appreciation of the individual lyrics, but to the formation of the grouping. Though he does not specify which 'lines on Lucy' he means, Myers' palpable borrowing from de Vere suggests that he is commenting on the Arnoldian grouping. A.J. Symington's study of 1881 also repeats de Vere's biographical suppossition, and prints the poems entire: 'I travelled,' 'Strange fits,' 'Three years,' 'A slumber,' and 'She dwelt' (1:128–32; Sykes Davies 150–1).[33]

One must keep in mind that Sykes Davies is seeking to give a non-Lucy reading of 'A slumber' 'a run for its money' (161) – a profoundly New Critical project not just in extricating the text from 'extrinsics' but also in avowing no purpose of its own beyond this operation. His history of the grouping is therefore expressly intended to explode the 'Lucy Poems' as a mere (and indeed silly) editorial creation; but if we are more concerned to understand the grouping than to dismantle it, his account must be qualified in at least two particulars. First, in resisting the editors' assimilation of 'A slumber' to poems that do name 'Lucy,' Sykes Davies overstates the case for its distinctness in Wordsworth's own arrangement. He claims, for instance, that the editorial groupings constitute 'the first time' that '"A slumber" was linked, conspicuously and apparently inseparably, with the poems containing the name "Lucy"' (151), and that 'It is not easy to see how Wordsworth could have made his final editorial decision about "A slumber" more obvious or ostentatious' (145). But Wordsworth always placed 'A slumber' after a poem naming Lucy, and if he had wanted it to stand unambiguously alone he could easily have dissociated it more distinctly: by classing, ordering, or writing it differently, or more simply by titling it.

Second, and partly therefore, one must qualify Sykes Davies' account of the editorial grouping's motivation. In his account, the grouping is formed to satisfy the Victorian biographical curiosity evinced by De Quincey's, de Vere's, and Myers' inferences of an original 'Lucy.' To display this supposition of a biographical subtext is to embarrass the grouping, especially from New Critical premises: no longer being subject to the Victorians' 'vulgar curiosity,' Sykes Davies implies, we can now lay their sentimental fiction to rest. But it is far from clear how including 'A slumber' with the 'Lucy Poems' could enhance their collective biographical bearing in the first place – a question Sykes Davies avoids raising, though he attacks the grouping only to extricate 'A slumber.' Biographical curiosity is not a sufficient cause for the editorial assimilation of 'A slumber' to the 'Lucy Poems,' but is more like a handy stick to beat the editors with. By overstating the textual distinctness of 'A slumber,' Sykes Davies in fact obscures the more obvious factor in its assimilation, which is the profound ambiguity of Wordsworth's own arrangements and the responsive tendency of interpretation – its 'positive capability' – to foreclose on uncertainty. The 'Lucy

Poems' grouping is less an editorial creation (in the sense that Sykes Davies calls de Vere 'its creator' [151]) than an editorial *decision*, an *interpretive* simplification, an objectifying and fixative effort. Its fundamentally interpretive or decisive nature is indeed illustrated by an ironic parallel with Sykes Davies' own argument, which responds to the same anxiety of ambiguity but disambiguates 'A slumber' in the opposite direction: whether the poem ends up firmly enclosed in the grouping or firmly excluded from it, both efforts reflect the same will to give it a definite status, which is also to objectify it. To minimize the poem's liminal position is to minimize our subjective role in *taking* it *as* one thing or another, though the poem's liminality seems designed to call attention to this subjectivity in the first place.

In short, if Wordsworth's ambiguous placement of the 'Lucy Poems' exacerbates criticism's self-consciousness, the editorial grouping objectifies the poems to alleviate the same. Thus the grouping exemplifies interpretation at its fixative and objectifying extreme; if any interpretation justifies the arguments 'against interpretation,' this one does. Comprehending the editorial grouping as interpretation also positions us to see that the impulse to closure is not a merely rational 'grasping after fact and reason,' but obeys an aesthetic imperative. Interpretation often presents itself as filling gaps, solving puzzles, or closing cases, but it does these things in accordance with its own Occam's razor: the right solution satisfies current aesthetic criteria, or makes art art – good art, by contemporary standards. That such criteria change periodically explains why the nineteenth-century simplification of 'A slumber' assimilates it to a sentimental tale, while a New-Critical simplification takes it as a self-enclosed whole. (My own explanation of the poem as a provocation of readers is, no doubt, explicable in the same terms, as a simplification with a dated aesthetic bias, reader-response.)[34]

Sykes Davies skips at least two critics who suggest a 'Lucy Poems' grouping before Arnold and de Vere, and both of them suggest the possibility that the grouping's motivation is aesthetic. The earliest is Thomas Powell's comment of 1831: 'Although the poem stands by itself ... yet we are to know, from the penetration of Mr. Wordsworth's admirers, that it is a sequel to the other deep poems that precede it, and is about one Lucy, who is dead' (563). The comments to which Powell alludes are unknown; his remark reflects that, having been largely oral, much of the early criticism of Wordsworth has not survived.[35] This makes it uncertain which poems 'A slumber' was supposed to continue, but Powell is unequivocal in referring the poem to Lucy.[36] And since this comment pre-dates De Quincey's remarks and makes nothing of Lucy's biographical status, it may be that 'Mr. Wordsworth's admirers' were reading the poem as a sequel for aesthetic motives.

The other critic is more explicit. In urging the grouping in 1871 (after Palgrave, but before Arnold), Margaret Oliphant appeals to both biographical curiosity and aesthetics. Attempting to explain why Wordsworth's mind reverted to England from Goslar, Oliphant writes:

> perhaps ... there was in truth as well as in poetry a dead Lucy left behind in one of these peaceful solitudes, whose ending had driven him away to this strange place. There is no information whatever to be found on this subject, either from himself or his friends. The five exquisite little poems which bear that name, snatches as they seem of some sad and tender story, have no explanation whatever attached to them. ... [Yet] they all hang together with a unity and reality which makes it very difficult to believe that they meant nothing. Why they should be separated and kept out of their natural arrangement, as they are in all the editions of Wordsworth we have seen, it is very hard to tell. Three of them we find included in the 'Poems Founded on the Affections,' and two in the 'Poems of the Imagination,' – a curiously arbitrary distinction, made, we suppose, by Wordsworth himself, either to veil the personal meaning contained in them, or in obedience to some solemn crotchet ... but a future editor would do well to piece together these broken threads, and put the five little lays which embody all we know of Lucy, together under her name. They belong as truly to each other as do the poems out of which Mr Tennyson's 'Maud' is formed. We should be disposed to place the verses in the following order: –1st, 'Strange fits ... ;' 2d, 'She dwelt ... ;' 3d, 'Three years ... ;' 4th, 'I travelled ... ;' 5th, 'A slumber ... ' Any one who reads them in this succession will see at a glance what a consistent story they convey, and with what an exquisite tenderness and natural feeling it is told. It differs from 'Maud,' not only in being much shorter and less definite, but also in the strange sad calm given by the fact that the whole is written after Lucy's death – a fact which makes it still less likely that Lucy herself was a mere creature of the poet's imagination; and in every other respect their unity and distinctness is not less than that of Mr Tennyson's exquisitely constructed tale. ('A Century' 315–16)

Oliphant's appeals to 'unity,' 'consistent story,' and pathos, but above all the repeated comparison with *Maud*, are aesthetic appeals. 'Anyone who reads them in this succession will see at a glance what a consistent story they convey': there is less 'vulgar curiosity' here than pleasure in a creative perception of unity. The same impulse is still clearer in

Oswald Crawfurd's comment of 1896: if 'she' in 'A slumber' refers 'to the dead girl ... the lines have a very beautiful and a still more pathetic meaning' (434n). The reading-supposition is justified by its aesthetic result.

If an aesthetics of interpretation figured in the initial grouping of the 'Lucy Poems,' the neglect of Sykes Davies' critique since 1965 testifies to the persistence of this factor: his essay is cogent, but inconvenient. There appear to be two main aspects of the aesthetic motivation for devising and/or keeping the 'Lucy' grouping: the enhancement of 'A slumber' and the 'discovery' of narrative. I consider the former here, and the latter in the next section. Because of the grouping, Sykes Davies notes, 'A slumber' 'acquired a prominence in the whole body of Wordsworth's work which it had not previously enjoyed, and which it has never since lost' (151). Though he barely documents this observation, if anything he understates the degree to which 'A slumber' has been 'made' by the editorial grouping.[37] De Vere and Swinburne, both writing after Arnold and to a large extent responding to his views on Wordsworth, both praise 'A slumber' extravagantly. Swinburne, it is true, does not explicitly mention the grouping, but the extreme economy of expression for which he praises 'A slumber' is arguably the function of the grouping, which makes it possible to understand more than the poem itself says.

> in a lesser lyric than this [i.e., than 'Ode to Duty'] we find the same spontaneous and sublime perfection of inspired workmanship. None but a poet of the first order could have written the eight lines in which the unforeseeing security of a charmed and confident happiness is opposed to the desolate certitude of unforeseen bereavement by a single touch of contrast, a single note of comparison, as profound in its simplicity as the deepest wellspring of human emotion or remembrance itself. No elaboration of elegiac lament could possibly convey that sense of absolute and actual truth, of a sorrow set to music of its own making, – a sorrow hardly yet wakened out of wonder into sense of its own reality, – which is impressed at once and for ever on the spirit of any reader, at any age, by those eight faultless and incomparable verses. (776)

By the turn of the century, 'A slumber' was receiving a significant share of critical attention. Josephine Miles indicates its centrality by the mid-twentieth century, observing that it is quoted in three out of seven essays in a critical collection (*Wordsworth: Centenary Essays*, ed. Gilbert Dunklin [1951]) where no other 'Lucy Poem' is mentioned (Miles 128).

In 1959 David Ferry finds 'A slumber' 'at the powerful center of this poet's art' (76), but Miles' doubts are worth considering: 'These are of course the terms, this the poetry, of our own era, and therefore the selection of it may reflect us primarily' (128). And as the rest of Ferry's statement suggests, it is not solely modern tastes but also the Victorian grouping that makes 'A slumber' central. Having just read 'She dwelt' and 'Three years,' he says: 'All this brings us to the lyric which is at the powerful center ... '

The power of 'A slumber' in this context is more than an accidental effect of the editorial grouping. The grouping makes it, as Powell suggests, a sequel, and something always accrues to sequels from the lead. The other 'Lucy Poems' are, arguably, as good alone as in the group: we don't need 'She dwelt' to appreciate 'Three years,' or 'Strange fits' to understand 'I travelled.' This is not to say that the grouping does not subtly transmute them also. But the spareness of 'A slumber' and its want of a Lucy put it at once outside the 'Lucy Poems' grouping and at its centre. Having included it, one can argue that the very object of the poem, Lucy, has been left out, that the speaker neglects to mention what he most means: understood as a sequel, it is tailor-made for the hermeneutics of repression.[38] One also finds interpreters treating it almost as a punchline that detonates the sequence. D.W. Harding writes of 'Strange fits' in 1963:

> The symbolic reference of the first experience – the steadily descending moon, the almost tranced man watching it and journeying on as if guided by it, but not foreseeing the end of its descent – is certainly not exhausted by the meaning that the lover's cry makes explicit. Nor does the implication of the 'sweet dream' come out until we have read 'A slumber ... ' (82–3)

Frederick Garber writes in 1971 that 'The last two Lucy poems,' 'Three years' and 'A slumber,'

> have to be taken as text and commentary or thesis and antithesis, with the poem on the beneficent fostering of Nature being loaded with phrases that turn savagely ironic when read in the light of its companion piece. (117)

In the same year Spencer Hall 'resists the temptation' to analyse the poem closely: 'Suffice it to say that in "A Slumber" the theme of sleepy unconsciousness and sudden awakening reaches its most economical, and most powerful, structural expression' (168). 'A slumber' can afford its minimalism because so much may be interpolated from its neighbours; it is compressed because they store its baggage, powerful by drawing on their reserves. In this sense the Lucy reading of 'A slumber' may be the grouping's *raison d'être* – if not a motive in its formation, certainly a factor in its persistence.

The 'Lucy Poems' grouping displays undeniable artistry, though it is not altogether Wordsworth's, and though it is therefore also liable to criticism as corruption of the authorial texts. In this respect the grouping typifies anthological works. The anthologist's ethical profile is essentially the same as the interpreter's: the transformative work of either may be celebrated as a creativity or deplored as a corruption, but it is in any case ultimately unavoidable. Observing Percy's arrangement of his *Reliques of Ancient English Poetry*, Karl Kroeber notes that 'Percy created the first, possibly the only, ballad compendium which makes even a modest claim to be a work of art in its own right' (*Romantic Narrative Art* 34). But no modesty hinders Francis Palgrave from advertising that his 'arrangement' of poems in the *Golden Treasury* seeks the most 'poetically-effective order,' that it has 'a certain unity,' and even that it is modelled on 'the symphonies of Mozart and Beethoven' (xi–xii); his arrangement is praised by Arnold in similar terms (3:252). Laura Riding and Robert Graves present the other side of this argument in their *Pamphlet against Anthologies* (1928): a 'private anthology ... becomes, when published, an organized theft of the signatures of the original poets, for it is the whole intention of a private anthology to make the included poems the anthologist's own' (35). From this perspective the very artistry of the anthologists is what makes them 'dangerous':

> The greater the integrity of the private anthology, particularly when the author is a well-known poet, the more dangerous is it when put on the market: by its publication it appears to be an act of criticism instead of a mere expression of taste. (36)

The statement is wholly appropriate to Arnold's Wordsworth, but in particular to the 'Lucy Poems' grouping. Sensitive to the effects of rearranging poems (28) and even of simply electing them for anthologies (ch. 5), Riding and Graves suggest that including 'A slumber' in the *Hundred Best Poems*, alongside Kipling's 'If' and Jonson's 'Epitaph on the Dowager Countess of Pembroke,' must induce 'sub-logical' readings of a 'supra-logical' poem.[39]

Pro- and anti-anthologists may disagree about legitimacy, but they agree in viewing anthologization as an activity that changes the ways poems are read. Whatever our views of the 'artistry' of Palgrave, Oliphant, and Arnold, they succeeded in fostering meaningful relationships between poems, in creating a textual family. The 'Lucy Poems' grouping is, in its effects, the Victorians' most important interpretive achievement with these poems, but *as* an interpretation it is unusual. In one sense, it is unusually mediatory: in its falsification of Wordsworth's text it seems an egregious case of interpretation's displacement of its original; and in presenting the 'Lucy Poems' as a textual sequence it imposes, as we shall see, sequential readings. In another sense, however, the grouping seems like the least imposing of interpretations: without explicitly dictating the meaning of the poems, it merely suggests their interrelatedness. To a considerable extent, I think that the grouping owes its endurance to this ambiguity: however useful in rendering the poems more definite, it does not *seem* officious or dictatorial, and thus it escapes the internal censors of its inheritors. One can take or leave a conventional interpretation, such as Sykes Davies' alternative reading of 'A slumber' as a description of mystical trance. By contrast, the 'Lucy Poems' grouping both facilitates and demands subsequent participation. It imposes more order while seeming to impose less, or none at all.

4. Tales of Lucy: The Narratization of Lyric

Piecing the 'Lucy Poems' together in 1871, Oliphant remarked 'what a consistent story they tell.' Besides clarifying and enhancing 'A slumber,' the nineteenth-century grouping imposed closure by narratizing lyric. In arguing this, I do not mean to claim that the poems *are* lyric in an objective and absolute sense, but on the contrary that they appear as lyrics in some settings, as narrative in others; what I call the 'narratization of lyric' is a transmutation of appearances, not essences. As Adena Rosmarin has argued, generic categorization is not a matter of fitting contingent works to essential categories, but of 'expedient error' with heuristic or 'explanatory power': we wilfully view works as instances of various kinds for the sake of posing certain expectations and/or highlighting certain qualities.[40] It is tempting to suppose that Wordsworth was himself concerned with this dynamic, since the interpretive problems presented by the 'Lucy Poems' derive from their generically liminal dispositions, both as parts/wholes and as 'lyrical ballads.' In other words, our modern theoretical dubiety as to the objectivity and stability of genres, typified by Rosmarin's powerful analysis, and our correlative self-consciousness in using them to 'describe' works, seem to derive from, and are certainly aggravated by, romanticism's flagrant crossings of genre;[41] conversely, the decisions within practical criticism that the 'Lucy Poems' *are* one kind of thing or another appears as the repression or containment of such romantic indecision and of the 'crisis' it brings. In their crossing of part and whole, lyric and ballad, the 'Lucy Poems' constitute another case of those Wordsworthian 'borderers' which generally have two opposite but correlative effects: they make you self-conscious regarding the taxonomic principles you ordinarily employ without thinking, but they may also goad you to suppress this disabling self-consciousness through summary invocation of those same principles. In this case, the historical decision has favoured narrative.[42]

But there is also a historical point in insisting that this narratization has not just decided the status of texts straddling a generic divide, but has fully recast texts that initially and individually appeared 'lyric.' In an argument that in some ways resembles Rosmarin's, William Dowling holds that narrative 'is really not so much a literary form or structure as an epistemological category' – which is to equate narratization with understanding itself, or to pose it as a synonym for interpretation.[43] I would qualify Dowling's statement, however, to recognize that narrative is both: even if narrative is 'an epistemological category,' to say that lyric is already essentially narrative (Dowling 96–7) is to forget that narrative and lyric remain terms for historically *conventional* 'literary forms.' Thus one can argue, what might seem nonsensical in the strict confines of Dowling's argument, that lyric, a historically conventional form opposed to narrative, will nevertheless tend to be narratized in the reception. This is a process dramatically illustrated by the sequential editorialization and interpretation of the 'Lucy Poems.'

At first, as Sykes Davies shows, editors invoked a putatively objective biographical narrative to justify grouping the 'Lucy Poems'; since then, even where the biographical reference was no longer supposed, their grouping has served to perpetuate narrative reading. The modern narrative readings of the poems, even when most fully interiorized or fictionalized, thus retain the vestiges of an early biographical criticism. To appreciate these interpretive implications of the Victorian grouping, we will have to take account of the narrative readings it continues to generate.

That most of the 'Lucy Poems' first appeared in *Lyrical Ballads* might be taken to suggest that they are simply half-narrative, but 'lyrical ballad' may also suggest a departure *from* ballad *toward* lyric. In considering the debts of the 'Lucy Poems' to the traditional ballads of Percy's *Reliques*, Herbert Hartman observes 'the unsuitability of Wordsworth's genius for the strict ballad form and spirit,' and cites the poetry's own disclaimer: 'The moving accident is not my trade' (136).[44] In a similar spirit, pointing out that the 'ballad revival' was an event of the eighteenth century and not of the romantic period, Karl Kroeber argues that 'the Romantics put the ballad to the service of lyricism': 'The evolution of Romantic lyricism is, in some measure at least, the gradual transformation of simple narrative structure as the basis of lyric organization into a discontinuous, non-narrative structure' which was 'demanded by the poets' efforts to express that which is not objective.'[45] Kroeber is not referring specifically to *Lyrical Ballads*, but he could be; both in its animus against 'frantic novels, sickly and stupid German Tragedies, and deluges of idle and extravagant stories in verse,' and in its famous specification of the point of Wordsworth's own poetry – 'the feeling therein developed gives importance to the action and situation, and not the action and situation to the feeling' – Wordsworth's Preface speaks of a retreat from narrative (Owen 74, 73). The notion of de-narratized ballad fits the 'Lucy Poems' in particular, and from this standpoint their editorial-interpretive renarratization appears curiously retrograde.

Individually, the 'Lucy Poems' can be read to bear out this non- or even anti-narrative characterization. It is suggestive that while 'Lucy Gray' is more aptly called 'lyrical *ballad*' than any of the canonical poems, those who 'eviscerate' it to create a 'Lucy Poem' essentially cut out the narrative elements to leave the lyric.[46] Of the five canonical poems, 'Strange fits' comes closest to ballad, yet even its narrative qualities seem to belong to anti-narrative or parody. As Geoffrey Hartman put it in 1971, its 'almost plotless story is an anticlimax' (*WP* xix). His explanation curiously evokes the proposals for eliding the middle of 'Lucy Gray':

> the poem's middle – the narrative proper – barely keeps beginning and end apart as they converge. In 'A slumber did my spirit seal' (where the slumber corresponds to the trance of 'Strange fits') this convergence has already taken place, leaving only two stanzas as poles of the vanished narrative, and the center a blank. (*WP* xx)

Thus Hartman expresses his sense of the sacrifice of narrative in 'A slumber,' in the process conceding to 'Strange fits' a minimally narrative quality. But the latter is less an anti-climactic narrative than an anti-narrative climax: the nature of its event, the mere 'thought' or emotion that 'befel' the speaker, forbids narrative development. The poem's superficially balladic form thus emphasizes the inapplicability of received ways of telling to a radically subjective message. Though the plodding transit between the lyrical first and last stanzas develops some narrative expectation, even this turns out to be spurious, for the climactic event – 'At once, the bright moon dropped' – is, objectively taken, too preposterous to be believed. One makes sense of the moon's fall only by internalizing it, as a trick of the eye, which is to explain it away. Only once the poem's narrative tension has been defused does it manifest the real event, the appearance of 'wayward thoughts.' Our experience in reading this poem is thus likely to follow a pattern of disappointment and mild surprise such as Wordsworth described once in 'There was a Boy,' and again, according to De Quincey, in personal conversation:

> I have remarked [says Wordsworth], from my earliest days, that, if under any circumstances, the attention is energetically braced up to an act of steady observation, or of steady expectation, then, if this intense condition of vigilance should suddenly relax, at that moment any beautiful, any impressive visual object, or collection of objects, falling upon the eye, is carried to the heart with a power not known under other circumstances. (*Recollections* 160)

Rather than an expectation that builds to a conclusion, this is a pattern of baffled expectation *and* unlooked-for mental event. Simply to occur is an inward thought's mode of happening: it is not narrative but lyric.

In all of the 'Lucy Poems,' thoughts and 'feelings' are more important than objective events or 'actions,' specific points in time more than temporal process. The poems specialize in points where temporal and emotional perspectives are reversed. If we approach 'She dwelt' – to take only one more example – as a story, we find that it is over before it has begun. It is not only that Lucy 'is dead before we so much as hear of her,' as Oliphant remarks (*Literary History* 1:307), though that is important. The tone of the poem's beginning is not narrative but descriptive, or more specifically pre-narrative. Like 'There was a monster who lived under a hill,' 'She dwelt among the untrodden ways' implies that a story is about to be told. By line 9, 'She lived unknown, and few could know,' the tone is still pre-narrative; there is no suggestion that Lucy has died until the next line, 'When Lucy ceased to be,' declares everything to be over. Now it turns out (and this may be why the first edition italicized *'liv'd'*) that 'dwelt' and 'lived' *were* narrations of an action, the beginning, middle, and end of Lucy's life. Lucy seems to begin the poem alive and to end up in her 'grave,' yet her death never arises; we discover her having-died.

I turn to narrate the reception/narratization of these lyrics. As Sykes Davies shows, those who first serialized the 'Lucy Poems' did so under the pretext that they already reflected (or refracted) a biographical story. The creative strain behind this 'discovery' appears in certain contradictions. Approving of Arnold's 1879 selection, Oliphant remarks, 'We are glad to see that Mr. Matthew Arnold ... has *put them together*, and permitted them at last *to tell their own tale*' (*Literary History* 1:309, emphases added). She is not disconcerted to find that Arnold's order differs from the 'natural arrangement' she herself advertised thus in 1871: 'Any one who reads them in this succession will see at a glance what a consistent story they convey.' Now, apparently following Arnold, she cites 'I travelled' rather than 'A slumber' as 'the conclusion of all.' The variability of early editorial sequences likewise suggests that the Lucy 'story' was exceedingly cryptic to these readers, however obvious it seemed that there was one.[47]

How the poems can 'tell their own tale' despite a variable sequence scarcely constitutes a problem for the early commentators, for the very presumption of an objective biographical referent makes it natural that the poems should disguise as much as they reveal: as in allegory, some obscurity is expected. Once reference is presumed, contradictions, confusions, and even the dearth of evidence may *be* evidence that a 'history' (Myers 34) has been hidden or disguised. Modern psychobiography makes the same assumptions but then scrutinizes the text as, by definition, the only clue to the repressed referent.[48] In early criticism, referential assumptions more commonly produce identification-studies, which largely bypass the text (it won't tell the truth anyway) in search for the referent, literally dead-ending in the *corpus delicti*. Biographical critics name various originals for Lucy,[49] especially Dorothy,[50] but seldom bother to articulate the poetic 'story,' which has importance only as scaffolding, as an opening assumption.

The project of identifying Lucy belongs predominantly to the early twentieth century, but that, I suspect, is less because we have evolved beyond the 'vulgar curiosity' of these critics than it is because they exhausted the candidates for Lucy. In any case, I shall also use later examples which tend to be more fully elaborated. In 1926, Anton Bertram can simply demand: 'Is it not as clear as day that the Lucy Poems are a revelation of the actual past?' (480). In a biographical study of 1953, H.M. Margoliouth argues that the 'hitherto mysterious' 'Lucy Poems' refer primarily to Mary Hutchinson's younger sister Margaret ('Peggy'), who died of consumption in 1796, and secondarily to Mary herself (51–3, 58). Margoliouth's most substantial evidence is that the poems are written after Peggy's death. Therefore his argument relies on the poems no more than on other texts such as letters, and it illustrates how the assumption of an objective story can work to justify a certain inattention to the poetry's version, especially where there are conflicting details.

> In the first of the new poems Lucy lives in a remote spot 'beside the springs of Dove'. There is no evidence that the Hutchinsons ever lived there, ... but Wordsworth habitually does what he likes with incidents and places of 'real' life. He was a dedicated and professional poet. His business was to create. (54)

Nor does it matter, Margoliouth takes care to point out, that Lucy, according to a cancelled manuscript, 'dies of a "slow distemper,"' whereas Peggy died 'of a galloping consumption' (55). Rendel Harris, who seeks in 1935 to identify Lucy as a Welsh girl whom Wordsworth met while visiting Robert Jones in the Vale of Clwyd in 1791, is more scrupulous about such details, and seeks to establish objective, physical referents. Harris identifies 'the springs of Dove' as the Welsh stream *Dyfi* and provides such hard evidence as a map, photos of 'the springs of Dove' and the 'orchard plot,' and a detailed description of 'Lucy's cot' (13–15). 'The valley,' he notes,

> is filled with the 'murmuring sound' of which Wordsworth had spoken as passing into Beauty's lines on Lucy's face. After an exploration of the glen, we found ourselves seated on a boulder covered with moss – there were many such – between the cottage and the stream. Was it possible that they were the original of Wordsworth's own language? Were there violets also in the vale? We had only to look around – the ground was covered with them ... and we could trace them right up to the mossy stone itself. Thus every detail seemed to accord with the description and to fit the 'happy dell' of the 'Lucy poems.' (18)

Harris even seeks Lucy in the parish register and lists a number of candidates – Elizabeth Jones, d. 5 Feb. 1787, and so on (14) – but he finds no 'Lucy' and is forced to invent a poetical explanation for her English name.

The search for Lucy's bones is an illuminating because both extreme and graphic version of the 'referential fallacy,' and it was, with the rise of formalist analysis, castigated as such.[51] As befits a 'fallacy,' one is inclined to regard it simply as a critical naïveté, and to locate its essential failure not in the inability to prove a specific objective referent, but in the more basic failure to consider what *that* could prove. It seems to turn on a fundamental error as to genre, on a mistaking of the fictional for the factual. Yet there is an important sense in which this has also been an 'expedient error,' a canny simplification facilitating interpretive mastery. In calling the poems 'hitherto mysterious,' Margoliouth implies that his biographical identification dispels their mystery; Harris proposes his as 'a solution of a literary problem of long standing,' and envisions himself as holding 'the key in the lock: presently we shall be able to turn it' (5, 11). The lock-and-key is an image both of revelation and of closure. In taking the poetry's speaker(s) for Wordsworth, in ignoring its fictionality or 'literariness,' and in conceiving it as a lock or puzzle with a single definitive solution, such approaches reduce its manifold indeterminacy to one empirical question – 'Who was this Lucy?' (Harris 3) – which *might* be answered decisively. But these simplifications and pretensions to closure are, it seems to me, more to be doubted than the referential assumption on which they are based. For as Richard Matlack cogently argues in resurrecting the question 'Who was Lucy?' for purposes of psychobiography, 'The charge of irrelevance cannot be made categorically. Issues are relevant or irrelevant with respect to contexts of preoccupation, not a priori' (46). The important matter is what critical practice an assumption of reference serves.[52] Hence, though the referential assumptions of the identification-readings have been in disgrace in recent years, I think it would be mistaken to dismiss them altogether.

Identification-readings were accused of something like the 'referential fallacy' by their contemporaries and indeed by their predecessors. One is tempted to assign such criticism to one period and its repudiation to the next, but 'progress' has not been so simple; Jameson's point that '*several* modes of production [exist] all at once' (*Political* 93–5) applies to the production of literary criticism as well. Though the historical objections to these biographical readings also come from diverse quarters, and are virtually never articulated in formalist vocabulary, it remains useful to think of them broadly as symptoms of the 'formalist revolution' in literary study.[53] In 1916 C.T. Winchester closes a sentimental commentary on the 'Lucy Poems' with the caveat: 'It is an idle curiosity that would seek to penetrate the secret of that memory, pure, passionless, holy ... ' (56). H.W. Garrod's lecture on 'Wordsworth's Lucy' (1929) opens with a bemused discussion of possible identifications, and notes, 'all these inquiries start from a premiss which I have never felt at full liberty to accept. They assume of the poet what I should hesitate to assume of any man – that he can never be in love with the moon' (78). In 1930, Herbert Read ungallantly rules out Mary Hutchinson as Lucy because the poems 'give expression to some passion that is too strong to be merely visionary and too idealistic to be associated with mundane emotions' (167). And in 1936 Peter Burra declares that, 'While ... acknowledging what Mary and Dorothy contributed far back to the making of Lucy, the identification of her with either of them is unnecessary' (87). Despite their differences, whether the grounds are irreverence or irrelevance, the dismissals of the Lucy-identifications recall attention to the opacity of the text, effectively reopening a case prematurely closed.

Abandoning the quest for a biographical Lucy inevitably entails a greater emphasis on poetic form – and hence, I will argue, a drastic reconception of her 'story' – but it also initiated other attempts at solution, such as the production of 'literary' originals. In dismissing biographical inquiries, Garrod merely displaces the quest for origins, citing poems by Thomas Tickell, Baron George Lyttelton, Edward Moore, Thomas Chatterton, and especially Samuel Rogers (90–1); Herbert Hartman, whose essay on 'Wordsworth's "Lucy"' (1934) is equally important, approves these remarks and adds William Collins to the possible influences (138, 141). Harold Bloom's reformative theory of poetic influence responds to the tendency of literary source-hunting to degenerate into something much like biographical source-hunting; in so far as either activity simply assumes the explanatory virtue of the 'source' or 'referent,' it becomes sterile. But just as the identification of Lucy with biographical originals can, in the hands of a sufficiently dialectical psychobiographical method, encourage rather than foreclose inquiry, so literary precedents may prove useful in the grasp of a sufficiently dialectical understanding of poetic development. However subject to dead-ending, the increasing attention to these sources in the early twentieth century is an important facet of the shift not just toward formalist analysis, but also toward the dialectical literary history espoused by formalism.[54]

The rejection of biographical identifications has equally profound implications for the reading of Lucy's 'story' in that she is henceforth assumed to be more fictional than real. Now the poems generate Lucy, not the other way around; now she is symbolic and significant, not primarily an existential signified; now her 'story' is the centre of interest, no longer a background assumption posited to be forgotten. But while this story remains as cryptic as ever, now the old ways of explaining-away its obscurity – by invoking the poet's 'reserve,' by revering his privacy, by diverting attention to objective physical referents – are no longer available. Formalism makes it necessary to read Lucy's story to the letter.

The 'Lucy Poems' criticism continues to be shaped by this invitation or challenge to narrative reading, as I illustrate by using three modern commentaries. In *The Heart's Events* (1976), Patricia Ball attempts to articulate the Lucy narrative:

> Do the Lucy poems ... tell a story? It is possible to summarise them so that they do. The speaker of the poems loved a girl of grace and beauty called Lucy, who lived in a secluded country spot and occupied herself with the usual domestic employments. He used to visit her frequently at her cottage, his horse knowing the path there without any guidance. The love affair was happy, the lovers trusted each other, Lucy being ready to tease him for his moods. Despite being momentarily visited by inexplicable fears that she might die, the lover is shocked when that event occurs, and his view of his native place, and the earth in general, remains deeply affected by it. (10)

Ball is hardly uncritical of this way of telling the 'story' and proceeds well beyond it. But her formulation clarifies the nature of the problem: though certain details are drawn from most of the poems, the plot, such as it is, must be developed out of 'Strange fits.' There is not much room for narrative after Lucy dies in 'She dwelt,' the next poem in Ball's sequence. As Ball notes (11), she must draw on the cancelled stanza of 'Strange fits' to flesh the story out; as she does not note, the statement that the lover is 'momentarily visited by inexplicable fears' jibes with 'Strange fits,' but maybe not with 'A slumber' ('I had no human fears'). But the central problem is the obvious deficiency in narrative interest, or plot. If the poems imply a story, it is hard to pretend that that is their point. 'Such a bald account,' Ball comments, 'is an obvious way of demonstrating that theirs is a lyric vitality. None the less, that lyricism does depend upon the narrative or historical framework, slight though it is' (10). This states in a nutshell the difficulty of narrative readings, but it characteristically understates the debt of this 'narrative or historical framework' to Victorian interpretation and editing, and fathers it on

Wordsworth. Ball acknowledges the poems' ambiguous status in the authorial text of 1850: 'they are neither one poem broken into five parts,' she says, 'nor are they five independent poems' (10). But her unquestioning assumption that there are five and that 'A slumber' is one of them (17–18) and her misleading statement that Wordsworth 'regarded their being placed in a certain sequence as important' (10) evince the Victorian influence; surely 'sequence' is a leading term for poems that are not all contiguous in any Wordsworth edition.

Ball's answer to a lyric 'sequence' that seems not 'to deal ... with the sequence of facts' (13) is to construe it as an internal narrative, or 'inner history' (6) of 'the heart's events.' This strategy is characteristic of modern readings, though the procedures for narratizing the inner history vary. Ball's procedure is to consider each poem in 'sequence,' tracing the speaker's psychic development. But her description of the poems as 'an imaginative effort ... to articulate an extended process of inner shock' (9) glimpses the irreconcilability of the poems' lyric form and sequential exegesis. When Ball charts this psychic progress, the result is less than compelling: in 'I travelled,' 'the sense of exploring an emotional situation is strongly advanced'; this poem 'finds a more oblique way of approaching the fact of Lucy's death'; 'The "difference" has been more precisely plotted.' In 'Three years,' 'nature and Lucy are brought together far less literally to aid Wordsworth's continuing attempt to find ways of representing adequately what Lucy was' (14–15). Ball's reliance on comparatives shows the strain imposed by the editorial sequence. One could reorder the poems and still argue the same thing, which is to say that 'the extended process of inner shock' is being read into rather than out of them. The 'Lucy Poems' are, frankly, short on plot, whether we take their 'events' to be objective or subjective; sequential readings are therefore inherently dutiful, compelled rather than compelling. Why consider all five, even if we have nothing new to say about 'Strange fits,' and 'I travelled' only waylays the argument? The grouping exerts its pressure.

The majority of critics do not consider all five poems; one might add that the best criticism does not. But the pressure toward narrative reading remains: any grouping still encourages it, while the poems themselves act as obstacles. One interesting solution is to seize this very difficulty as one's advantage, and emphasize the story's non-narrativity as its genius. This paradoxical strategy is implicit in Oliphant's account of Lucy's 'story, which is no story' (*Literary History* 1:307), but it is best elaborated by James Averill:

> Elegy, particularly as Wordsworth practices it, is suspended between narrative and lyric. ... The 'Lucy' poems, particularly, act as appendices to tragedy. The story they tell us by glimpses is familiar both in life and literature, but the remarkable feature of the poems is what is absent from them. After reading the four 'Lucy' poems in *Lyrical Ballads* (1800), the reader knows little about such rudimentary facts as who the lovers were, where they lived, who their families were, let alone what specifically their relationship was or what happened to the girl. Our expectations of a conventional love-found-love-lost narrative would be to learn some such details. It is as if Wordsworth set out to write a tragic story without plot or even characters, to achieve the sympathetic response by centering on the bare fact of death and on the survivor's reaction to it. In place of moving accidents, there is the drama of consciousness: for the excitement of the death, we are asked to substitute an uncanny premonition in 'Strange Fits of Passion' or the ironically pathetic vulnerability of having been 'without human fears' in 'A Slumber Did My Spirit Seal.' (*Wordsworth* 207–8)

Averill draws an interesting parallel between 'Wordsworth's desire to internalize the action of narrative poetry' and the practice of Henry James. He compares Wordsworth's statement that 'incidents are among the lowest allurements of poetry' (*Letters* 1:234) and James's 'What is character but the determination of incident? What is incident but the illustration of character?' (Averill 208–10). While the 'internal narrative' reading is not new with Averill, he evinces the credibility of this genre by reading several *Lyrical Ballads*, not just the 'Lucy Poems,' into it. But the paradoxical bent of his reading is evident in that the 'Lucy Poems' become its cornerstones precisely because they are *least* like narrative of all Wordsworth's 'narrative' poems. Despite Averill's recourse only to the 'four' in *Lyrical Ballads*, his treatment of them as narrative owes as much as Ball's to the Victorian tradition; the one point he does not have to demonstrate is the crucial one that they are narrative in the first place. 'It is as if Wordsworth set out to write a tragic story without plot or even characters': it is as if Wordsworth set out to write lyric. Like modern readings that marvel at the 'elision' of Lucy in 'A slumber' (see note 38 above), Averill's might be described as presenting an apple as an extraordinary orange. Discussions of 'A slumber' as being about Lucy without mentioning her, and of the grouping as a narrative 'without plot,' are fundamentally similar in that they defamiliarize the works, presenting them as what they evidently are not. It may seem equally illegitimate for me to declare what they are and are not, yet I think Averill's presentation of them as narrative is interesting and educative precisely to the degree that his presumed genre is askew. As Rosmarin points out, if genre criticism makes 'the edifying mistake of classification' (22), 'what the critic seeks is not a "fit" but the most suggestive "misfit" ' (45). But rather than invent his own misfit, Averill exploits the 'edifying mistake' imposed by the Victorian editors.[55]

In construing the 'Lucy Poems' as internal narrative, both Ball and Averill associate them with later developments in internal narrative, which Wordsworth is supposed to have anticipated or influenced. Ball asserts that 'the Lucy poems are Wordsworth's *In Memoriam*' (19), and she uses them to introduce a book-length study of Victorian poetry. Averill argues that '[i]n opposing character and incident, Wordsworth anticipates the Victorian discrimination between novels of plot and of character,' citing 'Austen, Trollope, James, Woolf, and Forster' (*Wordsworth* 209). Informed by the editorial grouping but ignoring its historical constitution, these arguments effect a subtle but significant historical reversal. Subjective as the 'Lucy Poems' are, their appearance as subjective *narrative* is largely due to Victorian decisions and probably would not have been recognized in Wordsworth's broken and shifting lyrical orderings. It is possible to see the 'Lucy Poems' as anticipating *In Memoriam* (1850) by fifty years only by forgetting that *In Memoriam* preceded Palgrave's serialization of them by eleven years, or that Oliphant's serialization (1871) explicitly invokes *Maud* (1855) as a model. Here Tennyson is merely synecdoche for the broader development at mid-century of lyrical series as media for subjective narrative – a development the 'Lucy Poems' do not so much anticipate as get caught up in. Other works of the period – Poe's 'The Poetic Principle' (1850), Whitman's *Leaves of Grass* (1855), and even the narratization of painting[56] – suggest a widespread interest in lyrical series. Understandably, Poe is sometimes taken to mark a movement away from narrative poetry, but in holding that *Paradise Lost* can be 'regarded as poetical, only ... as a series of minor poems,' and on the other hand that 'a poem may be improperly brief' (71–3), he justifies precisely the lyrical series then being, or soon to be, developed by his contemporaries, including the anthologists. Implicit in the disjunctive serial form is the discontinuous narrative of subjectivity.[57] Not that this development can be ascribed merely to the accidents of formal mutation: the strain both to produce and to accept it may best be seen in the fate of a work that Clifford Siskin (*Historicity* 114–24) treats as yet another arrangement of famous Wordsworth lyrics – *The Prelude*. That *The Prelude* appeared in the same year as Poe's essay and Tennyson's *In Memoriam* is not entirely coincidental, if one considers that one cause for its delay was Wordsworth's own inability fully to endorse the art he himself was producing: a thoroughly subjective art in a narrative, that is public, mode. If it is easy now to 'recognize' the 'Lucy Poems' as early instances of 'internal narrative,' this category was not fully viable when they were *first* composed.

These developments – the writing of the poems from ballad toward lyric, their reconstitution as narrative, and the rejection of the simpler biographical explanations for both their 'connections' and their obscurity – constitute a complex situation to which the complexities of modern criticism still respond. To explore as economically as possible both the problem and the response, I consider one more narrative reading at length – one that remains, I think, the most intricate and challenging reading of these poems.

Geoffrey Hartman read the 'Lucy Poems' in 1964 as a major skirmish in Wordsworth's psyche between nature and imagination, in which Lucy's loss to Nature entails the poet's humanization. Such a reading centres in 'Three years' and 'A slumber' and draws much from the Wordsworthian philosophy of compensation as expressed in the Immortality Ode and 'Elegiac Stanzas,' where 'humanization,' as Hartman says, 'is conceived as a precarious transition from imagination to the philosophic mind' (*WP* 160). In 'Elegiac Stanzas,' of course, this 'transition' ensues from the death of a loved one, so it is clear how that poem might serve to illuminate the death in the 'Lucy Poems.' But however familiar and comprehensible Hartman's conclusion, I begin with it because I find his argument more difficult to pursue through all its details. I stick my neck out to say so because, finding Hartman clearer elsewhere, I think the difficulty of his discussion of these poems reflects, in part, the difficulty of this editorially created narrative text.

I have already passed over the central difficulty in Hartman's account by saying that Lucy's loss to nature 'entails' the poet's humanization. This would imply a biographical Lucy behind the scenes. But one is tempted to think Hartman means Lucy is merely imaginary, and that her loss symbolizes his humanization. It is difficult to determine what in Hartman's opinion happens, for he resists specifying who or what Lucy is. He speaks, projectively, of *Lucy*'s 'ambivalence in mode of being,' not merely of *our* uncertainty:

> We wish to know about Lucy as a person, yet she represents more than a person. Who is Lucy, what is she?
>
> Lucy is a boundary being, nature sprite and human, yet not quite either. She

> reminds us of the traditional mythical person who lives, ontologically, an intermediate life, or mediates various realms of existence. Nymphs, both watery and human, are an example; heroes, insofar as both human and divine, another. Because of this ambivalence in mode of being, they seem to possess a supernatural element.
>
> Wordsworth's Lucy, however, is an intermediate modality of consciousness rather than an intermediate being. She is seen entirely from within the poet, so that this modality may be the poet's own, and Lucy the 'inner maiden.' Except for this inwardness she belongs to the category of spirits who must still become human, and the poet describes her as dying at a point at which she would have been humanized. (*WP* 158)

This wavering passage might be supposed to wean us from strictly biographical identifications. Even after insisting that Lucy is strictly a 'modality of consciousness,' Hartman admits that 'she is seen entirely *from* within the poet,' which is to suggest that her existence is objective. Hartman never clarifies Lucy's ontology: his statements that the poems 'center in a death or a radical change of consciousness' (157), that 'She never is fully a person, or we never see her as one' (158), are typical. Even the mode of her ambiguity is ambiguous: at times it is unclear whether she is human or 'nature sprite,' at others whether she is inner or outer. If we begin to think he refers to an objective Lucy, Hartman's description of 'A slumber' gives us pause. 'The first stanza describes the illusion and the second simply speaks its epitaph' (159): that is '*its* epitaph,' the illusion's, not Lucy's. But even if the death of Lucy is the death of an illusion, can Lucy herself be merely an illusion? Hartman is bewilderingly hesitant to resolve this ambiguity:

> if Lucy avoids the crisis of separation, the poet does not. She dies at the threshold of humanization, but he survives with 'The memory of what has been, / And never more will be.' The emphasis, I would repeat, is not on her death, but on the consciousness of the survivor. What he loses is more than a loved person. It is something *unique*, and the loss he feels includes the consciousness *that* it is unique. (160)

Hartman's use of 'emphasis' still allows that 'her death' is at issue. If so, what loss can be 'more than a loved person'? What is, *as opposed* to a loved one, 'unique'? Hartman suggests not only that the death of Lucy 'humanizes' the poet by stripping away his illusions, but that it is the *means* by which this is done; Lucy's death is subordinated to the loss of the poet's innocence. He loses Lucy, but this is secondary to the loss of his 'soft delusion' (160) of Nature's beneficence and sufficiency, or of Lucy's invulnerability to its touch. Hartman's reluctance to state more bluntly that the essential loss is inward, is, I suppose, a species of tact. The claim that 'What he loses is more than a loved person,' might even be taken as eulogy. Only the next sentence suggests that it is something quite different.

Ultimately, I think Hartman's ambivalence regarding Lucy's ontology is necessitated by his reading of the poems as a consolatory *narrative*, by his need to plot them, and thus by the Victorians' sequential grouping. Hartman appeals to *Lyrical Ballads* to determine which poems are in 'the group,' thus excluding 'I travelled,' but he also appeals to 'the later ordering' (158, 158n). If this appeal to Wordsworth's texts seems to father 'the group' on Wordsworth, the practice of picking one textual feature from one edition and another from the next edition hardly constitutes a coherent appeal to authorial intention; at best, it rhetorically rationalizes and objectifies the Victorian sequence. 'Given' this sequential ordering, narrative exegesis is all but inevitable; and Hartman's brilliant assimilation of the poems to Wordsworth's consolation plot is his way of meeting this demand. In both the 'Ode' and 'Elegiac Stanzas,' loss is followed by consolation or recompense, and Hartman sees the calm following Lucy's death in 'Three years' and 'A slumber' as implying the same. In the 'Lucy Poems,' however, Hartman raises this mere sequentiality into *felix culpa* or, more pointedly, into an 'orchard plot.' Consolation, recompense, calm, are not for Hartman fortuitous discoveries of the poet's meditation on Lucy's death, but are rather the purpose for which Lucy had to die. Hartman's reading centres, in other words, in the Wordsworthian doctrine of consolation raised to a 'teleological principle,' 'the deep intent of nature' (161). Obviously, however, if Lucy is seen to die with the *purpose* of providing 'abundant recompense,' and if she is also conceived as a real beloved human rather than a mythical or 'inner maiden,' the Wordsworthian long view becomes not merely consolatory but murderous. This may explain why Hartman is so evasive regarding Lucy's ontology. On 'Three years,' in which the blandishments of Nature are followed hard by the news of Lucy's death, Hartman writes:

Wordsworth never lays blame in any explicit way. The reason for his suspension of judgment will become clear. ... For Wordsworth ... nature's deception is a necessary lure 'To make her Foster-child, her Inmate Man, / Forget the glories he hath known' [Ode, lines 83–4]. Not to forget them entirely, but to naturalize imagination, to prevent it from losing its anchor in this world. (160)

Hartman makes of the 'Lucy Poems,' in short, a psychic murder-story in which Nature sacrifices Lucy to humanize the poet's soul, and the poet connives at it because he knows that Nature knows best; losing Lucy, he receives a psychic reward. Hartman even speaks of the poet's 'legacy' from Lucy.

Lucy's death is also more than loss, for it brings a new consciousness to birth. It is through Lucy's death that Wordsworth learns that nature does betray the heart which loves her. Yet the betrayal is not absolute; it has its point of comfort. It reveals not merely a delusion but also nature's strength in having *fostered this according to a teleological principle.* ... Thus if the poet has lost he has also gained. 'She died and left to me / This heath, this calm, and quiet scene, / The memory ... ' The lines indicate a legacy: 'left to me' has this connotation, if only in passing. The poet is calm *because he has learned the dignity of his mind as well as the deep intent of nature.* (161, my emphasis)

As with any powerful interpretation, it is possible to object to Hartman's narratization as a 'distortion,' but in turning to his distortions now I would rather emphasize their genius. Individually, the poems have nothing of the plot or purposefulness Hartman attributes to them. Meditative calm appears always to follow the mention or suggestion of Lucy's death; or more precisely, as Hartman notes, it coincides with it: 'death and the humanizing consciousness of death are almost simultaneous: Wordsworth does not dramatize the interval' (161). But this calm is always unexplained and apparently fortuitous, like the 'thoughts' that 'will slide / Into a Lover's head'; why the calm appears, or what it means, is something the poems do not explain. The speaker's attitude in stanza 2 of 'A slumber,' for example, is not necessarily 'humanizing consciousness'; it could as easily be read as numbness or unconsciousness. Hartman's accomplishment, then, lies in plotting the poems.

Like Palgrave, who invokes Mozart, or Oliphant and Ball, who invoke Tennyson, or Averill, who invokes Henry James, Hartman comprehends and reforms the poems on the pattern of other works. His plot, I have noted, is drawn from the Immortality Ode and 'Elegiac Stanzas,' but the conflation of these is no obvious or neutral matter. As Hartman's citation of lines 83–4 shows, Wordsworth's Ode presents nature's thefts as purposeful and ultimately beneficent. But Hartman's originality appears not so much in applying this idea to the 'Lucy Poems' – it would make a weak plot indeed – as in his conflation of the Ode's motifs of lost light, purposeful Nature, and 'abundant recompense,' with the lost loved one and ensuing 'humanization' of 'Elegiac Stanzas.' While something like consolation or recompense follows loss in both these poems, their 'consolations' are of entirely different orders. The Ode is a retrospective idealization of altered vision as entailing abundant recompense, especially in the relief of darkness itself ('shadowy recollections') and 'In years that bring the philosophic mind' (lines 150, 187). 'Elegiac Stanzas' also describes the loss of vision (lines 33–40), but here the occasion is the loss of a loved brother. The speaker still claims to attain calm, to renounce delusion, and to join 'the kind,' but he does not, and indeed could not, describe this 'humanization' in the terms of the Ode, as 'joyous' (line 169), nor does he envision nature's role here as teleologically providential. To do so would be to imply, and to accept, that nature had killed the brother *in order to* humanize the speaker. It is only by conflating these two very different, though in some respects parallel, elegiac poems that Hartman derives a narrative plot of such haunting psychological power for the 'Lucy Poems': it is not that when Lucy dies the poet is humanized (this would be 'Elegiac Stanzas'), and it is not that the poet must lose his *illusion* in order to gain 'the philosophic mind' (that would be the Ode), but instead that Lucy and the illusion she synecdochally represents must die to humanize the poet, make him 'forget,' and bring 'the philosophic mind.' When Hartman says 'Humanization ... is conceived as a precarious transition from imagination to the philosophic mind' (*WP* 160), he is reading the whole Ode into line 36 of 'Elegiac Stanzas' ('A deep distress hath humanised my Soul'). This plot has the dual virtue of apparently deriving from Wordsworth (the relevance of one poem's meaning to another's necessarily goes unquestioned) and of harmonizing with the most frightening surmises of modern psychology.

Hartman's reading illustrates the two most important, but in some respects contradictory, effects of the 'Lucy Poems' grouping, its impetus toward narrative reading and its tendency – odd one out – to highlight 'A slumber.' It would be no exaggeration to say that Hartman's is a narrative reading of 'A slumber,' into which other poems ('Lucy' and otherwise) are read when necessary. This strategy enables Hartman to avoid the implausible sequential development and to give this 'heart's event' unity of action. Hartman's reading also exemplifies in several respects the closural tendencies of most 'Lucy Poems' criticism, (1) in assimilating the incomprehensible to comprehensible, or at least familiar, mythic and aesthetic patterns (the fortunate fall, the Immortality Ode), (2) in narratizing the poems, especially as 'interior narrative,' or, what is much the same thing, in motivating sequences that themselves appear blankly successive and asyndetic (the 'teleological principle'), and (3) in objectifying 'the group' and 'the ... ordering' by ostensibly deriving them from Wordsworth.

At the same time, Hartman also represents a certain resistance to closural interpretation, and I would argue that this is what makes his practice exemplary in the positive sense. This resistance is nowhere more powerful than in his insistent ambivalence as to Lucy's ontology – which, in effect, admits that she is unknowable, and refuses to decide her status. Once the biographical identification of Lucy was found wanting, there was considerable pressure to symbolize her, to read her as the signifier of a metaphysical, usually literary, value such as imagination or light.[58] Hartman's peculiar virtue as a reader of these poems is to resist decision for either the biographical or the formalist-symbolic. 'We wish to know about Lucy as a person,' he admits, 'yet feel she represents more than a person. Who is Lucy, what is she?' (158). Perhaps Lucy must be made to 'mean' if these poems are to be read for more than cryptic biographical documents, yet Hartman makes one conscious of something monstrous in this necessity: why must she *mean* rather than *be*? how can she mean more than she naturally means simply as a function of being a person? Why do we feel the need to make her significant – an impulse I think most of us must admit to, at least to the extent that we hold biographical identifications in contempt? By declaring that Lucy is part human, part spirit, partly out there, partly in here, Hartman reflects not only a special ambivalence in the poetry, but also the uneasy balance of concept and existential fact which is, in small, one of the dilemmas of modern literary study. Does it relate to (the) life, or does it transcend and exclude it? Hartman's ambivalence is an effort to bridge these mutually deficient alternatives. His position between 'formalism' and 'beyond,' or his tendency to move through formalist analysis of the text's being toward surmises of psychological, religious, or mythical meaning, occurs here as vacillation between his declaration that 'we cannot distinguish' (159) and his achievement of distinguishing the poems as Wordsworth's secular myth of the Fall.[59] A far simpler register of Hartman's resistance to interpretive closure is that, in the twenty years following *Wordsworth's Poetry* (1964), he published ten more discussions of 'Lucy Poems,' most of them on 'A slumber.' This practice, which bears comparison to John Wilson's repeated assaults on Wordsworth, implies, to my mind, both a doubt that any interpretation can or should be sufficient, and a faith that it is worth pursuing anyway. Hartman's position is ultimately a middle one, between strong reading and anti-interpretation. Himself a 'borderer,' he therefore cannot so much conclude this survey of closural criticism as suggest that its opposition to anti-closural modes is far from absolute. My next chapter nevertheless attempts to explore a fully anti-closural practice by reading nineteenth-century parody and literary allusion as forms of 'creative criticism.'

3 Parody and Closural Criticism

If the Ruskinian pronouncements, the Arnoldian selectivity, and the simplifying projects of biographical identification discussed in my first chapters were a fair sampling of nineteenth- and early twentieth-century criticism, it would be hard not to regard this period in the 'rise of English' as naive, unself-critical, and happily outmoded. But as the early nineteenth-century reviewer who accuses the critical mainstream of 'quackery and humbug' suggests, the certitudes of the major critics do not stand alone; they are, at least in part, counter-assertions to scepticism.[1] To see nineteenth-century criticism whole, one must keep both sides in view: on the one hand, embodied in the projects and precepts of the major critics, is authoritative interpretation, a practice that reifies the 'author' as meaning's donor in order to authorize itself as sole or best executor. On the other are oppositional practices that emphasize textual complexity to challenge the definitive spirit of the mainstream critics. Using the critical activity surrounding the 'Lucy Poems' in illustration, this chapter argues that parody, including what is more often regarded as 'allusion,' constitutes the bad conscience of nineteenth-century criticism, and that only an institutional repression has prevented its being appreciated as such.

That is to present parody both as meta-criticism and as an exploration for (if not as the full-blown form of) an alternative criticism. In the latter, more constructive function, parody is an answer to what Michel Foucault has called the 'paradox' of endless finality in literary commentary. Commentary, he observes, 'permits us to create new discourses ad infinitum,' though its 'only role is to say *finally,* what has silently been articulated *deep down*' ('Discourse' 221). On a dimmer view, Foucault's 'paradox' marks the central deceit of authoritative interpretation, its pretence to finality when no interpretation has ever been adequate or final in real experience. If interpretation the process is endless, then interpretation the product is ultimately defensible only in non-ultimate terms, or as heuristics: it should be considered as an intertext for comparative purposes, not as displacing the text or mediating it for the reader.[2] Not coincidentally, this alternative model of interpretation as an intertextual and non-authoritative practice is also a description of parody. To reconsider parody *as* that alternative interpretive practice is not an arbitrary experiment of the 'let's view X as Y' variety; on the contrary, I propose it as a conjectural restitution of parody's historical function, based on a restitution of its oppositional position, within the competitive scene of nineteenth-century interpretive practices. But even as a whimsical experiment, viewing parody as a non-authoritative form of interpretation may have its relevance for contemporary practice and theory. Since the lateral, non-mediatory, and anti-closural disposition of interpretations I've just idealized is not wholly a matter of how interpretations have been constructed or of what they are in themselves, but depends in large part on how readers are disposed to use them, it may be useful to practice taking interpretations as intertexts; and it seems reasonable to begin by considering intertexts as interpretations. If reviewing nineteenth-century parody's assault on authoritative modes does not produce a reform or defence of interpretation *per se*, it may help specify the proper place for interpretation in critical procedure – *beside* the text.

Parody's subversion of authoritative interpretation is no exception to the general rule that neither subversion nor containment lives alone. We can hardly appreciate parody's subversion of interpretation so long as what we think we know as 'parody' is a form of parody recuperated and contained by interpretation itself – never, that is, until it has been de-interpreted. It will be necessary, in other words, to distinguish a subversive 'essence' of parody from the parody of innocuous and trivial reputation.[3] In the present critical establishment, the usual view of nineteenth-century English parody is celebratory. The *Princeton Encyclopedia* calls this 'the Golden Age of p[arody] in Eng[lish] poetry'; George Kitchin claims that 'No age and no country can show anything approaching the combined sparkle and finish of the mid-Victorian parodists.'[4] Such assessments are common, and they seem confirmed by the Victorians' dominance even in recent parody anthologies.[5] But they are much at odds with Mikhail Bakhtin's view that parody flourishes in medieval literature and declines thereafter. 'Parody has grown sickly,' he complains; 'its place in modern literature is insignificant' (*DI* 71).[6] While we might dismiss Bakhtin's dissenting judgment as showing only that his conception of parody is incompatible with Western conceptions, the nature of the incompatibility suggests a certain containment. This chapter privileges a Bakhtinian conception of parody to suggest that, as usually conceived in Western criticism – as genre, as communicative vehicle, and especially as a playful form of criticism – parody is a tamed creature. In Bakhtin's conception, parody is not a genre, but a degree of dialogism; by virtue both of its dialogism and of its generic indistinctness from non-parodic forms, it challenges critical discernment and authoritative interpretive practice. It therefore appears that the impoverishment of which Bakhtin complains may be a transitive rather than spontaneous affair, an effect of interpretation's self-protective repression of parodic subversions. To clarify the complex role of 'Lucy Poems' parodies in the general field of criticism, this chapter both emphasizes the subversive potential of parody and some of the ways in which Western criticism has therefore sought to contain it, from legal 'parody trials' to contemporary parody theory.

A serious difficulty confronting any effort to conceive of parody 'itself,' without the containment – a difficulty that can be pre-acknowledged but not fully overcome – is how to allow for containment when the presumption that a given text *is* a 'parody' is among the very means of this containment. Put differently, how far can we trust an interpretation of parody on the score of parody's subversion of interpretation? For the moment I merely suggest with Shelley that we 'imagine that which we know,' that we resist assuming that what we behold as 'parody' at any point is parody fully uncontained. The nineteenth-century parodic practice surrounding the 'Lucy Poems' ranges, inevitably, from obvious parodies, like those of 'She dwelt' by Hartley Coleridge, Phoebe Carey, and F.B. Doveton collected in Walter Hamilton's massive anthology of 1888, *Parody of the Works of English and American Authors* (5:94–5), to less obvious and even dubious cases: in Conrad's *Heart of Darkness*, when Marlow notes that 'the wilderness ... sealed [Kurtz's] soul to its own' (69), are there deliberate parallels here with the phrasing of 'A slumber' and with Lucy's loss to 'Nature' in 'Three years,' or am I merely imagining them, and would such parallels constitute parody? At this end of the scale it will often seem 'forced' to consider a text as a parody, yet these marginal cases and the very doubts they raise are essential for an understanding of parody's anti-authoritative function. Conversely, it will become clear that obviousness may be an effect of containment, so that obvious parody should not be considered to represent the essence of parody, but quite the reverse. Hamilton's anthology, which selects only the most obvious parodies in the first place (lyrics of the same length and stanza and with high percentages of identical words), and then marshals them under the explicit label of 'parody,' and even points out and reprints the texts that they resemble to ensure that their points are not lost through ignorance, typifies nineteenth-century efforts to contain and rationalize parody. What Hamilton sells is definition: more than just specify the generic status and 'targets' of these particular texts, he markets the assumption that parody is *in general*, or as *genre*, well defined; the possibility of distinguishing parodies from originals is, after all, one condition for making sense of each. It may be objected, of course, that all literary taxonomy entails some such 'containment,' and also that the parodies Hamilton collects are both obvious and tame without his services. Hartley Coleridge's description of Wordsworth as 'A bard whom there were none to praise, / And very few to read,' epitomizes the clever but frivolous subversion for which nineteenth-century English parody is famous. The problem is that Hamilton's treatment of parody cannot be appreciated as containment in the full sense, as pursuing a repressive/self-defensive agenda, until it is clear what needed repressing, or how parody 'unbound' would appear; and yet that knowledge is what gets lost or muted in the containment.

1. Parody of Interpretation/Parody as Anti-Interpretism

To appreciate interpretation's hostility to parody, one must first appreciate parody's threat to interpretation, and here it is best to begin not with Hamilton's anthology but with an essay by Samuel Butler, 'Quis Desiderio ... ?', published in the same year, 1888. Sending up 'my literary experience' essays and Victorian literary ideals generally, Butler's essay subverts interpretation so powerfully that it may seem a loaded example. But its extremity makes it a useful point of departure for exploring the subversive potential of all parody. Butler uses a persona (whom I shall call 'Butler' for convenience) whose self-indulgence and eccentricity, both as writer and as reader, put the communicative function of writing much in doubt. He writes, he claims, 'in order that I may have something to read in my old age when I can write no longer' (100). Then, with a brilliant misreading of Wordsworth's 'She dwelt' as a murder mystery, he presents reading as an equally circular process of veiled inference and false discovery: in both functions, as a writer of essays and as a reader of Wordsworth, Butler reads himself. To illustrate his parodic subversion of interpretation, I must quote the misreading of Wordsworth at length. When the British Library loses Frost's *Lives of Eminent Christians*, the only book that Butler can use as a writing desk, he is bereaved: 'For mere reading, I suppose one book is pretty much as good as another; but the choice of a desk-book is a more serious matter' (100). Comparing his sorrow to the way 'Wordsworth is generally supposed to have felt' upon losing Lucy, he explains:

> Now I think of it, Frost's *Lives of Eminent Christians* was very like Lucy. The one resided at Dovedale in Derbyshire, the other in Great Russell Street, Bloomsbury. I admit that I do not see the resemblance here at this moment, but if I try to develop my perception I shall doubtless ere long find a marvellously striking one. In other respects, however, than mere local habitat the likeness is obvious. Lucy was not particularly attractive either inside or out – no more was Frost's *Lives of Eminent Christians*; there were few to praise her, and of those few still fewer could bring themselves to like her; indeed, Wordsworth himself seems to have been the only person who thought much about her one way or the other. In like manner, I believe I was the only reader who thought much one way or the other about Frost's *Lives of Eminent Christians*, but this in itself was one of the attractions of the book; and as for the grief we respectively felt and feel, I believe my own to be as deep as Wordsworth's, if not more so.
>
> I said above, 'as Wordsworth is generally supposed to have felt'; for anyone imbued with the spirit of modern science will read Wordsworth's poem with different eyes from those of a mere literary critic. He will note that Wordsworth is most careful not to explain the nature of the difference which the death of Lucy will occasion to him. He tells us that there will be a difference; but there the matter ends. The superficial reader takes it that he was very sorry she was dead; it is, of course, possible that he may have actually been so, but he has not said this. On the contrary, he has hinted plainly that she was ugly, and generally disliked; she was only like a violet when she was half-hidden from the view, and only fair as a star when there were so few stars out that it was practically impossible to make an invidious comparison. If there were as many as even two stars the likeness was felt to be at an end. If Wordsworth had imprudently promised to marry this young person during a time when he had been unusually long in keeping to good resolutions, and had afterwards seen someone whom he liked better, then Lucy's death would undoubtedly have made a considerable difference to him, and this is all that he has ever said that it would do. What right have we to put glosses upon the masterly reticence of a poet,

and credit him with feelings possibly the very reverse of those he actually entertained?

Sometimes, indeed, I have been inclined to think that a mystery is being hinted at more dark than any critic has suspected. I do not happen to possess a copy of the poem, but the writer, if I am not mistaken, says that 'few could know when Lucy ceased to be.' 'Ceased to be' is a suspiciously euphemistic expression, and the words 'few could know' are not applicable to the ordinary peaceful death of a domestic servant such as Lucy appears to have been. No matter how obscure the deceased, any number of people commonly can know the day and hour of his or her demise, whereas in this case we are expressly told it would be impossible for them to do so. Wordsworth was nothing if not accurate, and would not have said that few could know, but that few actually did know, unless he was aware of circumstances that precluded all but those implicated in the crime of her death from knowing the precise moment of its occurrence. If Lucy was the kind of person not obscurely portrayed in the poem; if Wordsworth had murdered her, either by cutting her throat or smothering her, in concert, perhaps, with his friends Southey and Coleridge; and if he had thus found himself released from an engagement which had become irksome to him, or possibly from the threat of an action for breach of promise, then there is not a syllable in the poem with which he crowns his crime that is not alive with meaning. On any other supposition to the general reader it is unintelligible. (101–4)

To read this as 'parody as criticism' in the usual way would be to locate an obvious target, 'She dwelt,' and to unfold its 'implications' as explicit commentary. The more fully we belabour and document such an interpretation of Butler, however, the more vulnerable we seem to his reflections on this very activity. How does one interpret a parody of interpretation? It mimics whoever interprets it, thus making one self-conscious and subverting one's interpretation. On the other hand, if one *is* interpreting it, it must not really be subverting interpretation: even in interpreting it, one must be in some way suppressing it. Either interpretation *is* subverted, struck dumb, or it must admit to having already contained the subversion, and interpret in bad conscience. I propose that the logical embarrassments of reading this passage as a parody of interpretive bad faith might best be negotiated through a series of scaffolding moves, or self-renouncing readings, the first gleaning Butler's 'commentary' on commentary, even while exercising upon his text the very interpretive power of containment that his text subverts, the later readings denouncing such interpretive containments and lapsing mute.

A. *The explicit attack on claims of explicitness.* It seems obvious that Butler's passage is a parody not merely of Wordsworth's 'She dwelt' but of interpretations of it, even of interpretation itself. It might parody a particular interpretation or a historically specific kind of interpretation, the false scientism and biographical fallacy of late-nineteenth-century readings. It might parody broader historical trends such as interpretive sensationalism ('cutting her throat') and 'the hermeneutics of suspicion' (the sleuth emulated by Butler's literary interpreter is itself, of course, a nineteenth-century literary invention). It might even parody authoritative interpretation generally, with its self-confirming suppositions of genre (the murder mystery), or the hermeneutic circle;[7] its impatience with rival interpretations; its presumption of false surfaces concealing real depths ('reticence,' 'euphemism'); and its aesthetically wilful, teleological argumentation, especially evident in the quest for an organic saturation of meaning ('not a syllable ... that is not alive'). In any case, it is a parody of the fundamental interpretive deception, which is to interpret the interpreter's subjectivity as objectivity, or to pose invention as discovery. Though Butler begins by admitting his inability to 'see the resemblance' between two texts (which is what, in one sense, Lucy is), at the same time he supposes the objective existence of '*the* resemblance,' thus facilitating the presumption that, by merely 'develop[ing his] perception,' he can 'find' it; it then becomes 'obvious.' Likewise, the claim that Wordsworth has 'hinted plainly' first registers ('hinted') but then denies ('plainly') the interpreter's need to construe. Through such self-deceptions, the interpreter who begins with mere supposition – 'Sometimes, indeed, I have been inclined to think' – can yet convince himself that he is convinced by objectivities: 'On any other supposition' the text 'is unintelligible.'

As a parody of interpretation, Butler's essay represents a historically popular subgenre that has formed, as it were, where parody and the protest 'against interpretation' intersect.[8] Not atypically, Butler's reading of Wordsworth accentuates two distinct kinds of duplicity involved in interpretation – not only the interpretive lie itself ('Don't you see that X is really ... A?' [Sontag 97]), but also its posterior rationalization – in this case, the pseudo-scientific apparatus that objectifies Butler's 'findings.' By accentuating the interpreter's self-projections, parody of interpretation also points to the real, wilful, idiosyncratic subject who hides Oz-like behind them; it resurrects the self-consciousness that interpretation *per se* needs to repress, the spectre on which de Man has blamed the 'crisis' of criticism.[9]

Whether parody-of-interpretation is properly a 'sub-genre' may be moot, but the term does reflect the marginal place it typically receives in the care of critics, who easily contain its disruptive potential by presenting it in passing, as a curiosity, or by assuming that it targets only 'overreading[s],' 'absurdly serious interpretations' (Fletcher 9n). To appreciate its force properly one must resurrect it fully both as parody and, indeed, as interpretation. If, as I have suggested, a parody of interpretation seems to reveal the 'real' self-projections of interpreters, this stance of revealing the 'real' constitutes its own participation in the interpretive activity it parodies. A discursive argument 'against interpretation' may well complain that interpretation says, 'X is A,' but to do so it must assume (and how without its own interpretation?) that what interpretation calls 'A' is 'X' in the first place. To counter-assert this explicitly would be to make the anti-interpretist's own interpretive activity visible; but parody-of-interpretation need only exaggerate the interpretive act to which it objects, leaving its own counter-interpretation implicit, and thus winning for it the appearance of objectivity. Thus a parody-of-interpretation pits against interpretation the putatively uninterpreted fact, and for this reason one may even say that the protest 'against interpretation' *must*, by tactical necessity, use parodic means – as indeed Sontag does in her paraphrase of the interpreter: 'don't you see that X is really ... A?' In short, the radically dialogical parody-of-interpretation is at once exaggeratedly interpretive, anti-interpretive, tacitly re-interpretive, and ostensibly non-interpretive. The absurdity of the parodic readings offered by Sontag and Butler assumes a contrast with an implied 'common-sense' reading, 'X is really X' (which is equally, 'don't you see that "A" is really X?'). Thus they simultaneously disclaim interpretation and objectify a 'natural' or 'common-sense' reading precisely by leaving it to be gathered by the reader: what need to state what must be known by all?

Such a non-interpretive stance is, needless to say, rhetorical, not real. Though it exploits the tendency to take as natural whatever ways of seeing are so general that they literally go without saying, what it affirms are not objectivities but entrenched appearances, the status quo of reading. In this light, the conflict between interpretation and its parodies is actually a conflict of powers *within* interpretation: between interpretation and its own self-consciousness, or between one 'school' of interpretation and another. Therefore the real political bearings of such conflict are never so simple as the terms 'subversion' and 'containment' may seem to imply. Here it will help to cite a case closer to home than Butler. A recent attack by *Newsweek*'s George Will on the politicizing tendencies of current academic criticism paraphrases the new 'decoders of literature' as arguing that:

> Shakespeare's 'Tempest' reflects the imperialist rape of the Third World. Emily Dickinson's poetic references to peas and flower buds are encoded messages of feminist rage, exulting clitoral masturbation to protest the prison of patriarchal sex roles. ... Melville's white whale? Probably a penis. Grab a harpoon! (Will 72)

Will does not notably exaggerate post-colonialist and feminist readings. He merely aligns summaries of them with the crude parody of the raising of a Freudian subtext to implicate them in the parody: *These* are like *that*. The harpoonist, like Butler's detective manqué, figures the 'real' idiosyncrasy of the academic interpreter, 'revealing' his landing of the subtext as the secret displacement of some bizarre cultural fantasy. In implicit contrast is Will's supposedly passive perception of Shakespeare's, Dickinson's, and Melville's obvious meanings. By not bothering to state his alternative readings, Will assumes the immediacy of a 'common sense' apprehension and claims non-interpretive status. And yet the readings he takes as obvious are only the naturalized ones; the new 'decoders,' he himself complains, 'supplant ... esthetic by political responses.' Like all parody of interpretation, Will's is subversive to a degree, but it illustrates that what poses as attack on interpretation from without is really a power struggle within, or between historically specific kinds, and thus that parodic 'subversion' cannot be assumed to have any absolute political allegiances. It is a technique; its political bearing depends on its political context. In so far as the post-colonial and feminist interpretations parodied by Will are themselves efforts to subvert a canon and a certain canonical hermeneutics, Will's subversion negates the negative and serves hegemony. Though it may be convenient for us to read Butler as parodying interpretation generally, or outdated modes, his contemporaries would probably recognize his essay as an intelligent version of Will's reaction against new modes. 'The rejection of interpretation,' which as Jameson notes is often merely 'the source of a new method' ('Metacommentary' 6), is equally liable to resurrect the old. But in either case parodies of interpretation are not the trivialities they have come to seem; they are wielded as instruments of power. Their trivialization is another manoeuvre in the dynamics of subversion and containment.

B. *The intertextual attack on explicitness.* The main problem with my reading of what seems explicit in Butler is an aporia like that of the statement, 'this statement is not true.' If we take Butler as commenting that interpretation is really invention posing as discovery, then (1) if this lesson is true it cannot be explicit – I must have invented it – and (2) if it is explicit it is not true, for its explicitness presumes the possibility of a discovery-mode of interpretation. The reading of Butler above implies the second alternative, thus *containing* the lesson in the form of a false paradox that may be interesting in theory, but is meaningless in practice. I suggest that the first alternative, true but not explicit, is actually correct, and that Butler's seemingly explicit 'lesson' was actually generated and inferred through intertextual dynamics. In section A we had a choice whether to take Butler as parodying interpretation of his own milieu or as parodying interpretation essentially. As this choice reveals, our reading of Butler's text as a parody depends on our own ability to supply the comparison text. If we know the interpretive practice of Butler's milieu, we 'discover' his reference to it; if not, we compare what we do know and 'discover' his reference to that. Butler's 'lesson' about interpretation in general is, in this light, produced by our identifying his peculiar interpretive practice (which he in no way generalizes) with interpretive practice at whatever level of generality we choose: 'overreading,' biographical reading, nineteenth-century reading, or all reading. The explicitness of the lesson is, then, an effect of the fact that Butler's interpretation of Wordsworth is revealed only through our own interpretation of him; our own interpretive practice provides a shadow which, being habitual, is easily identified as a 'natural' or general practice. By generalizing from the tacit comparison between Butler's practice and ours, we *produce* the effect of an explicit parody of 'the interpreter,' a fabricated type. But to take what we learned from Butler by comparison and inference as something communicated *by* him is also to disarm and unlearn it.

I think it follows that Butler's text is a parody of interpretation not, as it seems, because of its explicit thematic content, but simply because it is a parody. The affinity between parody and anti-interpretism works both ways: just as the protests 'against interpretation' are tactically drawn toward parody, parody itself tends to undermine authoritative interpretation, especially by making its interpreters self-conscious about their inferences and dubious of their conclusions. Etymologically, 'parody' (*para* + *ode*) can mean not only 'counter-poem,' as it is most often and easily taken, but also 'beside-poem'; as Marshall McLuhan puts it, ' "Parody" is one road running beside another road (*para hodos*)'

(169).[10] The latter etymology declines to pre-decide the question of a parody's intent toward its partner (what would 'one road running beside another' be good for?), but in either case, whether as 'counter-' or 'beside-poem,' a parody is an intertext, incomplete in itself, and its interpretation is therefore obtrusively dependent on the particular text(s) an interpreter chooses, or is able, to place it 'beside' – as we have seen with Butler's passage. This is, of course, a matter of degrees: the more a parody leaves us to infer its intertext and its attitude, the more it threatens to confront us with the extent of our own inferential activity and thus to cast our reading in doubt. The effect of parody at the less obvious end of the scale is literally to put us 'beside' ourselves: a reader of parody 'becomes what he beholds' in that the duplicitous text precipitates his own habitual interpretive duplicity, his invention-as-discovery. By virtue of its own intertextual structure, text resembling text and inviting comparison, or, in more Bakhtinian terms, by virtue of its dialogism, multiple voices competing within a single utterance (*DI* 75–6), parody demands more than usually precarious inferences from the interpreter who would clarify its 'implications' and reclaim it as commentary; and in this way it foregrounds the acts of inference that interpretation *per se* likes to suppress. To be precise, then, it is not so much that all parody tends to parody interpretation, as that it tends to demand extreme versions of our usual interpretive activity, and thus to *produce* parody of interpretation. (Recall that Butler's own exaggerated reading procedures begin in an essentially parodic challenge to define 'the resemblance' between two texts.) I speak only of 'tendency' throughout this discussion, for such effects can of course always be foreclosed, can always prompt and be preempted by interpretive containments. When we read parodies as though they spoke plainly to a point, just as when Butler reads Wordsworth as 'hinting plainly,' we are, in large part, deflecting their 'point' from ourselves.

C. *Why do we know that genre?* My section B seeks to show how the interpretation in section A contained Butler's anti-interpretism in the very process of 'unfolding' it as an implied commentary. But a parallel objection must be made to section B, entailing a further renunciation of certainty. For in assuming that Butler's text is parody in the first place, section B effects a containment like the one it denounces. To 'know' the text as parody is already to contain its resistance to interpretation, since to know its genre is to interpret it. This works in both directions – knowing the genre certainly enables us to interpret, but it also reflects that we have interpreted already – and in this hermeneutic circularity both the pragmatics and the problematics of this 'knowledge' become clear. Interpretation can always defeat indeterminacy by arbitrary foreclosure, in this case by presuming the genre it cannot prove, but in this it also loses by winning; it will know Butler's text *as parody*, but fail, through this foreclosure, to know it in fact. Reading Butler's text as parody can teach us *in principle* that interpretation is impossible, but *not* knowing its genre would be to know that in fact. Here lies the importance of the more subtle and even liminal degrees of parody, of the shadowy parallels and half-echoes that leave one wondering: is it, or isn't it?

I don't believe that the successive decontainments of parody can proceed beyond this sceptical limit. For once we surrender the claim to know that any given text is parody, we become unable to speak of parody at all, and interpretation is subverted indeed. What we gain in pursuing these decontainments is not, then, a ground on which parody might be understood non-interpretively, on its terms, but on the contrary the awareness that any treatment of it, even a purportedly delimiting one, must entail an arbitrary supposition at some initial level, and thus be to some degree distorting, even contrary. If parody is essentially inimical to interpretation, we can never adequately understand its challenge, since to understand it is to have reduced it. The very dialectic of motives, subversion and containment, that I posit as governing parody's relation to interpretation, while it helps explain the nineteenth-century use and treatment of parody, is by the same token a pragmatic hypothesis that may denature parody to explain the nature of parody. Since we cannot pretend to cross the limit of scepticism and treat parody on its own terms, I propose that we linger near this boundary to consider the acts of containing parody. In doing so, I hope to show how parody's subversive power is bound up with its generic indistinctness.

2. Definition and Anti-Definition: Generic Indistinctness as Subversion

If we start with the least improved etymological sense of the term 'parody' – as 'beside-poem' or 'intertext' – we can see how the more directionally developed definitions – e.g., as 'against-poem' – have bestowed on this blank parallelism a recognizable function, first recuperating it as a more or less abstruse case of commentary on the 'primary' text, and then delimiting the many interpretive possibilities to two. The most popular question in theories of parody is whether parody compliments or ridicules, and the most resourceful resolution to this question – 'both' – has the rhetorical virtue of seeming liberal while still exerting a tremendous focal, or bi-focal, control over the dissemination of meaning. Linda Hutcheon, for instance, surveys several definitions and concludes that parody

> is imitation with critical ironic distance, whose irony can cut both ways. Ironic versions of 'trans-contextualization' and inversion are its major formal operatives, and the range of pragmatic ethos is from scornful ridicule to reverential homage. (37)

Hutcheon allows a 'range' of comment, but the register is still a binary one, and, as in Hamilton's anthologization, the only theme conceived of is the parodied text. Ziva Ben-Porat's definition, cited by Hutcheon, exercises a similarly 'liberal' restriction to binary channels: 'parodic representations expose the model's conventions and lay bare its devices through the coexistence of the two codes in the same message' (Hutcheon 49). If this binarism of 'two codes' seems to correspond to the 'dialogism' that Bakhtin finds essential to parody, it should be kept in mind that Bakhtinian dialogism may be more properly understood as a multivocity of unspecified number than as literally double. There is another containment in Ben-Porat's notion of 'code,' which recuperates parody's disruption of communication as communication itself.

The extrinsic thrust of such definitions is equally important: by enforcing distinctions between parody and (what become) its near neighbours, such as satire and plagiarism, theorists of parody have presented it as one 'genre' among others. Hutcheon praises Ben-Porat's 'precision in making the distinction' from satire (49), and considers it a 'danger' of her own definition 'that it might appear to risk confusing the limits of the genre's boundaries even more than is already the case' (37). The latter statement is valuable as an admission both of the obstacles to such distinctions and of the will to impose them anyway.[11] Yet there is no inherent reason why parody must be viewed as a genre at all. An emergent tradition in parody theory, one I find more Bakhtinian, has occasionally pressed the limits of its definition and even presented it as generically indistinct, 'generically neutral,' or 'anti-generic' (Shlonsky 2:797). Joseph Dane observes that whether a text appears as parody or satire depends on 'the reader's choice of interpretants and referents' (153). Likewise Anthony Wall attacks the semioticians' efforts to specify objective 'markers' of parody:

> The systematic search for a set of parodic markers can perhaps best be seen as an attempt to transform parodies ... into the ever-same homogenized set of techniques and formulae ... . [D]reaming about using markers either to localize the symptoms of parody or, in the sense of C. Perri's allusion-markers, as ways of getting at the hypotexts ... keeps us from seeing the essential quality of parody: it is everywhere but it is impossible to pin it down. (61–2)[12]

Similar formulations of irony and of rhetoric as unmarked and undefinable deviations from 'normal' language may illuminate Wall's conception. Regarding irony, the point is most succinctly made by a witticism of J. Hillis Miller's. Feeling that a statement of his own has been misconstrued, Miller sighs: 'As someone has said, there should be a mark of punctuation for irony.'[13] A marked irony would, of course, cease to be irony, just as marked puns cease to be puns: irony consists, paradoxically, in that which leaves us in doubt whether or not it is ironic.[14] Similar is Paul de Man's reasoning that a question is a 'rhetorical question' not when a clear-cut 'rhetorical' sense prevails over the 'grammatical' one (that would make it possible to produce a grammar of tropes, thus reducing rhetoric to a second-order grammar and leaving no rhetoric per se), but 'when it is impossible to decide ... which of the two meanings ... prevails.'[15] Likewise, parody may best be understood as that which makes us question *whether* it is parody. Each of these formulations appears to employ tautology to produce an anti-definition: in redefining 'irony,' 'rhetorical,' or 'parody' they include reference to the same. Yet they are not really circular; they do not reference themselves, but rather the popular or 'common-sense' definitions of irony, rhetoric, and parody that they seem to reject. What such anti-definition achieves is the decentring of the more definite conception which it employs, so that (to focus on parody only) the clear-cut parody becomes the marginal or excluded case, while parody itself consists, only or chiefly, of the indefinites.

Paradoxical and overly theoretical as it may initially sound, this anti-definition is in fact better supported by empirical evidence than is the more definite, 'common-sensical' conception which it decentres – the reality has proved richer than its definitions. Generalizing from a notoriously broad range of literary works and kinds, Bakhtin asserts that '*play with the boundaries of speech types*, languages and belief systems is one of the most fundamental aspects of comic style' (*DI* 308), and he repeatedly cites parody to illustrate such liminality. Indeed, his generalizations from a broad empirical array furnish the most convincing and comprehensible version of the 'anti-definition' that shunts obvious parody to the margin:

> Except in those cases where it is grossly apparent, the presence of parody is in general very difficult to identify (that is, difficult to identify precisely in literary prose, where it rarely is gross), without knowing the background of alien discourse against which it is projected, that is, without knowing its second context. In world literature there are probably many works whose parodic nature has not even been suspected. (*DI* 374)

He repeatedly stresses that parody has a 'highly varied' range,

> from external and crude literary parody (where nothing more than parody is intended) to an almost complete solidarity with the parodied discourse ('romantic irony'); midway between these two extremes ... stands *Don Quixote*, with its profound but cunningly balanced dialogism of parodying discourse. (*DI* 413; see also 59, and *Problems* 194, 198, 203)

Bakhtin is, of course, having it both ways: for him parody *may* be marked, but it also fans out into indistinguishable variations. But he devalues instances of the former kind as 'gross,' 'grossly apparent,' 'external and crude,' while gravitating in his analyses toward the indistinguishables, parodies that are 'unstable, compositionally still unshaped, lacking a firm or definite generic skeleton' (*DI* 59). In the medieval literature he favours, Bakhtin emphasizes 'how flexible the boundaries were between the straightforward and the parodically refracted word' (*DI* 73), and how 'very difficult' this makes it 'to know where reverence ends and ridicule begins' (*DI* 77). If at this point he too poses a binary range from 'reverence' to 'ridicule,' the context of this formulation is negativing: he insists on the unreadability of such 'ethos,' in this case by pointing out that the borders between parody and non-parody are anything but distinct. In its emphasis on indistinct forms, Bakhtin's conception of parody resembles Wall's: parody may be 'everywhere' but unrecognized as such. At the opposite end of the scale, Bakhtin's admission of 'grossly apparent' parody may seem to contradict Wall's view that parody is *in essence* unmarked, but their views are actually similar if we consider that the obvious or 'crude' forms that Bakhtin scorns as trivial are the pinned-down or marked forms that, for Wall, really cease to be parody. Wall and Bakhtin disagree on the minor point of where the limit of containment should be drawn, but they agree in viewing parody such that the indistinct, hitherto 'marginal' cases occupy the centre.

The generic indistinctness of parody is no merely technical or theoretical matter; it is, in practice, a major aspect of parody's opposition to interpretation. The less distinctly a text declares itself as parody, the less distinctly it can declare 'its message,' and the more it implicates the reader in constructing such messages. Rather than openly pronounce a statement that might be rejected or condemned, parody provokes complicity in the 'discovery' both of its intertext and of any 'commentary' upon it. In overtly political situations this quality obviously gives parody the ability not so much to sow subversion as to confirm and precipitate it, since parody can 'tell' us only what we can tell ourselves already. The same line of reasoning suggests the difficulties 'the Establishment' will have in prosecuting parody – it was, in fact, a crucial factor in the acquittal of the English publisher William Hone in his singular 'parody trials' of 1817, discussed below. Speaking more generally, indistinct parody subverts the very mode of authoritative interpretation, for its great reliance on readerly inference and decision, even as to the generic status of the text, belies the monological model of communication in which author, content, and recipient are conceived as discrete functions. If we cannot tell what *is* a parody we are equally unable to tell what is not, which is to say that the arbitrary generic decision foregrounded by the indistinctness of a parodic situation is not peculiar but typical. By forcing interpretation to be more obviously arbitrary than usual, the generically indeterminate parody foregrounds the usual inception of interpretation in an act of power, brings its usual posture of discovery into question, and suggests that the usual relation of recipient to author is not truly passive and subordinate, but projective and promiscuous. Once it appears that authorship and interpretation are not entirely discrete, but in some senses identical, both must be, to put it blandly, rethought. Where interpretation's relation to authority has historically been most important, in church and judiciary, it has always justified authority (or power to pronounce) through an ostensive deference to authority (or original authorship). To reveal this deference as a sham, to suggest that interpretation's authority is written rather than read, arrogated rather than received, is to subvert its entitlement. That is what parody threatens, if not always what it achieves.

The clearest illustration of the mutual hostility between parody and authoritative interpretation just as 'the Golden Age of parody' was supposedly dawning in England are the 'parody trials' of William Hone, small-time radical hack and publisher, in December 1817.[16] In an effort vividly literalizing the figures of 'containment' and 'interpretive closure,' a Tory government antagonized by several of Hone's non-actionable publications sought to close his press and to incarcerate him by trying three of his publications as parodies on the church service, and thus as blasphemous libel. Conducting his own defense, Hone contested the crown's reading of his parodies by exploiting their dialogism: they did imitate the church service in form, he admitted, but what they *ridiculed* was the government (e.g., *TT* 2:40). Thus, as Olivia Smith remarks, 'Hone was probably the only radical who could legitimately defend himself by claiming that he had attacked the state' (180). This line of defence exploits the bi-planar principle of parody later stressed by Bakhtin, the principle that in parody language is both 'represented *and* representing' (*DI* 45; see 44–59), or that parody refers simultaneously by resemblance (to other uses of language) and by conventional linguistic means (to things). But Hone did more than assert another monological reading against the one for which he was being tried; he also turned his trials into public lectures on the nature and variety of parody, anticipating Bakhtin's emphasis on its generic indistinctness by over a century in order to put the literary judgment of his judges on trial. Loading his defence-table with books, Hone cited text after text to illustrate that there are '[p]arodies of all kinds,' 'an endless variety.'[17] 'How many [scriptural parodies] could he have taken from Chalmers' Poets,' he exclaimed; 'and was it meant, if he should be convicted, to have an *index expurgatoris* applied to this, and the numerous other works in our language which contained parodies upon the Scriptures?' (*TT* 3:34). He cited Milton as 'a parodist on the Scripture' (*TT* 1:35), thus challenging the jury's ability to tell parody from other forms of imitation: does the rewriting of Genesis in *Paradise Lost* constitute parodies lost on reverential readers? He observed that the biblical language he was charged with travestying was actually the language of translations (*TT* 3:24), and that Athanasius' Creed (specified as one of his targets) was itself considered a parody by some scholars (*TT* 3:37). In short, by challenging the generic distinction between parody and other relations – translation, imitation, emulation, influence – Hone both exploited and re-emphasized the interpretive uncertainty that indistinct parody induces.

Benefiting from Fox's Libel Bill of 1792, which made the jury 'judge of the matter as well as of the fact,'[18] Hone was acquitted on all three counts. Rather than showing that parody was not regarded as subversive, these acquittals suggest that some parody is too subversive to be prosecuted as such. Yet the triumph of Hone cannot be read as the prelude to an unambiguously 'Golden Age of parody' in England, either. The very effort to prosecute parodies (which was, Hone argued, unprecedented [e.g., *TT* 3:31]) heralds an age of containment; and where legal trials fail, other methods might prevail.[19] As I show next, the Victorian period's apparent wealth of parody marks not its prospering but rather its precipitation into a circumscribed genre – into recognizability. The nineteenth century is, to be precise, the golden age of parodies of a certain definition.

3. Scholarly Containments: Parody as Communication in Anthology and Theory

> 'She's neither fish nor flesh; a man knows not where to have her'
> – Falstaff

Since Hone's day the most powerful agent in the containment of parody has been the parody anthology, a textual round-up and registration service that confers on its conscripts both a definite generic status and a distinct unilinear reference, both of which greatly assist interpretation. In considering why Bakhtin sees parody's modern decline where others see its flowering, it is important to notice that parody anthologies as we now know them did not exist before the 1880s, when Hamilton's six volumes appeared. There are indeed ancestors, notably Isaac Hawkins Browne's *The Pipe of Tobacco* (1736) and Horace and James Smith's *Rejected Addresses* (1812); but nothing illustrates the modern anthologies' containment strategies like their contrast with these earlier volumes (which I shall call 'presentations'). Early parody presentations do not typically round up pre-existing texts, nor do they offer them *as* parody; rather, they present new works as original writing or as 'imitation.'[20] Under pretence of printing the best 21 addresses out of 112 rejected for the reopening of the Drury Lane Theatre, the Smith brothers present 'The Baby's Debut,' for instance, *as* a rejected address 'By W.W.' Though relatively transparent, these attributions leave readers to decide whether a poem is original, forgery, respectful imitation, hostile exaggeration, or something between. The paracritical effect of such play is reflected in the difficulties of a literary historian:

> it has sometimes been maintained that one or two of the poems in the [Smiths']

> collection are imitations rather than parodies. Scott was convinced that one of the pieces was his own work, although he could not remember when he had written it. ... James Hogg's *Poetic Mirror* (1816) [is another] curious volume with a curious history. As Hogg tells us in his autobiography, he took it into his head to beg a poem from each of the principal English poets, collect them in a volume, and so make his fortune. For one reason or another most of the poets failed to oblige, however, and Hogg decided that he himself 'could write a better poem than any that had been sent or would be sent to me, and this so completely in the style of each poet, that it should not be known but for his own production.' The status of the volume is a little difficult to determine, and the reviewers were in some doubt. In a sense it is a piece of literary forgery as much as a volume of parodies: at times Hogg seems intent simply on imitating, though in other cases ... he is clearly at the satirist's work ... (Ian Jack, 176–7)

Jack also refers, significantly, to the 'surprising' 'unevenness of the pieces' in the Smiths' presentation (176). But the critical bafflement in such cases should be taken as an essential, not, as he implies, as an accidental effect of the volumes. To turn to our other example, Browne's subtitle reads: 'In Imitation of Six Several Authors.' The dismal fate of his poems among later parody-anthologists illustrates the function served by this rubric in *not* declaring intent or genre, for they were far more successful as 'imitations' than they have been as 'parodies.' Dwight Macdonald apologizes for including two of them in *Parodies: An Anthology* (1960): 'They are pleasant and accurate, though with not much bite, but for some reason they were much admired and long remembered.' Simon Brett finds them too feeble to include in the *Faber Book of Parodies* (1984): 'Browne's verses ... are interesting historically because there weren't too many books of parodies around in 1736. So what? They make pretty dull reading today ... they lack that spark of mischief that makes a parody appealing' (Macdonald 34, Brett 17; see also Jump 19). But if these poems' 'mischief' lies in the subtlety of their deviations from serious imitation, it is the anthologies that ail them, not they that fail the anthologies. For parody's subversive potential resides in the possibility that one may take it seriously, at least in the first instance, and is realized precisely where one remains in doubt. Early presentations of parody still challenge the ability of criticism to distinguish: original or imitation? serious or ridiculous? In rounding up extant poems and branding them 'parody,' modern anthologies serve the opposite function of preventing critical embarrassments.

Parody anthologies generally assist readers also by referencing the 'original' or 'target' poems or authors.[21] Walter Hamilton's anthology, for instance, gathers 'Parodies of William Wordsworth' in one section (5:90–106); 'She dwelt' appears in a column with parodies by Hartley Coleridge, Phoebe Carey, and F.B. Doveton below it. This apparatus has two effects, particular and general (or genrefying): it assures that particular parodies are readable – that we literally 'get the point' – while also implying that parodic reference is generally so simple. It is true that most of the parodies Hamilton includes would be recognized as 'targeting' Wordsworth without the assistance of his apparatus – for instance, Doveton's 'Emancipation' (1886):

She dwelt within unyielding stays
  That kept her bolt upright –
A nymph whose waist won doubtful praise,
  She laced so very tight.

A maiden by a kirtle dun,
  Half hidden from the eye,
A single skirt – when only *one*
  Was worn by low and high!

She burst her bonds at last, and so
  With perfect ease can stir!
She wears *'Divided skirts,'* and oh!
  The difference to her![22]

In the 'targeting' of such a poem, the general effect is more important than the specific one. By selecting only 'grossly apparent' parodies in the first place, Hamilton's volumes implicitly identify parody itself with the 'grossly apparent' and uni-referential. But even Doveton's parody is more complex than Hamilton's targeting makes it seem. The question muted by the anthology is (as for Hone's parodies) whether 'Emancipation' is derived from the text it resembles or directed against it. In Hamilton's placement, it appears to target Wordsworth's poem while employing the theme of emancipation incidentally, and read in this way it seems utterly trivial. But taken outside this context, it might also appear to use 'She dwelt' incidentally while targeting 'emancipation,' and if it trivializes the agitation for women's rights as a matter of women's fashions, it seems somewhat the less trivial itself. My point is not to pursue or recommend here the political reading that Hamilton's apparatus discourages, but to recover the double possibility, for this is what implicates the interpreter as yet a third 'target' of the poem. 'Emancipation' has a bi-planar referentiality, referring to events by conventional linguistic means and to texts by resemblance. Inasmuch as such duplicity tends to subvert interpretive confidence, it appears that the service of Hamilton's 'targeting' is not merely to train parody's scatter-shot pattern on a single object, but at the same time to divert it from us as interpreters.[23]

The anthological containment of parody has been confirmed and clarified by parody theorists, and particularly by their efforts to define parody as a genre and to (re-)function it as criticism.[24] The latter efforts, fundamentally coherent with the anthological 'targeting' of parody, assume above all that parody is a communicative vehicle.[25] As Linda Hutcheon puts it, every parody conveys an 'ethos,' which is the 'ruling intended response achieved by a literary text. The intention is inferred by the decoder from the text itself.'[26] The emphasis on coding may complicate, but does not otherwise compromise a highly specific communicative function; according to Hutcheon, 'it is part of the particular strategy of parody and irony that their acts of communication cannot be considered completed unless the precise encoding intention is realized in the recognition of the receiver' (93). Hutcheon's elaboration of the communicative model usefully consolidates and clarifies the implications both of the anthologies and of less developed theories. But recuperating parody as encoded commentary leaves two problems: first, since parody can never have the precision and articulation fundamental to good commentary, it is generally credited with only the crudest of critical functions, the judgmental. Thus, when George Kitchin presents parody as criticism, he presents it as a bludgeon for 'frauds,' 'absurdities,' and 'silliness,' a vehicle for 'the reaction of custom to attempted change' (ix–xiii; compare Riewald, Macdonald 560). Seeking to 'broaden' this overly narrow conception, Hutcheon and others point to 'loving parody' as well, but still conceive of its critical function as primarily judgmental.[27] Parody doesn't know much, but it knows what it likes. The other problem with considering 'parody as criticism' is that it becomes, as that phrase suggests, superfluous. However precisely we pretend that a parody can comment on its 'target,' it can hardly compete as commentary with actual commentary; indeed, this conception only licenses us to insert our own commentary on the parody, *as* the parody's commentary on its 'target.' The point of viewing 'parody as criticism' is apparently not, then, to glean what parody has to offer as criticism, but rather to make sense of parody itself, to have it somewhere, to contain it.[28]

4. 'Two Voices are there': Parody's Self-Containment and Escape

So far I've depicted parody's containment from the outside, as the effect of supervening legal and scholarly apparatuses, and ultimately of an authority that considers itself threatened. But containment is seldom so unilateral, and this one is complicated by apparent self-containments, that is, by texts that play into the conception of parody as a genre and as communication. As we have seen, Hamilton's apparatus produces obviousness, but it also deploys parodies that are obvious already, such as Hartley Coleridge's 'On Wordsworth' (1834):

> He lived amidst th' untrodden ways
>   To Rydal Lake that lead;
> A bard whom there were none to praise,
>   And very few to read.
>
> Behind a cloud his mystic sense,
>   Deep hidden, who can spy?
> Bright as the night when not a star
>   Is shining in the sky.
>
> Unread his works – his 'Milk White Doe'
>   With dust is dark and dim:
> It's still in Longman's shop, and oh!
>   The difference to him![29]

The explicit referencing of Wordsworth (not just in the title but in proper nouns throughout) marks this as criticism, while the line-for-line parallelism declares it as parody. There is little to problematize either construction; even the bi-planar ambiguity of reference that complicates 'Emancipation' is missing, since this poem's reference by resemblance and its conventional linguistic reference converge in one object, 'Wordsworth.' Our difficulty would be greater if Coleridge merely mimicked Wordsworth without commenting on him; as usual, explicitly targeting the writer puts the reader out of range. In short, Coleridge's poem is easily apprehended as commentary because it is little more than that; it is not a parody we can read 'as criticism' but criticism in the form of parody.

If so, the proliferation of such texts in the nineteenth century hardly marks a 'Golden Age of parody,' but it does not mark a spontaneous atrophy of parody either. So-called 'parodies' like Coleridge's are best regarded as infiltrators, secret agents of criticism, whose most ingenious means of containment has been to underrepresent parody from the inside. Only the existence of such obvious examples has made it possible to precipitate parody into a distinct genre, and in the process to disimplicate Literature-Proper of parody's taint. Unlike Hone and Bakhtin, we know a hawk from a handsaw, Milton from a parodist on scripture, and on this discernment stands much of modern criticism's authority.

Yet the proliferation of 'grossly apparent' parody can hardly keep more subtle parody from thriving wherever it used to thrive. Catherine Fanshawe's 'Fragment in Imitation of Wordsworth' (1834 or earlier) illustrates the survival of uncontained parody in the period of containment:

There is a river clear and fair,
  'Tis neither broad nor narrow;
It winds a little here and there –
It winds about like any hare;
And then it takes as straight a course
As on the turnpike road a horse,
  Or through the air an arrow.

[three stanzas omitted]

There's little Will, a five year's child –
  He is my youngest boy;
To look on eyes so fair and wild,
  It is a very joy:–
He hath conversed with sun and shower,
And dwelt with every idle flower,
  As fresh and gay as them.
He loiters with the briar rose, –
The blue belles are his play-fellows,
  That dance upon their slender stem.

And I have said, my little Will,
Why should not he continue still
  A thing of Nature's rearing?
A thing beyond the world's control –
A living vegetable soul, –
  No human sorrow fearing.

It were a blessed sight to see
That child become a willow tree,
  His brother trees among.
He'd be four times as tall as me,
  And live three times as long.[30]

This too was corralled by Hamilton, but its broader ranges of 'ethos' and reference (including 'A slumber,' 'Three years,' 'Her eyes are wild,' and 'Peter Bell') make it more difficult than Hamilton's other specimens either to seize as parody or to translate into commentary; even Hamilton, unable to specify a single 'target' for it, can do no better than place it beneath the general rubric 'Wordsworth.'[31] Fanshawe's use of the label 'imitation' is important, as usual, but particularly noteworthy is her gentle crossing from quotation and what seems like serious imitation into comic exaggeration, a crossing so gradual that it becomes difficult to specify where it occurs. Though the final stanza, wishing that 'little Will' might 'become a willow tree,' has obviously passed into absurdity, this passage only renders what precedes it more dubious: is the line wishing Will to be 'a living vegetable soul' serious or comic? The uncertainty brings the Wordsworthian sublime into ridicule – or reveals its proximity to the ridiculous – and yet the parody is not, like Hartley Coleridge's, solely 'On Wordsworth.' It also challenges *our* ability to discern between sublimity and its opposite, parody and imitation, Fanshawe and Wordsworth.

More than this, it can be said that Fanshawe challenges our capacity to tell one Wordsworth from another, the deep from the inane. And in mimicking the interplay of these well-known voices in his poetry, she does not merely parody him, but also suggests how large a part parody already plays in his own writing. For what Fanshawe 'imitates' is the 'art of sinking in poetry' widely known as the 'Wordsworthian anticlimax.' That critics since Coleridge have so often lamented this extreme lability of voice begins to make new sense once we consider it as parody, and hence as *essentially* inimical to criticism.[32] Gilbert Highet says that '[i]n all English poetry there is no self-parodist to equal William

Wordsworth' (79). He is using 'parody' as a term of censure, much as when Francis Jeffrey finds an 'air of parody' throughout *Poems, in Two Volumes* (*RR* 2:431), but the quality in question can be better appreciated today as parody in the Bakhtinian sense, as the intricate crossing of 'two languages' (*DI* 76) by which a text may at once mock authority, resist asserting authority, and fend off authoritative appropriations of itself. The famous lapse in 'Simon Lee,' from Milton-Wordsworth's 'oh the heavy change!' to Simon's 'ankles swoln and thick' (lines 25, 35; *PW* 4:61–2) is technically such a parodic crossing of languages (and 'self-parodic' in that it too is a 'heavy change'); if we lament the decline in music, we might also sense a challenge to the literary hierarchy which registers the transit from abstract moralizing to concrete descriptions of human decay only as a 'sinking.' Geoffrey Hartman cites a less obvious case when he asks of 'She dwelt': 'Is this not a tender parody of Lyttleton's pointed inanities?' ('Beyond' 48).[33] The suggestion recalls both Hone's and Bakhtin's suggestions that many solemn works would emerge as parodies if we only knew the the relevant 'background' (*DI* 374). But that Hartman must hedge his proposed classification as a question also reflects the power of uncontained parody to put interpretation and criticism on the most speculative basis: *is* it parody, or not?

One could hardly ask for a better illustration of this tendency in Wordsworth and of its confrontation with containments than one finds in comparing the much-anthologized 'Sonnet' by J.K. Stephen ('Two voices are there') (1891) with the sonnet by Wordsworth to which it refers, 'Thought of a Briton upon the Subjugation of Switzerland' (1806–7). At the risk of seeming merely perverse or fanciful, I shall argue against appearances here: of these two sonnets, by far the more thorough and serious parody is Wordsworth's; though witty and deservedly famous, Stephen's poem illustrates the containment of parody in every feature. In challenging the 'obvious' appearance that his poem belongs to parody while Wordsworth's does not, I hope to bring the canon of obviousness itself into question, to suggest how thoroughly our common-sense notion of 'parody' has been produced by the Victorian containment, and to illustrate and exercise the contrary, Bakhtinian perspective. Moreover, if I am at all successful in presenting the apparently solemn 'Thought of a Briton' as parody, or even in raising doubts as to its status, I hope this will suggest, *a fortiori*, how much more extensive the implication of parody is among our literature than the Victorian containment has allowed to appear.

For ease of comparison I quote both together, Wordsworth first:

Thought of a Briton on the Subjugation of Switzerland

Two Voices are there; one is of the sea,
One of the mountains; each a mighty Voice:
In both from age to age thou didst rejoice,
They were thy chosen music, Liberty!
There came a Tyrant, and with holy glee
Thou fought'st against him; but hast vainly striven:
Thou from thy Alpine holds at length art driven,
Where not a torrent murmurs heard by thee.
Of one deep bliss thine ear hath been bereft:
Then cleave, O cleave to that which still is left;
For, high-souled Maid, what sorrow would it be
That Mountain floods should thunder as before,
And Ocean bellow from his rocky shore,
And neither awful Voice be heard by thee! (*PW* 3:115)

A Sonnet.

Two voices are there: one is of the deep;
It learns the storm-cloud's thunderous melody,
Now roars, now murmurs with the changing sea,
Now bird-like pipes, now closes soft in sleep:
And one is of an old half-witted sheep
Which bleats articulate monotony,
And indicates that two and one are three,
That grass is green, lakes damp, and mountains steep:
And, Wordsworth, both are thine: at certain times
Forth from the heart of thy melodious rhymes,
The form and pressure of high thoughts will burst:
At other times – good Lord! I'd rather be
Quite unacquainted with the ABC
Than write such hopeless rubbish as thy worst. (Stephen 83)

Stephen's discovery of 'two voices' in Wordsworth anticipates Bakhtin's conception of 'double-voiced discourse' (*DI* 374) more than superficially; the oddity, from a Bakhtinian standpoint, is that a so-called 'parody' should find 'two voices' something to complain about. My explanation would be that Stephen's poem, like Hartley Coleridge's, is criticism masking as parody. Though the very first line, taken from Wordsworth, 'marks' the sonnet as parody, beyond this line it does not parody Wordsworth so much as comment on him: the quotations (lines 1, 12) are not significantly re-accentuated, nor is there, as in Fanshawe's poem, any re-creation of a specifically Wordsworthian style. But for the present argument, the special interest of Stephen's sonnet lies in the fact that this ontic containment of parody (the self-presentation as parody where parodic means have actually been virtually entirely displaced by commentary) is so amply confirmed and elaborated at the thematic level, in the overt hostility of that commentary to Wordsworth's two-voicedness. In a significant sense, and both in means and in message, Stephen's poem is anti-parodic.

It should be clear, moreover, that these anti-parodic elements harmonize with and support the projects of contemporary criticism. In idealizing the authoritative voice 'of the deep' and lamenting its adulteration, Stephen expresses a wish common in Wordsworth criticism, the grounds of which are easy to suspect: the more consistently authoritative Wordsworth, the more authoritative his commentators may be. To some extent, indeed, Stephen has even imposed what he idealizes by underrepresenting Wordsworth's multivocity as a merely temporal alternation ('certain times,' 'other times') between two quite distinguishable timbres, one 'articulate monotony' and another.[34] Fanshawe to the contrary, Stephen would have us think we can tell when Wordsworth nods. More than incidentally, this confidence that the essence of Wordsworthian authority can be precipitated from the babble reflects the program of contemporary editors, such as Arnold, who sought to purge the Wordsworthian ore, including the 'Lucy Poems,' of the dross.[35] The pointed and witty Victorian parody, the contemporary parody anthology, the hostility to Wordsworth's more mobile and liminal voices, and the authoritative but humourless Wordsworth of popular reputation – Auden's 'bleak old bore' (58) – are demonstrably cognate artifacts of criticism's will to discernment and 'knowledge.'

Hence the odd circumstance that one poet should have reputations both for bathos and for monotony: the latter is a critical evasion of the former. Wordsworthian monotony is, indeed, hard to verify first-hand. In contrast both to Stephen's wish and to his poem, Wordsworth's 'Thought of a Briton' *is* duplicitous, it does have 'two voices' (or rather more), but they are not easily disentangled. Wordsworth's sonnet is ambivalent to authority itself, paradoxically entertaining it as *one* voice even while undercutting it with another. Whether we read it politically or against a Miltonic intertext, we confront this doubleness; I begin with the former reading. Wordsworth presents 'Liberty' as having enjoyed the 'Two Voices' of sea and mountains, presumably those of Britain and Switzerland, before these 'two' were reduced to one by 'a Tyrant': presumably, Switzerland has lost the ear of Liberty while Britain's voice remains. But since the 'subjugation of Switzerland' involved a notorious imposition of univocity *within* Switzerland, and in fact created 'Switzerland' out of a loose confederation, it is also possible to read this collapse of 'Two Voices' into one as referring to the internal unification of the heterogeneous Swiss cantons.[36] Especially since centralizing Switzerland required suppressing resistance in the traditionally self-determined Alpine regions, a voice of 'mountains' no longer heard by Liberty suggests not only the silencing of the Swiss voice among nations, but also its own silencing of internal dissent; at this level, a voice 'of the sea' may refer to Switzerland's own lower lake regions (Lake Constance is *Boden See* in German).[37] The effect of the double construction is a profound ambivalence to the country apparently honoured by the poem: Switzerland is both victim and tyrant, a voice silenced by Bonaparte's imperial project to univocalize Europe, and an autonomous monologism that has emerged by silencing its own dissonance. This contradiction appears at more abstract levels as well: for instance, if tyranny consists in the reduction of two voices to one, then 'Liberty' must consist in multivocity; but Liberty is also figured as consistent with *uni*vocity, for she is expressly bidden to 'cleave to that which still is left.'

These are contradictions in theme, but there is a similar dissonance between the dominant message of Wordsworth's poem and its mode. Consider the phrase, 'a Tyrant': it is commonly presumed to represent Bonaparte, and in its singularity it represents univocity/authority itself. But historically speaking, Wordsworth's single 'Tyrant' is, itself, a reductive figure: as J.C. Maxwell points out, it is a synecdoche for plural aggressions that preceded, and exceeded, the agency of Bonaparte.[38] It is the same here, then, as in the use of 'Two Voices' to represent two internally multiplicitous countries: even while decrying the univocalization of Europe (or Switzerland) as tyranny, Wordsworth's poem acts 'a Tyrant' itself. It might fairly be said that the Miltonic sonnet's compression of such vast political processes in such 'narrow room' requires the very univocalizing power that this Miltonic sonnet also correlates with tyranny; or to turn it differently, it might be said that Wordsworth must act the 'tyrant' in order to speak with any coherence against tyranny. But in any case the sonnet speaks in two voices, actions and words, for and against the reduction of multivocity, and does so in a way that makes it impossible simply to align multivocity with or against the cause of 'Liberty.' This dilemma of aesthetic representation may itself, however, fairly represent the dilemma of political representation confronting the Swiss cantons in their resistance to external pressure from France and Austria: if 'united they stood' to combat consolidations imposed from without, their defence had to replicate, to some degree, the very univocity it sought to resist.[39]

These double positions and parallels – the 'tyrant' silencing Switzerland *ab extra* and Switzerland silencing its highlands; the reduction of multivocity in the political sphere and again in the poem's representation of that sphere – are redolent of the comparative dynamics of parody: we become conscious of parallels, but their 'ethos' and meaning are not immediately clear; whatever commentary the poem does include seems to be undercut or obscured rather than confirmed by them. A clearer suggestion of the parodic mode is the overarching parallel between the unification (or 'Subjugation') of Switzerland, on which the sonnet explicitly focuses, and the unification of Britain, to which its title barely alludes. The speaker's self-identification as 'a Briton' rather than an Englishman is difficult to read for attitude at a time when the brutally suppressed Irish rebellion (1798) and, consequently, the most recent Act of Union (1800) were fresh in memory – these events were, indeed, virtually simultaneous with the 'Subjugation of Switzerland.' The word 'Briton' might be read simply as accepting or affirming the newly 'United Kingdom of Britain and Ireland.' But I myself would find this too obtuse for a poem that specifically laments another imposed unification across the channel, and am therefore inclined to suspect a conscious irony or use of persona. (One indication of such irony is the curiously emphatic singularity of the phrase, '*Thought* of *a* Briton,' which might be read as a casualness or even as a humility, but which also emphasizes the representative pretension of one individual to speak for the whole.) While Wordsworth himself seldom refers to the most recent Act of Union, it is true that he cites it in 'The Convention of Cintra' (1809) as

> yet another case in which a People may be benefited by resignation or forfeiture of their rights as a separate independent State; I mean, where – of two contiguous or neighbouring countries, both included by nature under one conspicuously defined limit – the weaker is united with, or absorbed into, the more powerful; and one and the same Government is extended over both. ... Who does not rejoice that former partitions have disappeared, – and that England, Scotland,

and Wales, are under one legislative and executive authority; and that Ireland (would that she had been more justly dealt with!) follows the same destiny? (*Prose Works* 1:322–3)

One might respond, of course: many Welsh, Scottish, Irish, and even English people.[40] Yet even here there is some ambivalence with regard to Ireland, and the 'Thought of a Briton' provides a more troubled reflection on these events if one appreciates the 'Subjugation of Switzerland' as a parallel for the unification of Britain and Ireland. Whether or not it is recognized by the speaker or intended by the author (a quandary of a sort entirely germane to parody), the parallel casts certain shadows on its speaker's authority; the sonnet's very voice, as the singularizing 'Thought of a Briton,' becomes structurally comparable to the univocalizing 'Tyrant' to which it objects. Though it seems to deplore a specific univocalization, Wordsworth's sonnet has a basically pyramidal representative structure, in which any unity, including its own voice, turns out to 'represent,' or to have devoured, more primitive multiplicities.[41]

The relation of this sonnet to parody and its ambivalence to the authoritative voice may both become clearer if we take account of its echoes of the Miltonic 'trumpet,' specifically of the sonnet 'On the Late Massacher in Piemont' (1655/1673):

Avenge O Lord thy slaughter'd Saints, whose bones
  Lie scatter'd on the Alpine Mountains cold,
  Ev'n them who kept thy truth so pure of old
  When all our Fathers worship't Stocks and Stones,
Forget not: in thy book record their groanes
  Who were thy Sheep and in their antient Fold
  Slayn by the bloody *Piemontese* that roll'd
  Mother with Infant down the Rocks. Their moans
The Vales redoubl'd to the Hills, and they
  To Heav'n. Their martyr'd blood and ashes sow
  O're all th'*Italian* fields where still doth sway
The triple Tyrant: that from these may grow
  A hunder'd-fold, who having learnt thy way
  Early may fly the *Babylonian* wo. (*Complete Poetical Works* 84)

The resemblance between 'thy Alpine hold' and Milton's 'the Alpine mountains cold' suggests that the suppression of Switzerland's mountain voice (however this be taken) is comparable to the Florentine massacre of the Waldenses. (Piedmont was formally incorporated in France in September 1802, just before Bonaparte's second invasion of Switzerland, but its geographical proximity to the Alpine regions of Switzerland known to Wordsworth, particularly the Simplon, is probably sufficient to explain the association of the Swiss and Piedmontese.) Wordsworth's 'a Tyrant' corresponds to Milton's 'triple tyrant,' his tyrannic univocity oddly intensifed by the loss of Milton's rhetorical intensifier, a numerical diminution that also corresponds to Napoleon's progress from consul to emperor (with the Pope's blessing) between 1799 and 1804. As 'holy glee,' the cantons' nationalist resistance is assimilated to the Waldenses' religious persecution, while phrases such as 'age to age' and 'cleave, O cleave' echo Milton's echoic theme. Such comparabilities will more likely be read today as 'allusions' than as parody. But comparing recent events to historical ones, or, more precisely, fitting them to the textual patterns by which historical events have already been solemnized, always runs a risk of parodic sinking. The comparability of Wordsworth's sonnet and Milton's has basically typological potential: the same event appears to have come again. But in this case the parallel deflates rather than exalts, and the deflation works both ways. On the one hand Wordsworth's sequel deflates both Milton's authoritative affirmation that Heaven listens and the note of hope on which he closes; on the other, it discredits the present, not so much for falling short of the past as for repeating it. Milton affirms that the 'moans' of mother and infant rolled down the rocks were redoubled 'to the Hills' and 'To Heav'n'; but Wordsworth, while subtly reproducing Milton's image of the human waterfall, insists that the auditor is absent: 'not a torrent murmurs heard by thee.' The recurrence of the assault on nominally different Alpiners by a nominally different tyrant makes the ear of Heaven seem deafer. In its quotations of Milton no less than in its theme, then, Wordsworth's sonnet is ambivalent toward the authoritative voice: while borrowing Milton's authoritative vehicle of invocation and exhortation, it also undercuts its prophetic authority. 'Two Voices are there,' and they are not harmonious. One might be tempted to complain that this poem shows Wordsworth's multivocal mode crossed by the lure of Miltonic authority, and thus that it typifies his productivity at the latter end of the 'golden decade'; but it also stands to reason that a true multivocity cannot be consistently hostile to authority; authority is, precisely, one of its voices.

Undeniably, both Wordsworth's and Stephen's representations of the 'two voices' involve a certain reduction of real multivocity. Even what Stephen celebrates as Wordsworth's 'one [voice] of the deep' contains a successive mimicry of 'storm-cloud,' 'sea,' and 'bird' – just as the 'Two Voices' celebrated by Wordsworth contain the innumerable actual voices of countries. To some extent, such arbitrary reductions are endemic to representation (my own use of Wordsworth and Stephen to represent classes of 'free' and 'contained' parody not excepted).[42] The issue here, then, is not this unavoidable reduction of multivocity but a fundamental difference in its disposition. In asserting that 'grossly apparent' parodies such as Stephen's are monological in nature, I mean primarily that they mediate a 'primary' voice rather than ramify or enter in dialogue with it; they are assertive and generalizing, and their commentary does not encourage comparative verification. Though entertaining in itself, 'A Sonnet' simply does not function as a 'beside-poem': rather than rewrite or force a rereading of Wordsworth's poem, and rather than invite recognition of itself as a (mis)representation, it stands as an independent, authoritative statement on Wordsworth. It is true that its representation of Wordsworth might be compared with Wordsworth's actual practice, against its behest, as I have been attempting. But even then, so far from initiating a real reconsideration of Wordsworth (or of our reading of him), its statements tend to license the breezy dismissal of any peculiar or dissonant feature as 'hopeless rubbish.' Confirming first impressions and blaming the writer for problems, Stephen's sonnet thus brings to a scene of confusion the comfort of a simplified order. Perhaps this encouragement of interpretive complacency has something to do with its popularity.

Wordsworth's representation of political multivocity works very differently, discouraging political and interpretive complacency alike. The very obscurity as to what his 'Two Voices' of sea and mountains represent demands a restitution of context, and the possibility of reading either one voice or both as 'Switzerland' (or indeed as Britain) emphasizes both the arbitrariness of the figure and its simplification of voice. Leaving these referents to be inferred also implicates the reader in the representational act and at the same time undermines her interpretive certitude. Likewise in the relation to Milton's sonnet: does it assume the authority of Milton's form, or challenge it? Is it allusion or parody? Does it represent Milton at all, or is this reading 'forced' on it? These are the doubts with which the more subtle degrees of parody afflict the interpreter; these are the doubts which Hone emphasized to secure his acquittal.

It may seem that I have finessed the important question of Wordsworth's declared hostility to parody by considering a political sonnet that is, at best, only marginally parodic and only 'about' parody in a figurative sense.[43] But precisely because it is both thematically ambivalent toward authority and undecided between authoritative and dialogical modes, the 'Thought of a Briton' prepares us to appreciate that a contradiction between Wordsworth's parodic practice and his explicit critical antipathy to parody may be both normal and irreducible. Contrary to Stephen's comforting diagnosis, Wordsworth's authoritative voice, including his voice as critic, is not a standard voice subject to unfortunate accidents or false notes, yet remediable through critical-editorial discernment: it is simply one voice among many. It is one thing to pronounce that a distinct voice 'of the deep' exists, but the difficulty in practice of discerning this voice from the others constitutes multivocity's active challenge to authoritative interpretation. Is the authority of a particular statement heard in it or attributed to it? That even on the subject of parody Wordsworth should be of two minds, precept and practice, is a basically parodic situation; it will embarrass any critical representation of him that is unwilling simply to privilege one voice over the other. Maybe Wordsworth's stricture against parody refers to 'obvious' forms, or false parody; the 'parodies' of *Peter Bell*, for instance, are full of simple commentary on Wordsworth. Or the contradiction might be resolved chronologically, by consigning parody to the early period and authority to the period of maturity and self-revision.[44] The lure of such resolutions is precisely that they contain parody, in the first case by interpreting dissenting precepts into harmony with the practice, in the second by consigning the parodic practice to a distinct 'period.' Either solution produces a comprehensible Wordsworth, but both fail to comprehend the full challenge of his example. If much nineteenth-century 'parody' contains its own subversive potential by announcing itself as a discrete genre, and indeed joins ranks with commentary, Wordsworth illustrates how true parody may escape under false rubrics (bathos, anti-climax, allusion) to fight another day.[45]

6. Parody, Alias Novelistic Allusion

At this point my argument may appear critically retrograde, for the conventional problem for formalist scholarship of intertextualities has been to distinguish one kind from another. In *Wordsworth's Art of Allu-*

sion, for instance, Edwin Stein attempts to distinguish among a range of textual relations including 'allusion,' 'echo,' 'borrowing,' 'imitation,' 'influence,' 'quotation,' 'parallel,' 'evocation,' and 'indebtedness,' producing classifications such as 'non-allusive echoes.' Stein comments on the difficulties in telling an echo from an allusion: 'It helps to develop a decorum in dealing with any poet's work, a sense of where to draw the line between truth and mere ingenuity in interpretation.'[46] Drawing this line enables Stein to produce statistics – e.g., 'Milton's works will be found the source of about 550 echoes out of a grand total of some 1,300' – subject to the note of qualification: 'To pretend to an exact count ... would be misleading, partly because some can be disputed, and partly because some no doubt have been overlooked' (10, 224n8). Without wholly denying the value of Stein's findings, his diffidence on this point, and his anxiety concerning 'mere ingenuity in interpretation,' are significant symptoms of the real resistance of intertextuality to the formal classifications he seeks to impose. If it is so hard to tell whether a similarity with another text constitutes an allusion, or in Stein's terms to tell 'echo' from 'allusion,' one may either force the critical distinction or consider the salience of the indistinction. I pursue the latter course here, though this may appear like lumping 'distinct' genres of intertextuality – in this case imitation, allusion, and parody – together.

The comparability between Wordsworth's sonnet and Milton's, considered above, provides one example of the difficulty of 'draw[ing] the line' between imitation, allusion, and parody. But the primary issue here is not so much Wordsworth as the practice of those who rewrite him. In this sphere, though Fanshawe's 'Imitation' represents a certain 'escape' of parody from the usual critical containments, it too was contained, as we have seen, at least for a certain readership, by Hamilton's anthologization. If we seek, alongside the multifarious nineteenth-century containments of parody, the 'return of the repressed,' we must look where Hamilton did not, to novelistic allusion. In keeping with my anti-definition stipulating that true parody is not clearly parody, this is not to offer a formalist argument that novelistic allusion *is* parodic, but a phenomenological suggestion that it may be considered *as* parodic, or that it is parodic *in effect*. And here its very ambiguity of status, which puts readings both of itself and of its intertexts into question, is essential.

Bakhtin practically identifies parody with the dialogical novel, particularly with novelistic mimesis of speech patterns.[47] Hone's precedents for parody of Scripture extend similarly to apparently marginal cases of dramatic and novelistic imitations of religious speech. Hone observes that Jonson's plays have parodic passages and quotes 'the Hypocrite' and 'Foot's Farce of "The Minor" ' to show how religious language was 'caricatured upon the stage' (*TT* 2:33, 3:32). He quotes at length from another contemporary 'farce,' 'The Weathercock,' to show 'the use of scriptural language tolerated on the stage, for the very purpose of ridiculing ... the *Quakers*' (3:33–4). And he demands: 'Why did not the Attorney-General prosecute Mr. Walter Scott, for "Tales of My Landlord," a work which abounded with Scriptural phrases, set in the most absurd and ridiculous view?' (3:31). As Hone's citations are meant to show, the dramatic and novelistic reproduction of speech patterns, shading into caricature, constitutes a rich field of uncontained parody. And it does so for the same reason as do the verse 'imitations' by Fanshawe and her predecessors: while it consists, like parody, in textual parallelism, it is free of the labelling and targeting that render parody 'grossly apparent' and assimilable as commentary. A reader still finds comparabilities, or 'echoes' of other discourses, but their meaning remains an open question.

As even Fanshawe's 'Imitation' illustrates, the intertextual dynamics of such parody depend on both similarity and difference, or on the parody's partial re-creation of textual patterns such that deviation becomes significant. The close of Fanshawe's imitation, where similarity turns into exaggeration, exemplifies such deviation:

> It were a blessed sight to see
> That child become a willow tree,
>   His brother trees among.
> He'd be four times as tall as me,
>   And live three times as long.

If we accept the preceding lines' apparent invitation to compare Fanshawe's text with the 'Lucy Poems,' particularly with 'Three years,' these lines deviate from Wordsworth's usual practice in at least three significant ways: first, by making the child's assimilation by material nature explicit ('That child become a willow-tree'); second, by making the speaker's attitude to this assimilation explicit ('a blessed sight'); and third, by rationalizing the speaker's approval ('He'd be four times as tall'). In all three cases, Fanshawe does not really exaggerate so much as provide information lacking in Wordsworth's texts, which avow, at most, that 'She died,' that she is '*With* rocks, and stones, and trees,' and that her death makes a 'difference to me.' Even aside from its specific absurdity, Fanshawe's rationale constitutes precisely the type of information Wordsworth typically avoids providing, most certainly in the 'Lucy Poems.' As Geoffrey Hartman has emphasized, '*Wordsworth's understanding is characterized by the general absence of the will to attain relational knowledge*, that is, knowledge which may be obtained in direct answer to the Why, the What, the Wherefore, and the How' (*Unmediated* 5). But Fanshawe's provision of such information works in at least two ways. On the one hand, it emphasizes by contrast the bare facticity of Wordsworth's verse. On the other, it renders her text an 'Imitation' less 'of Wordsworth' than of what his text becomes in a typical reading; in its very lack of correspondence to Wordsworth's texts, the concluding rationale parodies the inferential rationalizing which his flat statements elicit. Maybe no one would seriously ascribe *this* rationale to Wordsworth, but the pressure to make sense of his asyndetic statements provokes most interpreters to forge similarly rational links between verse and verse, and to ascribe them to the poet under the rubric of the 'implicit.' Here, indeed, Fanshawe anticipates one of the most important developments in the interpretations of 'Three years,' though we may doubt whether it can be considered to 'parody' interpretations before the fact. Most critics have read 'Three years' either as showing how beneficent Nature fosters the human (usually ignoring the death in stanza 7) or as lamenting Nature's betrayal (stanza 7 becoming anticlimactic all in all). What Fanshawe anticipates is Garrod's pivotal reading of 1929, which argues the *continuity* between Nature's tutelage and Lucy's death, and supposes Wordsworth's quietistic acceptance.[48] The acceptance, in Fanshawe's poem, of Will's metamorphosis into 'a willow-tree' suggests what Garrod argues, Wordsworth's acceptance of Lucy's death as the fulfilment of nature's 'work.' Likewise, Fanshawe's crude Ovidian metamorphosis may also help us recognize Wordsworth's subtle use of metamorphosis myth as a euphemism for death.[49] As Wordsworth's 'Nature' promises, 'The floating clouds their state shall lend / To her, for her the willow bend.' Depending on how we read 'state,' this may mean Lucy becomes a cloud or vapour; if so, why not a willow tree?

In sum, Fanshawe's 'Imitation' invites a comparative use by way of suggestively incomplete parallelism, while its deviations from parallel suggest points of observation to the comparer. If one is tempted to say 'it comments' through such deviation, the interreadings I have just attempted are in many ways too tenuous to be mothered on Fanshawe:

it is far from certain, for instance, that the insight into Wordsworth's avoidance of 'relational knowledge' is derived from comparative use of Fanshawe rather than imposed on her with the assistance of Hartman and hindsight; it is not clear even that Fanshawe is to be interread with the specific text(s) I have adduced, or that any given detail is to be interread in the relations I have used (emphasis by contrast, emphasis by exaggeration). These uncertainties are essential to criticism-by-parody: however useful heuristically, Fanshawe's text does not pronounce upon Wordsworth's and does not easily lend itself to pronouncements of our own. If anything, if I am right to suggest that its principal absurdities lie in *additions* to Wordsworth, it tends to mock interpretive rounding-out.

Novelistic allusions to the 'Lucy Poems' have similar effects, as I shall illustrate with examples from Shelley's *The Last Man* and Melville's *Pierre*. But it is worth stressing that not all allusion works in this way; one must distinguish novelistic allusion from more authoritarian practices, such as D.H. Lawrence's allusion to Lucy in 1924:

> The simple innocent child of nature does not exist. If there be an occasional violet by a mossy stone in the human sense, a Wordsworthian Lucy, it is because her vitality is rather low, and her simple nature is very near a simpleton's. You may, like Yeats, admire the simpleton, and call him God's fool. But for me the village idiot is a cold egg. (624)

Lawrence does not question the meaning of 'Lucy' but assigns a meaning to her. Though Wordsworth's Lucy had become something of an idiom even by the time of his death, what she is or stands for has never been an obvious matter of agreement. Lawrence presents his idiosyncratic view of Lucy as 'the village idiot' as something to be taken for granted, but at the same time he is forced to specify this meaning through apposition. What does such a manoeuvre achieve? Why allude to Lucy, to Hamlet, or to Quixote when one must still identify or even re-create these characters, when their ostensive functions as fixed tokens or symbols are so fallible that they must be supplemented with explanation? Lawrence's example suggests that such allusions have a rhetorical function as false vehicles: though he must attach his own concept to Lucy, she lends it a semblance of common currency.[50] In this respect Lawrence's allusion lies close to, and may even be considered a drastically conflated form of, authoritative interpretation. By contrast, novelistic allusion to the 'Lucy Poems' merely begins with explicit reference or quotation (in the case of Melville even this is omitted) and consists chiefly in more oblique parallelisms, such that it may indeed be questioned whether allusion is intended. Rather than identify or interpret Lucy, novelistic allusion raises questions about both the 'primary' text and the nature of our interpretive relation to it.

SHELLEY'S 'THE LAST MAN'

Geoffrey Hartman observes, '[a]s a curiosity,' that 'the first person to draw attention to [the] contrast implicit in the violet-star image [of 'She dwelt'] is Mary Shelley in *The Last Man* (1826)' ('Beyond' 44n). He refers to an early passage in the novel, spoken by the narrator Lionel Verney:

> I have detailed the perfections of my sister; and yet she was utterly unlike Idris [whom Verney eventually marries]. Perdita, even where she loved, was reserved and timid; Idris was frank and confiding. The one recoiled to solitude, that she might there entrench herself from disappointment and injury; the other walked forth in open day, believing that none would harm her. Wordsworth has compared a beloved female to two fair objects in nature; but his lines always appeared to me rather a contrast than a similitude:
>
> [quotes stanza 2 of 'She dwelt']
>
> Such a violet was sweet Perdita, trembling to entrust herself to the very air, cowering from observation, yet betrayed by her excellences; and repaying with a thousand graces the labour of those who sought her in her lonely bye-path. Idris was as the star, set in single splendour in the dim anadem of balmy evening; ready to enlighten and delight the subject world, shielded herself from every taint by her unimagined distance from all that was not like herself akin to heaven. (36)

Though in one respect Verney's allusion could not be more straightforward, Shelley's allusion is more complex than Hartman indicates. It does not end here, but continues, more tenuously, with the later appearance of the character Lucy Martin (née Clayton); moreover, particularly in a novel abounding in thinly veiled but inconsistent 'portraits' of contemporaries, it is doubtful that a comment by Verney can be taken simply as a comment by Shelley.[51] In context, this discussion of 'She dwelt' is dialogical, having what Bakhtin calls a 'twofold direction ... both toward the referential object of speech ... and toward *another's discourse*, toward *someone else's speech'* (*Problems* 185): it is not just Verney's commentary on Wordsworth's poem, but also Shelley's thickened representation of such commentary. Verney's interpretive manoeuvres are of familiar kinds: he wilfully construes Wordsworth's simple juxtaposition of images as comparisons with the 'beloved female'; he establishes the relevance of these images by appropriating them to his own experience; and he rationalizes what appears to him as their 'contrast,' or contradictory qualities, by predicating them of two distinct women. Thus far his appropriation of Wordsworth's stanza is not just an interpretation but a compact epitome of interpretive process; it can be read both ironically and 'straight.' But the passage is dialogical in a deeper sense also. The women to whom Verney applies the stanza are, suggestively, his sister and his wife-to-be; he and his sister have grown up in the Lake District, their father has been unhappily connected with the court, their mother is the native 'daughter of a poor cottager,' and both parents die when the children are very young (5–7). The parallels here (Verney = Wordsworth, Perdita = Dorothy, and, by extension, Idris = Mary) are imperfect and shadowy, and they are not extended in the sequel (Perdita, for instance, marries); but they are sufficient to cross Verney's commentary with a perspective not belonging to him. From this perspective, Verney re-presents Wordsworth rather than commenting on him, and 'Lucy' proves to have been two women, his lover and his sister. Thus, even while Verney explicitly *re*writes Wordsworth's Lucy in the register of his own personal experience and understanding, from the supervening perspective his rewriting stands as the poem's prewriting, or subtext, and we come upon a suspicion that the historical Wordsworth is the one who has rewritten his (multiple) personal relationships as 'Lucy.' This *á clef* reading is fully consistent both with the quasi-biographical romancing of Shelley's novel and with the biographical speculation that typifies nineteenth-century 'Lucy Poems' criticism, and thus it is at least plausibly attributable to Shelley. But since Verney's voice can be heard equally as Shelley's voice, as the voice of Wordsworth's all-too-typical reader, and as Wordsworth's own, and since this makes it possible to read several contradictory commentaries, the sum effect of Shelley's allusion is a 'commentary' not so much on Wordsworth as on commentary itself. Her inconsistent parallelism invites us to question whether the parallels we 'find' are really 'there' and thus to be self-conscious about our own inventive selectivity. If we seek to sort out these contradictory voices, are we not in danger of recognizing, in Verney's simplification of Wordsworth's contradictory text, our own reflection?

These effects of a dubious parallelism are compounded by the later appearance of the character Lucy Martin, whose similarities with Wordsworth's Lucy might indeed be dismissed as coincidence were it not for the earlier reference to 'She dwelt.' *The Last Man* envisions an extinction of humanity by plague in which the English appear to be the last affected, Lionel Verney the last to survive. Just as the last English survivors are gathering to flee south for the winter, Lionel receives a written plea for help from Lucy, a resident of his neighbourhood who has lingered to nurse her ailing mother. Lucy, we learn (252–66), is of humble origins and multiply unfortunate: she loses her 'little cottage' to fire, makes a marriage of inconvenience to provide for her mother, is rediscovered too late by the suitor of her choice, and is finally abandoned by her 'brutal and quarrelsome' husband. Though Lionel and Idris, now married, have themselves forgotten Lucy in preparing to depart for France (255), they respond to her plea with alacrity. They set out in bad weather, though Idris is ill, and when Idris dies en route of cold and neglect, Lionel, having paused to inter Idris, continues alone for Datchet to save Lucy. He finds her 'humble abode' open to the snow and Lucy within sewing a shroud, for Lucy's mother has left her, during the night, 'the lone survivor of a dead nation.' Lucy still feels bound to her mother, but Lionel persuades her to accompany him by invoking 'duty' – with Idris gone, he needs a caretaker for 'the orphan children' (255–66). Lucy has to insist on burial for her mother, and they leave for Dover and eventually cross to France. The next we hear of Lucy, she brings news of the death of an orphan girl, and her own death appears in the next sentence: 'Poor Lucy herself only survived, till we arrived at Dijon' (301).

Shelley can unfold Lucy's tale almost entirely in retrospect because it is superfluous to the plot of her novel; whatever significance it has lies in its symbolic dimensions, established largely through allusion to Wordsworth, but also in its metacritical reflectivity upon the construction of this symbolism. In reflecting upon Lucy's death, Lionel presents her as a 'type':

> Poor Lucy herself only survived, till we arrived at Dijon. She had devoted herself throughout to the nursing the sick, and attending the friendless. Her excessive exertions brought on a slow fever, which ended in the dread disease whose approach soon released her from her sufferings. She had throughout been endeared to us by her good qualities, by her ready and cheerful execution of every duty, and mild acquiescence in every turn of adversity. When we con-

signed her to the tomb, we seemed at the same time to bid a final adieu to those peculiarly feminine virtues conspicuous in her; uneducated and unpretending as she was, she was distinguished for patience, forbearance, and sweetness. These, with all their train of qualities peculiarly English, would never again be revived for us. This type of all that was most worthy of admiration in her class among my countrywomen, was placed under the sod of desert France; and it was as a second separation from our country to have lost sight of her for ever. (301)

To a reader of Wordsworth, Verney's identification of Lucy with 'qualities peculiarly English' will likely recall Lucy's identification with England and English womanhood in 'I travelled,' just as Verney's 'second separation' will recall, with a certain irony, that poem's ominous promise: 'Nor will I quit thy shore / A second time' (6–7). Like most allusion, this one may be said both to take and to give. If it takes over from Wordsworth the ready identification of 'Lucy' not just as elegiac object but as a 'type' of English womanhood, what it adds is a certain reflection on the paradox of this characterless and even self-effacing 'type' and on its social and historical specificity. Verney's 'type,' 'distinguished for patience, forbearance, and sweetness,' has virtually no character or life of her own. Indeed, if we consider the etymological sense of 'character' as 'an instrument for marking and engraving' and hence 'a distinctive significant mark ... or symbol' (*OED*), Lucy is, strictly speaking, an anti-type, the passive complement and blank opposite of a 'character.' An 'exemplary sufferer,' as she is called elsewhere (255), she is known only for 'patient endurance,' for 'sacrificing herself for the comfort and welfare of her parent' (253). But if Wordsworth's characterless Lucy is associated with nature, Shelley's anti-type is a product of ideology: not only does Verney praise her self-effacement as her 'good qualities,' 'worthy of admiration' (301), but Lucy herself considers passivity as virtue, praising her own mother's 'patien[ce] in many sufferings' (256). Being so selfless and transparent, the wonder is not that this feminine Anchises is initially forgotten in the exodus, but that she ever can call herself to the attention of people as self-involved as Verney.[52]

Verney's eulogy is, like his earlier commentary on 'She dwelt,' dialogical: it can be read, at the least, both as Shelley-Verney's characterization of Lucy and as Shelley's characterization of Verney. In the first case it refers straightforwardly to Lucy's character; in the second, it mimics 'another's discourse,' specifically the masculine construction of the 'peculiarly feminine.' On the second level, where Verney appears less as the subject than as the object of scrutiny, Lucy's self-effacing character appears to the reader no longer as objective datum but as a salient of Verney's interpretation. While her characterlessness appears as the construct and the complement, in short the imprint, of Verney's own egotistical type, his myopic, neglectful, and thoroughly self-serving construction of Lucy also typifies her treatment by her family, her parents, her neighbours, her negligent suitor, her 'brutal' husband, and, in short, her culture. The irony of Verney's eulogy is that the death of Lucy which it laments pales beside the ideological consensus that kept her from living in the first place; and yet the eulogy also perpetuates this stifling. Thus far it is not difficult to construe Verney's eulogy of Lucy as parody reflecting on the egotistical objectification of Lucy by Wordsworth's epitaphic poems, or on what Crabb Robinson admired as 'the opposition,' in 'She dwelt,' 'between the apparent strength of the passion and the insignificance of the object.[53] But this reading is significantly crossed by voices at the former level. Verney's eulogy of Lucy does not merely caricature chauvinism, but also strikes notes of enlightenment or correction, in which one seems to hear the voice of Verney's feminine creator. Only at first does this speech stereotype Lucy's self-abnegation as a 'peculiarly feminine' virtue; thereafter it progresses to type her more sensitively, not just as 'peculiarly English' but as peculiar to a 'class' and even to a period: having left England both temporally and geographically behind, Verney recognizes that Lucy's character can 'never again be revived.' As this seems to acknowledge, Lucy is not the universal-eternal feminine; if Wordsworth's 'I travelled' gets as far as nationalizing the feminine, Shelley's male speaker, benefiting both from the gendered insight of his creator and from his imaginative end-of-time perspective, sees still more clearly the cultural specificity of her self-abnegating 'type.'

The cost of this advance is, it seems, a certain incoherence in Verney, who appears partly as Shelley's butt and partly as her mouthpiece. One might dismiss this incoherence as an aesthetic or mimetic flaw, especially since more seriously taken it challenges the instinct to judge novelistic speech by the coherence of the individual character. But the multivocity of Verney's eulogy may be justified even as realism; our difficulties in distinguishing his speech and his ideological positions from Shelley's are not fundamentally different from the difficulties posed by the texture of real speech, with its constant interchange of quotation, received opinion, ideology (all these in various stages of digestion and conflict), and more considered opinion. The central point here is that, even if in Verney's eulogy of Lucy Martin, as in his earlier reading of Wordsworth's poem, both an authoritative voice of Shelley and the fallible, all-too-typical voices of Verney and his culture seem to be provisionally distinguishable, the challenge of knowing which speaks when, of deciding precisely which utterances are serious and authoritative, is in practice insurmountable. Both passages mix real insight with egotistical projection and appropriation, but the mix is inextricable. Verney's multivocity renders his commentaries not just unstable and unauthoritative, in the sense that no particular utterance can be reliably attributed to its author, but literally untrustworthy – heuristic, but inconclusive. The force of their unreliability is to make the reader compare and in effect formulate his or her own commentary; and these, it seems to me, are the basic means and ends of any genuinely intertextual criticism.

MELVILLE'S 'PIERRE; OR, THE AMBIGUITIES'

> Is it possible then, thought Pierre, that there lives a human creature in this common world of every-days, whose whole history may be told in little less [sic] than two-score words, and yet embody in that smallness a fathomless fountain of ever-welling mystery? (Melville 165)

Source studies of Melville's *Pierre; Or, The Ambiguities* (1852) had turned up everyone except Wordsworth until 1973, when Maxine Moore observed that its allusions to Wordsworth are impossible to overlook. Moore's documentation of them is not exhaustive but is thoroughly convincing: besides many salient verbal allusions, she notes a close congruence between Melville's plot and characters and Wordsworth's biography. The elder Pierre (the hero's father) has an adoring sister named Dorothea, a wife named Mary, and an illegitimate daughter begotten in a hushed-up pre-marital affair with a Frenchwoman. The novel opens with the younger Pierre's courtship of Lucy, but it brings the lovers to ruin on the revelation of the father's indiscretion – or rather on the son's foolish/idealistic handling of it. Especially in the idyllic account of Pierre's courtship, the novel is liberally sprinkled with reminiscences of the 'Lucy Poems.' For instance:

> ... from Lucy's mouth and cheek came the fresh fragrance of her violet young being.

'Smell I the flowers, or thee?' cried Pierre.

'See I lakes, or eyes?' cried Lucy, her own gazing down into his soul, as two stars gaze down into a tarn ... (42)

This complex allusion to 'She dwelt,' stanza 2, which also suggests 'There was a Boy,' lines 24–5, and Wordsworth's association with the Lake District, is characteristic of *Pierre*'s reference to Wordsworth throughout. On the one hand, Wordsworth is nowhere directly named or quoted (while *Hamlet*, *The Inferno*, and several other intertexts are); on the other hand, a broad hint appears in the opening pages:

An excellent English author of these times enumerating the prime advantages of his natal lot, cites foremost, that he first saw the rural light. So with Pierre. It had been his choice fate to have been born and nurtured in the country, surrounded by scenery whose uncommon loveliness was the perfect mould of a delicate and poetic mind ... (9)

If, with Moore, we make the initial association with Wordsworth, the following pages are dense with allusion. Yet there can be little point in distinguishing proper allusions from more tenuous resemblances; the novel, as its subtitle suggests, is about 'the ambiguities,' both of life and of art, and the very indistinctness of Wordsworth's presence – 'half-hidden from the eye' – reflects this theme. Even assuming the *fact* of its allusion to Wordsworth, its attitude, or 'ethos,' is equally ambiguous. Under the witty subtitle 'Intimations of Immorality,' Moore presents *Pierre* 'as a parody on the life and work of Wordsworth' (89). By focusing on the parallel between Wordsworth and the elder Pierre, one can indeed read it as parody in this judgmental sense, as deriding Wordsworth's respectability in light of his suppressed liaison with Annette Vallon.[54] But as Melville's subtitle suggests, the novel also dwells on interpretive problems anterior to such judgment, and Moore's simple ethical reading is therefore, I think, overly simple. Significantly, such a reading tends to reflect itself: the closural reading of Melville's text presents *it* as a closural reading of Wordsworth's. But the nature of the novel's 'ambiguity' makes quite different reflections possible. I would argue that precisely in resisting our own authoritative interpretation of itself, *Pierre* resists (being taken as) authoritative interpretation – and judgment – of Wordsworth.

Pierre's apparent echoes of Wordsworth's poetry include not just the 'Lucy Poems' but also (in an impressionistic order of importance) *The*

Prelude, 'Ode to Duty,' the Immortality Ode, 'Resolution and Independence,' and 'Anecdote for Fathers.' It suggestively broaches several Wordsworthian topics also – mysticism, 'wise passiveness,' the mutual fittedness of mind and nature. While I cannot, therefore, do justice here to the novel's engagement with Wordsworth, its allusions to the 'Lucy Poems' suffice to illustrate the anti-closural *mode* of this engagement. The novel opens with the nineteen-year-old Pierre's courtship of Lucy Tartan, a blonde, blue-eyed 'angel' who, like Pierre, comes from a wealthy and respectable American family. But Pierre's courtship is complicated almost from the beginning by rival affections, or more specifically by his typically romantic inability to make simple distinctions between filial, fraternal, and sexual affections. The only child of the widowed Mary Glendinning, he has long wished for a sister with something like connubial longings (12). Meanwhile he addresses his mother as 'sister Mary,' yet his bantering attentions are as much 'loverlike' (22) as fraternal or filial. Jealous of Pierre's affection, Mary favours his marriage to Lucy, who at seventeen appears pliable and unthreatening. And in the opening idyll there appears to be no bar to this happy resolution. But we are warned, in a passage reminiscent of 'Three years':

> In the country ... Nature planted our Pierre; because Nature intended a rare and original development in Pierre. Never mind if hereby she proved ambiguous to him in the end; nevertheless, in the beginning she did bravely. (19)

'[W]e shall yet see,' Melville adds, 'whether Fate hath not just a little bit of a word or two to say in this world' (20). Like Wordsworth's, and like his father's before him, Pierre's affections are soon divided among three women, Lucy, Mary, and his illegitimate half-sister, Isabel. These women are rather bluntly identified as Pierre's Fates.[55] By running Pierre through the eerie moonlight journey of 'Strange fits' three times, once with each woman, Melville curiously suggests both Pierre's own debilitating ambivalence and the multiple identity of Wordsworth's Lucy. In the triplification of Lucy and of the journey toward her, Melville's rewriting ramifies rather than simplifies the complexity of Wordsworth's poems.

On the first journey Pierre accompanies Mary, 'early of a pleasant moonlight evening,' to visit a sewing circle where his entanglement with the Fates is first adumbrated. As Mary and Pierre enter the home of the Miss Pennies, two 'pious spinsters' who have arranged the circle, they are announced by 'a gratuitous old body, seated with her knitting near the door' (54, 56). As the knitting Fate announces the Glendinnings, Pierre is struck 'through his heart' by 'a sudden, long-drawn, unearthy, girlish shriek' (56); and though he does not yet know that the 'strange thing' struck by this fit of passion is his half-sister Isabel, Pierre is strangely affected by her abrupt entrance into his life. On the way home his mother comments on his 'strange' behaviour – the word is repeated five times (59) – and Pierre's explanation again recalls 'Strange fits': 'I believe I was dreaming – sleep-walking, or something of that sort' (59).

His sister Isabel having so 'slidingly' (154) entered his life (cf. 'Strange fits,' line 25), Pierre begins to be haunted by mystical visions of her, and he is foolish, or honest, enough to complain of them to Lucy. In an interlude conceived in the language of 'A slumber,' this honesty complicates Pierre's marriage proposal, but here it is Lucy who has strange premonitions. Is there 'no flower that, in the bud ... may untimely perish, ere the June unfolds it?' she asks (cf. 'Strange fits,' lines 5–6). 'A joyful manliness invests thee, Pierre; and thy intrepid heart never yet felt the touch of fear; – But –' and she breaks off (cf. 'A slumber,' lines 1–3). Lucy has forebodings of 'endless dreariness' (46). When she declares she cannot marry Pierre unless he swears to keep no secrets, Pierre exclaims: 'Something seizes me. Thy inexplicable tears, falling, falling on my heart, have now turned it to a stone. I feel icy cold and hard; I will not swear!' (47). It may be that Pierre is named after the 'rocks, and stones' of 'A slumber'; indeed, the novel's tragic finale, the dead Lucy lying with the dead Pierre, who is 'arbored ... in ebon vines' of Isabel's hair (421), obliquely replicates the imagery of the poem's last line.

The second rendition of 'Strange fits' falls on the unmoonlit evening following Pierre's abortive marriage proposal. Pierre is scheduled to call on Lucy, and approaches her cottage through the pitch blackness. But

> He had not gone very far, when in the distance beyond, he noticed a light moving along the opposite side of the road, and slowly approaching. ... [A]s it silently drew nearer and nearer, the one only distinguishable thing before him, he somehow felt a nameless presentiment that the light must be seeking him. He had nearly gained the cottage door, when the lantern crossed over toward him; and as his nimble hand was laid at last upon the little wicket-gate, which he thought was now to admit him to so much delight; a heavy hand was laid upon himself, and at the same moment, the lantern was lifted toward his face, by a hooded and obscure looking figure, whose half-averted countenance he could but indistinctly discern. (75)

In this rendition, Wordsworth's speaker's presentiment of death is strikingly allegorized as the encounter with a hooded messenger. Modern commentators on Wordsworth often read this presentiment as a repressed wish, Lucy's death in the 'subsequent' poems as its fulfilment. Melville similarly implicates Pierre in Lucy's 'death.' The lantern-bearer brings Pierre his first earthly communication from Isabel, which drives the decisive wedge between him and Lucy. By advising him that he has an illegitimate sister – both the fulfilment of his boyhood desire and an embarrassment to his family's respectability – this letter not only aborts his present journey toward Lucy, but precipitates his rejection of her. Not wholly uninfluenced by her beauty, Pierre concludes that he must countenance and support Isabel, and that to do so without revealing his father's indiscretion he must present Isabel as his wife. His next meeting with Lucy in her tomb-like bedchamber, where she swoons at these false tidings, enacts the symbolic killing. Her maid accuses him, 'Thou hast somehow murdered her' (218).

The third rendition of 'Strange fits' is Pierre's first, night-time visit to Isabel in her natural, 'moss-incrusted' cottage. Here the suggestions of the poem are fainter. Pierre approaches:

> In front, three straight gigantic lindens stood guardians of this verdant spot. A long way up, almost to the ridge-pole of the house, they showed little foliage; but then, suddenly, as three huge green balloons, they poised their three vast, inverted, rounded cones of verdure in the air.
>
> Soon as Pierre's eye rested on the place, a tremor shook him. Not alone because of Isabel, as there a harborer now, but because of two dependent and most strange coincidences which that day's experience had brought to him. ...
>
> Strangest feelings, almost supernatural, now stole into Pierre. With little power to touch with awe the souls of less susceptible, reflective, and poetic beings, such coincidences, however frequently they may recur, ever fill the finer organization with sensations which transcend all verbal renderings. ...
>
> And now the thicker shadows begin to fall; the place is lost to him; only the three dim, tall lindens pilot him as he descends the hill, hovering upon the house. He knows it not, but his meditative route is sinuous; as if that moment his thought's stream was likewise serpentining ... (132–3)

Wordsworth's moon is supplanted by the three linden trees that 'pilot' Pierre, perhaps because their darkness better suggests the dark lady Isabel, perhaps because, in this final rendition, they represent the three-women-in-one with or toward whom Pierre is bent on his fateful journey. But enough remains to suggest that these lindens are a transformation of Wordsworth's moon – their 'sudden'ness in propinquity to the top of the house, their ghostly 'hovering upon' it, their association with the 'strangest feeling, almost supernatural, [that] now stole into Pierre.' But once the cottage door is opened, they are replaced by another version of Wordsworth's moon: 'holding the light above her supernatural head, Isabel stands before him' (134).

How are we to understand this curious relationship between the texts? The very multiplication of aspects entailed by these plays on the language and imagery of Wordsworth's poems makes it impossible to offer a precise or satisfying explanation of them as a coherent interpretation. While Melville preserves certain events, words, and images of the poems, he also alters them, especially by reassigning them. Lines and images associated with Wordsworth's Lucy are assigned most often to Pierre or Isabel. Maybe Melville is pointing to an identification between Wordsworth's Lucy and his own Pierre to suggest that Wordsworth's Lucy is an aspect of himself;[56] maybe he is suggesting that Wordsworth's sister came between him and the original of the 'Lucy Poems'; maybe just that 'Lucy' is an amalgam of the several women in Wordsworth's life. Melville's practice suggests both that all of these 'explanations' may be relevant and that none is conclusive. While he does appear to build on a biographical interpretation of the 'Lucy Poems,' his treatment of them goes far beyond identification-readings, and is ultimately far more concerned with the poems' mysteriousness as an artistic fact than with unravelling them to discover biographical fact.

That the intertextual relationship resists any simple resolution of Wordsworth's mystery makes it, implicitly, a commentary on commentary. Most significantly, Melville's practice suggests that hermeneutic mystery is not merely an effect of tricky texts but derives from the obscurities of life itself.[57] As an interpreter of his own complex obligations, Pierre is caught painfully in their 'ambiguities' just as readers of the 'Lucy Poems' are caught in theirs. The three women, who at first appear realistic characters, gradually develop more ethereal and Fate-like identities until one wonders, not just which of them most deserves Pierre's allegiance, but also whether any one of them is to be considered 'real' and not merely a literary allegory of the forces of Pierre's destiny. In thus crossing realism and allegory, Melville reproduces the central historical quandary regarding Lucy – actual or symbolic? – but also suggests that this quandary obtains whether one reads life or literature. This is only one way the hermeneutic challenges of the literary text and of being are fused. The continuity between the interpretation of language and the interpretation of life is posed more explicitly when Pierre considers that a tale's mystery may constitute its very truth to life. Pierre listens to Isabel's account of herself, an account so veiled and uncertain that it can climax only in a meaningless redundance of the word 'mystery.' She takes her guitar and sings:

> Mystery! Mystery!
> Mystery of Isabel!
> Mystery! Mystery!
> Isabel and Mystery! (151)

Being possessed of a good critical intellect, Pierre is at first made uneasy by the silly song and by Isabel's revelry in mystery, and he wonders whether the 'mystery of Isabel' does not lie merely in her telling. But soon he grows less distrustful of 'the clew-defying mysteriousness of Isabel's narrative' (163):

> He saw, or seemed to see, that it was not so much Isabel who had by her wild idiosyncrasies mystified the narration of her history, as it was the essential and unavoidable mystery of her history itself, which had invested Isabel with such wonderful enigmas to him. (165)

In the phrase 'or seemed to see,' the narrator avoids solving the mystery of mystery for us. The theory that narrative mystification, the mystery of the text, can be adequately explained in terms of its correspondence with the mystery of being remains just one theory among others, and this irresolution lies at the centre of all. To Pierre, who to the very end is driven to understand the enigmas of his world and of his existence in it, this ambiguity – whether there is ever any sense in searching out meanings, or whether meanings are unattainable by their very nature – is fundamental.

Pierre never escapes this ambiguity. He never ascertains whether Isabel is, as he first believes, a victimized girl to whom he owes his love and protection, or, as he later suspects, a dark angel sent to ruin him. Her status being left uncertain, he can never know whether he has acted foolishly or nobly by her; neither can we. His entanglement in Isabel's hair at the tale's end is portentous but fully as ambiguous as the final line of Wordsworth's 'A slumber,' which it echoes. In Pierre's insoluble quandary, the novel portrays our own difficulties reading any text and, no doubt, Melville's in reading Wordsworth's. Indeed, it appears to reflect on a Wordsworthian belief in the hopelessness of reducing life to a single order and certainty:

> Hard task, vain hope, to analyse the mind,
> If each most obvious and particular thought,
> Not in a mystical and idle sense,
> But in the words of Reason deeply weighed,
> Hath no beginning. (*Prelude* 2: 228–32)

The echo in *Pierre*:

> In their precise tracings-out and subtile causations, the strongest and fieriest emotions of life defy all analytical insight. ... The metaphysical writers confess, that the most impressive, sudden, and overwhelming event, as well as the minutest, is but the product of an infinite series of infinitely involved and untraceable foregoing occurrences. Just so with every motion of the heart. ...
>
> Idle then would it be to attempt by any winding way so to penetrate into the heart, and memory, and inmost life, and nature of Pierre. (82)

This acceptance of the overwhelming intricacy of causation may explain the novel's habit, much like Wordsworth's, of shunning 'relational knowledge.' There may be reasons why Pierre behaves as he does, but it would be fruitless to attempt to trace them, and he seems to infer the same for Isabel. The result is a very Wordsworthian mysteriousness of the matter of fact. In view of the novel's Wordsworthian appreciation of ethical complexity, it is hard to take *Pierre* simply as chiding Wordsworth for his relations with Annette, Dorothy, and Mary.[58] Indeed, Melville's treatment suggests the opposite of a judgment on Wordsworth's life; by stressing our inability to comprehend that life in all its complexity, or to separate it from the art, it forces a suspension of judgment.

My point in this chapter has not been to argue that nineteenth-century parody deliberately or even consciously opposed the editorial and critical projects that were attempting to define and make sense of the 'Lucy Poems.' On the contrary, in keeping with my figure of it as the 'repressed' of institutional criticism, parody appears to have been mostly unconscious of its own oppositional functions (perhaps one should say potentials) both as commentary upon commentary and as an alternative form of commentary. The cases of Hartley Coleridge and J.K. Stephen even suggest that when 'parody' assumes a deliberate critical function it does so at the cost of its function as parody. Pure and simple, parody is just a textual parallel, a 'beside-poem'; it does not comment. And yet the apparent obliviousness of the most dead-pan parody to contemporary critical efforts is not tantamount to irrelevance in this field: criticism's persistent efforts to define parody, to sort it from non-parody, to dismiss it as trivial, and to recuperate it as 'coded' yet fundamentally monological commentary, all suggest otherwise. Parody's greatest challenge to criticism may indeed consist in its very tacitness, in its neglect to declare an errand. Its unexplained parallelism may not only call attention to the 'cruxes' that authoritative interpretation presumes to resolve, but also compounds them with the question of the purpose of the parallel. While it is, I believe, fair and useful to regard this parallelism as a form of interpretation, parodic interpretation is in every way the opposite of definitive.

4 Proving Grounds: Modern 'Theory' Polemics and the Use of 'A slumber'

> ... everything is tedious when one does not read with the feelings of the Author.

> It is no tale; but, should you think,
> Perhaps a tale you'll make it.

My epigraphs, both from Wordsworth, could serve as mottos for both sides in one of our recent literary-theory debates.[1] The first is from Wordsworth's expostulation with Sara Hutchinson for misreading – that is, disliking – 'The Leech-gatherer.' So that she might better entertain 'the feelings of the Author,' Wordsworth even attempts 'to explain to you in prose my feeling in writing that Poem' (*Letters* 1:366). The assumptions of this letter come close to the intentionalist arguments of E.D. Hirsch, Jr, and others that 'a text means what its author meant' (*Validity* 1). But that is precisely what the second quotation seems to deny. As these lines from 'Simon Lee' imply, the thinking reader has the power to determine or redetermine the genre of the text, and thus its meaning – a position compatible with W.K. Wimsatt and Monroe Beardsley's famous argument that '[t]he poem belongs to the public' and that the author's intention is, as a critical standard, irrelevant (5).[2]

Whether a text has a determinate meaning that an interpreter may seek to discover or whether its meaning is determined or co-determined by its interpreter is, I suggested in chapter 2, a fundamental question for a history of criticism: on the former view, the historian may feel justified in producing an account of misreadings leading toward or away from a single 'correct' reading; on the latter, she may have difficulty finding grounds to evaluate or differentiate readings. It has been widely assumed that this question will be fundamental for criticism itself, that one's theory of where meaning resides will shape one's critical practice. If meaning is fixed by or in the text, the reasoning goes, one may be scrupulous in discovering it; if not, one may make sense of it as one likes. Still more broadly, this question has been seen as consequential for the claims of literary study to disciplinary status: in arguing that the meaning of a text is objective and unalterable, and that a critic's aim is therefore to achieve a 'valid' reading, Hirsch claims that '[a]t stake ultimately is the right of *any* humanistic discipline to claim genuine knowledge' (*Validity* viii). On the other hand, he recognizes the objection that an extreme historicist view may deny a text's relevance, may 'deaden past texts and cut them off from our present lives.'[3] No wonder there have been many attempts to have it both ways, as Wordsworth does. It is one thing to renounce in theory the pro-disciplinary assumption of literary meaning's determinacy, but quite another to renounce it in practice; as recent debates over the interpretation of the 'Lucy Poems' suggest, and as I shall elaborate here, much of modern theoretical criticism is surreptitiously informed by the assumptions it officially renounces. This chapter explores such double positions not as mere inconsistencies but as rhetorical sleights in which the 'discipline' of English is grounded.

Since the 1960s, when Hirsch first published his theory, the theory that theory is consequential has itself come under attack. Arguing 'against theory,' Stanley Fish and others have viewed it, usefully for some purposes, as

> an attempt to *reform* practice by neutralizing interest, by substituting for the parochial perspective of some local or partisan point of view the perspective of a general rationality to which the individual subordinates his contextually conditioned opinions and beliefs.

As such, Fish argues, '[t]heory is an impossible project' ('Consequences' 110). Invoking Baconian method as an example, Fish reasons that our social-historical situation determines our presuppositions and purposes and hence our 'findings,' despite our theories, just as the hypotheses embedded in Bacon's tables of discovery would determine how nature 'reveals itself' to the scientist; on this view, the point of having a theory is not to guide or control practice, but merely to legitimize the practice one already has – and to impress, intimidate, or sway others.[4] The argument 'against theory,' then, itself assumes what Hirsch calls the 'relativist' theory of meaning. And though it seems to me that Fish overlooks important alternative meanings and functions of 'theory,'[5] his view of its *potential* use as a rhetorical means for projecting 'general' claims on behalf of inevitably 'local or partisan' views helps explain one of the more bewildering products of modern criticism: the 'theory' essay containing practical exercises, 'examples,' or 'illustrations,' that bear no discernible relation to the theory.[6] From Fish's perspective, it appears less that the 'practical criticism' in such essays is there to illustrate the theory, than that the theoretical framework is there to generalize, validate, and confirm the specific reading of the supposedly 'illustrative' text. Thus, for all their diversity in approach and in explicit theoretical claims, such essays have in common both an interpretive function and a persuasive or polemical one, or in aggregate a *determinative* interpretive function.[7] As such, these essays are useful for exploring the specifically polemical practice that accompanies most interpretive practice without quite being part of it – the practice by which a reader seeks to make his readings stick, or to claim their general acceptability.

Wordsworth's 'A slumber' has been used in such theoretico-critical essays with uncommon frequency, obligingly 'illustrating' arguments both for 'objective interpretation' and against it, both for specific theories of formalism, reader-response, and deconstruction, and 'against theory' in general.[8] The very fact that it can be used to illustrate and confirm so many theoretical arguments would seem to make obvious the futility of such confirmation – hence my suspicion that the 'exemplary' reading is usually less a means of proof than it is the point being argued. Since not all these arguments can be treated in detail, I focus on the dispute opened by Hirsch in 1960 and joined by theorists of formalism and reader-response, in which 'A slumber' is used to 'illustrate' arguments both for and against the possibility of 'objective interpretation.' In this dispute it is remarkable that, even while seeming to debate the possibility of determinate interpretation, and in spite of their ostensibly fundamental theoretical disagreements, the disputants on *both* sides (which for convenience I call, adapting Hirsch's terms, 'objectivism' and 'relativism') have read 'A slumber' in fundamentally similar ways, agreeing, in practice, not only on its interpretability but even, to a very high degree, in their interpretations. A partial explanation may be that by opening this dispute at a location so far to the closural right, Hirsch has made it possible to denounce him as a dogmatist while still remaining considerably right of centre – a 'Tempting region' where closural interpretation might work 'And never hear the sound of [its] own name' (*The Prelude* 11:228–31). The situation might also be explained in Fish's terms as showing that disagreements in theory do not necessarily entail differences in practice. But more than this, I think that throughout this 'debate' the 'illustrative' readings of 'A slumber' have functioned to minimize the threat of perspectival difference in practice even when, and sometimes because, the threat is embraced in theory. Hirsch avows that his theoretical and interpretive polemicism is motivated by the spectre of interpretive disagreement: worried that humanism's 'claim' to 'genuine knowledge' may be undermined by the disagreements of a burgeoning army of readers, he sets out methods of 'adjudication' to control the chaos. But this anxiety of difference is not necessarily absent when unexpressed.[9] I would argue that it motivates Hirsch's 'opponents' as well as himself, and indeed that they have contained relativistic interpretation more powerfully than he by embracing it in theory but not in practice.

This thesis may appear more concretely if we consider what constitutes the peculiar privilege of 'A slumber' in these arguments. Given the preliminary difficulties of this poem's relation to the (other?) 'Lucy Poems' and hence of its reference to Lucy, to say nothing of its countless internal difficulties (some of these are detailed in chapter 1, above), it is surprising to find it repeatedly used by objectivist theorists to demonstrate that meaning is determinate and even 'in' the text. Hirsch chooses 'A slumber' precisely because (aside from being brief and quotable) it is well documented as permitting more than one interpretation; if one can show that the meaning of *this* text is determinate, the same will seem to follow *a fortiori* for others. But the history of commentary plays a crucially double role in this argument: while seeming to establish the poem's complexity, it powerfully reduces it. Rather than read 'A slumber' for himself, which would at least complicate his argument by requiring him to decide on several ambiguities, Hirsch cites two established *readings* of the poem (by F.W. Bateson and Cleanth Brooks) which have already presumptively resolved most of these ambiguities. Taking the divergence of these readings upon a single crux to reflect the poem's actual ambiguity enables Hirsch to argue, simply by justifying his choice between them, that 'A slumber' is both superficially ambiguous and fundamentally determinate. In this manoeuvre the long tradition that 'A slumber' is 'simple' is, one might say, taken in the radical sense of the German, *einfältig*, one-fold, having a single ambiguity. Here, it seems to me, polemicism and the tradition of commentary combine to override real attention to textual indeterminacy; the will to understand proves weaker than the will to be assured that understanding is possible.

Surprisingly, the 'relativist' arguments using 'A slumber' in illustration rely almost as heavily on received readings, keeping us off 'the untrodden ways.' The typically hackneyed rather than idiosyncratic readings they admit are probably the clearest sign of these essays' complicity with the objectivist projects they purport to challenge. In all the modern reader-response criticism of 'A slumber' there is nothing, for instance, that approaches the real idiosyncrasy of Samuel Butler's murder-mystery reading of 'She dwelt' (discussed in chapter 3).[10] Gerald Graff's use of 'A slumber' to illustrate 'indeterminacy' for a recent theory primer is a somewhat loaded case (Graff is not much noted for relativism) but all the better for showing quickly how such arguments can contain the 'indeterminacy' principle while seeming to assert it. Graff presents 'A slumber' as '[a]n exemplary case of contextual indeterminacy in a work of literature' ('Determinacy' 168). Quoting the poem, but discussing only the crux cited by Hirsch, he disagrees with Hirsch's adjudication between Bateson's and Brooks's readings and remarks: 'There seems to be no alternative except to regard this as a poem of indeterminate meaning' (169). Since Graff, like Hirsch, has acknowledged nothing more than a single ambiguity, his theoretical claim is severely qualified by his practice, and this qualification makes its appearance a few pages later: 'though it may be unclear whether ['A slumber'] is a lament or a pantheistic celebration, it is not uncertain that a death has occurred' (174). This neglects to mention, of course, that the poem makes no explicit mention of 'a death' and that some critics have made perfectly good sense of it without supposing one.[11] Thus, even while pretending to argue the text's indeterminacy, in practice Graff determines its meaning considerably. One must bear in mind that a weak or understated relativist argument is, in effect, a devious objectivist one. The same manoeuvre is, we shall see, made by critic-theorists with better relativist credentials than Graff's.

This is not to denigrate the particular interpretations offered for 'A slumber' by these theoretico-critical essays – I assume that any reading can be faulted for 'error' and, conversely, defended as heuristics[12]– but only to observe that they are few in number, given the text, and to suggest that this consensus is not 'natural' but concerted. The issue here is the polemicism that has sought, overtly or covertly, to confine this text to a single reading or a narrow range of readings; if my analysis focuses more on argumentation than on what is being argued, that is why.

1. E.D. Hirsch, Jr, versus Relativism

Hirsch announces in 1960 that 'subjectivism and relativism' are 'some of the most serious faults of current criticism' (*Validity* 209), and he cites William Empson, René Wellek and Austin Warren, W.K. Wimsatt and Monroe Beardsley, and their unnamed followers as particular offenders. In response to these faults Hirsch presents principles and distinctions to facilitate, what is the title of his essay, 'Objective Interpretation.' In 1967, he reprints this essay and elaborates its argument under the title *Validity in Interpretation*. Hirsch's titles are anything but modest. 'Validity' is a term used in aesthetics in connection with 'universality.'[13] But since Hirsch actually acknowledges that no interpretation can be absolutely valid, and later falls back on this acknowledgment to deflect objections to his theories,[14] it is worth stressing the rhetorical function of what amounts to overstatement in the large print and retraction in the small. He claims to show that 'valid interpretation can indeed be achieved' (*Validity* xi), but then uses 'valid' interchangeably with 'probable': Bateson's 'reading must be deemed the more probable one until the uncovering of some presently unknown data makes a different construction of the poet's stance appear more valid' (*Validity* 240). This is not really to use synonyms; it is, rather, to associate terms of very different values such that either comes to mean, in Hirsch's discourse, 'probably valid.' *Validity in Interpretation* in the large print means something like 'probably valid interpretation' in the small. It is true that Hirsch repeatedly stipulates that 'validity' means 'probability': why then speak of 'validity' at all?[15] The slippage in terms makes it easier to grant his argument, but to the same degree minimizes its value.

Hirsch is able to argue the determinacy of textual meaning only through a similar slippage in the terms of his central distinction, 'meaning' and 'significance':

> There is a difference between the meaning of a text (which does not change) and the meaning of a text to us today (which changes). The meaning of a text is that which the author meant by his use of particular linguistic symbols. Being linguistic, this meaning is communal, that is, self-identical and reproducible in more than one consciousness. Being reproducible, it is the same whenever and wherever it is understood by another. However, each time this meaning is construed, its meaning to the construer (its significance) is different. (*Validity* 255)

Again:

> Significance is always 'meaning-to,' never 'meaning-in.' Significance always entails a relationship between what is in a man's verbal meaning and what is outside it, even when that relationship pertains to the author himself or to his subject matter. (*Validity* 63)

As Hirsch extends this distinction, 'interpretation' discovers meaning, and 'criticism' discovers significance. Theoretically, this appears an ingenious and useful distinction. It appears to allow the bracketing of the subjective element of one's reading to concentrate on what is, or should be, objective and constant. But whether such a separation is possible in practice is the very essence of the 'meaning' controversy; indeed, Hirsch's method of distinguishing these elements as 'meaning-in' and 'meaning-to' illustrates the practical problem. For *in practice* all meaning 'entails relationship' or must be 'meaning-to.' In practice there can be no meaning without someone to whom it means, and if it must be meaning to someone it becomes, in Hirsch's terms, 'significance.' To put it differently, if meaning is rigorously defined as 'meaning-in,' it is by definition unavailable to anyone and merely hypothetical. All that is left in practice is an ever-changing 'significance,' which does not advance us beyond the initial problem of changes in meaning. While Hirsch identifies the meaning/significance distinction as the 'crucial' one for his theory (*Validity* xi), it is also highly problematic.

To some extent it may nevertheless seem possible to distinguish between the objective and subjective elements in interpretation, or at least between the stable and unstable ones, and to this extent Hirsch's distinction is not only potentially useful but is, I think, a common-sense rule already used in virtually all reading. A 'meaning' that was verifiable and unchanging would have to comprise only explicitly coded information, that which might be proved to everyone's satisfaction by referring to commonly accepted lexicons and rules of grammar; all uncoded information that cannot be so proved, including implications, ironies, and ambiguities (or the inferences used to decide them), must constitute 'significance,' since this by definition is what will change from reader to reader and cannot be demonstrated. If we used 'meaning' and 'significance' in these senses, following Schleiermacher's principle that '[e]verything in a given text ... must be explained and determined exclusively from the linguistic domain common to the author and his original public,' the 'meaning' of a text might remain relatively stable while its 'significance' changed to suit the interpreter and the period.[16] Such appears to be the sense of Hirsch's terms at first, when he says, 'If criticism is to be objective in any significant sense, it must be founded on a self-critical construction of textual meaning, which is to say, on objective interpretation' (*Validity* 210).

Hirsch, however, does not contemplate so modest a scope for what he calls 'meaning.' Having stipulated that 'meaning' must be stable, rather than limit it to the most obviously verifiable elements, he *expands* the term to include implications, attempting to argue that they can indeed be verifiable. But since it is precisely in matters of implication that the differences between meanings *to* different readers become pronounced, and since implications are by definition neither explicit nor therefore objectively verifiable, it is hard to see how Hirsch can have 'meaning' both ways, both as an inclusive category and as the limited domain of verifiability.[17] In effect, admitting implication to be a part of 'meaning' makes the meaning/significance distinction a rhetorical sleight. It allows a text's meaning to one interpreter (say, oneself) to become its 'real meaning,' but only by making nonsense of the term's pretensions to objectivity. This is, I think, the central fault in Hirsch's treatment of 'A slumber.'[18]

Hirsch considers the 'expert' but 'divergent' readings of this poem by Cleanth Brooks and F.W. Bateson to show that, unlike other theories, his enables one to define 'in principle the nature of a correct interpretation,' and even to 'insist that Brooks is right and Bateson wrong (or vice versa)' (*Validity* 226, 229). In speaking of 'correct interpretation,' I remark again, Hirsch is speaking of 'meaning.' Differences in 'significance,' which would be matters of 'criticism,' do not concern him; 'significance' is by his definition what varies. His treatment of 'A slumber' is ostensibly a pre-critical exercise designed to determine which single meaning the poem must have, in itself, for all critics before they attach their own idiosyncratic 'significances' to it. It is not necessary to quote both readings at length to suggest the similarities and differences that concern Hirsch:

> the girl, who to her lover seemed a thing that could not feel the touch of earthly years, is caught up helplessly into the empty whirl of the earth which measures and makes time. She is touched by and held by earthly time in its most powerful and horrible image. (Brooks, 'Irony' 736)

> [The poem's] last two lines succeed in effecting a reconciliation between the two philosophies or social attitudes [of humanism and pantheism]. Lucy is actually more alive now that she is dead, because she is now a part of the life of Nature and not just a human 'thing.' (Bateson, *English Poetry* 59)

Hirsch blandly asserts that 'both the cited interpretations are permitted by the text' (228). As I have already suggested, using two carefully chosen readings of the poem rather than reading it anew enables him to simplify the interpretive problem as a single binary choice, between 'bitter regret and affirmation' (229). He can then, and with an appearance of liberality, allow the ambiguity, at least in principle: 'I do not ... imply that a poem ... must be unambiguous' (230). By construing the poem so similarly, as a description of the *death* of the speaker's *lover* (both are points of interpretive presumption), Brooks and Bateson have already done most of Hirsch's consensualizing for him; the broad ground of their consensus enables him to overlook all interpretive decisions on which they happen to agree, and which belong to prior stages of reading.[19]

In short, in the very act of 'demonstrating' how criticism may be solidly grounded in a verifiable pre-construction of verbal meaning, Hirsch fails to consider the most elementary interpretive problems, taking one reading for granted simply because two authoritative critics have, approximately, agreed upon it. Given his own emphasis on the priority of interpretation to criticism, one would expect him to question such things as the meanings of 'slumber,' 'spirit,' 'seal,' and 'human fears'; to question certain grammatical and syntactic relations, e.g., whether the slumber has sealed the spirit or vice versa, and whether line 2 means '*but*,' '*because*,' or '*that is*, I had no human fears'; to inquire into the probable reference of 'she'; and to consider whether 'she neither hears nor sees' verifiably *means* 'she is dead.' This is not to suggest that he could answer any of these questions objectively; that is just the problem with discussing the poem under the rubric of 'objective interpretation.' At no stage can one avoid answering one of these questions in a way to suit a prejudice or purpose. The 'meaning' one ascribes to 'slumber,' for example, is not wholly determined by the dictionary, but depends largely on how one wishes to read the rest. One inclined to read as Brooks reads may take 'slumber' as deceptive and malignant, since this makes sense of stanza 2 as a rude awakening. One more inclined to read as Sykes Davies does may likewise read 'slumber' as a genuinely benign trance, 'Kind Nature's gentlest boon.' In both cases the construction of the ambiguous evidence is to some degree teleological; one reads to achieve basically aesthetic effects such as unity, coherence, or irony, though nothing *in* the text says its parts must be concerted to one such effect rather than another. What this suggests is that the questions of the poem's 'significance,' in Hirsch's usage, are inextricable from those of its 'meaning'; that in practice one cannot perfectly distinguish a stage of 'interpretation' from a stage of 'criticism.'

Hirsch to a large extent if not entirely recognizes such problems. It is, in fact, to avoid such circularity between one's larger purpose and one's reading of particulars that he introduces authorial intention as a standard. Hirsch reasons that to be 'probable' a reading must satisfy the requirement of coherence, but that our perception of a 'coherence' among particulars depends on our assumed sense of the whole, or on our presuppositions about the text's genre.[20]

> The fact that coherence is a dependent quality leads to an unavoidable circularity in the process of interpretation. The interpreter posits meanings for the words and word sequences he confronts, and, at the same time, he has to posit a whole meaning or context in reference to which the submeanings cohere with one another. The procedure is thoroughly circular; the context is derived from the submeanings and the submeanings are specified and rendered coherent with reference to the context. (*Validity* 237)

The important consequence of this circularity is that 'there is no absolute standard of coherence by which we can adjudicate between different coherent readings' (*Validity* 238). So long as each reading of 'slumber' jibes with the supposed genre, each will appear acceptable unless one genre can be proved correct.

> *It is necessary to establish that the context invoked is the most probable context.* ... [W]e have to posit the most probable horizon for the text, and it is possible to do this only if we posit the author's typical outlook. ... This is not only the one way we can test the relative coherence of a reading, but it is also the only way to avoid pure circularity in making sense of the text. (*Validity* 238)

But even this does not end the 'pure circularity'; aside from the fact that our knowledge of any particular intention and of any 'typical outlook' is likewise suppositional, authorial intention is not itself an absolute standard but one of many possible standards – as Hirsch says in a later work, 'an ethical choice, not a metaphysical necessity' (*Aims* 83; see also 75–9,

85). Even if one could satisfy this standard, one could only say, 'This is the meaning to the author.' That would not be the 'meaning-in' in any absolute sense, but would be analogous to saying, 'This is the meaning when the poem is read as mystical trance.' Supposing each reading coherent with its given genre or standard, there is no way to show which is 'meaning,' since there is still no way to verify the standard.

An arbitrary choice must enter the interpretive process at some stage; it is merely by deferring this arbitration to a more general level (from 'criterion' to 'standard' or 'aim'; from 'genre' to 'authorial intention') that Hirsch can claim authority for his 'adjudication' between Bateson and Brooks. In practice as in principle, this reference to an author's probable attitudes is regressive (see Crosman 161). If it circumvents troubles in determining the meaning of a 'piece of language,' it presents equal or greater difficulties at the next stage, where one must determine the author's 'typical attitudes' from necessarily limited (and highly mediated) biographical data. A dead person is no doubt as difficult to read as a poem, and 'the problem of the text' is worse.

Bateson's reading of 'A slumber' and Brooks's differ, according to Hirsch, only in their understanding of the implicit attitude toward the 'bereavement ... which Wordsworth's poem explicitly [sic] presents' (*Validity* 239). For Bateson the attitude is pantheistic 'affirmation,' for Brooks irony and horror. Though Brooks's reading 'is clearly justified not only by the text but by reference to universal human attitudes and feelings' (*Validity* 239), Hirsch concludes that Bateson's is 'more objective':

> Instead of projecting his own attitudes (Bateson is presumably not a pantheist) and instead of positing a 'universal matrix' of human attitudes (there is none), he has tried to reconstruct the author's probable attitudes so far as these are relevant in specifying the poem's meaning. ... since Bateson grounds his interpretation in a conscious construction of the poet's outlook, his reading must be deemed the more probable one ... (*Validity* 240)

To present this as the adjudication between two pre-critical interpretations of *meaning* is to present Bateson's reading as the obligatory starting-point for all criticism, for all discussion of the poem's *significance*. But, in his own terms, Hirsch has already chosen a significance, not a meaning, for the poem. The Bateson-Brooks disagreement, concerning as it does the poem's meaning *in relation to* questions of faith and mutability, is, in Hirsch's own terms, a disagreement about significance. By calling this 'meaning' Hirsch argues, in effect, that the significance he prefers is 'objective' and should be generally accepted. His argument confers authority on a reading of 1950 based both on the traditional presumption that 'A slumber' refers to 'Lucy' and on certain dated assumptions about Wordsworth's religious development. The further we move in history from Bateson's reading, the easier it becomes to see its assumptions as historical rather than natural, and the more clearly Hirsch's 'validation' of this reading appears as a species of 'theory,' in Fish's description, as that which claims 'general rationality' for a 'local or partisan point of view.' And the problem is not just that Bateson's reading is dated, but that any reading must be.

Even if Hirsch's principles cannot deliver the interpretive 'validity' or 'objectivity' they promise, is the alternative as devastating as he says? His argument is, as he puts it, an ethical one. He believes that the 'theory of a changing meaning. ... should not remain unchallenged, since if it were correct, there could be no objective knowledge about texts' (*Validity* 212). It is of considerable importance that this reasoning does not begin in an insight into the falsity of relativist theories, but sets out to prove their falsity because their consequences are deemed unacceptable.[21] For even aside from the logical dubiety this casts on Hirsch's reasoning, it may be argued that the consequences of a relativist theory of meaning are hardly so dire as Hirsch assumes. Without invoking the new-pragmatist claim that 'theory has no consequences,' which I find too sweeping, I would argue that a relativist theory of meaning is not a 'theory' in the sense of a 'method of interpretation' but rather in the sense of a view or model of meaning. It has no direct bearing on the specific meaning one 'discovers.' What it does affect is how dogmatically one holds to one's interpretations once one has them, how widely one projects them, and how tolerant one is of others'.[22] Surely the worst situation is to interpret relatively, as one inevitably does, yet still 'validate' one's interpretation absolutely. Here I think Hirsch's fear of relativism and concern for consequences may be turned against him, or rather against his theory: the pretence to have a method for 'valid' interpretation is destined not to counteract but on the contrary to aggravate problems of perspectival difference.

Hirsch's anxiety for 'the right of *any* humanistic discipline to claim genuine knowledge' is not peculiar to him; the treatments of 'A slumber' that follow in his trail his all echo this concern. Yet there are different ways to claim 'genuine knowledge,' depending on how one defines it, and the way by claiming 'objectivity' is among the weakest. At one point Hirsch suggests a different way:

> ... there can be no apodictic certainty that our preliminary guess regarding a text's genre is correct. Yet that guess governs and constitutes what we subsequently say about the text ... our idea of genre is ultimately a hypothesis like any other. ... This identity of genre, pre-understanding, and hypothesis suggests that the much-advertised cleavage between thinking in the sciences and the humanities does not exist. The hypothetico-deductive process is fundamental in both of them, as it is in all thinking that aspires to knowledge. ('Appendix II: Gadamer's Theory of Interpretation' [1965], *Validity* 263–4)

In other words, if 'science' is our standard of knowledge, the standard itself can be reinterpreted: we can claim 'knowledge' for the humanities either by promoting humanistic knowledge to the level of science, or by demoting scientific knowledge to the level of the humanistic. In doing the latter, this passage suggests (what one would not guess from Hirsch's terms and titles) that one can be satisfied with some level of subjectivity and uncertainty in 'knowledge.'

To find uncertainty cause for satisfaction is not merely to make a virtue of a necessity. When reader-response theorists celebrate the 'open' text, it is sometimes asked if ambiguity and indeterminacy can be viewed as ends in themselves. But the intense activity surrounding 'A slumber' shows that uncertainties, or what Wolfgang Iser (274–94) calls 'gaps,' do have a function: they are the only things that have interested and engaged the poem's interpreters. No one discusses what is truly obvious to all. They focus, rather, on what does not appear to all (often, it is true, arguing that it should): on the implicit, the connotative, the suppressed. Yet these 'gaps' are not defects that must be filled, corrected, hidden, or explained away; an interpretation is not an end to which the text is a means. A conclusive interpretation that 'solves' the text as though it were a puzzle has a dead weight about it, and we even have pejorative terms ('facile,' 'totalitarian') for readings that manage to stitch up too many loose ends. David Hoy, taking 'interpretation' and 'meaning' in the narrowest senses initially proposed by Hirsch, objects: 'An "interpretation" such as "All the phrases of 'Les Chats' are in French" is valid but thin.' It is 'thin' precisely to the extent that it is 'valid': it comprises precisely what, if anything, is objectively true of the text. As Hoy elaborates,

> ... interpretation should contain elements that make it, if not necessarily completely verifiable, at least falsifiable. ... the interpretation must be debatable in terms of its own evidence, and there must be some considerations that may count against it. (34)

As this suggests, a truly 'objective interpretation' would not be a prologue to criticism, as Hirsch presents it, but a dead end. To some extent, even the bare pretence to objectivity has proved sterilizing. In the arguments about 'A slumber,' beginning with Hirsch's, interpretation-the-product has been privileged over interpretation-the-process; that is, a crux central to Brooks and Bateson in 1950 has been permitted to dominate the interpretive scene for decades, to the exclusion of novel perspectives. That this displacement of reading by readings has not even been remarked upon suggests only the strength of our will to be assured that understanding is possible, or the tremendous prevalence of our product-bias. Even in pretending to *illustrate* 'objective interpretation,' Hirsch does not seem to notice how very little of the text he actually reads, and those taking issue with his arguments have not noticed it either.

2. 'Objective Interpretation's Fine-Tuning

Several critic-theorists have responded to Hirsch's argument and to his use of 'A slumber' by accepting his contention that meaning is determinate while rejecting or modifying his intentionalist argument. I treat these briefly, and generally in tandem with Hirsch – as variations on a theme – if only because, in multiplying arguments toward a single end, they illustrate that Hirsch does not really stand alone versus 'relativism.' The nailing-down of 'A slumber' has been a genuinely institutional project.

In *The Possibility of Criticism* (1970) – a title fraught with the anxiety of 'crisis' – Monroe Beardsley objects that Hirsch chooses the right reading of 'A slumber' for the wrong reasons. Beardsley denies that 'a text means what its author meant' (17), but agrees that texts are determinate in meaning and that interpretation is verifiable. Accepting Hirsch's observation that 'the two interpretations [of 'A slumber'] cannot be reconciled; at least one must be false,' but challenging his assumption that 'both the cited interpretations are permitted by the text' (28; *Validity* 228), he argues that all the evidence needed to adjudicate between true and false lies in the text itself, which simply requires more cautious reading. In short, Beardsley reasserts the principles and procedures outlined in 'The Intentional Fallacy.' He attacks, not Brooks's failure to assume the author's world-view, but his reading of nuances.

Brooks's reading is (uncharacteristically) distorted. Lucy is not 'whirled'; she is 'rolled.' She does not fall back into a 'clutter of things,' but is placed among trees, which do not really suggest 'dead lifelessness.' An orderly 'diurnal course' is not 'violent motion.' Brooks has simply substituted words with connotations quite absent from the poem, and built his own 'horrible image' out of them. We do not need to appeal to the poet's biography to know that Brooks's bitter reading will not do. (29)

One might expect Beardsley, with his emphasis on close reading, to point out the dependence of both readings on traditional but undefended assumptions, and perhaps to question the poem's reference to Lucy. In overlooking these preliminary matters and focusing his argument instead on connotations, Beardsley essentially repeats Hirsch's procedure. The very fact that one can and must dispute these connotations should suggest that they are not the objective elements of 'meaning' Hirsch and Beardsley wish them to be. Beardsley seems at first to acknowledge that including connotations in a stable 'meaning' is problematic; he admits that, in itself, 'Rolled' (line 7) has a 'repertoire of connotations' ranging from 'boring' to 'scary.' But this 'admission' has already reduced the 'repertoire of connotations' to a single axis; assuming a simple register of degrees of scariness enables Beardsley to specify still more precisely by reference to context:

But what about the present context? Here what must strike us forcibly is the way the other words in this line qualify and specify the motion that Lucy has: it is a regular motion, with a constant rate; it is a comparatively slow and gentle motion, since one revolution takes twenty-four hours; it is an orderly motion, since it follows a simple circular path.

In none of these respects is it terrifying or demeaning; if anything, it is comforting and elevating. If we accept these connotations, the poem contains a hint of pantheism, or at least animism.

If these little exercises in close reading have a point, then, interpreting this poem is not a matter of willfully superimposing some precast intellectual scheme upon it. There really *is* something *in* the poem that we are trying to dig out, though it is elusive. (46–7, emphasis added)

The soothing rhythmic assertions of the first paragraph recall those of Hotspur: 'our plot is a good plot as ever was laid; our friends true and constant: a good plot, good friends, and full of expectation; an excellent plot, very good friends' (*I Henry IV* 2:3:15–17). Thus a certain rhetoric, not just of persuasion but of self-persuasion, pervades the matter-of-fact clarity of Beardsley's practical 'demonstration,' though its repetitive assertion is passed off as scientific observation, 'close reading.'

Like Hirsch, Beardsley recognizes that claims for 'determinacy' amount to virtually nothing if they concern only explicit and coded information, and contends further that 'the connotations and the suggestions in poetry really [are] part of the poem's meaning' (49). To rationalize this claim, he accepts William Alston's definition of meaning as 'illocutionary-act potential' (51–2) and uses cases of 'ordinary language' to show that such potential includes 'connotation' and 'suggestion.' In 'He took the pill and became ill,' he argues, causal relationship is merely suggested but indubitably a part of meaning (53). The sleight in this argument is not hard to see: Beardsley's use of 'potential' for 'meaning' enables him to include suggestions, but as a consequence 'meaning' is no longer what all should understand, but only what some *may* understand. In his example causality is not verifiably coded but inferred. It is evidently a rule of usage that when two statements are so connected, 'and' *may* mean 'and consequently'; *post hoc, propter hoc* is so predictable an inference that speakers rely on it to economize expression. What is dubious about this 'ordinary language' example is precisely its exemplarity, since the cost of such economies is a certain fallibility: since the possibility of this usage means that 'and' can mean either 'and' *or* 'and consequently,' it is impossible for an interpreter to be certain in every case that it means the latter. Even if one meaning might be called the norm, poetic texts are especially liable to deviation, and Beardsley does not bother defending the transferability of his principle to poetic uses of language. In 'A slumber,' where the relationship between verses is not explicit, one cannot infer a causal relationship between lines 1 and 2 with anything approaching the certitude that Beardsley's example of ordinary language suggests.

Both of Beardsley's arguments for the determinacy of connotations mask persuasion, even self-persuasion, as clear and logical demonstration. However trivial in themselves, these deceptions reflect how much is assumed to be at stake. The 'possibility of criticism' is assumed to be at stake in the possibility of determining meanings, and this dictates, from an institutional standpoint, that meaning *must be* determinate. At the same time, does not the polemical force brought to bear on this point reflect a consciousness that it *is* otherwise?

A.E. Dyson's essay 'Symbiosis in Wordsworth' (1973) does not acknowledge Hirsch (or any of the studies it draws on), but it uses his 'slumber' example, rehearses his formulation of its 'ambiguity,' and assumes his intentionalist principle finally to determine its meaning (41–3). In that it makes no effort to justify its procedures, it amounts to a popularization, and is useful as such for showing Hirsch's principles in application. Dyson begins by observing the binary 'complexity' of some apparently 'simple' poems: 'Quite a few of [Wordsworth's] poems seem like two poems occupying the same body, as if by symbiosis in the creative act' (41). Presenting the readings of 'A slumber' by Brooks and Bateson (more or less), he contends that

> the poem has two *total* meanings, each of which 'explains' everything in it; but one meaning [the ironic reading] 'explains' a degree more convincingly than the other, and it happens to be the one that is wrong. (42)

Brooks's reading is 'wrong' because these 'are not Wordsworth's own sentiments as we find them elsewhere.' 'All Wordsworth's poems,' Dyson assumes, 'are of a piece and mutually illuminating, and a poem simply tragic in content would violate the cast of his thought' (43). In somewhat parodic fashion, Dyson illustrates that Hirsch's criterion of typicality (*Validity* 238) is no guard against the contingencies of its application. In practice we cannot square a reading with the author's typical attitudes, but only with our own 'knowledge' or interpretation of them. Hirsch, whose first book was on Wordsworth, would understand the problem that 'all Wordsworth' does not seem to be 'of a piece' (the 'two voices' problem, to put it reductively), and that *The Borderers* (to cite just one work 'tragic in content') was written not long before 'A slumber.' Therefore Hirsch himself compares 'A slumber' only with contemporaneous poems, cautiously asserting that 'Wordsworth is, in a given period, more consistent than most poets' (*Validity* 240). But the same principle may, in practice, 'verify' as many other conclusions as there are people to apply it, since each will cleave to his own 'type' of Wordsworth. Even that Hirsch and Dyson affirm the same reading of the poem is no proof of the consequentiality of their principle; it may be attributable to the influence of Hirsch's judgment on Dyson, or it may be an accident made possible by their *a priori* limitation of the alternative readings to two.

At least two critic-theorists have borrowed Hirsch's interpretive problem to defend or modify his principles, both arguing (contra Beardsley) that even when one limits oneself 'strictly' to the text, one implicitly refers to intention. Most elaborate and challenging of these is

P.D. Juhl's 'The Appeal to the Text: What Are We Appealing To?' (1978).[23] Enlarging on a suggestion by Hirsch, Juhl argues that the appeal to any 'textual feature' to defend a certain reading of another 'feature' by any criterion, such as coherence or complexity, involves a tacit appeal to authorial intention.[24] In other words, the appeal to the author, which Hirsch allows is 'an ethical choice,' Juhl believes to be, indeed, 'a metaphysical necessity.'

The theoretical point is easy, but Juhl's exemplification of it is stultifyingly difficult to follow. His citation of 'A slumber,' via Bateson and Brooks, via Hirsch, via Beardsley, until one loses track of the distinctions between citation and assertion, readings and reading, is both tactical (Reader: skip this 'example' and take my conclusion as demonstrated, or at least accept that my evaluation of two other critics' readings of one ambiguous phrase is a fair 'example' of the real difficulty in interpreting 'A slumber') and, by now, an unavoidable part of the 'slumber' game.[25] Juhl's 'example' consists of Beardsley's argument regarding line 7 of 'A slumber,' 'Rolled round in earth's diurnal course' (Juhl 279). As we've seen, Beardsley contended that it was possible to adjudicate between Brooks's and Bateson's readings by using strictly non-intentionalist evidence: in particular, he held that a reading of 'Rolled round' as connoting 'slow and gentle' motion could be substantiated solely by an appeal to context, since the neighbouring phrase, 'in earth's diurnal course,' connotes 'slow and gentle' motion. As Juhl argues, such a proof assumes, among other things, that the line is *meant* to be coherent; it involves a 'functional explanation.'

> On the assumption that 'rolled round' connotes slow and gentle motion, it would be natural or plausible to suppose that the phrase is qualified by the words 'in earth's diurnal course' *because* the latter are an appropriate means to suggest a slow and gentle motion. (279)

Thus Beardsley's defence of Bateson's interpretation supposes a 'means to' a purpose, an authorial intention. Juhl runs this argument through a baffling circuit of possible objections, restatements, and suppositions of typing monkeys, but it is essentially complete as stated here. And while it is convincing in itself, it has no effect on Beardsley's argument; indeed, nothing at all seems to follow from it. For the authorial intention to which, as Juhl demonstrates, a reader necessarily 'appeals' is what has been called a programmatic rather than an active intention.[26] To interpret any element of a text one must assume that an author intended *something* by it, but both the existence of the intention and its specific content remain inferential. One always construes textual features, as Juhl says, according to 'some general criterion' such as coherence or complexity (278–9), and this involves, as he says, inferring what the author intended, but what he does not point out is that the criterion remains, from the interpreter's point of view, *a priori*: since there is no assurance that it *is* the criterion the author had in mind, its imputed intentionality is methodologically useless.[27] Even Wimsatt and Beardsley allow 'that we infer the intention of an artificer' (4), but they rightly rule out its relevance as evidence. What permits Juhl to lose track of this embarrassing inferential act is his ambiguous term 'appeal': when he says we 'appeal' to intention, it seems that we are appealing to something objective, not to something we ourselves are in the act of positing.

So what is gained by Juhl's argument? The same thing, I would say, as Hirsch's and Beardsley's arguments gained: a 'necessary fiction,' a fallacious yet evidently important assurance that textual meaning – all the way down to the subtle connotations of a phrase – can be reliably determined by appeals to objective evidence. His introduction claims not 'to provide a general method for interpreting ... or for resolving interpretive controversies; rather my aim is to help clarify what such controversies are about' (277). But his conclusion claims to have found a useful principle:

> I have argued that textual features are evidence for a claim about the meaning of a work *in virtue of* the fact that they are evidence of the author's intention; it follows that they are evidence for a claim about the meaning of a work *only insofar as* they are evidence for a statement of precisely the same kind, namely a statement about the author's intention, as facts about the author's beliefs, values, concerns, etc. whether revealed in his diaries, notebooks, letters, conversations, or in other literary works. That is, insofar as such facts are evidence of what the author intended, they will be no less relevant than textual features. (285)

Juhl has moved closer than at first to Hirsch's 'method ... for resolving interpretive controversies,' for now he claims to dictate what is 'evidence for a claim about the meaning of a work.' But while he *appears* to be claiming to have demonstrated that 'extrinsic' and 'intrinsic' evidence are of equal weight,[28] the intricacy, not to say contortion, of this passage makes it difficult to tell exactly how much he is claiming. I would suggest that his important claims are those made most in passing, and that they are misleading: 'I have argued that textual features are evidence for a claim about the meaning of a work *in virtue of* the fact that they are evidence of the author's intention.' Textual features are always 'evidence of the author's intention' to a trivial degree (e.g., evidence of an intention to put them there – and even in this, as editors know, they are not always reliable evidence) but they are not *sufficient* 'evidence of the author's intention' to mean *specific* things, which is the only version of this claim that would make it more than trivial. The interpreter's 'knowledge' of intentions to mean specific things is, as we have seen, inferred rather than directly deduced, and this makes these intentions, not 'evidence for a claim about the meaning,' but merely a different form of 'a claim about meaning.'[29] Moreover, if Juhl's principle of evidence seems unobjectionable for some kinds of 'intention,' it must be noted how, in his 'example,' it is unobtrusively extended to far more subtle and specific kinds of 'intention' than it can handle. For the issue in Beardsley's defence of Bateson's reading was (as usual in these arguments) connotation, specifically the claim that 'Rolled round' connotes 'slow and gentle motion.' Therefore when Juhl speaks of 'a claim about the meaning,' his 'example' suggests that he is speaking of claims about the specific connotations of a phrase, and it is therefore remarkable to see him offering an objective 'textual feature' as 'evidence' for such claims. The objective 'textual features' are what raise the dispute about connotation in the first place, which is to say their evidentiary value is ambiguous.

Empty as all this overt theoretical argumentation turns out to be, the *disposition* of Juhl's 'example' has meanwhile argued some things more covertly. When he first offers, as 'an example,' Beardsley's fallacious claim to have determined the connotation of 'Rolled round' contextually, Juhl remarks: 'I shall not argue for or against this claim; rather I shall try to show what it involves' (279). But his procedure effectively ratifies Beardsley's claim, just as Beardsley's project was to ratify Bateson's reading. Juhl sets up the problem as a rigorously controlled experiment with only one variable among other constants:

1. Immediately after quoting the poem, Juhl quotes Beardsley's argument that 'in earth's diurnal course' suggests 'slow and gentle motion.' This reading is not offered as fact, but it is never questioned, and no other supposition is offered. It is, itself, an interpretation of connotation, but it becomes hypostatized as stable 'context,' as a means to control the experiment.

2. Juhl next offers the variable: two possible connotations for 'Rolled round,' originating in the readings by Bateson ('slow and gentle motion') and Brooks ('violent motion').
3. He then offers the 'fact ... that "rolled round" is qualified by the words "in earth's diurnal course"' (279).

Having fixed these elements, Juhl can focus on Beardsley's appeal to 'coherence' (one reading of 'Rolled round' makes the line coherent, the other does not) and show that it is really an appeal to intention. But to make that point hardly requires setting up this array of fixed elements and running Beardsley's appeal to 'coherence' through countless variations and suppositions ('Now suppose that the poem ... has been accidentally typed out by a monkey' [279]). The only real function I can find for this bizarre mental experiment is to make Juhl's demonstration intimidatingly complicated while *repetitively* (repetition has a persuasive power) staging a reading process in which the actual difficulties of reading 'A slumber' have been reduced to manageable dimensions: a single ambiguity in a controlled context. Hypostatizing Beardsley's reading of 'in earth's diurnal course' gives Juhl, like Beardsley, a handle on the ambiguity next door. In this perspective Juhl's service is not really to challenge Beardsley (especially since his coda to Beardsley's 'appeal to the text' turns out to be empty) but merely to confirm Beardsley's confirmation of Hirsch's confirmation of Bateson's reading – which is unconfirmable. The experiment is, in the deepest sense, make-believe, a 'scene of reading' carefully constructed *not* to reproduce the conditions of actual reading. An actual reading will confront ambiguities not one by one, in successively stabilized contexts, but in droves, thus in mutually destabilizing contexts. It will not be a linear process in which each difficulty can be resolved by appeal to things already established, but a gestalt experience in which several 'textual features' suddenly fit together in one view – which makes their 'evidence' in each other circular, not absolute. While Juhl's experiment with his example does not prove his theoretical argument about the value of external evidence, both are profoundly coherent in their efforts to stabilize interpretation, or rather to depict it as more stable, more subject to regulation by the 'appeal to' evidence, than in fact it is. In this, Juhl to the contrary, both are also coherent with the arguments and the practice of Hirsch and his followers.[30]

By the time (1981) that James Phelan writes about 'A slumber,' it has come to seem easy meat for objectivist arguments. Otherwise it would be curious that Phelan should discuss this lyric at all in presenting a *Theory of Language in Fiction*, and en route to a discussion of Dreiser. But the appeal of its *Einfältigkeit*, as determined by Hirsch, is irresistible:

> Since what is at issue here is not the specific interpretation of *Samson Agonistes* [Phelan has just been debating a point with Fish, who uses this example] but the principle of how textual meanings are created by authors and understood by readers, I shall demonstrate the justice of the principle by considering a different, more manageable though perhaps more problematic text: Wordsworth's 'A slumber did my spirit seal.' This poem will also require us to consider Hirsch's challenge ... (91–2)

For Phelan, 'A slumber' is 'problematic'; he portrays Hirsch's presentation of 'two extremely different, yet quite persuasive interpretations' (92) as opening, not closing, Pandora's box, as a 'challenge,' not an assist, to Phelan's argument; and thus the Bateson-Brooks dilemma is trumped up as a fair example of complexity, yet 'manageable,' eminently useful for proving determinist 'principles' for subsequent applications. By this point it should go without saying that Hirsch's creation of this 'problem' is all that makes Phelan's argument possible. His response to Hirsch is that close reading shows deficiencies in both Brooks's and Bateson's readings (94–5), but that a third reading, on which the speaker simply accepts Lucy's death, is objectively verifiable. His theoretical rationale resembles Beardsley's in being strictly textualist, but Juhl's in claiming that the text is itself evidence of intention. On this point he is, indeed, less equivocal than Juhl. Whereas Juhl's use of the phrase 'appeal to' fudged the question whether intention is attributed to or discovered from the text, Phelan claims: 'our notion of intention is formed from the language of the text not from our interpretive assumptions or external knowledge of the author'; again, 'the intention is not ours, but Wordsworth's and it is embodied in a language which we share (or at least *can* share) with him' (96–7). Therefore, rather than argue, as Juhl does, for the validity of extrinsic evidence, Phelan argues to exclude it, streamlining the appeal to intention as an appeal to the text itself: as we have seen, Juhl's principle, rigorously applied, returns us precisely to Beardsley's practice of adjudication through close reading. What has been gained by this manoeuvre is a seeming coalescence of disputed authorities: if Hirsch argued that our authority lay in the author's intention, Beardsley that it lay in the text, and if it was some embarrassment to objectivists that they couldn't agree on the object, Juhl and Phelan prevent this embarrassment by collapsing the two. Both are authoritative, both are practically the same.

In practice, however, Phelan cannot be quite so consistent, for he wishes, like the others, to claim the validity of his own inferences, or, in Hirschean terms, to pretend that 'implications' lie in the realm of objective 'meaning.' In critiquing Bateson's and Brooks's readings he notes that 'one of the poem's most prominent features' is 'the lack of any *explicit* emotion in the second stanza.' 'It is this feature of the poem which makes it so problematic and which leads to such widely divergent readings: we must *infer* the emotions behind the speaker's descriptions' (95, emphasis added). I agree – at least that this is one of several problematic features. But rather than admit subjectivity and uncertainty, Phelan immediately continues:

> this feature itself helps us to decide what the emotions are, and provides an important piece of evidence in understanding Wordsworth's intention in the poem as a whole. ... [T]his factual description in both its tone and details helps us to see that the speaker has moved beyond grief and comfort to an acceptance of the facts about human mortality; indeed, acceptance is implied in full knowledge. (95)

Since full knowledge of death hardly entails acceptance for everyone ('Do not go gentle into that good night'), it is evident that Phelan has, as he says, inferred an attitude, whether one of his own or one he thinks typical. However plausible and interesting as an interpretation, this hardly works as a decisive or even probable determination of meaning (stanza 2's tacitness as to emotion might be explained also as reflecting other emotions, such as vexation, or the lack of emotion, numbness). The attempt to have reading both ways, both as admitted inference ('we must infer the emotion') and as discovery ('not ours but Wordsworth's') is more simply evident in Phelan's later claim that '[t]he implied grief is very clear' (96) – a contradiction in terms.

Phelan and indeed all who consider Hirsch's 'problem' assume that the poem describes a death. This assumption reflects the force of tradition and the peculiar way in which Hirsch has structured the problem, not a necessity posed by the text itself. Though Phelan criticizes Bateson and Brooks and offers a third possibility, his reading accepts what is common to the previous two, as though their agreement placed certain matters beyond question. Hirsch, writing before Sykes Davies' essay of 1965, may not have seen that the text would support a wholly different construction, that his case of ambiguity was just one interpretive dilemma within another. But the omission of Sykes Davies by so many who respond to Hirsch in subsequent years suggests that Hirsch's framing of the problem was too good to be exposed to complications. There may be some refined disputes as to how, and even whether, 'we can reconstruct the intention with a high degree of probability' (Phelan 97), but for the purpose of establishing 'the possibility of criticism,' these quibbles are less important than the representation of the challenge (and here there is consensus) as the simple ambiguity of 'A slumber.' As in children's books, illustrations are what stick.

3. Relativist Determinations

> Chaos is not
>
> The mass of meaning. It is three or four
> Ideas or, say, five men or, possibly, six.[31]

So far, Hirsch's opponents have been surprisingly meek. They may question his rationale, they may deny discipleship, they may speak of his 'challenge,' but they are careful not to upset his conclusions. They accept his representation of the complexity of 'A slumber,' they confirm his claim that its meaning (right down to connotations) can be determined by objective evidence, and for the most part they even confirm his judgment of what this meaning is. Hirsch's argument is confirmed and even extended behind a façade of opposition; enemies turn out to be agents. This aside, the simple fact that critics have not been able to leave Hirsch's exemplary demonstration be, but have had to keep rehearsing it, suggests that they have found it equally dubious and appealing – too good to be true. Is Hirsch's argument one we can't refute, or one we can't refuse? Critic-theorists contemplating the actual processes of composition and reading give Hirsch more serious opposition, but here, too, I think we find some sheep in wolves' clothing.

Beardsley's simple response to Hirsch's intentionalist 'adjudication' of readings invokes the New Criticism's well known principle that texts are self-sufficient. In *The Dramatic Impulse in Modern Poetics* (1967), Don Geiger draws on the New Criticism for a doctrine closer to Hirsch's own – that of the 'implied speaker' – and finds it useful for a more searching examination of Hirsch's procedures.[32] He cites the famous passage from Wimsatt and Beardsley's 'The Intentional Fallacy':

> The meaning of a poem may certainly be a personal one, in the sense that a poem expresses a personality or state of soul rather than a physical object like an apple. But even a short lyric poem is dramatic. ... We ought to impute the thoughts and attitudes of the poem immediately to the dramatic *speaker*, and if to the author at all, only by an act of biographical inference.[33]

The 'implied speaker' was the primary agent in the New Criticism's dramaticization of lyric, a barrier, semi-permeable at best, between lyric and 'reality.' But Geiger's argument is epistemological rather than ontological. He is interested not in doctrinaire denials of relationship between speaker and author, lyric and reality, but merely in our difficulty knowing, in any particular case, what the relationship is. Hirsch, he notes, first approves Bateson's reading of 'A slumber' for matching 'the author's probable attitudes,' but then concedes: 'A poet's typical attitudes do not always apply to a particular poem' (*Validity* 240; Geiger 135). But to admit the possibility of variance between specific utterance and 'typical attitude' seems to be to admit the 'implied speaker' who is potentially different from the poet. The problem is, as Geiger observes, that there is nothing to indicate 'whether or not a particular poem is atypical, or in what respect it is atypical' (135). A poem might even reflect its author's 'typical outlook,' but 'in unpredictable ways and measure' (136). By thus refusing any simply binary option between 'authorial' and the 'dramatic' utterance, Geiger provides a well-nuanced account of the ensuing interpretive complexities:

> The distinction between man and work affords the possibility of an interesting variety of simply harmonious or contrapuntal relations, even to the point of outright division where we might conclude that the work's typical outlook contradicts – as psychic compensation or self-persuasion of some sort or another – the typical outlook of the man. (137)

In short, without exactly denying Hirsch's principle that 'meaning requires a meaner' (*Validity* 234; see Geiger 16–17), he emphasizes the problem that remains in *ascertaining* that meaning, given the rich variety of possible ratios between intention and expression. While the arena remains, as Hirsch has defined it, sharply individualistic, the problem Geiger raises is analogous to what Marxist theorists call 'reflection' or 'refraction.'[34] Can interpretation assume, as Hirsch's procedure seems to do, an immediate and straightforward expression of typical attitudes? And if not, how reliable can these attitudes be as standards for 'verification'? It might be objected, of course, that the 'implied speaker' is itself merely a theoretical supposition. But we have to assume that there is *a* speaker, if we are going to read at all (as Hirsch, Juhl, and Knapp and Michaels all argue); what we don't have to assume is that this speaker is identical with the author. The burden of proof therefore lies on those who insist on this identification, not on those who suspend judgment. Wimsatt and Beardsley said it precisely: the speaker's identification with the author involves an additional 'act of biographical inference' (5). Geiger's challenge to Hirsch consists in stressing the shadow that may fall between.

Geiger's interest in dramatic utterance leads him to explore the possibility most opposed to Hirsch's expressionist assumptions. The author of a lyric, he suggests, is not so much expressing typical attitudes as experimenting with possible ones. Like the dramatist, the lyric poet

> is not ... committed before the writing of each new piece to consult his typical outlook to see what he should say next. Indeed, the poet ... may not know what his typical outlook is. He may only slowly discover his typical outlook by writing his poems, as his readers discover it by reading them. (137)

In short, the author-become-reader 'discovers,' selectively, her 'own' attitudes in statements at first merely tentative and exploratory.[35] While still allowing some connection between speaker and author, this view of the composition process reverses the formative relation between them, or so complicates it that Hirsch's procedures for 'verification' appear far from reliable; for it comes in question not just which trial 'attitudes' the author came to adopt, but how much of them she accepted, when, and so on. In thus suggesting that intention may be the *effect* rather than the cause of utterance (as it unavoidably is from the standpoint of interpretive practice), Geiger faintly adumbrates the more rigorous and sweeping Derridean attacks on the expressionist theory of meaning.[36] At the same time, his implied critique is severely circumscribed by the supposition that this reversal is only an occasional and irregular event made possible by dramatic genres; as in formalism generally, the critique of expressionism limits itself to the contention that *literary* language is not expressive.[37] By limiting this critique to artistic uses of language, it is possible to open a certain quarter of interpretive practice to 'play' without disturbing the rest; Geiger's response to Hirsch's argument would not extend to the interpretation of legal discourse or historical writing, and one may well suppose that it is meant not to.

Geiger's specific response to Hirsch's use of 'A slumber' is fully in keeping with this logic of restraint – or restraint of logic. Since Hirsch's example is certainly 'literary,' Geiger's objections should apply in full force; it should be not just possible but necessary to reconceive the speaker's meaning without reference to our preconceptions about Wordsworth's 'typical attitudes.' But rather than read the poem from so ungrounded a perspective, Geiger accepts Hirsch's interpretive dilemma and argues that both readings may be squared with a developmental conception of the author's consciousness. Between Bateson's pantheistic reading and Brooks's ironic reading of Lucy's death, 'there is a still more inclusive possibility' that Wordsworth began thinking as Bateson reads him and ended with the ironic insight registered by Brooks (142–3). 'When we speak of a poem's meaning ... I think we are stating what we think it is that, in saying what he says in the poem, the speaker reports himself to be discovering' (145). It must be said that Geiger somewhat relaxes the deterministic claims of the objectivist theorist-critics. He claims nothing like validity or probability for his own synthetic reading: it is merely a third 'possibility' (145). But only if we begin with Hirsch's formulation does three seem a large number. From any other standpoint, and certainly from the theoretical perspectives opened by Geiger himself, a range of three readings is reassuringly narrow.

Geiger borrows the 'implied speaker' from the New Criticism, but his view of the author's self-reading suggests phenomenological theory's 'implied reader.'[38] Meaning may be 'an affair of consciousness not of words' (*Validity* 4), but reader-response critics generally contend that it is, in practice, an affair of the *reader's* consciousness not the author's: Stanley Fish even recommends that the term 'meaning' should 'be discarded, since it carries with it the notion of message or point,' in favour of the term 'experience' (*Is There a Text* 65). While such a theory appears antithetical to Hirsch's effort to ensure 'objective interpretation,' it turns out that the practical illustrations of reader-response that follow him in considering the case of 'A slumber' are more in league than at variance with his disciplinary efforts to minimize its indeterminacy and claim 'knowledge.'

Norman Holland's 'Literary Interpretation and Three Phases of Psychoanalysis' (1976) is a literary critic-theorist's conversion-narrative and apologia. Using readings of 'A slumber' to measure his progress, he recounts his abandonment of formalism for a psychoanalytic version of reader-response theory. Beneath a transcript of the poem, Holland remarks:

> It is a poem that has meant differently to me at different times in my life.
>
> Once upon a time, so devout a New Critic was I, I could scarcely relate to the poem at all. It seemed too simple to admit the critical exegesis I admired and needed. Now, I find it so apposite to the psychological criticism I advocate, it came unbidden to my mind like a free association. (221–2)

If critical theories are religions, a poem is the spirit of God that descends to the believer – but some creeds block it, others let it through. At one and the same time, Holland claims that our apprehension of the poem is affected by our presuppositions and theories, and that the consequence of his new orientation is the poem's 'unbidden' appearance – a curiously passive stance for a devotee of reader-response. Holland is well known for his libertarian perspective on reading – as this essay puts it, 'There can be as many readings as there are readers to write them. Can be and should be' (233). Yet there remains a certain essentialism, a faith that the work remains itself, and that it appears more truly to some than to others.

Holland mentions neither Hirsch nor his representation of 'A slumber' explicitly; his essay targets formalist rather than Hirschean hermeneutics. Despite this obliquity, it turns the tables on 'Hirsch's challenge' in some detail. Hirsch, complaining of 'subjectivism and relativism,' proposed 'objective interpretation.' Holland complains that the quest for 'impersonal, generalizable ... quasi-scientific knowledge' has produced an 'essential inhumanity' in criticism, an 'objectivism' that abstracts the 'experience' of poetry from the 'particular experiencers.' His proposal is therefore that we reacknowledge readers in all their multiplicity: 'there are experiencers, and the great, gaping question for this kind of formalist criticism is, Why do their experiences differ so, even for so straightforward a poem as this?' (224–5). Having already noted that 'A slumber' 'has meant differently to me at different times,' Holland underscores the importance of the specific reader by citing a broader range of critical opinion than Hirsch's argument could handle: about five readings of the word 'she,' two alternatives to Bateson's pantheistic reading of the 'theme' (the failure to mention Hirsch at this point is curious), and six or seven readings of 'diurnal' (225–6). The fact 'that different readers take the same text differently' shows Holland, not the need for 'objective interpretation,' but rather 'the basic difficulty in this effort to put criticism on an objective or quasi-scientific footing.' 'I have not,' he complains, 'found any satisfactory way of accounting for this divergence within my tradition of formalism' (226).

Without exactly explaining why, Holland next surveys the psychic models associated with the 'three [historical] phases of psychoanalysis' and produces a reading of 'A slumber' corresponding to each. In rejecting each of the first two models, Holland notes their failure to 'account for the considerable variation in individual response' (227, 229), but it is hard to see how he could expect them to. The real aim of this virtuoso performance (three tunes on one text) seems to be to extend Holland's demonstration of the perceiver's importance. Each model of psychic process amounts to a different discovery procedure, a different set of presuppositions and questions that differently determines even a single reader's 'findings.' The first model instructs readers to expect 'a latent content,' and Holland obliges with a reading of 'A slumber' construing 'she' as the castrated phallus, 'rocks, and stones' as fecal matter, and so on – 'a primitive reading by today's standards,' he concedes (227). The second phase instructs readers 'to find ego strategies,' and Holland accordingly finds several modes of 'denial,' from the speaker's denial of 'human fears' in the first stanza to his multiple negations in the second: we may not know what, but 'something has been denied.' Even 'the lost rhyme of line six' ('hears,' buried in the middle of line 6, rhymes with 'fears' and 'years' at the ends of 2 and 4) suggests denial to the reader looking for denial; even 'omissions in the form correspond to denials in defense' (228–9).

Before considering Holland's 'third phase,' we might object to the contrivance of these experiments: can Holland really demonstrate the effects of models and presuppositions to which he himself does not seriously subscribe? Does his first reading, which he himself dismisses as 'primitive,' really follow *from* the model on which he premises it? Couldn't that model underwrite less 'primitive' readings as well? But if we allow that these exemplary readings are necessarily simplified, even caricatured (he himself admits that 'symbolic decodings by different psychoanalytic critics' vary [227]), this only confirms his major point that readings depend considerably on the individual reader. Meanwhile, however simplified they may be, Holland's phase-readings foreground an item of presupposition that is often overlooked: if all reading involves inference of intention (as Juhl, Phelan, and Knapp and Michaels assert), it must also assume *some* model of the psychic process by which 'content' is encoded. If one reader assumed a model of 'latent content' and one did not, the latter could not claim to be assuming no psychic model and hence to be less fallible; she would actually be assuming a 'no latent content' model. Since psychic processes are 'known' only by such models, and since there are several, this level of presumption constitutes a significant uncertainty factor for intentionalist interpretation.

The more serious objection to Holland's procedure concerns his dismissal of his own first-phase reading: 'That is a primitive reading by today's standards (perhaps by any standards).' What standards? Holland has admitted the problem of readers' 'divergence' far more extensively than Hirsch. Having admitted so much, what then? (How) does he control it? What standards can he invoke? Holland's explicit effort to address such questions proceeds from his third psychic model, 'identity theory,' which views a

> person as a continuing sameness within change. ... In effect, we can read one another like music, hearing ourselves play our lives like variations on a melody, an identity theme, which is, quite simply, our very essence. (230)

Since Holland has already suggested viewing '[t]he patient as text, the text as patient' (221), it is evident that this principle can be applied both to texts and to the people who read them. Its application to the text might be, 'The text remains the same, while readings vary'; but that is a statement of the problem, not its solution, and Holland does not formulate it.[39] Instead he applies his identity-principle to the reader – a peculiar move, since a reader's identity has not been the question.

> In effect, I can speak about a person as about a poem, achieving rigor but retaining uniqueness. I can talk fully and rigorously about the individual – person or poem – provided I remember that *I* am talking.
>
> Thus, this concept of identity adds a new dimension to all our games. Not only do we perceive, we also perceive ourselves perceiving. We become able to understand how our perceptions are themselves acts that express our identity themes. So too interpretation, so that when I read and comment on Wordsworth's lyric, I know that two seemingly inconsistent things are going on at once.
>
> On the one hand, I am bringing my skills as a reader to bear, my knowledge of Wordsworth, English Romanticism, and what others have written about them, but most important my own commitment to an honest search for a 'valid' interpretation, one that will command assent from others besides myself. We

call this being 'objective.' Yet at the same time I know I can only do this in a way which is wholly authentic for me – 'subjective.'

These are only seemingly inconsistent, however. All my acts, perceptions and relationships are functions of my identity, including my relation to this lyric, for that is what identity is: my thematic sameness plus my variations on it. My relation to the poem includes *both* my emotions *and* my characteristic use of the critic's discipline. ... It is precisely because I feel emotion toward the poem that I can re-imagine it in my own characteristic way, yet my tactics and commitments I share with other critics.

Identity theory enables me to understand that interaction of firm critical hypotheses with exciting, shimmering fields of personal knowledge. This third phase is not a retreat to subjectivity. It is giving up the illusion that I can only understand reality (or a text) by keeping myself out. (231)

I quote at such length to show the multiplicity of Holland's own denial strategies. A professional critic cannot admit the problems of subjectivity and 'divergence' as fully as Holland has done without at some point explaining how criticism can function as a 'discipline.' They may be held at arms' length, in quotation marks, but the two Hirsch-words, 'valid' and 'objective,' cannot be kept out perpetually; Holland is willing to admit 'subjectivity,' but unwilling to make it a sovereign principle. Therefore he must have it both ways: subjectivity and objectivity are 'only seemingly inconsistent.' To illustrate this, however, Holland begs the question of the poem's identity by stressing the reader's – 'my thematic sameness.' (The question, as he pointed out earlier, is really the 'thematic sameness' of 'A slumber,' for critics 'differ even more about its theme' than about its 'subject' [225].) His other strategies are equally evasive. His assertion that 'I can talk fully and rigorously ... provided I remember that *I* am talking' assumes, reassuringly, that admitting subjectivity serves to control it,[40] but the term 'rigorously' is carefully chosen to sound disciplinary without specifying what is being claimed: knowledge of the object? Holland does appeal to some apparent objectivities ('knowledge of Wordsworth' and of 'English Romanticism') and to other stabilizers ('the critic's discipline,' 'firm critical hypotheses'), but these are circular appeals to what still needs demonstrating. If there can and should be as many readings of 'A slumber' as there are readers, it is precisely this knowledge of Wordsworth and romanticism, not to mention 'the critic's discipline,' that are in question; and Holland's own purported conversion from formalism suggests that 'critical hypotheses' are anything but 'shared' and 'firm.' Ultimately the passage does little more than admit subjectivity while anxiously denying it: 'I can only do this in a way which is ... "subjective". ... This third phase is not a retreat to subjectivity.'

It is, of course, Holland's extensive admission of subjectivity and 'divergence' that sets his argument apart from other responses to 'Hirsch's challenge.' This admission is most pronounced in his last reading of 'A slumber,' correlative with the 'third phase,' but it too is crossed by objectivist counter-claims:

> The poem says to me – or I say through it – that to be close to another person, you must unseal yourself in a world of perhaps indifference or perhaps intrusion. Either way, you must risk yourself, but it is worth it, because you can gain both intimacy and the safety of a larger being. (233)

'The poem says to me – or I say through it': is this an act of indecision or of revision? Is Holland still having it both ways, or is he, in an afterthought, fully admitting subjectivity? The same cautious duplicity appears in Holland's conclusion, where he generalizes from this practice:

> my last move – which you will share with me, I hope – makes criticism into an act of personal discovery. ... There can be as many readings as there are readers to write them. Can be and should be. For criticism from the third phase of psychoanalysis risks intimacy in order to restore individuality. The best interpreters will speak from self-knowledge as well as from the knowledge of literature. How to do this? That, the third phase tells us, we each will have to find for ourselves. (233)

Does the phrase 'personal discovery' mean that the reader discovers *herself*, or that she personally *discovers* what she is reading? By permitting both readings, the phrase seems to admit subjectivity but also to make way for criticism's disciplinary claims (whichever you wish to hear); but the latter sense contradicts Holland's earlier invocation of the anti-foundationalist tenets that 'perception is a constructive act,' that 'the human being' is 'a freely emitting center of meanings,' that 'we confer meaning on events instead of letting the world shove its meanings down on us' (232). If we take these statements seriously, 'discovery' is a term deceptively objectifying what is really invented and projected. So how can Holland's conclusion assert 'discovery' and even '*the* knowledge of literature' (my emphasis) without submitting them to the *epoche*? As he shows, one can admit subjectivity and still claim objective knowledge – through sheer inconsistency.

I dwell on these gestures of anxiety and retreat precisely because Holland comes closer than most to admitting the full extent of the problems in really producing knowledge of 'A slumber.' That *even he* retreats to objectivist claims reflects, I think, the force of the interpretive imperative to present invention as discovery,[41] or (what is much the same thing) the disciplinary imperative to square interpretation with 'knowledge.' Holland may seem Hirsch's polar opposite, but their differences are in degree or emphasis; both are arguing, and using 'A slumber,' to the same end. Using a two-phase structure that has become traditional for literary-theory essays (see chapter 2, above), Hirsch and his followers pretend to offer an interpretive problem and then to solve it, but their real 'solution' is to present the problem reductively in the first place. After admitting the problem of 'divergence' more extensively than most, Holland denies the consequences of this admission in an eleventh-hour philosophical argument that assumes what needs to be demonstrated. But precisely because he seems to marshal, perhaps even to magnify the problems, it is important to note that he too has actually minimized them. Before presenting his list of cruxes, he intones the 'simplicity' of 'A slumber': 'It seemed too simple,' 'A simple "slumber" rid me of fears,' 'this so intensely simple and human poem,' 'the simplicities of a Lucy poem,' 'so straightforward a poem as this' (222–5). He then cites a narrower range of interpretive disagreements than really exists even in the published commentary, neglects to mention that even the text is available in several varieties, and then ranges his psychoanalytic readings in successive 'phases,' as though of increasing validity, appealing to an unexplained 'standard' to dismiss the first as 'primitive.' These devices, which encourage one to think the problems smaller than they are, are more important than Holland's summary claims for 'knowledge of Wordsworth' and 'the knowledge of literature' at the end; they are what make these claims seem the less impossible.

This is not to identify Holland's argument with Hirsch's. Both have it both ways: Hirsch in his manipulation of the term 'meaning,' Holland in both admitting to invention and then claiming 'knowledge' by 'discovery.' But something is gained, I think, by Holland's way of doing so. In two conspicuous ways his argument differs from the others we have considered: he defers his claims to 'knowledge' long enough to admit the obstacles more fully, and he leaves these claims empty; he does not finally attempt to persuade us that his opinion is 'knowledge,' or that a specific reading is the most 'valid' or 'probable' (except in so far as this is implied by his successive phases). He argues, in effect, for the compatibility of indeterminacy and knowledge. Since the kind of knowledge he refers to (*the* knowledge of literature) is not, I think, finally compatible with his allowance that meaning is so largely determined by the specific reader, the effect of this argument is to rationalize an *attitudinal* shift toward indeterminacy: don't deny it, accept it (if only by denying the consequences of this acceptance). To say this argument is attitudinal is also to say that it is not logical, as it presents itself, but ideological. Though couched in respectably scientific terms, the appeal to 'identity psychology' is an appeal to liberal ideology: 'the individual – person or poem' – is constant though apparently changing, real though appearances deceive. It has a 'very essence,' though no one can know what it is. This assumption of a poetic 'essence' corresponds to Hirsch's positing of 'authorial meaning,' but here their phenomenologies part: Holland is content to believe *that* it is, while Hirsch thinks it necessary to determine *what* it is. Though Holland speaks reassuringly and in general terms of 'knowledge,' in practice he lays claim, at most, to what Hirsch calls 'significance' ('the poem says to me'). Believing *that* there is an essence makes the exercise of perspectives seem sufficiently 'valid.' At this level – to return to the figures of his opening – Holland's acceptance of readerly difference is not just ideological but theological, a rejection of pontifical interpretive authority in favour of personal witness.

One might well expect reader-response studies to have realized Hirsch's fears of critical 'perspectivism and relativism.' But more often they serve as rhetorically concessive arguments to strengthen his disciplinary claims. The more we can acknowledge, or seem to acknowledge, the constitutive role of readers and then still claim 'the knowledge of literature,' the less assailable our critical and pedagogical endeavours appear. Holland's claims to validity, objectivity, knowledge, and discipline are (however hedged) cases in point, yet for all his disciplinary back-pedalling Holland concedes *more* force to the actual variety among readers than has been common in reader-response theory. By substituting an ideal reader, a 'competent reader,' a 'super-reader,' or simply '*the* reader' for the real horde, or by arguing that real readers cannot help but resemble one another by virtue of co-membership in 'interpretive communities,' theorists have been able to acknowledge the response-factor in interpretation while still repressing the uncertainty factor raised by the differences between interpreters.[42] This stabilization gives rise, in effect, to a circuitous formalism: if we no longer speak of an objective meaning in or of the text, 'the effect' or 'the experience' attributed to it is still regarded as communally stable or normative.

A treatment of 'A slumber' in this more strenuously pro-disciplinary mode of reader-response is Brian Caraher's recent book-length study reflecting on his own interpretation of the poem as an exemplary critical-theoretical process producing 'critical knowledge.' Caraher describes his own project as a study of 'real readers reading' (1), and he stresses the importance of 'particular readers' (246). He compares himself to Holland in his 'awareness of how important the activity of the reader is to an interpretation of the poem' (88), and faults Fish and Iser for 'treat[ing] the reader as an ideal construct' (249). At the same time, he presents his study as 'a closely reasoned investigation of what is involved in generating and securing warrantable interpretations of specific literary works' (1) and even claims that his own putatively pre-interpretive 'analysis' of 'A slumber' 'involves the production of reflective, criticized, and cognitively responsible critical knowledge' (185). In short, though he specifically rejects Hirsch's intentionalist 'adjudication' of Bateson's and Brooks's readings (71–6), his project is to reconcile full acknowledgment of 'real readers reading' with the full force of Hirsch's disciplinary claims to knowledge. His argument is a very true copy of Hirsch, but in the reader-response mode, and writ large.

Caraher argues, by both precept and example, for an 'inductive' 'realign[ment of] the relation of critical practice and theoretical conceptualization' (2, see also 241) – that is, for a combination in which theory waits upon practice. His study therefore divides in two, part 1 building and defending an interpretation of 'A slumber' (if you read line 1 as 'My spirit did seal a slumber,' the poem 'confesses a murder' [44–6]), part 2 'inductively drawing upon ... [this] act of interpretation' (130) and glossing it with theories of knowledge taken from John Dewey, Stephen Pepper, and others. But part 2 can also be seen as retrospectively authorizing and rationalizing Caraher's own interpretive procedure, as in the claim that it has produced 'cognitively responsible critical knowledge': does the example of 'practical criticism' illustrate the theory, or does the theory promote the 'example' to the status of 'general rationality'?

That the theoretical apparatus serves to generalize and confirm Caraher's reading is sufficiently evident from his putatively pre-theoretical 'practical criticism' alone (part 1). To present this interpretive process as 'inductive' and pre-theoretical is itself highly theoretical; not for nothing is 'Baconian method' the first example Fish thinks of in arguing 'against theory' ('Consequences' 110). Taking pains to present his process *as* inductive, Caraher both builds his reading up linearly from what he considers 'basic fact' (21), and delays extensive theorization until part 2 of his study. But while this inevitably prolongs the presentation of his reading, it does nothing to ensure that his reading *is* inductive; the temporal ordering of his own reading experience serves only to hide its inevitable guidance by *a priori* hypotheses such as what Hirsch calls 'genre presuppositions.' In defending his inductive claims in his Prologue (1–12), Caraher offers the literary detective, 'a Dupin or a Holmes,' as a model for his 'inductive' reader (12). But these exemplary discoverers of clues and revealers of the truth are themselves fantasies, which makes them dubious models for inductive critical inquiry. Perhaps more instructive here is the curious parallel with Samuel Butler's murder-mystery reading of 'She dwelt,' which Caraher does not mention. Butler's mock-reader (see chapter 3, above) similarly emulates the literary detective, and that both he and Caraher discover murder in the subtext illustrates precisely how a reader's (pre)occupation may shape his discoveries. Butler's detective and Caraher's 'critical sleuth' (12) both look *for* something that does not appear, hence for something that has been suppressed, hence for something that needs to be suppressed, hence for something like 'murder.' Not much is really inductive about that – Caraher to the contrary (5n), Sherlock Holmes is right to call his own method 'deductive.'[43]

Most surprising, however, given Caraher's emphasis on 'real readers' and his complaint that they are neglected by Fish and Iser, is his own unrepentant idealization of the reader in order to present his own experience of the text as 'fact.' The basis of his interpretation is the observation that 'she' (line 3) may refer to either 'Lucy' or 'spirit.' This dual possibility produces an 'experience of a confusion' which Caraher insists is not merely his: 'the experience of a confusion in the reference of "she" is very real' (16); 'we do experience a confusion about who "she" is' (21). Recognizing that his 'we' may be questioned, Caraher defends it: 'I have used "we" ... because this confusion is something we all *can* experience' (21). But 'can' and 'do' are different things. Caraher's further justification exemplifies the double bind in which reader-response theory often finds itself, its need to both admit and repress subjectivity:

> Now, it would be unreasonable to claim that every reader does or must experience a referential confusion in reading 'A slumber.' However, the 'we' must and

does begin with an 'I.' It is myself, one reader, who experiences the confusion over the reference of 'she'; it is *my* experience, and I know it to be so. However, in this instance, what makes *my* experiences *possible for me*? A number of things do, but what is important about them is that I share them with a great many other readers. Specifically, my knowledge of how pronouns are used in English is routinely called into play here. ... A more refined but still shared and shareable form of knowledge is an awareness of the literary uses of the pronoun 'she'. ... in designating human and divine spirits. ... [T]hese general competencies are necessary to any individual reading of 'A slumber did my spirit seal.' (21–3)

To paraphrase, not every reader 'does or must,' but competent readers can – hence 'we do.' Even accepting what I would dispute, that a reader without a 'refined' knowledge of feminine pronouns is incompetent to read 'A slumber,' both competencies Caraher stipulates are necessary rather than sufficient conditions of 'the experience' he seeks to generalize; they make this experience 'possible,' as he says, but not inevitable or normative. His 'we do experience' is premature generalization of 'I do experience.' (Even a reader with both competencies *may* assume that 'she' refers to a girl or woman without ever noticing its potential reference to 'spirit'; many published readings *do* this, and what has happened is, as Aristotle says, 'manifestly possible.') In what Caraher himself advertises as a 'closely reasoned' procedure, this neglect of basic distinctions between necessary conditions and sufficient ones, between 'can,' 'ought,' and 'do,' seems to reflect oversight less than will to knowledge.

Generalizing his experience as 'the' or 'our' experience enables Caraher to constitute it as pre-interpretive fact, thus giving rise to what I have called 'circuitous formalism':

I propose that this experience of a confusion is a basic and necessary piece of literary evidence in any comprehensive experience and explanation – that is to say, interpretation – of 'A slumber did my spirit seal.'

Before I offer an interpretation, it is best to start with a ground-level accounting of how and why a referential confusion is not only possible but plausible in reading or in rereading this poem after some time away from it. The first two lines introduce a slumbrous and insensitive speaker ... (16–17)

The effort to distinguish pre-interpretation (which Caraher sometimes calls 'reading') from interpretation corresponds to Hirsch's effort to separate the 'objective interpretation' of 'meaning' from 'criticism' of 'significance,' but Caraher concedes less than Hirsch to the 'probable.' That 'we do experience a confusion about who "she" is' constitutes, for him, 'a *basic fact* involved in reading this particular lyric' (21, my emphasis). Putting aside merely theoretical objections to the claims of pre-interpretive fact, in practice Caraher includes interpretations in what he says lies 'before ... interpretation,' just as Hirsch includes 'significances' in what he presents as 'meaning.' His notice of 'a slumbrous and insensitive speaker' is by no means pre-interpretive; without interpreting we know neither that the speaker is 'insensitive' nor whether he is, has been, or merely claims to have been 'slumbrous.' Indeed, on Caraher's own alternative interpretation of the line as 'My spirit did seal a slumber,' it is not clear even that the slumber pertains to the speaker. Thus, what Caraher wishes to present as 'the experience' or 'basic fact' of the poem is built upon interpretation, is itself interpretation, and is, as such, subject to variation among readers and to controversy. The wonder is that he should argue otherwise.

Caraher's further construction upon his 'basic fact' traces a now familiar pattern. Unlike most others, he does address the challenge of Sykes Davies, who in 1965 read 'she' as referring to 'my spirit' so that the poem as a whole appeared to describe a mystical trance. As I have suggested, Sykes Davies' counter-interpretation was long forgotten because it had to be: not only did it participate in a challenge to the popular 'Lucy Poems' group, but it also recovered certain ambiguities repressed or presumptively resolved by Hirsch's 'adjudication' between Brooks and Bateson: what does 'she' refer to? Does stanza 2 describe a death? Thus it upset Hirsch's simple phrasing of the interpretive problem; far more seriously, it threatened to show that Hirsch's pro-disciplinary demonstration of the possibility of turning interpretation to the production of 'genuine knowledge' required certain distortions. Caraher readmits Sykes Davies into the 'slumber' problem, but takes no notice of the issues involved in his historical exclusion; indeed, he uses Sykes Davies exactly as Hirsch used Bateson or Brooks, to produce *Einfältigkeit*: 'The situation, then, is that two ways of reading "A slumber" are possible and defensible; yet neither one can be ruled out in favor of the other' (43). Two? Now there is 'the line of interpretation derived from Davies' and 'the conventional line of interpretation' (43). Now the question is not 'bitter or affirmative?' but ' "spirit" or "Lucy"?' – but the strategy is a perfect rehearsal of Hirsch's, and its effect of reducing 'A slumber' to a tidy ambiguity is the same. And now Sykes Davies has been figured in.

Like Geiger and Phelan, Caraher chooses a 'a third way' (45) of reading rather than choose between the two traditions. The 'referential confusion' of 'she' is, he suggests, authorially intended (37), its intent being to force a close rereading of the first stanza. During such rereading, a hitherto unnoticed detail 'is almost certain to appear': line 1 may mean 'my spirit did seal a slumber' (44). This will suggest that the speaker is active, not passive, and it follows that he 'confesses a murder' (45–6). This, while clearly a possible experience in reading the poem, strikes me as involving too many detours and contingencies to be common or predictable, let alone intentional or 'almost certain.' But Caraher claims for his reading more than mere plausibility or passing interest. It is a 'determination of meaning' (65), 'the experience,' not just 'my experience.' From the strong vantage point of Hirschean *Einfältigkeit*, this is not hard to prove. Only one or two competitor readings must be ruled out. Caraher's reading

> does not so much supplant the other two as supplement them. It articulates what is lacking in both and turns squarely to address what precisely is at stake in a work that appears at first to send its readers off along two divergent pathways of interpretation. (63)

That the traditional readings are 'lacking' means, of course, that they *are* being supplanted. Their actual dismissals were delivered earlier, both on somewhat delusory grounds. Of the 'Lucy' reading, Caraher writes: 'Strictly speaking, the ascription of "Lucy" as the reference or antecedent of "she" in line three is completely unwarranted' (19), apparently forgetting that Wordsworth always printed the poem after poems naming Lucy ('not completely warranted' would be true). The 'spirit' reading he dismisses as inconsistent with the death in stanza 2, even though stanza 2, on the 'spirit' reading, has nothing to do with a death (35; see note 11, above). Supposing, however, that we accept Caraher's exclusion of these alternatives, the Hirschean ambiguity-structure does the rest. If we believe Caraher, there are 'two ways of reading "A slumber,"' both of which prove 'lacking.' This leaves his 'third way' the only adequate way to read, however odd it may seem that no one discovered it before 1991.

It is more than just ironic that demonstrating that critical inquiry can produce 'cognitively responsible critical knowledge' (185) should involve so much deception. The deceptions I have examined are not singular – they are representative of many others both in Caraher's argument and in the Hirschean 'slumber' project as a whole. The question is what to make of them. I have argued that some such deception is endemic to interpretation, that interpretation necessarily involves presenting, at some level, invention as discovery, inference as efference, fiction as fact, subjectivity as objectivity, particularity as generality, or interpretation as knowledge. But if the persistent deceptiveness of the Hirschean 'slumber' project substantiates this view, doesn't this view likewise excuse the deceptions? What is the point in dwelling on them? There would be no point, if all deceptions were equal. Derrida's comment on another necessary duplicity, or 'double gesture,' may be pertinent here. He argues that after deconstruction one must continue to use concepts whose 'truth value' is in question, and that '[t]his necessity is irreducible; it is not a historical contingency.' 'But,' he adds, 'if no one can escape this necessity, ... this does not mean that all the ways of giving in to it are of equal pertinence.'[44] The need to posit that what *we* understand is what *the text* says is, I think, very real, but in practice interpreters have many different ways to 'give in' to this need. As in Holland's 'The poem says to me – or I say through it,' the supposition may be entertained and questioned or discarded almost at once. The opposite extreme would lie, not in argumentation of the kind we have been examining, but in supremely confident statement: 'A means X.' What makes the 'slumber' project remarkable as a whole is its earnest communal underscoring of the word 'means' in that sentence. Here the (self-)persuasive gestures endemic to interpretation overshadow interpretation *per se* until, with Caraher, an entire book of strategies – false induction, contextual and consensual confirmation, disproval of rival interpretations, invocation of philosophical authorities on 'knowledge' – is required to satisfy the will to knowledge about an eight-line poem. Only the severest doubts in the possibility of interpretive knowledge could produce a will so strong in the first place, only the sincerest fears of 'perspectivism and relativism.' Or so the situation speaks to me, or I say through it, especially in supposing that the whole 'slumber' project speaks by way of denial. Even if the necessity of interpretive deception is not, in Derrida's phrase, 'a historical contingency,' this particular earnestness in deception is not business as always.

It may appear that my study has neglected to specify the reasons for the emergence of this complex of strong 'disciplinary' anxiety and self-deception. Not fully believing in the possibility of explaining such phenomena by reference to a determining historical exterior, or rather fearing that my own efforts to trace such determinants would mainly produce simplifications, but without denying that they might receive their due in another kind of study, I have sought instead to document in detail the existence of this complex, to trace its internal development, and to infer its causes on a more immanent or semi-autonomous model. But for an emblem of its motivation where the internal meets the external, one could do far worse than point, once again, to the survey of reading 'protocols' in the first part of I.A. Richards' *Practical Criticism*, that 'field-study in comparative ideology' (6) that dared to begin asking how differently real readers really read.[45]

5 Lucy's Modern Meanings

My last chapter plotted a strand of 'Lucy Poems' criticism in the context of criticism's efforts to claim 'knowledge.' If poetry may be about poetry, perhaps we should not grumble when criticism is really about criticism. From Pope's 'Essay on Criticism' to Hirsch's 'Objective Interpretation' and its sequels, literary commentary has never been able entirely to overcome its doubts regarding its own disciplinarity, doubts to which the reiterative Hirschian projects ironically testify. In my opinion, such projects have not succeeded in their specific tasks of rendering criticism 'objective,' 'valid,' or determinative, but their negative results remain valuable as illustrations that some element of self-projection, personal or cultural, is inseparable from genuine interpretation. It is indicative that objectivist critic-theorists seeking to minimize the idiosyncratic misapprehension of 'A slumber' by reflecting on their own methods have succeeded only in so far as they abstained from interpretation itself. But confirming and reconfirming a pre-existing reading like Bateson's is hardly the same thing as achieving objectivity; it is only willed consensus, an agreement to agree.

If critical self-consciousness cannot purify our understanding of literature in itself, it may nevertheless improve our understanding of understanding, and that is something. Moreover, it is precisely because interpretation is not 'objective' that it can become an object of historical interest in its own right. As in Fredric Jameson's call for a 'metacommentary' that 'takes in its own mental processes as well as the object of those processes' ('Metacommentary' 4), critical self-consciousness is increasingly recommended not in order to control subjectivity, but out of the very recognition that, aside from its ostensible function as an eye-piece on 'the object,' criticism also has a life of its own: a complexity of social and ideological determinants, a broad range of lateral functions and ulterior purposes. This does not make 'the object' any less its *raison d'être;* it only means that when the object is being scrutinized most closely, other functions are also being filled. These functions are what make the history of commentary more than a mere series of 'true' insights and near misses. With them in mind, this chapter focuses more on the actual twentieth-century interpretations of the 'Lucy Poems' and less on their claims to knowledge – though the latter cannot be avoided entirely.

1. A Question of 'Nature'

Notwithstanding efforts to fix them, the meanings (or what Hirsch calls significances) of the 'Lucy Poems' have changed in the past century, and to understand this change I think we must change our own interpretive horizon. Since self-consciousness only inhibits interpretation, real interpretation occurs when self-consciousness is most in abeyance, and real interpretive shifts will reflect shifts in the least conscious presuppositions. Undoubtedly the greatest interpretive 'gap' presented by the 'Lucy Poems' is the one disputed by Bateson and Brooks, the relationship between the 'human' ('I had no human fears') and 'nature.' What is to be made of 'Kind Nature's gentlest boon' in 'Strange fits,' of the dual 'Nature' and nature in 'Three years,' of Lucy's rustication and disappearance in 'She dwelt' and 'I travelled,' of what Cleanth Brooks ('Irony' 736) calls the 'clutter' of natural objects in the last line of 'A slumber'? What is to be made of Lucy's life and death in 'nature'? Or what does the speaker, or what does Wordsworth, make of these things? The reader *of* these poems has no greater challenge than to understand the reader *in* them. But the poems themselves provide so little guidance as to attitude that on this point their readers are left almost wholly to the projection of assumed attitudes.[1] Hence the shifts that have occurred in the interpretation of the 'Lucy Poems' cannot help but reflect cultural shifts in the interpretation of 'nature.'

Unavoidably, these shifts also involve shifts in the interpretation of Wordsworth's interpretation of 'nature' – a complexity I shall simplify to the extent of using 'Wordsworthian nature' to mean 'Wordsworth's interpretation of and attitude toward nature.' Wordsworth criticism, that is, has two distinct ways of reflecting changing attitudes toward 'nature.' First are simple changes in attitude toward Wordsworthian nature, taken as a fixed quantity, such as Aldous Huxley's declaration in 1929 that Wordsworth's interpretation is false:

> it is only possible for those who are prepared to falsify their immediate intuitions of Nature. ... 'Let Nature be your teacher,' says Wordsworth. The advice is excellent. But how strangely he puts it into practice! Instead of listening humbly to what the teacher says, he shuts his ears and himself dictates the lesson he desires to hear. ('Wordsworth in the Tropics' 116–18)

Travel in the tropics, suggests Huxley, would have 'somewhat rudely disturbed' Wordsworth's 'pantheistic worship of Nature' (113). While Huxley simply takes the dominant Victorian reading of Wordsworthian nature for granted and rejects it as naïve,[2] his own darker view also reflects a contemporary shift that led to more subtle rereadings of Wordsworth's views. The pronounced swerve in readings of 'Three years' in about 1930 is only the most blatant case in which criticism of the 'Lucy Poems' reflects this reinterpretation. H.W. Garrod's pivotal essay on 'Wordsworth's Lucy' (1929) focuses, as we have seen, on the transition to stanza 7, and comments:

> The truth is, as I believe, that between Lucy's perfection in Nature and her death there is, for Wordsworth, really no tragic antithesis at all. ...
>
> The real difficulty ... of understanding Wordsworth proceeds from our finding it so hard to believe that he means what he says. Of what he says upon the subject of man's place in nature, we miss a large part by being sceptical from the beginning.[3]

Garrod's latter remark suggests that by 1929 Huxley's scepticism was growing common, but it is also important in urging the close re-reading of Wordsworthian nature itself.

2. Nature and Symbol

More important than Garrod's comments in marking the shift from the Victorian view are A.C. Bradley's *Oxford Lectures* on Wordsworth (1903; pub. 1909). Though Bradley scarcely mentions the 'Lucy Poems,' he does much to explain the subsequent readings of them by critics such as David Ferry, Geoffrey Hartman, and Paul de Man. Finding the conception of Wordsworth as naïve nature-lover insufficient to account for his greatest work, Bradley urges closer attention: 'the road into Wordsworth's mind must be through his strangeness and his paradoxes, and not round them' (101). Quoting passages that seem anomalous from within the Victorian assumptions, including a declaration to 'Almighty God' that 'Carnage is thy daughter,'[4] Bradley remarks:

> This last ... is a startling statement; but is it a whit more extraordinary than the others? It is so only if we assume that we are familiar with thoughts that lie too deep for tears, or if we translate 'the soul of all my moral being' into 'somehow concordant with my moral feelings,' or convert 'all that we behold' into 'a good deal that we behold,' or transform the Wanderer's reading of the silent faces of the clouds into an argument from 'design.' But this is the road round Wordsworth's mind, not into it. (102)

Bradley is ahead of his contemporaries in attacking the presumptive interpretation that dominated Victorian criticism, but his desire to make the interpretive moment at least wait upon closer examination is a central feature of subsequent critical development. Citing numerous passages ill fitted to the then-prevalent conception of Wordsworthian nature, he concludes that these 'nature' poems frequently involve 'the expression through sense of something beyond sense' (132). It would be hard to overstate the importance to the subsequent reading of Wordsworth of this transcendentalist inference and its various restatements:

> [Wordsworth was not a great love poet because] he did not strongly feel ... that the *passion* of love is a way into the Infinite; and a thing must be no less than this to Wordsworth if it is to rouse all his power. (113)

> He apprehended all things, natural or human, as the expression of something which, while manifested in them, immeasurably transcends them. (127)

> [I]n the kind of experience which forms our present subject, there is always some feeling of definite contrast with the limited sensible world. The arresting feature or object is felt in some way *against* this background, or even as in some way a denial of it. (131)

Equally important is Bradley's comment on the *Prelude* passage describing the speaker's wait for the horses that would take him home for the Christmas holidays:

> ... the wind and sleety rain,
> And all the business of the elements,
> The single sheep, and the one blasted tree,
> And the bleak music of that old stone wall,
> The noise of wood and water, and the mist
> That on the line of each of those two roads
> Advanced in such indisputable shapes. [*Prelude* 12:317–23]
>
> Everything here is natural, but everything is apocalyptic. And we happen to know why. Wordsworth is describing the scene in the light of memory. In that eagerly expected holiday his father died; and the scene, as he recalled it, was charged with the sense of contrast between the narrow world of common pleasures and blind and easy hopes, and the vast unseen world which encloses it in beneficent yet dark and inexorable arms. (134)[5]

In suggesting that Wordsworth uses nature to transcend nature, Bradley develops the dialectic between nature and imagination that has, via Ferry and Hartman, come to dominate modern Wordsworth criticism. If 'the narrow world' is fundamental to Wordsworth's imagination, the two are also deeply opposed; Bradley's conception of nature as Wordsworth's symbol for 'the Infinite' has the far-reaching implications of leaving Wordsworth's allegiance to *this* world, both human and natural, in doubt. Bradley can assert that 'No poet is more emphatically the poet of community' (143), but only as a concession to counterbalance his profound sense of the alienation involved in Wordsworth's devotion to the eternal. His comment on 'Lucy Gray,' in the same vein as his comment on love poetry (above), illustrates the point of dehumanization:

> there is too much reason to fear that for half his readers his 'solitary child' *is generalised into a mere 'little girl,'* and that they never receive the main impression he wished to produce. Yet his intention is announced in the opening lines, and as clearly shown in the lovely final stanzas, which give even to this ballad the visionary touch ... (143, my emphasis)

There is, no doubt, some justification for Bradley's animus against realist and biographical readings. One may recall Wordsworth's own description of Peter Bell as a man for whom a primrose is a primrose and 'nothing more.' But to call them 'generalis[ation]' is the wrong charge, and is indeed the one to which Bradley's own reading is liable. Why is it considered reductive to refer the poem to a 'mere "little girl"'?

Compared to what is she 'mere'? In by-passing the dead-end of biographical readings, Bradley argues a more general symbolic or literary value for Lucy Gray ('the visionary touch'); but in the process he obliterates her status as human pure and simple, or, what is the same, underrates the importance of this status. Bradley's 'mere "little girl" ' reflects, in short, the rarefying and alienating power of transcendental symbolic reading.[6] In this, as in emphasizing the 'apocalyptic' in Wordsworth generally, Bradley creates the problems addressed by Hartman's powerful book of sixty years later.

But the dehumanizing tendencies of the transcendentalist reading of Wordsworth are first most powerfully developed in David Ferry's study, *The Limits of Mortality* (1959), which also articulates the implications for the 'Lucy Poems.' Ferry argues that 'Wordsworth's poems are major documents in the history of symbolism'; their ' "inner" or "final" or "deeper" meanings are not mere extensions or generalizations of the implications of [their] surface' (14). Natural objects are for Wordsworth 'signposts to that metaphysical place to which he wants to go'; like all signposts, however, 'if they tell us the way to get there, they also tell us that we have not gotten there. They are the sign of the incompleteness of our mission' (10–11). There are two natures for Wordsworth, then, vehicle and tenor, and Ferry's specific contribution is to argue that Wordsworth has patience with the former *only* as a vehicle for the latter. Wordsworth, for Ferry, is a metaphysical poet. Since the distinction will be important later, it is worth stressing how this conception, what I would call low or transcendental symbolism, differs from the high or immanent symbolism usually associated with romantic poetics through the advocacy of Coleridge and Schelling. High symbolism stipulates that the symbol has value both in itself and as a symbol for something beyond it; being, as Paul de Man has suggested, essentially synecdochal, it has being and meaning, and its core of being is what makes it inexhaustible to interpretation: there is always a remainder. But in the conception Ferry attributes to Wordsworth, the symbol is a 'signpost,' significant but worthless in itself.[7] Ferry's famous assertion that 'Wordsworth is not a great lover of man but almost a great despiser of him' (52) follows reasonably from this conception. He argues that this makes the poetry anti-humanistic (and 'remote ... from the ordinary reader') only 'in a certain sense' (51). Wordsworth still values the human, but only if 'we are willing to accept a definition of man by which he is enlarged – or reduced – to a glorious abstraction and simplification of himself, the exponent purely of his metaphysical capability' (50). Yet it seems to me that this is to make the poetry anti-humanistic in the only sense that matters. This anti-humanism appears, for instance, in Ferry's description of 'Tintern Abbey': the speaker learns 'not only that love of man which is another form of the love of nature, but a corresponding hatred and fear of the ordinary experience of men' (111).

The implications for the 'Lucy Poems' will be plain enough. Lucy will be 'enlarged – or reduced – to a glorious abstraction,' to the status of a symbol, and loved for that, and her death will not be immovable brute fact but rather significant of her belonging elsewhere. Ferry argues that in Wordsworth 'death' can mean 'to be related to the eternal truths of things' (71), and that is the sense he ascribes to it in the 'Lucy Poems.' Of 'She dwelt,' he remarks:

> only a poet like this speaker was wise enough in the truth of nature to love her and to know *what she stood for*. That she was a violet says not only that she was humble and pretty enough, but that she was one with nature, that she had achieved the ideal human condition of being hardly human at all. (74, emphasis added)

Ferry does hesitate to reduce Lucy *entirely* to the status of 'signpost,' but only temporarily, and he implies that she would be better could she be so reduced. In 'Three years,' he says, readers

> are asked to feel at once the pathos of the physical death (and the grief of the bereaved) and at the same time the rightness of it. For she has not 'really died,' she has only gone away to live forever with immortal nature ... (76)

In 'A slumber,' which he calls 'a distillation' of 'Three years,' Ferry again attempts to have it both ways. He says that the poem 'recognizes and accepts' mortality 'not fatuously, blandly, nor gladly, but with a full realization of the pain that change involves for human beings' (78). But while this seems to attribute a human actuality to Lucy and her death, it is not quite true to Ferry's symbolic model: if Wordsworth loves the human only as 'the exponent purely of ... metaphysical capability' (50), there is no room for love of incarnation. In the end the transcendent symbolic model wins out:

> Her death was right, after all, for by dying she was one with the natural processes that made her die, and fantastically ennobled thereby. ... Eternal [as opposed to material] nature is her true lover, and the poet's first idealization of

her was right after all, for she had nothing to do with humanity or mortality, and her true relation was to the world of eternity, from which he is excluded. (78)

If she died, how could she have 'had nothing to do with humanity or mortality'? Only by being purely symbolic and dying symbolically. There are no grounds within Ferry's argument for his claim (which anticipates Hartman) that the women of 'Louisa,' 'To a Young Lady,' and the 'Lucy Poems' are 'half-goddesses though also wholly human'; he is more consistent when he says 'It is the poet's imagination which is *finally* the subject matter of these poems' (79, my emphasis). Though Ferry presents the poems as consolatory or elegiac, he has so emphasized Wordsworth's love for 'eternal nature' that the need for consolation is inexplicable. If the hatred of incarnation is as Ferry says, to him Lucy's death can *only* be a good thing.

Geoffrey Hartman's first reading of the 'Lucy Poems' (1964) is discussed above, in chapter 2, but it belongs here also. Hartman, I argued, tries to mediate between the biographical identification of Lucy and the symbolist trading-away of Lucy by grounding her meaning *in* her humanness. If Ferry occasionally claims an ambiguous or dual nature for Lucy, Hartman does so persistently: 'We wish to know about Lucy as a person, yet feel she represents more than a person'; she is 'nature sprite and human, yet not quite either'; she is both outer and 'inner maiden' (*WP* 158). But only by giving the human value equal emphasis can Hartman justify his claim that she is also 'something more.' My purpose in considering Hartman out of place was to stress the pressure the Victorian editorial grouping has exerted on modern interpretations, but the displacement also dramatizes Hartman's continuity in the modern period. Taking his argument out of its historical sequence made it hard to follow because it literally did not follow: it is, in large part, a response to problems formulated within Wordsworth criticism only after (and in response to) the Victorians. The Victorians, who read Wordsworth as the great mediator, would not understand the need to mediate him. Inheriting Bradley's and Ferry's interpretation of Wordsworthian nature as a 'signpost' to the infinite, hence their conception of his erring loyalties, Hartman seeks in *Wordsworth's Poetry* to show how Wordsworth laboured to heal this duality, 'humanizing ... imagination,' 'binding imagination to nature or world' (xi, xvi). For a history of criticism, the revealing point is that Hartman's account is not, therefore, transparently descriptive of Wordsworth: his narrative of Wordsworth's 'labour' is equally Hartman's reinterpretive labour to rejoin the halves into which symbolist interpreters had fractured Wordsworth, or to mediate between symbolic interpretation's quest for significance and biographical and high-formalist anti-interpretism's respect for being ('the individual – person or poem' – 'should not mean but be').[8] Lucy's ontological liminality in Hartman's conception may best be viewed as the projection of his own resolute indecision, his resolution not to decide what she is, or rather whether she is or means: to say that she both is and means is in one sense to interpret her, but in another sense to refuse.

Hartman's critical inheritance of a 'wound' between the worlds of nature and of imagination in Wordsworth helps explain his insistent reading of the word 'seal' in 'A slumber' as 'heal.'[9] But the simplest illustration of his effort to save the symbolist understanding from its own liabilities is his reading of 'Strange fits' in the 'Retrospect 1971' prefaced to his 1964 study (xviii–xx). Speaking of the lover's focus on the moon, Hartman asks: is his mind 'not over-anticipating, taking the moon as its mark, so that it is already where it wishes to be – with the beloved, and beyond a changeable, sublunar world?' In other words, isn't Ferry right? Hartman's answer lies in ambivalence:

> In mood, style, and subject, his poems are a defense against ecstasy of this kind. Ecstasy, in which the soul goes out of the body, becomes ordinary and almost funny (a 'fit'). We sense the psychopathology of everyday life as the rider approaches an invisible boundary, the point at which he will go through into another world. He never does; when he wakes from his trance or dream he is very much in this world, and we do not know where his mind has been. The crash – the moment proper of discovery – is leaped or avoided. The poem swerves from this 'center' or hovers between natural events and the intimation of an ecstatic sphere. ...
>
> The poets, we know, anticipated Freud, but depth analysis will not explain this poem any more than romance does. It is with both and with neither. (*WP* xix)

The fundamental revision of Ferry is, in one sense, minor. Ferry stressed the willingness of Wordsworthian ecstasy and a correlative hatred of material being. Hartman accepts his dialectical assessment of Wordsworth's understanding of nature, revising only with respect to Wordsworth's attitude. By positing his ambivalence, his defensive 'distrust of pure imagination – of ecstasy' (*WP* xvi), Hartman produces, I think, an immeasurably deeper conception of Wordworthian nature. The poem becomes human in its very ambivalence toward the human, its 'wandering,' as Hartman calls it, between two worlds. It is a poetry of 'error' in Hartman's terms, a poetry of second sight but also of second thoughts.[10]

3. Nature as Traitor: Disenchantment Readings

Symbolist readings engage the question of material and spiritual levels in Wordsworthian nature, but another tradition, proceeding more directly from Huxley, and focusing instead on the question of Wordsworthian nature's benignity, treats the 'Lucy Poems' as 'second thoughts' in a different sense, that is, as disenchantments. Since this tradition intervenes, roughly speaking, between Bradley's transcendentalist reading and Hartman's engagement with it, I turn to consider it, including deconstructionist disenchantment-readings, before returning to Hartman's third and fourth thoughts.

Were it not for Bradley, the dialectic of nature and imagination might not be so big an issue in Wordsworth studies. The simpler question about Wordsworthian nature – at least in the phrasing – is whether his nature is benign. The answer to this question is usually, for good reason, ambivalent. When Carson Hamilton speaks in 1963 of 'the destructive split in Wordsworth's concept of Nature,' he refers not to the symbolists' division between real and ideal nature, but to one between hostile or indifferent and benign (159). In Hamilton's formulation, Wordsworth found nature benign to 'animate and inanimate objects,' but hostile to humans. He further distinguishes Wordsworth's 'two Natures' as the 'transcendental Nature' found in the lyrics (using 'transcendental' for 'benevolent,' not in the sense of Bradley and Ferry), and the 'animate and elemental Nature' in the narratives (169). Though the 'Lucy Poems,' being lyrical ballads, fall somewhere between, Hamilton's reading stresses elemental nature far more than is usual. 'Nature's influence,' he argues, is 'untrustworthy, even fictitious' in these poems, and he uses the cancelled stanza of 'She dwelt' to show that

> Wordsworth was not as mystical as some critics make him out to be in the series. The girl had something the matter with her that we might have called consumption. ... Without healing, without so much as sustaining, Nature deserted her. The whole series presents a Nature that could not do anything to prevent change, either growth or decay, except to end all change. (177–8)

Strangely enough, though, Hamilton says 'Wordsworth intended ... to make the treatment almost entirely lyric and therefore about what is, in this study, termed transcendental Nature' (178). Thus the poems have a truth to 'real' nature despite Wordsworth's idealizing intentions, which Hamilton finds especially in 'Three years.' If nature 'exhibit[s] a benign aftercare,' it is 'only in the sense that Lucy is an impersonalized, unfeeling, and otherwise impotent part of a pantheistic universe' (178).

If the last point marks a similarity with Ferry's reading, there is a profound change in attitude. Hamilton stresses the poems' revelation of nature's indifference to the human, Ferry the poet's imaginative ability to transcend the human and natural altogether. On the other hand, the contrast between both Ferry's and Hamilton's readings and, for instance, Ruskin's reading of 'Three years' shows the moderns' common ground in an *a priori* rejection of any significant beneficence of nature.

Similar to Hamilton's view are those of Spencer Hall (1971), Alan Grob (1973), and John Hodgson (1980). These critics pose the 'Lucy Poems'' ambivalence not by second-guessing Wordsworth's idealizing intentions, but by placing the poems in the context of his development. For them, the poems mark the difficult transition from pantheistic faith in 'one life' to the acknowledgment of nature's otherness and human mortality. 'Three years,' with the sting in its tail, is understandably central to this reading. Hall and Grob both read it as describing rivalry between the speaker and Nature for Lucy's hand in marriage (Hall 166–7; Grob 244). According to Grob, the 'Lucy Poems'

> express serious misgivings as to whether any purely natural theodicy ... can give meaning and purpose to such tales as that of Margaret and her ruined cottage. ... Perhaps the principal importance of the 'Matthew' and 'Lucy' poems ... is in suggesting the presence of seeds of discontent even in a period of seemingly assured faith. (Grob 204)

Hall argues that '[i]n all of these poems, nature would seem to betray the heart that loves her' (166), and he expressly rejects Ferry's assertion that the poems show '"the ideal human condition" as that "of being hardly human at all," of being "one with nature."' The poems focus on 'the difficult contradiction between the life of nature and the life of man' (168).

The poems give so little evidence of Wordsworth's or even of the speaker's attitudes that such argument amounts to little more than assertion and counter-assertion. These disenchantment-readings are obliged to fetch their plot from somewhere else; the uncertainty as to the poems' order is, as for all narrative readings, both a problem and an opportunity. Hodgson, whose reading is most historical and most interesting of these three, accepts Bateson's view of 'A slumber' as an 'eschatological vision' that 'accords perfectly with Wordsworth's "one life" tenets.' He then remarks: 'But now Wordsworth is patently disturbed by such a fate, less than wholly consoled by such a vision: "But she is in her grave, and, oh, / The difference to me!"' (53–4). The transit from 'A slumber' to 'She dwelt' enables Hodgson to hang his narrative of faith and disenchantment on the 'But' of 'She dwelt' (the only 'Lucy Poem' that uses the word as a conjunction) – which he deftly temporalizes as 'But now.' That putatively chronological ordering is not demonstrably wrong, for none is demonstrably right – but it is demonstrably concerted for a specific narrative effect.

The betrayal plot of these narrative readings derives from the famous lines in 'Tintern Abbey,' 'Nature never did betray / The heart that loved her,' invoked by both Hall (166) and Hodgson (53). But using these lines to plot the 'Lucy Poems' illustrates only the regressiveness of interpretive appeals to contextual, contemporary, or 'similar' passages. What the betrayal-readings of the 'Lucy Poems' really invoke is the ironic *reading of* these lines as 'Nature *did* betray,' and this reading, popular as it is, cannot be taken for granted. The context in 'Tintern Abbey' suggests that the betrayal lines refer to 'human nature,' not external nature:

> Oh! yet a little while
> May I behold in thee what I was once,
> My dear, dear Sister! and this prayer I make,
> Knowing that Nature never did betray
> The heart that loved her; 'tis her privilege,
> Through all the years of this our life, to lead
> From joy to joy: for she can so inform
> The mind that is within us, so impress
> With quietness and beauty, and so feed
> With lofty thoughts, that neither evil tongues,
> Rash judgments, nor the sneers of selfish men,
> Nor greetings where no kindness is, nor all
> The dreary intercourse of daily life,
> Shall e'er prevail against us ... (lines 119–32; *PW* 2:262)

The contrast with 'the sneers of selfish men,' etc., suggests that 'Nature' may mean 'blood' or 'kin,' so that the lines in question mean 'kin are kind': 'as siblings we are certain not to betray (or be betrayed by) the sibling hearts that love us.' My counter-interpretation is uncertain itself, of course, but its mere possibility illustrates how the ironic reading of these lines, invoked to support interpretations of the 'Lucy Poems,' *is* a reading, and one shaped in turn by contentious readings of Wordsworth's general experience and understanding of nature.[11] Bradley remarks that '[t]he best commentary on a poem is generally to be found in the poet's other works' (133), and the assumption is widespread; but in such cases it is not ultimately the poet who is commenting.[12]

As I argued in chapter 2, the same problematic informs Hartman's modelling of the 'Lucy Poems' on the Immortality Ode and 'Elegiac Stanzas.' In general, twentieth-century symbolist readings of Wordsworthian nature draw not only on these major poems, but also on a certain darkened notion of nature's 'ministry of fear' in *The Prelude*. But while supposing a more severe nature than Wordsworth himself ever made explicit, they ultimately subordinate its severity to an overarching benevolence – albeit a benevolence on nature's own terms. That is the qualification Hartman makes when he cites the 'betrayal' lines: 'Yet the betrayal is not absolute; it has its point of comfort' (*WP* 161). It is this consolatory view that the more strictly diachronic disenchantment-readings reject: 'In the Lucy and Matthew poems,' Hodgson (rather unaccountably) asserts, 'Wordsworth *explicitly* acknowledges the inadequacy of his belief in the "one life" fully to sustain and console him in the face of human loss' (61, my emphasis).

After Bradley's and Ferry's symbolist readings of Wordsworthian nature, these more strictly 'naturalist' readings – and Hartman's as well – served to return the poems to this-worldly human concerns: Lucy's death is not 'right, after all,' after all. But in all cases Wordsworthian nature has changed since the Victorian period, and the 'Lucy Poems' are read more darkly within its shadow. My guess is that darker readings of Wordsworthian nature are in turn functions, not just of increasing astuteness, but of darker readings of nature, period. Can we claim to have found that Wordsworth was more pessimistic than the Victorians supposed? Or is it just that we are unable to suppose him less pessimistic than ourselves, without dismissing him (à la Huxley) for naïveté? I think the latter at least largely true, especially since the problem of dissonance noted by Bradley now obtains in reverse. Now it is as hard to accept Wordsworth's cheerful affirmations – 'Nature never did betray' – as it once was to countenance the others – 'Carnage is thy daughter.' But now the way 'round' his 'strangeness and his paradoxes' lies in converting 'Nature never' to 'Nature did.' This is to say, not that the Victorians were right, but that it is hard for Wordsworthian nature not to reflect our own because it is hard for us not to credit Wordsworth with our own wisdom: so much for what Hirsch calls Wordsworth's 'typical attitudes.' The wisdom of the 'Lucy Poems' grows with Wordsworth's wisdom, which grows with ours.

In readings by Paul de Man and other deconstructionists, the views get darker still. That de Man credits Wordsworth with an 'authentic' vision I think illustrates my point; what can it mean except that, as de Man interprets Wordsworth's vision, it agrees with de Man's? What makes the deconstructionist view darker is that with deconstruction, as Derrida has put it, 'language invaded the universal problematic.'[13] For de Man, as we shall see, 'A slumber' speaks not merely of a moral breach between nature and human, but of an epistemological one.

4. Deconstruction: The Nature of Language

> How did we come to think that autumn
> Was the veritable season ... ?[14]

At the end of 'The Rhetoric of Temporality' (1969),[15] Paul de Man interprets Wordsworth's 'A slumber' as an instance of what he calls 'allegory.' His interpretation is not altogether new. Though in calling it allegorical he explicitly denies that the poem is 'ironic' (223), his reading of it as a tale of enlightenment, as moving from 'mystification' to 'wisdom' – or to 'insight into the rocky barrenness of the human predicament' (225) – puts one in mind of Cleanth Brooks's famous 'ironical' reading. Brooks claims that 'her unnatural slumber ... has waked him out of his' and that he now beholds her 'held by earthly time in its most powerful and horrible image' ('Irony' 736). But whatever debt or continuity it has with previous readings (none are mentioned), de Man's does more than illustrate the interpretive projection of a contemporary conception of nature. For de Man 'Nature' is itself a linguistic effect, and therefore what he calls the 'human predicament' is determined not by nature but by the nature of language. 'Death,' he says elsewhere, 'is a displaced name for a linguistic predicament' (*Rhetoric of Romanticism* 81). 'The Rhetoric of Temporality' is a particularly famous and influential essay – in Culler's phrase, 'the most photocopied essay in literary criticism' (*Blindness and Insight* xvi) – and it uses 'A slumber' as a main support for a revisionary historical argument of considerable sweep. Since this argument also involves a surprising degree of apparently deliberate deception, it makes a good introduction to the ethic of strong misreading.

De Man's essay has two sections, the first discussing 'Allegory and Symbol' as antithetical modes, the second, though it is titled simply 'Irony,' making a parallel argument about irony and 'nineteenth-century realism' (222). These revisionary arguments – I concentrate on the former here – have three distinct levels: historical, theoretical, and (though de Man deplores 'the association of rhetorical terms with value judgments' [188]) evaluative. On the historical level de Man challenges 'the assumed predominance of the symbol as the outstanding characteristic of romantic diction' (198), arguing chiefly against the literary histories of Earl Wasserman and M.H. Abrams. On the theoretical level, he contends that the usual mode of distinguishing allegory from symbol, as different modes of reference, is 'of secondary importance,' since their primary distinction is temporal. Symbol is a synchronic and 'spatial' mode, whereas allegory is diachronic: 'in the world of allegory, time is the originary constitutive category,' for 'the allegorical sign refer[s] to another sign that precedes it' (207). Thus the Derridean view of all language as differance is identified with a particular literary mode; the regressive signifying operations of allegory are held to acknowledge both the true nature of language and our 'truly temporal predicament' (222).[16] Hence the third level of de Man's argument, his reversal of 'the valorization of symbol at the expense of allegory' (188). Symbol is 'self-mystification,' and the distinction between the two 'becomes a conflict between a conception of the self seen in its authentically temporal predicament and a defensive strategy that tries to hide from this negative self-knowledge' (208).

The 'self-mystification' with which de Man arraigns the symbolic mode, chiefly in Coleridge's theorization, is the myth of continuity between self and nature, subject and object – in Coleridge's phrase, 'the one life within us and abroad' (quoted, 194). If de Man were criticizing Coleridge and his critics merely for locating 'the unifying principle ... within nature' (194), or for asserting 'the priority of natural substances over the consciousness' (196), it would be easy to reply with quotations more cognizant of the subject's imposition of this continuity: 'in our life alone does nature live.'[17] But de Man himself notes that Coleridge can 'insist on the need for the self to give life to the dead forms of nature'

(196). The genius of de Man's critique lies in the suggestion that the very wavering or indecision commonly seen in romantic epistemology, between an objectivist insistence on the 'presence of nature' and a subjective-idealist 'assertion of a radical priority of the subject' (196), is indissociable from symbolist assumptions, and is itself the evasion.[18] The symbolist world-view, he contends, imposes a 'genuine impasse' (198) or 'confusion' as to the 'priority' of subject and object (196-8). Though he implies that this 'confusion' (both senses of the word are operative) is a strategic evasion of the undesirable consequences that would ensue from decisively prioritizing either self or nature, he questions whether the confusion is the romantics' or the critics': it seems 'the main romantic problem,' he notes, only so long as we assume the 'predominance of the symbol as the outstanding characteristic of romantic diction' (198). In other words, if we understood the romantics as allegorists, the subject-object question could not arise because there would be no object; the subject would be in relation purely to language and time.[19] But in suggesting that the subject-object 'confusion' in romanticism is itself the function of our own interpretive assumptions, de Man poses a shrewd and bedevilling analogy: the romantic is to nature as the symbolist interpreter is to romanticism. In each case the subject or reader is craftily 'confused,' happily uncertain as to whether the object is invented or discovered. But in each case the impasse or confusion is really an evasion of the 'painful knowledge' (207) that the subject cannot know the object at all, since the object is a delusive effect of differance.

What follows, then, is de Man's decision of this 'genuine impasse' in favour of differance. Paradoxically, however, this decision consists in claiming knowledge of his own immediate object, in affirming the actual historical predominance of allegory over symbol in romantic writings. Arguing first for the role of allegory in 'French pre-romanticism,' specifically Rousseau's *La Nouvelle Héloïse* (199–205), he then generalizes fantastically from this single case: 'Similar allegorizing tendencies ... are present ... in all European literature between 1760 and 1800' (205). The 'are present' is a remarkably, and I think deliberately, decisive objectivism in contrast with de Man's own indecision and meta-confusion a few pages earlier ('Does the confusion originate with the critics, or does it reside in the romantic poets themselves?' [198]). For there, as we must recall, the question was precisely one of the '*presence* of nature' (196, my emphasis) to the romantics. Since their indecision turned out to be, according to de Man, a self-comforting strategy comparable to and indeed constitutive of symbolism itself, since it permitted the vacillation between prioritizing subject (hence the possibility of interpretive freedom) and object (hence the possibility of knowledge and communication), de Man now presumptively rejects indecision. Now, as his sole example of 'allegorizing tendencies ... in all European literature,' de Man pits a decisively allegorical Wordsworth against the symbolical Coleridge.

Even the case for Wordsworth is built on only two examples. The first is an early passage from the first of the three 'Essays upon Epitaphs' (c. 1810), a passage that de Man presents as 'an allegorization of the geographical site' (206). M.H. Abrams holds that romantic loco-descriptive poems describe a 'present, particular, and almost always precisely located' landscape whose meaning is 'brought to it by the private mind which perceives it.'[20] On the contrary, de Man argues, the romantics were actually rediscovering the old allegorical mode after the loco-descriptive movement of the eighteenth century:

> in observing the development of even as geographically concrete a poet as Wordsworth, the significance of the locale can extend so far as to include a meaning that is no longer circumscribed by the literal horizon of a given place. The meaning of the site is often made problematic by a sequence of spatial ambiguities, to such an extent that one ends up no longer at a specific place but with a mere name whose geographical significance has become almost meaningless. Raising the question of the geographical locale of a given metaphorical object (in this case, a river), Wordsworth writes:
>
>> 'The spirit of the answer [as to the whereabouts of the river] through the word might be a certain stream, accompanied perhaps with an image gathered from a Map, or from a real object in nature – these might have been the letter, but the spirit of the answer must have been, as inevitably – a receptacle without bounds or dimensions; – nothing less than infinity.'
>
> Passages in Wordsworth such as the crossing of the Alps or the ascent of Mount Snowden [sic], or texts less sublime in character, such as the sequence of poems on the river Duddon, can no longer be classified with the locodescriptive poem of the eighteenth century. In the terminology proposed by Abrams, passages of this kind no longer depend on the choice of a specific locale, but are controlled by 'a traditional and inherited typology' ... (189–90/206)[21]

As Clifford Siskin has pointed out (30–1), de Man not only takes his Wordsworth passage out of context, but seriously misquotes it in order to present it as 'allegory.' In Wordsworth's context the passage illustrates a point de Man would surely regard as 'self-mystification': that 'intimation or assurance within us, that some part of our nature is imperishable.' In introducing his essay on epitaphs, Wordsworth discusses the function of epitaphs and monuments. He argues, via the passage discussed by de Man, that even before they have reason enough to understand it perfectly or to wish for remembrance, 'very young children' have a 'sense of immortality':

Never did a child stand by the side of a running stream, pondering within himself what power was the feeder of the perpetual current, from what never-wearied sources the body of water was supplied, but he must have been inevitably propelled to follow this question by another: 'Towards what abyss is it in progress? what receptacle can contain the mighty influx?' And the spirit of the answer must have been, though the word might be sea or ocean, accompanied perhaps with an image gathered from a map, or from the real object in nature – these might have been the *letter*, but the *spirit* of the answer must have been *as* inevitably, – a receptacle without bounds or dimensions; – nothing less than infinity. We may, then, be justified in asserting, that the sense of immortality, if not a co-existent and twin birth with Reason, is among the earliest of her offspring ... (*Prose* 2:50–1, emphases in original)

The thoroughness with which de Man alters this passage and suppresses its context suggests that he does so on purpose. The Wordsworthian child is concerned, not merely with the stream's 'whereabouts,' but with its source and destiny; the stream itself is not 'metaphorical,' but is supposed to be actual ('*the* real object in nature'); the 'spirit of the answer' presents itself not allegorically, 'through the word,' as de Man's misquotation has it, but 'though the word,' in spite of the letter. That Wordsworth poses this as a child's reading of landscape (another detail de Man elides) suggests that it depends on a natural symbolism, not on a 'traditional and inherited typology,' of which a child-interpreter would be unaware. De Man follows his analysis of this passage with a generalization:

Whether it occurs in the form of an ethical conflict, as in *La Nouvelle Héloïse*, or as an allegorization of the geographical site, as in Wordsworth, the prevalence of allegory always corresponds to the unveiling of an authentically temporal destiny. This unveiling takes place in a subject that has sought refuge against the impact of time in a natural world to which, in truth, it bears no resemblance. (206)

The clash between this conclusion and Wordsworth's own rhetoric of 'infinity' and 'immortality' is so extreme that one almost suspects a hoax. It would not be easy to find worse passages in Wordsworth than those cited by de Man to illustrate 'the prevalence of allegory' in de Man's sense of the term. The Alps passage, presenting crag, stream, and clouds as 'types and symbols of Eternity' (*Prelude* 6:639), is one of the very few places where Wordsworth actually uses the word 'symbol' in its Coleridgean sense, for natural rather than conventional signifiers.[22] The Snowdon passage not only offers a very specific geographical scene as 'the type' and 'emblem of a mind / That feeds upon infinity,' but explicitly emphasizes the 'mutual domination' and 'interchangeable supremacy' that de Man derides as symbolic 'confusion' of subject and object (*Prelude* 14:66–71, 81–4). The apostrophe to Imagination preceding the Alps passage (6:592–616) has a similarly confusing function, and so does the passage from the 'Essays upon Epitaphs': does the river itself betoken 'infinity,' or is the point that a child's mind will 'find' infinity wherever it looks? In short, de Man does not merely oppose allegory in Wordsworth to the symbolical 'self-mystification' of Coleridge; he does so by manipulating Wordsworth's most apparently symbolic passages. Yet aside from the extremity of the deception (even de Man's page reference for the prose passage is wrong), there is little to indicate that he is anything but in earnest.

De Man's treatment of his second text, 'A slumber,' is more subtly deceptive. Having discussed the structure of irony, he questions if there are texts that have 'transcended irony without falling into the myth of an organic totality or bypassing the temporality of all language.' And after musing over this question, he concludes:

> it might be better to approach the question ... by making a brief comparison of the temporal structure of allegory and irony.
>
> The text we can use for our demonstration has the advantage of being exceedingly brief and very well known. It would take some time to show that it falls under the definition of what is here being referred to as 'allegorical' poetry; suffice it to say that it has the fundamentally prefigurative pattern that is one of the characteristics of allegory. The text clearly is not ironic, either in its tonality or in its meaning. We are using one of Wordsworth's Lucy Gray poems:
>
> [quotes 'A slumber,' 1850 version]
>
> Examining the temporal structure of this text, we can point to the successive description of two stages of consciousness, one belonging to the past and

mystified, the other to the *now* of the poem, the stage that has recovered from the mystification of a past now presented as being in error ... (204–5/223–4)[23]

De Man develops this reading for two pages, stressing the contrast between the speaker's 'mystified world of the past, when the temporal reality of death was repressed,' and the 'present that, however painful, sees things as they actually are' (224). He then heavily stresses something so 'obvious' it might be missed: the poem is organized 'as a temporal sequence,' such that the speaker remains self-identical ('unique throughout') and 'the difference has been spread out over a temporality ... in which the conditions of error and of wisdom have become successive.' This, he argues, is a point of modal idealization: it 'is possible within the ideal, self-created temporality engendered by the language of the poem, but it is not possible within the actual temporality of experience' (225). But if, as a 'successive mode,' allegory idealizes temporality, it knows its 'illusion of a continuity ... to be illusionary.' It is 'determined by an authentic experience of temporality' (226).

The important point of this argument is, I think, what is most casually assumed rather than argued: that 'A slumber' 'falls under the definition of what is here being referred to as "allegorical" poetry.' Whatever de Man means by 'the fundamental prefigurative pattern,' it does not 'suffice' that the object have 'one of the characteristics of allegory.'[24] The demonstration he begs is the crucial one. As Hirsch observes, 'an interpreter's preliminary generic conception of a text is constitutive of everything that he subsequently understands,' but it is also 'highly presumptive, since the interpreter may easily mistake the text's genre' (*Validity* 74, 236n). While I would question Hirsch's assumption that the text has an objectively correct genre, his basic contention holds for de Man's modal presumption as well: reading a text *as* allegory may make it *seem* allegory, but cannot prove that it *is* allegory. Even the alternative de Man poses is highly presumptive: by locating this discussion in the 'Irony' section, by citing 'A slumber' so casually for 'a brief comparison of the temporal structure of allegory and irony,' and by declaring that 'the text clearly is not ironic,' he encourages even a sceptical reader to object that the poem is not allegorical but ironic. Either way, of course, he wins, for whether as 'irony' or 'allegory' (in his sense of these terms) the poem will be in a mode 'determined by an authentic experience of temporality' (226) – which is 'the void of ... temporal difference' (207). However it may have been intended, de Man's mere assumption has been immensely successful in persuading his readers, not that 'A slumber' may be read as, but that it is allegory.[25]

The presumption that 'A slumber' is allegory serves de Man's argument on all levels. On the historical level, de Man can quickly project the allegorical wisdom he reads in the poem onto the author, as 'Wordsworth's wisdom' (226), and by extension onto romanticism in general, in support of his thesis that 'allegorizing tendencies ... are present ... in all European literature between 1760 and 1800' (205). Even if this wisdom about our 'truly temporal predicament' (222) is not the wisdom of all romanticism, it is the wisdom romanticism must come to: as an allegory of 'two stages of consciousness' (224), 'A slumber' is an eight-line literary history of the very transition de Man is arguing, from symbolic mystification (pre-romantic analogism, Coleridge) to allegorical enlightenment (Wordsworth, post-romanticism, de Man). On the theoretical and evaluative levels, the presumption that allegory is 'present' gives de Man a claim to knowledge and clarity in sharp contrast with the symbolist 'confusion' as to the priority of subject and object. Taken by itself, that 'confusion' appeared to respond to a 'genuine impasse,' to a stark impossibility of knowledge. Only by contrast with the certainty to which de Man pretends does it seem a discretionary and wilful 'repress[ion]' (224) of a possible knowledge, hence 'self-mystification' (208), 'bad faith' (211).

And yet these accusations are in turn the main supports for de Man's own claims to 'insight' and 'wisdom'; on this point his logic is perfectly circular. Rather than *demonstrate* the 'authenticity' of 'the temporal relationships that exist within a system of allegorical signs' (208), de Man contrasts symbol and allegory in a quasi-puritanical opposition between self-indulgence and sufferance, in order to associate allegory with self-renunciatory virtue.[26] Symbol is systematically aligned with 'sensualis[m]' (205), 'seductiveness' (206), 'nostalgia and the desire to coincide,' and 'illusory identification with the non-self' (207); allegory, with 'painful knowledge,' 'negative self-knowledge' (207–8), a 'truly temporal predicament' (222), or 'insight into the rocky barrenness' (225). Of course, only if the symbolist 'impasse' is viewed as discretionary is it possible to suspect its 'confusion' as a matter of desire and seduction, and only on this view does the contrary stance, associated with ascetic 'renunciation' (205, 207) and 'pain,' appear to be knowledge, a consciousness imposed on the unwilling subject from without. In short, the only argument de Man presents for his view as 'knowledge' and 'authenticity' is its association with pain, just as his only demonstration for symbolism's falsehood is its association with comfort: what is painful must be true. This rhetoric – I call it 'pessimism as epistemology' – turns on the insight that myths are made for comfort, but fallaciously infers that no one would create a painful falsehood; more simply, it turns on the epistemological posture of passivity: if it is suffered, it is not imagined. In Jameson's version, 'History is what hurts.' But this resource for claiming knowledge is common to romanticism itself: 'Sorrow is knowledge'; 'welcome ... frequent sights of what is to be borne!'[27] But what it overlooks is the self-comforting role of its own epistemological claims: 'sorrow is knowledge' is comfort and happiness, and, on its own reasoning, is falsehood. From this I conclude only that pain cannot be used, as de Man uses it, for a marker of knowledge. But in associating symbolism with 'seductiveness' and the 'desire to coincide,' and allegory with 'rocky barrenness,' de Man's argument also has the sexist overtones indissociable from its ascetic tradition. Symbol would appear to be woman. If I am right to understand his allegory-reading of 'A slumber' as an allegory of the literary history he advocates, 'the lady' who has died represents symbol, with all its 'seductiveness,' *femme fatale* to ascetic knowledge; hence the 'de-mystifying power of [her] death' (224). De Man's reading is overtly anti-symbolist, but it nonetheless approximates the effects of the transcendental symbolist readings in conceptualizing and dehumanizing the 'she,' and even in making her death seem 'right, after all' (Ferry 78).

Putting aside the evaluative argument, de Man brings a revisionary historical argument of considerable breadth to rest on little more than two readings of Wordsworth, one involving a gross misquotation, the other merely presuming its central point.[28] Two questions arise: how and why does he make so much hang upon so little? And why have his contentions been so successful? In answer to the first question, I think the possibility of a solemn hoax, or parody, must be entertained. De Man's argument combines a severe scepticism with routine claims to 'wisdom,' 'knowledge,' and 'insight.' The paradox is most stark in his comments on the 'successive' structure of allegory in 'A slumber':

> The *difference* does not exist within the subject, which remains unique throughout. ... The difference has been spread out over a temporality which is exclusively that of the poem and in which the conditions of error and of wisdom have become successive. *This is possible within the ideal, self-created temporal-*

> *ity engendered by the language of the poem, but it is not possible within the actual temporality of experience.* (225, second emphasis added)

Why should the growth through error and suffering to 'wisdom' be 'not possible within the actual temporality of experience'? Because, according to de Man, temporal succession is merely an effect 'engendered by ... language.' '[F]actual experience,' he explains in connection with 'irony,' is 'a succession of isolated moments lived by a divided self' (226). But while allegory creates 'the illusion of a continuity,' it also 'knows [this continuity] to be illusionary' (226). On de Man's reading, then, 'A slumber' is a narrative of enlightenment, but in a narrative mode that 'knows' itself to be illusionary; its wisdom consists in knowing that wisdom is illusionary. Like all 'allegory,' this one is 'authentic' only in that *while* it falsifies experience it acknowledges its falsification. The superiority of allegory to symbol is its acknowledgment, or foregrounding, of the differential structure and constitutive function of all language.

This view of narrative is, of course, eminently applicable to the history propounded by de Man's essay. If he reconstructs literary history from a few small and tenuous examples, in doing so he suggests that whatever history we have is always, already a construction. The logic might be compared to what Bakhtin calls the 'gay deception,' which is motivated by 'a radical scepticism toward any unmediated discourse and any straightforward seriousness.' As Bakhtin explains, such 'a *lie* [is] justified because it is directed precisely to *liars*' (*DI* 401). But de Man's contemporary essay, 'Literary History and Literary Modernity,' suggests that his own reasoning may derive rather from Nietzsche's *On the Use and Misuse of History for Life*. In the last paragraph of that essay, de Man proposes:

> To become good literary historians, we must remember that what we usually call literary history has little or nothing to do with literature and that what we call literary interpretation – provided only it is good interpretation – is in fact literary history. (*Blindness and Insight* 165)

As literary history, 'The Rhetoric of Temporality' has a parodic potential that highlights this linkage of history and interpretation. In projecting a momentous revisionary narrative on the basis of a few highly selective examples, in projecting attitudes upon authors, and thence on periods, on the basis of highly presumptive reclassifications and forced readings, even in taking a passage out of context and misquoting it, de Man does little more than exaggerate standard procedures – and standard problems – in literary history.

In this sense, de Man's procedures should make his readers suspicious not just of him but also of themselves. When he contends that 'allegorical tendencies are present ... in' romanticism, I am happy to criticize his 'myth of presence.' But when he presents Wordsworth's Alps or Snowdon passage as allegorical, I am tempted to argue that both are symbolic. Can I be sure, or am I merely falling back on the 'assumed predominance of the symbol' that he puts in question? Is not my insistence on the symbolic nature of these passages as presumptive as his presumption that 'A slumber' *is* allegory? To take another example, when de Man reads 'A slumber' as allegory, projects his own wisdom on the speaker, and then claims it as 'Wordsworth's wisdom,' this seems to reverse Hirsch's procedure of referring to the author's 'typical attitudes' in order to determine genre and meaning. But when we consider both that what Hirsch considers 'typical attitudes' are unavoidably inferred from the received but fallible interpretation of other texts, and that there is no reason to assume that the text he is attempting to interpret is typical, is de Man's procedure any less certain? De Man articulates and illustrates the problematic of literary history as profoundly as anyone, and simultaneously warns us that to fall back on a high moral tone may be to have missed 'the lesson of Paul de Man' entirely.

In suggesting de Man's 'parodic potential,' I would, however, stress the word 'potential' and defer almost infinitely the question of intent. Whatever their intent, I think the potential of his extremely leveraged arguments remains the same, and that we will learn most from them when we take them personally, as versions rather than opposites of our own 'accuracy.' At the same time, the short-term effects suggest that de Man's parody was misjudged, and perhaps over-subtle. His essay has been read far more as authority than as a questioning of authority; its strength has been more evident than its misreading. That is a danger of 'strong misreading': in taking authoritative or closural interpretation to an extreme, it may foreground itself, or it may simply impose itself.

Two notable readings in the train of de Man's illustrate both the mode of his influence, or appropriation, and the typicality of the concerns projected on the poetry by his view of nature as a linguistic effect. In 'The Lucy Poems: Wordsworth's Quest for a Poetic Object' (1973), Frances Ferguson reads the usual five together as a 'renunciatory' sequence that 'call[s] into question the very possibility of locating an object of representation or a signified,' and thus marks Wordsworth's 'recognition of the primacy of words' (*Wordsworth* 176, 174). By taking Lucy as the generic 'object of representation,' or transcendental signified, Ferguson reads the poems in which she 'is repeatedly and ever more decisively traced out of existence' (174), in which it is found that 'that love is compounded of nothing but *absence*' (184), as the 'poetic history of various stages in the poet's accession of knowledge' (187). Wordsworth learns 'that Lucy is essentially unknowable' (193), that is, that poetry is not referential.

Like de Man's, this 'renunciatory' or 'ascetic' reading denies the subject-object dialectic and attributes to Wordsworth the paradoxical expression of a 'cryptic wisdom' (192) that both expression and knowledge are impossible.

> With the Lucy poems, Wordsworth's poetics move into an almost unimaginably ascetic stance in which poetry appears to admit that it can justify itself neither as self-expression nor by an appeal to the reality of its subjects. Self-expression becomes a conspicuously vexed enterprise as the poet keeps continually expressing the deficiencies of his previous, deluded notions; and the 'reality' of the poetic object comes to seem beside the point in poems which finally assert that such 'reality' can never be known, whether it exists or not. (193–4)

Yet Ferguson's reading depends, like de Man's, on certain presumptions to the knowledge of *her* object: first, on the generic presumption that the poems form a narrative sequence, and second, on the presumption that Lucy is not, and cannot be, an actual object of reference. Again like de Man, Ferguson notes that a narrative of enlightenment is paradoxical: 'Adequate critical discourse on these poems can only try to balance their scheme of temporal progress against the recognition that the progress is itself delusive' (180). But note that she is speaking of '*their* scheme of temporal progress.' Her establishment of this 'progress' is, necessarily, deceptive:

> Problems about discussing the Lucy poems as a group should ... be outlined. Only four of the five poems appeared in the same edition until 1820, and it was 1815 before Wordsworth shifted the order of them to give 'A slumber did my spirit seal' the final position (which 'Three years ... ' had originally occupied). ... Critics have from Wordsworth's day felt the continuities among the Lucy poems so strongly as to suggest that they are commentaries upon one another,

but the nature and limits of those continuities can emerge most clearly through following Wordsworth's final order for his five ways of looking at Lucy. His order for the poems – along with its notable shift from the 'love poems' of the affections to the imagination – justifies itself, in so far as it too provides an implicit commentary on the poems by establishing for them the logical structure of a negative quest romance. (177)

Ferguson's factual error (all five of the poems appeared in 1815) is probably unimportant. But the rest, while ostensibly historical and critical, seems designed to repress the grouping's genesis in Victorian editorial practice. Saying that 'Wordsworth shifted the order of them to give "A slumber ... " the final position' implies that Wordsworth conceived of a grouping, that he shifted his ordering *for* this poem, hence that he included it, and hence that it refers to 'Lucy.' (That supposition is crucial for Ferguson's subsequent argument that 'A slumber' 'is the first poem *in the Lucy cycle* in which the name of Lucy never appears' [192, my emphasis], and hence that it actually elides Lucy.) The claim that 'Critics have from Wordsworth's day felt the continuities among the Lucy poems' makes the grouping seem to pre-date the editors' efforts, but it has never been proved. (A note appended to this remark cites only Ferry's *The Limits of Mortality*, which does not date 'from Wordsworth's day.') The earliest faint suggestion of such a grouping dates, as we have seen, from 1831, and thereafter there is no mention of it until well after Wordsworth's death. Moreover, to speak of 'Wordsworth's order for the poems' is to imply that they proceed in one line. Ferguson notes that they fall under two headings, but not that eighty-one poems separate them (in the 1850 edition). In appearing to concede 'problems' with the grouping, she actually rationalizes it.

The second presumption on which Ferguson's reading relies is that Lucy *is* merely an effect of the 'primacy of words.' On this point she is initially tentative: noting how little the poems actually state about Lucy, she suggests that 'there may be a fundamental category mistake in seeing her as a human being – she is, perhaps, a flower (or a simile, or a metaphor)' (175). But the possibility of Lucy's human existence is increasingly denied, not by the poems but by the critic: 'Lucy ... did live unknown; no one had seen her alive' (184); she 'now seems never to have been born' (191); 'he had profaned the idea of Lucy by supposing that she could have lived,' and 'had diminished the idea of Lucy by supposing that she could have been human' (192); 'Lucy *properly* exists in the poet's mind as an idea unanalogized, unimaged, unnamed' (193, my emphasis). Like the symbolist critics, Ferguson makes sense of Lucy by attributing to her a purely conceptual status; her observation on 'I travelled,' that the speaker 'rightly sees the path to the love of absence as lying through the love of sense' (186), wittily reproduces the symbolist view of Bradley and Ferry, only with 'absence' written in the place where they wrote ideality. But to the symbolist reduction of Lucy to sign-post or signifier, Ferguson's value terms ('properly,' 'rightly') add a positive caveat *against* assuming her actual existence: that way lies delusion. Tracing Lucy 'out of existence' is not for Ferguson a fault in Wordsworth but a virtue, an ascetic 'wisdom.'[29]

Yet a third version of de Man's reading, in J. Hillis Miller's 'On Edge: The Crossways of Contemporary Criticism' (1979), is couched within an institutional argument and so helps to locate the political or disciplinary bearings of Lucy's allegorization. Miller enumerates the signs of a crisis in the American 'discipline of literary study': fears of irrelevance, mounting evidence that students are not learning to 'write well' or to 'read well either,' and a proliferation of 'alternatives in literary methodology.'[30] Literature departments must follow the dinosaur, he asserts, or 'make changes which would allow them to survive in a new cultural situation' (97), but he does not explicitly offer a program for such changes. Instead he offers a reading of 'A slumber' 'to "exemplify" one mode of ... interpretation,' deconstruction (110). The curious emphasis Miller places on the survival of the 'discipline' rather than on the achievement of its functions recalls the pro-disciplinary polemics of Hirsch and his followers; his willingness to rest a world of consequences on his reading of this tiny poem recalls not just them but de Man also. For whatever reasons, 'A slumber' has become Archimedes' fulcrum for the discipline of English studies.

Miller's closing generalizations on deconstruction show the point of leverage:

In a passage in *The Will to Power* Nietzsche says: 'To be able to read off a text as a text without interposing an interpretation is the last-developed form of "inner experience" – perhaps one that is hardly possible.' If it is hardly possible, it may not even be desirable, since interpretation, as Nietzsche also elsewhere says, is an active, affirmative process, a taking possession of something for some purpose or use. In the multitudinous forms of this which make up the scene of literary study, perhaps the true fork in the road is between two modes of this taking possession, two modes of teaching literature and writing about it. One mode already knows what it is going to find. Such a mode is controlled by the presupposition of some center. The other alternative mode of reading is more open to the inexhaustible strangeness of literary texts. This enigmatic strangeness much literary study busily covers over. The strangeness of literature remains, however. ... The strangeness lies in the fact that language, our Western languages at least, both affirm logic and at the same time turn it on edge, as happens in 'A Slumber ... ' If this is the case, the alternative mode of literary study I have tried to exemplify both can and should be incorporated into college and university curricula. (110–11)

In contrasting deconstruction, as a mode of interpretation, with that which 'already knows what it is going to find' and which 'covers over,' Miller appears to be claiming to have found Nietzsche's way of 'read[ing] off' – a hermeneutics that dispenses with pre-understanding, that is non-reductive, that reveals '*the* ... strangeness of literary texts.'[31] Moreover, in offering deconstruction as the new mode of 'objective interpretation,' he assumes the same disciplinary consequences for this discovery as Hirsch assumed for his.

Like de Man's and Ferguson's, Miller's interpretation combines a posture of epistemological scepticism with a tendency toward dogmatism. In this case, the scepticism targets the 'referential,' 'metaphysical,' and 'dialectical' (101) assumptions of conventional readings, while the dogmatism appears in the deconstructionist reading by which they are displaced. His reading of 'A slumber' alternates between 'dialectical' exercises, which turn out to be ironic, and more earnest deconstructionist operations. Thus, the poem 'seems at first to be organized around a systematically interrelated set of binary oppositions,' of which Miller offers an extensive catalogue: 'slumber against waking; male as against female; sealed up as against open ... ' (102). These abstracted binaries then serve to produce reductive generalizations: 'The second line, for instance, repeats the first, and then lines three and four say it over again' (103). But since logical binaries are merely logical, and are 'both present and at the same time undermined by the text' (101), this parody of interpretation must give way to its renunciation and enlightenment: 'My account has been a little too logical ... ' (105). Miller's central example of a 'dialectical' reading is a psychobiographical one (105–7), and as such it is (though not in particulars) reminiscent of Hartman. Lucy is identified with Wordsworth's mother, who died when he was eight; since 'the poet wants to efface that death' but also finds in that death 'the condition of life and poetry,' he must 'have it both ways.' According to this reading, Wordsworth resolves the problem by reenacting the mother's death in Lucy's, who remains 'both alive and dead, still available in life and yet already taken by Nature' (106–7). As a both-and solution, this idealization is notably similar to the convenient 'confusions' of which de Man accuses symbolist reading. Miller's sceptical turn upon it recalls de Man's view of allegory as a narrative form that 'knows' itself to be 'illusionary':

> 'A Slumber ... ' dramatizes the impossibility of fulfilling this fantasy, or rather it demonstrates that it can only be fulfilled in fantasy, that is, in a structure of words in which 'thing' can mean both 'person' and 'object,' in which one can have both stanzas at once, and can, like Lucy, be both alive and dead. ... To have it as wordplay, however, is to have it as the impossibility of having it, to have it as permanent loss and separation, to have it as the unbridgeable gap between one meaning of the word 'thing' and the other. (107)

Assuming that the poem's 'fantasy' is as Miller says (a point I have some difficulty seeing), there is nothing very remarkable about his demystification of it except his attribution of this demystification to the text. How does the poem *demonstrate* that the fantasy 'can only be fulfilled in fantasy' – does it say, 'I am only a fantasy,' or does it merely present its content in a mode its interpreter assumes to be fantasy? In a move that rounds out the de Manian pattern, Miller first credits the speaker with this renunciation of his fantasy, but then, recognizing the claim to enlightenment as another idealization, renounces it:

> The speaker was 'sealed,' as she was. Now he knows. ... To know, however, ... is to speak from the impersonal position of death. It is to speak as death. ... The speaker's movement to knowledge, as his consciousness becomes dispersed, loses its 'I,' is 'the same thing' as Lucy's death. (108)

In sum, Miller presents this speaker's 'movement' from delusion to a knowledge-that-is-not-knowledge as an allegory of the modern development of interpretive practice, from metaphysical delusion to deconstructionist wisdom. In viewing the poem as a 'parable' of 'the relation of metaphysics and the deconstruction of metaphysics' (101), thus as a literary history in small, he is only slightly more explicit than de Man.[32] Yet it is important to note that Miller is not *attempting* to read the poem in order to admit that reading is impossible; he is *reading* the poem *as showing* that reading is impossible. This is no frivolous paradox, but rather the containment and nullification of the very deconstructionist insights Miller pretends to wield.[33] The poem's binaries, he repeatedly asserts, lead to 'an aporia or boggling of the mind,' 'an oscillation in meaning' (101). 'The reader is caught in an unstillable oscillation'; the poem 'shimmers' (108). I think these sceptical claims are upsetting because only too true; 'A slumber' has too many variables to be stabilized. But these claims are not compatible with the 'reading off' of 'A slumber' as a history of metaphysical criticism. And yet Miller cannot resist concluding with a virtuoso old-style allegorical reading, in which the 'oscillation' is not felt in the least:

> ['A slumber'] enacts one version of a constantly repeated occidental drama of the lost sun. Lucy's name of course means light. To possess her would be a means of rejoining the lost source of light. ... The fear of the death of Lucy is the fear that the light will fail. ... The fulfillment of that fear in her actual death is the loss both of light and of the source of light. It is the loss of the logos, leaving the poet and his words groundless. ... The consciousness of the poet has survived all these deaths of the light to subsist as a kind of black light. His awareness is the light-no-light which remains when the sun has sunk and Lucy has died ... (109–10)

If this reading is in some respects dark, it remains a reading of a conventional kind; thus it stands as reassurance as to the continuity of interpretation as a 'discipline,' even as it imagines the end. Identifying Lucy as 'light' and 'grounding,' even in order to read the poem as dramatizing the loss of these things, falls back on basic referential assumptions. The epistemological scepticism of deconstruction proper is at once affirmed within the fiction, and denied in Miller's practice; it is thematized. To put it differently, reading the poem as a 'drama' of the loss of 'ground' confines this loss to the theatre, and Addison's explanation for the pleasures of tragedy applies equally well to explain the appeal of Miller's contained deconstruction: 'When we look on such hideous objects, we are not a little pleased to think we are in no danger of them. We consider them at the same time, as dreadful and harmless.'[34]

Miller's containment of deconstruction as a 'mode of ... interpretation' is, of course, indissociable from his pro-disciplinary priorities. Literature departments need to 'incorporate' this 'mode' (111) if they are to 'survive' (97), but the incorporation of deconstruction in such a face-saving program entails drawing its teeth. A predominantly anti-interpretive theory that puts 'truth' in question is recuperated as a new hermeneutic method productive of new knowledge, thus illustrating Jameson's observation that 'the rejection of interpretation' may be 'itself the source of a new method' ('Metacommentary' 6). When I refer to 'deconstruction proper' and call it 'anti-interpretive,' I mean that for Derrida (the only name Miller associates with it besides the 'certain critics' at Yale [100]), deconstruction consists above all in the theory that all our knowledge is always, already *constructed* – specifically, by language – or, in Nietzsche's pre-poststructuralist version, that 'facts are precisely what there is not, only interpretations' (Nietzsche 267).[35] Derrida's efforts to demonstrate this theory are anti-interpretive not in that they renounce interpretation (by their reasoning nothing can do that), but on the contrary in the sense that they renounce the claim of any given interpretation (which is, to be consistent, everything, including 'description,' 'commentary,' 'explanation,' and deconstruction itself) to truth of a referential, representational, or correspondential kind. Derrida recognizes the necessity of preserving concepts despite their deconstruction, or of 'preserv[ing] as an instrument something whose truth value [is] criticize[d].'[36] This rigorously sceptical procedure of bracketing concepts while using them, which 'separate[s] *method* from *truth*,' becomes in Miller's hands a serial procedure in which conventional interpretations are exploded to make way for the so-called deconstructionist one; it is not accidental that Miller's reading ('Lucy's name of course means light') appears only at the end of his essay, out of further questioning. In so far as this interpretation poses itself as non-interpretation, as matter 'of course,' as mere 'explanation of Wordsworth's little poem' (110), as not determined by pre-understanding, and as passively 'open to *the* ... strangeness of literary texts' (110), it evades its own claims to scepticism.[37] Just as Miller presents 'A slumber' as reaching knowledge-no-knowledge, 'light-no-light,' he offers his 'mode' as interpretation-no-interpretation – that familiar disciplinary dream. But rather than acknowledge 'Lucy' to be unknowable, he has read her decisively, again as in the transcendental-symbolist readings, as an intellectual abstraction: 'light.'

Yet Miller himself represents such a procedure, taken as one discovered *in* the poem, as a violence:

> The poet has himself somehow caused Lucy's death by thinking about it. Thinking recapitulates in reverse mirror image the action of the earthly years in touching, penetrating, possessing, killing, encompassing, turning the other into oneself and therefore being left only with a corpse, an empty sign. (108)

The question is whether the abstractive gesture is the poem's or its reader's. Is it impossible to read 'A slumber' without finding the 'she' 'an empty sign'?

5. The Actual and Significant Lucy

I have suggested that Hartman's dialectical readings of the 'Lucy Poems' attempt to do just that. By undeciding Lucy's status, or by projecting his indecision as *her* liminal ontology (she is 'a boundary being' [*WP* 158], inner and outer, spirit and human, symbol and 'thing' in herself), I think Hartman's interpretive practice achieves a superior mediation of the contradictory imperatives to which interpreters typically respond: Interpret! Don't interpret! His practice is also truer than others', I shall argue, to high symbolism's emphasis on the duality of the symbol, to the deconstructionist both-and, or double gesture, and to Wordsworth's own anti-mediate and stereoptical interpretive mode. This is not to claim rightness or authority for Hartman's interpretations, but it is to claim virtue of some sort for them. Where none can be exclusively valid, other claims to virtue in interpretation come to the fore. Harold Bloom suggests strength, while Stanley Fish suggests (and retracts) interestingness (*Anxiety* 19–20; *Is There a Text* 174). Less selfish virtues are imaginable.

In his later treatments of the 'Lucy Poems,' Hartman's vocabulary changes and his references broaden, but his fundamental concerns remain the same. He continues to read the poems as 'healing the wounded consciousness,' as reconciling its other-worldly allegiances with the natural and human. That is also to say that he himself continues to resist readings of these poems that reduce them to purely ideal or metaphysical meanings. As he writes of 'A slumber,' stanza 2, in 1984,

> There is loss, but there is also a calculus of gain and loss which those two stanzas weigh like two sides of a balance. Their balancing point is the impasse I have mentioned: such a death could seem better than dying into the light of common day. Yet to think only *that* is to make immutability of such value that human life is eclipsed by it. (*Easy Pieces* 152)

The 'impasse' Hartman comes to is the one de Man describes as the evasive 'confusion' imposed by symbolism; it is also what Miller describes as the 'fantasy' of 'having it both ways.' But in Hartman's view it is an ethical and not an epistemological dilemma; it is one that *ought* to make us pause. The final sentence responds, consciously or not, to Ferry's contention that the death is 'right, after all.' The oddity is Hartman's attention to the implications or consequences of that decision. Rather than simply seek to 'read off' the poem in an objective, totalizing, or persuasive fashion, Hartman tries to make its speaker recall the 'value [of] human life.' Yet he does not 'eclipse' the speaker's error, either, the terrible 'calculus of gain.' Maybe the second thought obeys no obligation, but only posits that the speaker, if he is human, must think both ways.

Hartman's double postulations can be understood as efforts to save the actual from the reductionism of transcendental-symbolist reading, but they can be understood also as functions of his own liminal theoretical stance. His essay of 1966, 'Beyond Formalism,' is easily misconstrued as a renunciation; hence the note of disappointment in Christopher Norris's observation that, '[i]n the last analysis his criticism moves not so much "beyond formalism" as round and about its ambiguous fringes' (99). Norris is right, but Hartman never claimed to leave formalism. His essay on the move 'beyond' argues that 'There are many ways to transcend formalism, but the worst is not to study forms' (56; see also Atkins 16–17). To F.W. Bateson's attack on formalism for narrowness, Hartman responds simply by broadening the term to include both formalist study and humanist (or humanizing) interpretation: 'Bateson defined *formalism* as a tendency to isolate the aesthetic fact from its human content, but I will here define it simply as a method: that of revealing the human content of art by a study of its formal properties' (42). There is a sort of historical oxymoron in this extension of formalism, in itself originally an anti-interpretism, to hermeneutics, to 'revealing ... content.'

In his practice, Hartman never forgets to mark this tension, usually with a pun. Hartman illustrates his extended sense of 'formalism,' or his move 'beyond,' by looking at readings of 'She dwelt' by Bateson and Cleanth Brooks – thus visiting, from a certain distance, the dispute officiated by E.D. Hirsch. Rather than adjudicate between them, Hartman observes that Brooks's and Bateson's 'faults are alike': 'neither critic is enough of a formalist' (42). Both are 'nonhistorical'; they generalize about Wordsworth's style without relating it to his contemporary work or to the tradition of form. Placing the poem in the context of eighteenth-century 'pointed,' 'witty,' or 'epigrammatic' style reveals its reactive or parodic qualities. Thus far, Hartman's is a more or less typical exercise in formalist literary history. But his transit toward the 'human content' is not so typical. He continues:

> The history of style itself seems to urge us beyond formalism by asking, What is the point of *point*? Conversely, what is achieved by Wordsworth's creation of so pointless, so apparently simple a style?
>
> ... It can be charged that neoclassical poetry, or lyricism Old Style, was a didactic and digital poetry – calculating, pointing, computing too much by fingers and feet. It knew its weakness, certainly; and much of the theory of the time cautions against false wit and excessive *pointe*. ... Perhaps Wordsworth comes to reveal rather than teach, and so to free poetry of that palpable design which Keats still charged him with. All truth, said Coleridge, is a species of revelation.
>
> Revelation of what? The question cannot be answered without a certain kind of pointing, as if truth were here or there, as if life could be localized, as if revelation were a property. Yet Wordsworth's concepts of nature, of natural education and of poetry, are all opposed to this reduction. ... Pointing is to encapsulate something, strength, mind, life. It is to overobjectify, to overformalize. It implies that there is a fixed locus of revelation or a reified idolatrous content.
>
> Yet pointing in this larger sense cannot be avoided: it seems inextricably tied to the referential nature of signs or the intentional character of thought. All Wordsworth can do is to emancipate the direction of the reference. The Lucy poems, taken as a sequence, remove the mimetic dependence of imagination on reality, or on any fixed order of 'this then that.' We cannot tell whether the poet is reacting to an imaginary thought or to an actual death, or which of the two came first. ... Lucy is a fiction integral to the mind: if she did not exist, she would have to be invented. Her mode of being, therefore, cannot be reduced to the imagined or the real by a temporal principle of anteriority or an ontological one of priority. (49-50)

I have elided somewhat, but I think the passage still illustrates Hartman's characteristic method. The difficult transition from form to 'human content' he negotiates through the pun on 'point,' which has both a formal and a 'larger sense.' One hesitates either to accept this pun as a conceptual connection or to write it off as mere play. Wordsworth's both-and relation to didactic 'pointing' leads to Hartman's characteristic conclusion that Lucy is not merely a pointer or symbol (Ferry's 'signpost' to the infinite), but must fall, at least to our knowledge, between the real and ideal. Thus Hartman's puns, though sometimes seen as mere playfulness, have an important function analogous to Wordsworth's own discreet flirtation with 'point'; they point without pointing, or 'emancipate the direction of the reference,' making Hartman's points just less than clear. It would not, indeed, be frivolous to compare Wordsworth's transcendence of nature (as understood by Hartman) and Hartman's transcendence of formalism. In both there is both an impatience with and a strong loyalty to, a gesture beyond with one foot within. Like Lucy's status both as herself and as signifier, Hartman's more-than-pun opens vistas beyond the formal feature and yet pauses, as he might say, on the 'threshold.'

In *Saving the Text* (1982), Hartman's treatment of 'A slumber' falls in the final chapter, 'Words and Wounds,' which is his 'counterstatement to Derrida' (though 'not a refutation') (121). In this chapter, 'for those interested in the *value* of literature' (118), Hartman poses the Keatsian and Arnoldian question: 'what kind of a physic is literature?' (122). Derrida's view of writing as 'a sort of disaffiliation' implies 'that writing cannot be an antidote to anything except itself.' In response, Hartman seeks, through 'a restored theory of representation,' to have it both ways: if 'presence is ... a ghostly *effet de réalité* produced by words,' the *effect* may still be real.

> I will try to show that the reality of the effect is inseparable, in literature, from the reality of words that conduct voice-feeling; this reality, in its discernible, empirical nearness, in its moral and mimetic impact, is the subject of 'Words and Wounds.' (121)

The reversal of literature's mere 'effect of reality' to produce 'the reality of the effect' turns on a pun ('special effect'/'effectiveness') and has a saving effect that is itself Derridean.[38] Hartman's 'counter-statement' consists in using, despite Derrida's challenges to the privilege of speech, 'voice-feeling' to describe the words of literature and hearing to describe its reading. But despite the engagement with Derrida, Hartman's project remains similar to his former efforts to move from literary form to 'human content' (or, here, human effect) without reducing the former to mere means or vehicle for the latter.

That words can 'wound' Hartman grants (123), or rather supposes, since this serves at least to establish the 'reality of the[ir] effect' (thus, in inception, Hartman invokes a rhetoric of pain not unlike de Man's). He elaborates the effectiveness of curses (123–6). All he admits into question is the effectiveness of blessing, or how words can also 'heal.'

Using 'A slumber,' among other texts, to answer this question, Hartman argues by way of a pun on 'closure' (formalist closure/healing). Indeed, his reading of the poem ends one subsection and overflows into the next, which is titled 'closure,' thus straddling the concept itself. The necessity of connecting 'the formal structure of art' with 'art as essental human experience' (149) is foremost in Hartman's mind now as in 1966, yet now he turns on himself, questioning his own punning bridges:

> who has succeeded in going from closure understood formalistically ... to art in its immediacy? Closure remains a relatively bloodless notion. ... Precisely at this juncture the impotence of aesthetic theory is felt: we are tempted to become associative and metaphorical, asserting, for instance, that the feeling of closure conveyed by Wordsworth's 'A slumber' is due to his converting a wounding thought of death into a beautiful irony. (148–9)

No better answer is offered. But Hartman's reticence in this case is no different from his offering so tenuous a connection as 'point' to bridge the stylistic character and human wisdom of 'She dwelt.' The pun is on the table, whatever it is worth; in neither case is it clear that such sound-connections are conceptually sound, but in both cases they are suggestive; they open inquiry rather than close it. And *that* sort of closure, the closure imposed by interpretations 'to stem the drive toward endless interpretation,' is not surprisingly the topic with which Hartman diverts us from any answer about the poem (149). The evasion may be frustrating if we are waiting to hear how words can finally 'heal,' but it is just this sort of passive expectation in the auditor, Hartman suggests (123, 131), that allows words to 'wound' in the first place; having 'emancipate[d] the direction of the reference,' he hesitates to do more. Hartman's sound-connections are not entirely persuasive, then, yet their function lies in this avoidance. In their very tenuousness they acknowledge not only the breadth of the chasm between the literary concerns of formalist criticism and 'human content,' but also the extent of the critic's will to bridge that chasm. Unlike de Man and Miller, Hartman does not labour to persuade, and this studious avoidance of interpretive closure is, I think, his virtue.

His unclosed reading of 'A slumber' has all the complexity of a genuinely self-reflective investigation: braving the 'confusion' of subject and object repudiated by de Man, Hartman discusses closure or 'healing' not merely as a power of the text, but also as an option of its reader. Assuming that 'A slumber' describes Lucy's death, Hartman beholds its 'mystification' of this death as its 'healing' effect, and likewise (contra de Man, though he is not mentioned) resists seeing any decisive demystification within the poem.

> The poet-slumberer ... wakes into the consciousness of death, but instead of pity or terror or the human fear that had been elided, his recognition expresses an irony: now indeed Lucy cannot feel 'The touch of earthly years.' She is what she seemed to be. His image of her has come true, but as a curse he may have laid on himself unawares. (147)

In reading the speaker's 'wake[ning] into the consciousness of death' as 'irony,' Hartman skirts the readings of both Brooks and de Man, which do find the speaker 'demystified' or disillusioned. But Hartman presents irony as a liminal mode falling just short of demystification: it falls among '[w]hat Bakhtin labels as "genres of reduced laughter"' (146); it is a mode of containment or euphemism. To presume that a text is euphemism – 'soft names,' 'flowers of speech,' as Hartman calls it – is to presume that its 'real' meaning lies hidden, which is also to license oneself to infer ('recover') this meaning. Yet Hartman's divergence from de Man and the other deconstructionists on this point is revealing. De Man criticized symbolism for its fictiveness and self-delusion, while Hartman *values* euphemism on much the same basis. He lays all the emphasis on the value of the euphemism itself *as* a mystification, as the softening of language's capacity to 'wound.' In this poem euphemism is the essence of language's 'healing' capacity. Having suggested, then, that the poet has laid a curse 'on himself unawares,' Hartman continues:

> Yet is it a curse? ... Wordsworth quiets language till myth is present only in 'unheard' form and irony is the point-zero between curse and blessing. Wordsworth's second stanza, as if a new sealing had taken place, is tonally unreadable, *leaving consciousness where it was*, strangely intact like Lucy herself. Irony leans toward silence. ... This muteness, however, is close to a mutilation, a 'blinding' of the ear and an ultimate defense against the unquiet imagination. (147–8, emphasis added)

In sum, Hartman appears to accept the de Manian reading of the poem's self-mystification but in two senses to reject the second step of demystifying it: he denies that the poem itself records a demystification, and sees no need to demystify it himself.

'Our best critics have always demystified this turn to beauty,' Hartman remarks. His example is not from de Man but is Kenneth Burke's substitution of 'Body Is Turd, Turd Body' for the closing lines of 'Ode on a Grecian Urn' (quoted, 167n25). 'Burke's interpretive readings,' says Hartman,

> erode forms of closure in art and concepts of beauty in aesthetic theory: he exhibits their illusory or purely conventional force and opens a text so much that to close it again may seem impossible. Must the aesthetic charm, then, gradually disappear from the interpreted work of art, and leave us but an intellectual construct, one with a fascinating, fallacious, teasingly evasive mode of being? (149)

Burke's concept of text as euphemism is notorious also in de Man, and particularly in Freud. But all of these interpreters are demystifiers, opening the text's euphemistic closure to 'reveal' what lies beneath as 'real' though 'latent' meaning. This accomplished, the interpretive process is closed; it is significant that de Man, for instance, never returns to 'A slumber' in print. Without wholly repudiating this procedure, Hartman questions its conclusiveness, seeking a way of 'saving the text' in its merely apparent form, mystical 'effect of reality' and all. Without arguing 'against interpretation,' he questions why latent meaning, even if it were demonstrable, should be valued to the exclusion of the ways in which it is refracted – why pain should be of better significance and interest than pleasure, 'wound' than 'healing,' depth than surface. To grant the text its own 'closure' is necessarily to leave the interpretive process open, for it is to recognize the residual surface that demystifying interpretation alone, in seeing through, cannot see. Just as Lucy must have both meaning and being, the text must have not just its significance but also its insignificance.

Hartman's style makes few concessions. One risks reading him for aperçus, not for argument, and, at the other extreme, of reducing these to a 'certain kind of pointing' he himself studiously avoids. The difficulty is not, however, entirely a matter of style. The elliptic and associative style serves Hartman's efforts to reconcile the insights of analytical or demystifying interpretation with the beauty and comfort enjoyed by weaker modes of reading. In 'The Interpreter's Freud,' the 1984 Freud Lecture at Yale, Hartman redevelops his earlier reading of 'A slumber' as euphemism; this lecture is more condescending, as befits its inclusion in the volume *Easy Pieces* (1985), but still by no means 'easy.' Here again, Hartman borrows Freud's understanding of the dream-text as euphemism while rejecting the Freudian impulse to demystify it. Psychoanalytic interpretation, like Burke's, is 'kakangelic,' a Hartman coinage for 'pessimistic' with excremental overtones. Hartman's desire is 'to understand yet delimit Freud's kakangelic mode of interpretation' (*Easy* 153). Thus his reading has two aspects: the unfolding of the text as euphemism, and the explanation why it cannot be reduced entirely.

Hartman presumes that the text is euphemistic, or that it talks of death without doing so, and he uses this presumption, much as Ferguson and James Averill use theirs, to marvel at its silences.[39] In law, there is a principle that '*Aliud est celare, aliud tacere*: To conceal is one thing, to be silent is another' (Black 73). But assuming a literary genre defined as suppression makes every silence pregnant. Some of the poem's words, Hartman suggests,

> even show Wordsworth's language penetrated by an inappropriate subliminal punning. So 'diurnal' (line 7) divides into 'die' and 'urn,' and 'course' may recall the older pronunciation of 'corpse.' Yet these condensations are troublesome rather than expressive; the power of the second stanza resides predominantly in the euphemistic displacement of the word *grave* by an image of *gravitation* ('Rolled round in earth's diurnal course'). And though there is no agreement on the tone of this stanza, it is clear that a subvocal word is uttered without being written out. It is a word that rhymes with 'fears' and 'years' and 'hears,' but which is closed off by the very last syllable of the poem: 'trees.' Read 'tears,' and the animating, cosmic metaphor comes alive, the poet's lament echoes through nature as in pastoral elegy. 'Tears,' however, must give way to what is written, to a dull yet definitive sound, the anagram 'trees.' (149–50)

If 'it is clear' that 'trees' is really 'tears,' it was never clear to anyone before Hartman. But in seeming to rule this word out at the end, he actually posits its priority: it 'give[s] way to what is written,' 'the anagram "trees."' The first puns are presumably 'inappropriate' in that they work the other way round: rather than being occluded as are 'grave' and 'tears,' these death-words – 'die,' 'urn,' 'corpse' – are unnecessarily spoken. But 'what is the point?' If the euphemistic hypothesis is granted, the puns – at least the latter ones – impose relevance, connecting form and 'human content': the 'tears'/'trees' 'anagram' suggests the theme of grieving nature, connecting the poem with the elegiac tradition.

The important question is how Hartman can 'delimit' the euphemistic de-coding licensed by his genre-presumption. If we presume euphemism, how can we rule out a 'kakangelic' reading such as this one proposed by Norman Holland?

> The maid is invulnerable, yes, but inert. Untouched because she is unable to touch. The earthy rocks and stones would ... symbolize dirt or, in the body sense, feces. She has become lifeless and worthless – like excrement. The trees and rocks might also symbolize a phallus. In effect, she has not lost a phallus – she has become one. (Holland, 'Literary' 227)

Beside such a reading (which Holland himself judges 'primitive'), the subtext that Hartman reveals seems positively restrained; the interpreter has, perhaps, his own euphemistic resources. Hartman's way of rationalizing the curb on readings such as Holland's is absurdly simple. 'A slumber' itself, or rather Hartman's reading of it, is made to answer. In 'A slumber,' he says, 'Wordsworth leaves that illusion [i.e., of stanza 1] its moment of truth as if it were natural, and not in any way out of the ordinary. He does not take pains to demystify it' (146–7). Surely this is to deny de Man's reading again. More fully, Hartman says:

> As out of Adam's first sleep an Eve arose, so out of this sealed but not unconscious spirit a womanly image arises with the same idolatrous charm. Wordsworth's image seems to come from within; it is a delusive daydream, yet still a revision of that original vision.
>
> There is, however, no sense of an eruption from the unconscious: brevity and condensation do not lead, as they do in dreams, to remarkable puns, striking figures, or deviant forms of speech. Nor is it necessary to be psychoanalytic to recognize that the trance is linked to an overidealization of the loved person. The second stanza, which reports that she has died, should, in that case, express disillusionment. Yet remarkably this does not occur: the poet does not exclaim or cry out. Both transitions, the passage from slumber to dream, and the breaking of the dream, are described without surprise or shock. (145-46)

Hartman's negative report on stanza 2 is, I think, truer to the features of the text than is de Man's assertion that it records a demystification; the poem is blank as to attitude, and Hartman refrains from presuming one. Perhaps there should be a demystification – one expects it, at least – but there is no explicit sign of one.

> Wordsworth does not actually say he projected his starry emotions upon the

girl. It is, rather, *our* habit of giving priority to the psychological state of the writer, *our* inability to consider his euphoria as a contagious identification with the girl, that makes us assume it is a dream and a delusion. (150)

Thus far Hartman is surely correct, except in slipping in the word 'euphoria,' which is as difficult to find in the text as is a demystification. But the appeal to what the speaker 'actually say[s]' is no argument for what he actually means, especially in the context of Hartman's own presuppositions of euphemistic suppression. Hartman has retreated from his role as interpreter to offer a report on interpretation. But even if darker psychoanalytic suppositions reflect '*our* habit' of reading, that is no proof that our habits are mistaken. To put it differently, Hartman's stance amounts to the interpreter's emulation of the poet's (or speaker's) own interpretive restraint; but an appeal to the poet's *mode* of reading is as helplessly regressive as the appeal of a Hirsch or a Bradley to statements or attitudes 'found in the poet's other works.' Hartman's restraint reflects ultimately his own will, pure and simple, not to demystify, to respect the 'closure' of the text.

The stand-off between Hartman and de Man returns in some respects to the one between Bateson and Brooks. The feeling of *déjà vu* is especially strong when Hartman insists that

Divided into two parts, separated formally by a blank and existentially by a death, the epitaph does not record a disenchantment. The mythic girl dies, but that word seems to wrong her. Her star-like quality is maintained despite her death, for the poet's sense of her immutability deepens by reversal into an image of *participation mystique* with the planet earth. (152)

Bateson stressed the 'pantheistic magnificence of the last two lines' (*English Poetry* 29). Hartman's appeal to things such as Wordsworth's typically eudemonic attitudes in order to justify his non-demystified reading (151–2) likewise recalls Hirsch's defence of Bateson. But there is an advance over the Brooks-Bateson dispute. Hartman does not need, as he seems to think he does, to insist on his reading over the demystified readings. The important point is that his reading itself is already twofold; rather than reiterate or ratify Bateson's reading, Hartman mediates Brooks's *and* Bateson's to insist, once again, on Lucy's dual ontology, her status both as lost person (as in Brooks) and as 'image of *participation mystique*' (as in Bateson).[40] The earlier comparison of Lucy with Eve (145), who exists both within and outside of 'Adam's dream,' marks this double conception. In this ambivalence, Hartman implies that the poem can and indeed must be read at more than one level. Even if a 'kakangelic' reading, stressing a fall or absolute loss, finds that the poem 'records a disenchantment,' the poem's illusionary, euphemistic, or 'healing' surface demands equal acknowledgment.

Yet Hartman's twofold readings differ significantly from the deconstructionist 'double-readings' of de Man or Miller in that they are not sequential. He does not read the poem once and debunk this reading, so that the text or the rival interpreter seems to have stated 'in a mode of error' what he puts right. Instead he calls attention to the coexistence of depth and surface, such that neither seems sufficient alone, and such that their very inequality continues to be a point of wonder. His 'double intention' should not, I think, be seen as a matter of any particular brand of interpretation, such as allegorical, symbolic, or formalist. It is, rather, a function of being properly any one of these things, or properly between them. Historically, the movements against allegory and toward symbolism, from symbolism to formalism, and from formalism 'beyond,' have all been motivated by a similar discontent with the oversimplification of the image, specifically with the subordination of the signifier to the signified. Coleridge criticizes allegory for 'abstraction from objects of the senses,' even though allegory originally had, in figura, a double mode of reading historical events both as themselves and as prefigurations of other events. In reaction, Coleridge stressed the combinatory nature of the symbol – 'a medium between the *Literal* and *Metaphorical*' – 'It always partakes of the Reality which it renders intelligible.' But as symbolism in turn declined toward the purely transcendental conception (a late version of which we see in Ferry), it was in turn repudiated by the formalists, who re-emphasized thingness. High formalism erred, if anything, too much in the direction of insignificant thingness, but it too has declined into hermeneutics. The symbolic tension of actuality and significance has seemed impossible to sustain for long, though it is constantly being recalled to mind. Lukács's dialectical materialism is one example of post-formalist efforts to recapture a duality similar to that which Coleridge sought in the immanent symbol. Hartman has not only gestured 'beyond formalism' toward a 'human content,' but has also, in his earliest reading of Lucy, sought to pull back on transcendental-symbolic readings to recall a human being. Both efforts to recapture the image's tensional nature accept interpretation as a project while denying its claims to sufficiency. Something always remains behind to be gathered.[41] Hence, perhaps, Hartman's constant return to these poems: they are his *omphalos*, his version of the 'holy site' or 'strait between worlds' around which, he argues, Wordsworth's obsessional 'spot syndrome' revolves (*WP* 122–3).

Hartman's practice implies a rejection of the common conception of interpretation as the displacement of the object by its representation or misrepresentation. To interpret an object in terms of its 'deep' meaning is to account for it precisely as it does *not* appear, but Hartman insists that if we must do this, we must also take account of the text as it shows itself, that is, non-interpretively. The only thing that might help us do that is apparently the text itself.

6. Conclusion: Objective Resistance and Critical Self-Discipline

> How do you know but ev'ry Bird that cuts the airy way
> Is an immense world of delight, clos'd by your senses five?
>
> – Blake

As this study has been written and rewritten (between 1984 and 1994), literary studies appear to have moved, at least in North America, from preoccupations with reader-response and deconstructionist theories and methods to apparently more extrinsic social and political preoccupations. Partly in response to this shift, this book, initially conceived as a reception-study, has been reconceived as a case-study in the emergence of English as a 'discipline.' It is important to concede that I have necessarily neglected some important political and historical problems, questions such as the relation between the popular success of Hirschean projects and their cold-war and post-Holocaust setting, or the reasons for the virtually total absence of feminist readings of these poems. That I have not considered such problems here is not, I stress, to deny their importance or even my own interest in them. But I have chosen to focus on a politics more intrinsic to interpretive argumentation. In conclusion I would like to emphasize, however, that this politics of determination and consensus, if I may call it that, is far from being as narrow in its relevance as it may seem. The political dangers of pro-disciplinary arguments that presume or pretend to greater 'knowledge' than is available, and the virtues of critical procedures that resist or defer such claims, are at issue not only in the narrow theatre of literary hermeneutics but wherever there is a question of knowing a simple or complex other, be it an artifact, a person, a species, a place, or a culture.

By the same token, I would like to emphasize that my argument should not be taken as a wholesale attack on 'the profession' or 'discipline,' or as a denial of the possibility of knowledge; it is not anti-disciplinary in so absolute a sense, though it does aspire to make some discriminations. The large body of 'Lucy Poems' criticism affords an array among which no example can be said to determine the poetry's meaning, and yet some seem superior to others. By what standards, in what terms?

Believing that the issues raised by the interpretation and knowledge of literary works are similar, even continuous, with those raised by the interpretation and knowledge of other subjects, including humans, I have assessed critical procedures in this study according to what are, I think, basically moral standards. In considering modern readings of the 'Lucy Poems,' for instance, I have usually concentrated on the ways Lucy and her death are apprehended, whether as actuality, symbol, or allegory. Early commentaries emphasizing Lucy's biographical existence found a definite but narrowly specified human content in these poems. In extreme cases, the poems became biographical documents, the word 'violet,' for instance, being given factual evidentiary value rather than symbolic meaning. At the other extreme, symbolist and so-called deconstructionist criticism emphasized meaning while denying reference to human content: for Ferry to celebrate Lucy's premature death as 'right,' for the new allegorists to read the poem(s) as allegorizing specialized developments in literary history, was to understand Lucy as a sign, or 'signpost,' and her death as something quite different from death itself.

Where none is fully and demonstrably right, one can hardly fault such readings as wrong. Yet each is one-sided in its own way; each rules out a possible realm of meaning without being able to demonstrate its irrelevance. Conversely, the virtue of the reading process exemplified by Geoffrey Hartman lies not in correctness or verifiability, but in its determination to rectify such simplifications – though at the considerable cost of its own claims to determinate knowledge. I have suggested that Hartman's portrait of Wordsworth's inner struggle toward the 'humanization' of his imagination is equally Hartman's struggle to 'humanize' these texts, especially after they had been radically dehumanized by Bradley and Ferry, and in the process to undecide Lucy's status. I have taken Lucy's ontological ambiguity, her existence on a 'threshold' between human and symbol, as the central feature of this reading. But I have also noted that Lucy's ambiguity might be viewed as a projection of Hartman's own ambivalence, hence as an interpretation that is falsifiable like any other, and I would not be understood as proclaiming that it is 'right' or 'true.' Lucy is not obviously or necessarily the 'liminal' creature Hartman claims, or he would not need to claim it so often. Even the fact that most critics stress either Lucy's plain biographical existence or her significance – that she is constantly falling to one side or the other – does not prove that *she* is ontologically mediate or dual. A similar reading by Karl Kroeber, which makes the both-and more explicit than is usual in Hartman, may better illustrate this point:

> Wordsworth's Lucy possesses a double existence, her actual, historical existence and her idealized existence in the poet's mind. The latter is created out of the former but is neither an abstraction nor a conceptualization, because the idealized Lucy is at least as 'concrete' as the actual Lucy. ...
>
> Lucy is both actual and idealized, but her actuality is relevant only insofar as it signifies her idealization, which, in turn, is valuable only insofar as it makes manifest the significance implicit in the actual girl. (*The Artifice of Reality* 106–7)

It is by no means verifiable that Lucy 'possesses a double existence,' as Kroeber says, or that she is 'a boundary being, nature sprite and human, yet not quite either,' as Hartman says (*WP* 158). So if even in attempting to have it both ways, these interpreters cannot tell us what is happening in the poem itself, what value can their arguments have?

I believe that their value lies in a pragmatic rather than veridical register; they are superior to more determinate readings *in effect*. It is not insignificant, to begin with, that both 'humanize' the poems. Their insistence on positing Lucy's actual humanity (the objective correlative of their own uncertainty and vacillation regarding her) is not a necessary deduction but something more in the order of an ethical insistence. When we categorically deny the existence of the real human and more specifically of the woman in these poems in order to seize her more securely as a metaphysical significance, Lucy suffers a second death, or what Gayatri Spivak (171–4) calls a 'double displacement.' The postulation of a human Lucy is, of course, a feature of more simple biographical readings also. But in their double postulation of Lucy's being *and* meaning, or 'actual historical existence' and 'significance,' Hartman's and Kroeber's readings also refuse the closures of the biographical school. Like readers of parody, and like readers of Wordsworth's own interpretive practice, a reader of these readings is asked to look twice and compare, but without being led to a definitive resolution. And Lucy is most profoundly humanized, I think, in the acknowledgment that she cannot be wholly known.[42]

What sets these readings apart is not merely their doubleness, then, but also their simultaneity; by not sequentializing their dual perspectives, they resist conclusory simplification. De Man, Ferguson, and Miller all offer double interpretations in which the allegorical reading is corrective and apparently final. Ferry attempts a double reading as well, and the finality he attributes to the symbolic one is precisely what dehumanizes the poem:

> Her death was right, *after all*, for by dying she was one with the natural processes and fantastically ennobled thereby. ... Eternal nature is her *true* lover, and the poet's first idealization of her was right *after all*, for she had nothing to do with humanity. ... It is better *after all* to become immortal than to be the mortal object of a human relationship ... (78–9, emphasis added)

The back-and-forth quality of a more stereoptical reading such as Kroeber's amounts to a kind of 'negative capability'; like Wordsworth's 'A Spirit, yet a Woman too,' it is dialectical but resists synthesis. Both appearances of the object must be preserved out of respect for its unknowability: neither near nor far, truth nor beauty, being nor meaning, constitutes adequate knowledge.[43]

Such resistance to interpretive closure may get associated today with the 'infinite play' of philosophy or aesthetics and even find itself rejected as apolitical temporization or reactionary politics.[44] It is therefore worth pointing out that, in contrast to so-called deconstructionist approaches, these readings do posit reference to a complex 'actuality,' and indeed that their anti-closural impulses reflect a fundamental respect for the object rather than the reverse. It is equally important to observe how the apparent alternative, the overtly politicizing interpretive program, may miss its object entirely in the presumption to pin it down and 'have it somewhere.' A recent essay that aspires to criticize the 'Lucy Poems' on progressive political grounds illustrates that such impatience may be directly retrograde in effect to its own best intentions. In *Romantic Discourse and Political Modernity: Wordsworth, the [sic] Intellectual and Cultural Critique* (1993), Richard Bourke comments at length (175–97) on Wordsworth's 'insidious eradication' of Lucy from 'Nutting'; though Lucy is named in an early manuscript draft or version, she does not appear in any authorially printed version.[45] Bourke's reading closely follows Frances Ferguson's reading of a hypostatized

'Lucy cycle' in which 'Lucy is repeatedly and ever more decisively traced out of existence' (Ferguson 180, 174); but where the deconstructionist Ferguson praises Wordsworth's supposed 'renunciation' of referential poetics and hence of his 'claims to knowledge' of an object, where she celebrates his access to the 'ascetic' and 'cryptic wisdom' of deconstruction (192–3), the cultural critic Bourke reads the omission of Lucy from the revised 'Nutting' as a typical violence on Wordsworth's part. In 'Nutting,' he argues, 'the poet's rapacious subjugation of "untamed nature" brings into play an attitude of usurpation and domination.' The poem directly translates 'the arrogant presumptuousness of commercial and industrial civilisation' into

> the sexualised expenditure of self-interested desire, the merciless ravage of a 'virgin scene'. Lucy must consequently be written out of the text because she acts as a reminder of the fact that the encounter with nature is necessarily fraught with difficulty; that nature does not necessarily yield to human interest. (174)

In attributing the poem's thematized 'rapacity' directly to 'the poet,' this allows no distancing medium between the poetic surface and the political-economic 'subtext,' nothing even so elementary as an ironic or dramatic speaker. In Bourke's view, 'Sexual commodification supplants economic commodification' (185) directly. Thus his politicization, and arraignment, of the poetry depends on a blindness to its most basic complexities *as* poetry. Though nothing is particularly novel in this procedure, it does illustrate how determinative readings can actually create the sins they pretend to deplore. That Bourke's effort to gauge the falling-off in Wordsworth's early 'political radicalism' turns on an examination of both '*Nutting* and the Lucy cycle' (143) should come as no surprise, then; what he refuses to see is how much of Wordsworth's artistic and perhaps even philosophical radicalism he himself suppresses in his blind adoption of this editorial convenience (see 193, 195, 196), or how this adoption implicates him in precisely the 'critical dogmatism,' 'Victorian mystification,' and 'reification' that he pretends both to condemn and to avoid (143). Suppressing the history and the complex interrelationship of Wordsworth's texts makes it easier to extract a straightforward political thematics from them – e.g., as 'surrogate commodification' (144) – but it leaves Bourke perpetrating the very sort of appropriative violence (on the text) that he blames 'the poet' for committing (on Lucy and the landscape). This case illustrates why the 'history and politics' of literature cannot be adequately appreciated as simple thematics *in* literature, to be straightforwardly 'read-off': a literature's history and politics are also made up of the conditions that surround and befall it, conditions that cannot be pretended to exclude *us*, or the dynamics between its objective resistance and our will to knowledge.

Since I have repeatedly invoked Hartman's practice as an exemplar of more self-restrained and anti-closural modes of reading, it may be useful to consider also his more explicit reflections on the politics of closure. The essay 'Elation in Hegel and Wordsworth' (1987) will serve doubly, as both precept and example, since it explores 'the question of closure' through yet another reading of 'A slumber.' Beginning with an iconoclastic reading of the end of Hegel's *Phenomenology*, as opening in aesthetic 'elation' rather than closing in a totalizing synthesis, Hartman explains: 'When I assert ... that the movement of Hegel's prose is recognizably aesthetic, I refer to that rich difficulty of closing in a dialectic that leads to and postpones a final resolution' (186). In his usual fashion, he considers closure punningly, suggestively, repeatedly, and open-endedly. In 'final resolution,' one may hear a disturbing echo that aligns philosophical and hermeneutic totalization with political totalitarianism. The echo – and the doubt it puts me in as to whether it is right to take it as such – is characteristic of Hartman and yet far from the merely 'playful' punning he is sometimes reputed for. It is responsible in several senses of the word, culpable, wisely self-restrained, but also evocative: I too am responsible for 'hearing' it. Thus it poses a question both of comparison and of responsibility: Dare we compare textual totalization with historical-political totalitarianism? But also: Dare we assume that there is no connection?

Hartman comes to these questions again via 'A slumber,' 'one of the "Lucy" poems, which has been explicated so many times without its meaning being fully determined' (188). Even as he stresses indeterminacy, Hartman appears blind, as in some previous readings, to the considerable determinacy of his own genre-presuppositions: he presumes that 'A slumber' is a 'Lucy Poem' and 'a kind of epitaph' (188), and his reading turns, in part, on comparison with 'a previous poem in the same cycle' (189). Yet these moves take on a concessive logic within his reading; the poem remains indeterminate *despite* these determinations from without. Hartman's new reading recalls his previous readings, but also crosses their grain. While he still holds that '[t]he tonal assignment' of stanza 2 'is curiously open or beside the point,' he now attends also to the poem's own 'point' and 'closure': it 'is composed of a series of short and definitive statements, very like assertions. ... indeed the sense of closure is so strong that it thematizes itself in the very first line' (188). As an 'epitaph,' the poem 'marks the closure of a life that has never opened up' (188). And yet stanza 2, notes Hartman,

> does not close out the illusion; it preserves it within the elegiac form. The illusion is elated, in our sense of the word: 'aufgehoben' seems the proper term. For the girl is still, and all the more, what she seemed to be. (189)

Taking *aufhebung* as 'elation,' Hartman makes a term of philosophical resolution, par excellence, into one of irresolution, incomplete synthesis, self-difference: in 'the girl is still, *and all the more*, what she seemed to be,' he emphasizes the difference that remains even *within* the resolution of 'is' and 'seemed.'

Thus Hartman treats 'A slumber' as both closural and 'unclosured' (190) – giving a vacillating, 'unclosured' reading of its closure. Perhaps it is a poem that seeks to close but does not. And, characteristically, he moves to explain what he sees as its formal effort toward closure in terms of the most human emotions, and of the most pressing of human issues. Relative to 'Strange fits,' 'a previous poem in the same cycle,' this one marks 'a purification' (189).

> At the limit of the medium of words, and close to silence, what has been purged is not concreteness, or the empirical sphere of emotions – shock, disillusion, trauma, recognition, grief, atonement – what has been purged is a series of flashy schematisms and false or partial mediations: artificial plot, inflated consolatory rhetoric, the coercive absolutes of logic or faith.
>
> A question remains. Why is closure needed at all? Because the realm of the dead – the 'Geisterreich' – is not tranquil. Lucy haunts the poet as a virginal figure, an unconsummated force of life: she must have shape, if only in this tomb or crypt of words. There is the poet's guilt in living on, or living a life the other has not had. ... 'A slumber did my spirit seal': the seal is like a hymen over consciousness. (190)

The poem's formal drive to closure reflects the drive of a grieving man, but also that of an interpreter. It is explicable as a self-defensive effort to foreclose and heal, yet at the same time unwarranted, arbitrary, and violent: an 'unconsummated force of life' is buried. This account also suggests uglier forms of 'purgation,' 'purification,' and 'closure.' Wordsworth's formal 'purgation' calls to mind the criminals and the victims of the Holocaust, though these suggestions themselves resist ordering or resolution:

> I now face a traffic jam of thoughts. The anthropologist in me is interested in how closure and elation might enter rites of burial and purification. The psychoanalyst in me wonders what role the 'lost object' plays in mourning: an object that can be as evasive as musical meaning. The philosopher of language remembers how many utopian or racially motivated theories of language-purification have been put forward ... (190)

Hartman does little more than suggest that connections exist between the worst violence and the 'violence of intellect' (192) – a responsible caution. When critics used the discovery of de Man's collaborationist writings in 1987 to equate deconstructionist interpretation with Nazi politics, Hartman rightly dismissed the connection: 'Such a judgment is superficial' ('Blindness' 29). Yet the judgment would seem to go wrong, from his point of view, not in its general association between interpretive and political practices, but in its specific linkage of deconstruction's doctrine of the 'indeterminacy of meaning' with totalitarian politics. Hartman himself customarily treats interpretive modes as far more than just literary; but totalitarian thought he usually connects instead with interpretive 'closure' or 'totalization.' As he puts it,

> It is difficult, in short, to separate off Aesthetics as a field of inquiry, one based on distinctive features disclosed in experience by our experience of art. The claim for Aesthetics as such a field, or the only claim I can make, is that in conjunction with art it develops interpretive powers that bring us closer to all types of experience, not in their immediacy but in their mediatedness. Every work of art, from this point of view, is a criticism of life in terms of a criticism of mediations ... ('Elation' 191)

Paradoxically, Hartman's effort 'to separate off Aesthetics as a field' consists in positing its intimate connectedness with 'all types of experience.' And his considerable claim for its formative role turns on this redefinition; his 'Aesthetic,' once again, is not merely the domain of the beautiful, but refers 'to that rich difficulty of closing in a dialectic that leads to and postpones a final resolution.'

This claim for a reconstituted 'Aesthetics' as the locus of hermeneutic resistance, challenge, and exercise recalls Percy Shelley's contention that

'Poetry strengthens that faculty which is the organ of the moral nature of man, in the same manner as exercise strengthens a limb' (488). Yet it makes a most important qualification. The twentieth-century humanist disenchantment – the recognition of George Steiner and others that the 'humanities' have failed to humanize – centres in the recognition that art or 'Poetry' has not been enough in itself; and one reason why old-style humanism failed to humanize was that it entrusted art with inherent or self-sufficient values, determinate meanings, and predictable effects.[46] The corollary was passivity in the consumer. In questions of the 'determinacy of meaning,' much also depends, we have learned, on the determinations of readers, and so also on those of teachers and professional interpreters; and where there is reader-response there is also, as Hartman says, 'reader-responsibility.' This means that if art and aesthetics are to be called on to develop 'interpretive powers' of a 'moral nature' – and they certainly should be – they must first be cultivated by the same. Here, I believe, lies the political importance of anti-closural practices of reading, of the refusal to totalize, of the programmatic admission that she knows an object best who does not pretend to know it fully. This is not to deny that literary study can be a 'discipline,' but to say that it must begin with a discipline of self, self-discipline.

Appendix: Editions

This appendix presents editions of the usual five 'Lucy Poems' with an apparatus listing all published authorial variants and some, but not all, manuscript variants. The standard edition of Wordsworth, edited by Ernest de Selincourt and Helen Darbishire (1941–9), includes only those variants 'which seemed ... of the least significance' (*PW* 1:v); it does not note, for example, changes in the last line of 'A slumber,' from 'With rocks and stones and trees!' (1800) to 'With rocks, and stones, and trees.' (1836–50). Jared Curtis's Cornell edition of *Poems, in Two Volumes* gives the 1807 text of 'I travell'd' with all variants in apparatus (103–4), and the other 'Lucy Poems' have been so treated by James Butler and Karen Green in their Cornell edition of *Lyrical Ballads*. The editions below resemble those of de Selincourt and Darbishire, and differ from those of the Cornell editors, in that they use later authorial versions as copy-text.

I have no dispute with either of the Cornell editions – both are splendid re-creations of the earliest collections – but Wordsworth's later texts are clearly appropriate here, since most of the 'Lucy Poems' criticism refers to them (while neglecting, of course, the notorious late authorial organization). Beyond this, I am not convinced either that Wordsworth ruined his poetry over the years or that he neglected details such as accidentals when he published it, and I therefore see no reason to accept the increasing privilege accorded to the earliest versions. Indeed, I think that in some cases, where it involves the printing of ambiguous manuscript drafts or versions as completed 'poems,' this resurrection of the 'original' Wordsworth may be our generation's version of the Victorians' creation of the 'Lucy Poems.'

The initial practice of the Cornell editions (1975–) was archaeological: it presented Wordsworth's poems in their earliest published versions, earliest coherent versions, or even in their earliest versions editorially emended and punctuated into coherence. The rationale for this project has a long and complicated history with two prongs: the preference for the earliest versions and the justification for emending them, when necessary, as poems. I can only sketch the main lines here.[1] The preference for Wordsworth's earliest texts has much to do with the theory that he lost his competence as a poet sometime after 1807. As time passes, editors seem to lose patience with the later Wordsworth. Publishing the 1805 *Prelude* in 1926, de Selincourt said: 'No one would doubt that the 1850 version is a better composition' (xliv). But in 1941 he described Wordsworth's habits of revision as 'an obsession,' claiming that where 'revision effected a change in meaning, it is hard to defend it' (*PW* 1:vi). Publishing early versions of *The Ruined Cottage* in 1969, Jonathan Wordsworth declared that 'Wordsworth is almost exclusively known by his worst' texts – meaning his latest texts (*The Music of Humanity* xiii). Stephen Parrish quotes this statement approvingly in 'The Worst of Wordsworth,' his apologia for the Cornell editions (1976):

> the ageing Wordsworth failed to serve himself well. ... As he grew older his opinions, naturally, altered, his orthodoxies hardened, his creative energy fell off, and the old anxieties intensified. From the age of thirty onward, he turned compulsively, again and again, to his manuscripts to reshape, alter, and extend his poems ... (89)

In practice, it should be said, the Cornell editions vary considerably.[2] But Parrish, then general editor, said its purpose was 'to rescue these lost poems' from Wordsworth's revisions. Among his examples was 'Adventures on Salisbury Plain' (90–1), a 'poem' that Stephen Gill was able to 'rescue' for the first volume in the Cornell series only by pasting in 'The Female Vagrant' to fill a gap left in the manuscript by Wordsworth (Gill, ed., *Salisbury* 9–10, 131–8). The yet earlier manuscript of 'Salisbury Plain,' presented as another 'poem' in the same volume, required extensive editorial punctuation, and 48 of its 549 lines are missing. That an initially 'archaeological' project has at some points assumed the dimensions of revisionary history and even of proselytization is evident from its popularizations. In 1984, Gill included the partially emended 'Salisbury Plain' as a 'poem' in his Oxford Authors selection of Wordsworth; and he himself remarks that the two-part *Prelude* and 'The Ruined Cottage' occupied 'more than a quarter of the pages devoted to Wordsworth' in *The Norton Anthology* (4th edition), 'undoubtedly the world's most influential teaching anthology of English Literature.'[3] Since the publication of *The Salisbury Plain Poems*, Gill has thoughtfully pointed out how fine a line distinguishes editorial 'rescues' from editorial creations, but without admitting to the place of 'Salisbury Plain' among the latter. 'With no other major poet,' he says, 'has the definition of the essential poetry been so changed by recent scholarly work' ('Wordsworth's Poems' 189n). But the question is not merely what is 'essential poetry'; it is what are *poems*. Is it fair to present these things as poems rather than as drafts?

One must question not only why but also how scholars justify editorializing such texts as 'poems.' In part, the rationale turns on a particular conception of Wordsworth's punctuation and on a strangely contradictory conception of his revisions. On the one hand editors deplore Wordsworth's meticulous habits of revision as 'obsessive'; on the other they assume that he would or could not punctuate his own work, and this justifies consideration of early, very lightly punctuated manuscripts as fair copy ready for the press. To stick to the case of 'Salisbury Plain,' Gill claims that 'the way it had been entered in a fair-copy manuscript and evidence of letters suggest that it was regarded as completed and publishable' ('Wordsworth's Poems' 185–6). But in manuscript, stanza 8 of this poem reads (I give Gill's punctuation in brackets, though his edition adds it silently):

> Hurtle the rattling clouds together piled[,]
> By fiercer gales, and soon the storm must break,[.]
> He stood the only creature in the wild
> On whom the elements their rage could wreak,
> Save the bustard of those limits bleak[,]
> Shy tenant[,] seeing there a mortal wight
> At that dread hour[,] outsent a mournful shriek
> And half upon the ground, with strange affright,
> Forced hard against the wind a thick unwieldy flight[.][4]

Even aside from the fact that Wordsworth subsequently tore leaves out of this manuscript, this is not quite what most people would regard as 'completed and publishable.' Many of Wordsworth's early and unpublished manuscripts are lightly punctuated like this one; were they really considered completed?

The case for dismissing Wordsworth's punctuation as insignificant dates at least from William Hale White's presentation of the Longman manuscripts in 1897, including the manuscripts for the four 'Lucy Poems' of *Lyrical Ballads*. The poems directly preceding the 'Lucy Poems' are written on a sheet sent to Humphry Davy in Bristol (Wordsworth was in Grasmere at the time), with a letter to Davy including a compromising remark:

> You would greatly oblige me by looking over the enclosed poems and correcting any thing you find amiss in the punctuation a business at which I am ashamed to say I am no adept. (Letter of [29] July [1800], *Letters* 1:289)

White transcribes this letter, noting that

> Wordsworth's punctuation has been reproduced exactly, and it certainly justifies the appeal to Davy. The stops in the MS. of the poems are mostly in a different ink from that used in the rest of the MS., and we may infer therefore that they are Davy's. We may infer also that no superstitious respect need be payed to them. (8-9)

In light of the manuscript (now in the Beinecke at Yale), White's conclusions are dubious. It has all brown ink; some marks are darker than others, but this variation in colour (ranging almost to black) appears even in the letter to Davy itself. If we trust White and call the darker marks Davy's, all the bracketed material in the following passage from 'The Brothers' is his:

> 'These Tourists, heaven preserve us! needs must live
> A profitable life[:] some glance along[,]
> Rapid and gay[,] as if the earth were a[i]r[,]
> And they were butterflies to wheel about
> Long as their summer lasted[;] some[,] as wise[,]
> Upon the forehead of a jutting crag,
> [Sit perched, with book & pencil on their knee,]
> And look and scribble[,] scribble on and look[,]
> Until a man might travel twelve stout miles[,]
> Or reap an acre of his neighbor's corn[.]
>
> ('The Brothers,' lines 1–10)

The 'i' in 'air' and all of line 7 would be Davy's, for they are inserted in the same dark ink, but the interlineated line 7 is in the same hand as the rest (Dorothy's).[5] The similarity in ink between interlineation and punctuation does suggest that Wordsworth left punctuation to be inserted later, but it also suggests that it was inserted under Wordsworth's supervision, not by Davy. It is also possible that some of the punctuation in question is darker because of firmer pressure on the pen, or that Wordsworth punctuated sometime after the lines were written, with a newly inked pen. The period after his signature in the letter to Davy is as dark as anything in the manuscript, and it is unlikely that anyone would have added it later.

White makes much of Wordsworth's mispunctuation in his very request that Davy correct 'anything you find amiss in the punctuation a business at which I am ashamed to say I am no adept,' but he fails to note that in the manuscript 'punctuation' runs to the edge of the page and slants down into the margin; the missing comma is easily explained by the lack of space. Elsewhere White transcribes Wordsworth's abbreviation for 'volume' as 'vol;' – pedantically making a semicolon of a sloppy colon. These seemingly trivial misrepresentations are important not just because they have perpetuated the myth of Wordsworth's ineptitude in these matters, but also because they show an odd desire to make the case worse than it really is.

It is no doubt convenient for editors to assume that 'no superstitious respect need be paid' to Wordsworth's punctuation, but other explanations can be offered for his comments to Humphry Davy. He was far away and unable to supervise the printing, and there may be some flattery in his self-deprecation. Noting that he 'had a fresh copy prepared for this purpose,' Curtis says:

> Wordsworth, in his Grasmere 'cabin,' as he calls it in his letter, was in a poor position to undertake the painstaking but necessary job, especially since speed seemed essential; Davy, living in Bristol, where *Lyrical Ballads* was being published, and softened up apparently by Coleridge, was willing, able, and available to carry it out.[6]

But it may not even be a case of Wordsworth's wishing 'to avoid performing this difficult and time-consuming task,' as Curtis suggests (51). Mary Moorman points out that he was ill at the time of the letter to Davy and indeed during much of the preparation of the 1800 *Lyrical Ballads*. 'In July Wordsworth himself told Josiah Wedgwood that "ill health has for some time rendered literary labour inadviseable for me" '

(Moorman 1:489). Many of the papers sent to the printer are, as she notes, in Coleridge's hand (488), and the appeal to Davy may thus be explained as an extra precaution rather than as carelessness.

If the presumption against Wordsworth's punctuation were simply that he was unorthodox or 'no adept,' one could argue easily enough that his punctuation is worth preserving whatever it is like. As is often pointed out, poetic punctuation differs from usual punctuation. 'Verse,' says T.S. Eliot, 'is itself a system of *punctuation*; the usual marks of punctuation themselves are differently employed.'[7] Comparing editorial punctuation with a poet's will almost always reveal something sacrificed in the alteration. But modern editors appear to assume as much that Wordsworth neglected to punctuate his poetry as that he did not know how. How else can one explain all the 'fair copy' manuscripts without punctuation? This problem turns on the assumption that these *are* finished manuscripts, and I would suggest that Wordsworth added punctuation only when he considered a poem finished and ready for publication. This has been suggested before. A critic studying Wordsworth's 'To the Spade of a Friend' notes: 'as the manuscript of the 1807 *Poems* shows, punctuation was usually regarded as a separate operation preparatory to printing' (Kelliher 157). The manuscript facsimiles of the Immortality Ode in Curtis' edition of *Poems, in Two Volumes* (360–7) confirm Kelliher's deduction. The version in DC MS. 44 (ca. 6 March 1804, prepared for Coleridge) has hardly any punctuation, and in the Longman manuscript (prepared for the printer) most of the punctuation has been added in a separate stage after the writing. Curtis notes that these sheets were 'corrected and repunctuated by Wordsworth, probably at the time they were sent to the printer' (*Poems* 25; see also 52).

This curious practice may be explained in part by Wordsworth's haste in composition,[8] and in part by the quasi-oral character of the poetry. Wordsworth appears to have composed mentally, committing the poems to paper only afterward; even then they remained oral.[9] Marks of punctuation are precisely what would not be included in this compositional process, and they would not be necessary until the poetry went public. Wordsworth would know how to recite his own poetry without punctuation; even after publication, he considered it as designed for 'recitation' and allowed that readers should have a good degree of liberty 'to modulate, in subordination to the sense, the music of the poem' (*Prose* 3:29–30). But especially considering Wordsworth's parenthetical style, the length of the stops or pauses is important, and it is reasonable to suppose that, given shortages of paper and the purely mechanical difficulties in altering punctuation in ink, he might wish to wait until publication to insert it. The important point about this hypothesis is that the lack of punctuation in Wordsworth's 'fair copies' may actually signify, not sloppiness or diffidence, but a greater care than usual in these matters.

The question comes down to a fine distinction between 'poems' and 'drafts.' Without examining more evidence than I can do here, it would be fruitless to insist that all editorially 'rescued' texts are drafts rather than poems. What makes Wordsworth's compositional process important here is that the editorial practice of punctuating early texts and presenting them simply as poems tends to reinforce the prejudice against his ability and willingness to punctuate his own works; and this prejudice has historically served to justify not just the repunctuation of his poetry but the wholesale re-editing of it, including the dismissal of Wordsworth's challenging pseudo-organic arrangement, and the consequent atomization of his corpus. Yet his revisions suggest that he laboured over his punctuation as much as any author. Having studied the revisions in *Poems, in Two Volumes*, Jared Curtis finds that the evidence suggests 'that Wordsworth reviewed with care and extensively altered punctuation and capitals in proof' throughout their printing history (*Poems* 54). In a study of the 1832 edition of the *Poetical Works* which Wordsworth revised for the 1836 edition, Curtis concludes that the punctuation is authorial even at this late date:

> I have long been puzzled by the systematic changes in punctuation and capitalization which occurred in the 1836–37 edition, at a loss to say certainly whether these changes were initiated by the poet or by his new publisher, Moxon. The Wellesley manuscript, seconded by the Princeton authorially corrected proofs, confirms that Wordsworth himself made most of these changes. (Curtis, 'Wellesley' 14)

This conclusion is particularly important for the 'Lucy Poems' texts, for here the revisions are predominantly in accidentals and the poems were changed very little after 1836. Wordsworth emphasized the 'value' of his extensive revisions in the 1836 edition (Curtis, 'Wellesley' 5). The choice of copy-text, then, does not involve a question of Wordsworth's supervision of the later editions, but rather the question of his competence and authority in altering the poems thirty-six years after they were first published. The changes in punctuation, for the most part tending toward far more standard practice, affect the poems considerably, and historical editions of the poems' earlier versions are therefore of interest; but to me, Wordsworth does not seem to have made completely different works of the poems, or to have altered them for the worse. Therefore, considering the pains he took in revision, and his own assessment of the value of these revisions, I think it best to stick with the latest authorial texts.[10]

I emphasize that these texts are given as a convenience and not for their own sake, and as several editions, not as one; otherwise an edition of the 'Lucy Poems' might seem to reinforce their status as an unambiguous unit. It should be recalled that they were never presented as such by the poet. While I present them in the order in which they would be encountered in the final authorial edition, Wordsworth placed the first three together under 'Poems Founded on the Affections,' and the latter two together under 'Poems of the Imagination,' and many poems fall between them. The rationale for including these five and no others lies in the history of their criticism.

Manuscripts and Editions for the 'Lucy Poems'

A. MANUSCRIPTS

W–STC Letter from William and Dorothy to Coleridge, 14 or 21 Dec. 1798. Includes early versions of 'Strange fits' and 'She dwelt.' Wordsworth Library, Dove Cottage. I have not examined this manuscript, and rely on the transcriptions in *Letters* 1:236–8.

STC Letter from Coleridge to Thomas Poole, 6 April 1799. Includes Coleridge's transcription of 'A slumber,' entitled 'Epitaph,' which he says 'Some months ago Wordsworth transmitted to me.' Its textual authority is of course highly questionable (see Sykes Davies 139–42). British Museum. I have not examined this manuscript, and rely on Griggs's transcription in Coleridge's *Letters* (1:478–81).

Longman Longman Manuscripts, including 'Lucy Gray,' 'Three years,' and the letter 'directed to Mr. Davy,' 29 July 1800 (letter 1). Also includes 'Strange fits,' 'She dwelt,' and 'A slumber,' as well as 'The Brothers' (letter 2). Beinecke (Yale University); see also White, and *Letters* 1:289–90.

I copied from Yale's microfilm, then checked against manuscript.

Tinker — *Lyrical Ballads*, 1800, vol. 2, annotated with corrections and revisions in preparation for the 1802 edition by (according to *The Tinker Library ... Catalogue*) William, Dorothy, and an unidentified person. Beinecke (Yale University). Inside the front fly leaf of this edition is a note in pencil:

> This book is made up of proof sheets of the original edition; and the MSS corrections are by the hand of the Author's sister Dorothy Wordsworth and by the Author himself. This book belonged to the Author's nephew John Wordsworth, son of Richard Wordsworth [signed:] Chr W—

Includes 'Strange fits,' 'She dwelt,' and 'Three years.'

Tinker 2335 — *Poems in Two Volumes* (1807), with interpolations and revisions for Wordsworth's 1815 *Poems*. Beinecke (Yale University). No changes are made in 'I travell'd among unknown Men' (the only 'Lucy Poem' in this volume), though several changes appear in the 1815 *Poems* (see apparatus).

B. EDITIONS *(copies examined are listed below each entry)*

1800 — *Lyrical Ballads*. 2 Vols. London, 1800. Vol. 2.
Columbia University (2 copies); Yale University (1 copy); British Library (11642.aa.50, Ashley 2253, Ashley 2254, and C58.c.12/2)

1802 — *Lyrical Ballads*. 2 vols. London, 1802. Vol. 2.
Yale (Tinker 2332); British Library (11642.aaa.39 and Ashley 2255); Cornell (PR5869.L99.1800d [sic–vol. 2 is an 1802 ed.])

1805 — *Lyrical Ballads*. 2 vols. London, 1805. Vol. 2.
Columbia; British Library (Ashley 2256 [T.J. Wise's copy], and C.58.bb.23 [Southey's copy])

1807 — *Poems, in Two Volumes*. London, 1807.
Yale; Columbia; British Library (C.58.bb.3)

1815 — *Poems*. 2 vols. London, 1815.
Columbia; British Library (C.95.d.2); Cornell (PR5850.E15 c.15 [with Blake's annotations])

1820 — *The Miscellaneous Poems*. 4 vols. London: Longman, 1820.
Columbia (1 copy)

1827 — *The Poetical Works*. 5 vols. London: Longman, 1827.
British Library (11645.df.50); Cornell (PR5850.E27)

1832 — *The Poetical Works*. 4 vols. London: Longman, 1832.
British Library (11611.aaa.25–28); Cornell (PR5850.E32)

1836	*The Poetical Works.* 6 vols. London: Moxon, 1836–7. Columbia (1 copy); British Library (11611.b.11–16); Cornell (PR5850.E36c)
1840	*The Poetical Works.* 6 vols. London: Moxon, 1840 (from 1836 plates, with alterations). British Library (11611.bbb.35–40); Cornell (PR5850.E40)
1845	*The Poems.* 1 vol. London: Moxon, 1845. Columbia (SLF, Sutliff Collection); British Library (11632.ee.5); Cornell (PR5850.E45)
1846	*The Poetical Works.* 7 vols. London: Moxon, 1846. Cornell
1850	*The Poetical Works.* 6 vols. London: Moxon, 1849–50 (last authorial edition). Columbia; British Library (11607.ccc.1); Cornell (PR5850.E49b)

SYMBOLS USED

‸ = no punctuation
<> enclose editorial explanation or comment

TEXTS AND APPARATUS

'Strange fits of passion have I known'

Strange fits of passion have I known:
And I will dare to tell,
But in the Lover's ear alone,
What once to me befel.

When she I loved looked every day
Fresh as a rose in June,
I to her cottage bent my way,
Beneath an evening moon.

Upon the moon I fixed my eye,
All over the wide lea;
With quickening pace my horse drew nigh
Those paths so dear to me.

And now we reached the orchard-plot;
And, as we climbed the hill,
The sinking moon to Lucy's cot
Came near, and nearer still.

In one of those sweet dreams I slept,
Kind Nature's gentlest boon!
And all the while my eyes I kept
On the descending moon.

My horse moved on; hoof after hoof
He raised, and never stopped:
When down behind the cottage roof,
At once, the bright moon dropped.

What fond and wayward thoughts will slide
Into a Lover's head!
'O mercy!' to myself I cried,
'If Lucy should be dead!'

'Strange fits' variants in W–STC, Longman, 1800, Tinker, 1802–50

<stanzas unnumbered> 1800–50 <numbered 1–7> *W–STC*
1–4 <not in *W–STC*>

1 have I *1832–50*] I have *Longman, 1800–27* known: *Tinker–1850*] known, *Longman, 1800*
3 Lover's *Tinker–1850*] lover's *Longman, 1800*
5 When she I loved looked every day *1836–50*] Once, when my love was strong and gay, *W–STC*; When she, I lov'd, was strong & gay *Longman*; When she I lov'd, was strong and gay *1800–2*; When she I loved, was strong and gay *1805*; When she I loved was strong and gay, *1815–32*
6 Fresh as *1836–50*] And like *W–STC, Longman–1832*
8 an evening moon *1850*] the evening moon *Longman, 1800*; the evening Moon *W–STC, Tinker–1832*; an evening-moon *1836–46*
9 moon‸ *W–STC, 1800, 1836–50*] moon, *Longman*; Moon‸ *Tinker–1832* fixed *W–STC, 1805–50*] fix'd *Longman, 1800–2* eye, *Longman–1850*] eye‸ *W–STC*
10 lea; *Longman, 1800, 1827–50*] lea: *W–STC, Tinker–1820*
11 With quickening pace my horse *1836–50*] My horse trudg'd on, & we *Longman*; My horse trudg'd on, and we *W–STC, 1800*; My Horse trudg'd on – and we *1802*; My Horse trudged on – and we *Tinker, 1805–32*
13 we *Longman–1850*] I've *W–STC* reached *1805–50*] reach'd *Longman, 1800–2* orchard-plot; *1836–50*] orchard-plot, *W–STC, Longman*; orchard plot, *1800*; orchard plot; *Tinker–1832*
14 And, as *Longman–1820, 1832–50*] And as *W–STC, 1827* climbed *W–STC, 1805–50*] climb'd *Longman–1802*
15 The sinking moon to *1836–50*] Towards the roof of *W–STC–1832*
16 Came near, and nearer *1836–50*] The moon descended *W–STC–1800*; The Moon descended *Tinker–1832*
18 Nature's *1800–50*] nature's *W–STC, Longman* <*Longman* has 'Nature's' with 'n' written over 'N'> boon! *Longman–1850*] boon, *W-STC*
19 And all the while *W–STC, 1827–50*] And, all the while, *Longman–1820*
20 moon *W–STC–1800, 1836–50*] Moon *Tinker–1832*
21 horse *W–STC–1800, 1836–50*] Horse *Tinker, 1802–32* moved *W–STC, 1805–50*] mov'd *Longman–1802*
22 raised, *1805–50*] raised‸ *W–STC*; rais'd‸ *Longman–1800*; rais'd, *Tinker–1802* and *W–STC, 1800–50*] & *Longman* stopped: *1805, 1827–50*] stopped, *W–STC*; stopp'd, *Longman*; stopp'd: *1800–2, 1815–20*
23 roof, *1820–50*] roof‸ *W–STC–1815*
24 once, the bright moon *1836–50*] once the planet *W–STC–1800*; once the Planet *Tinker–1805*; once the bright moon *1815*; once, the bright Moon *1820–32* dropped *1805, 1827–50*] dropp'd *W–STC–1802, 1815–20*

25 What fond and wayward thoughts *Longman–1850*] Strange are the fancies that *W–STC*

26 Lover's *1800–50*] lover's *W–STC*; Lovers *Longman* head! *1836–50*] head, *W–STC*; head – *Longman–1815*; head! – *1820–32*

27 mercy!' to *1800–50*] mercy' to *W–STC*; mercy!', to *Longman* cried, *Longman–1850*] cried‸ *W–STC*

28 dead!' *W–STC, 1800–50*] dead! *Longman*

<*W–STC* has an additional stanza:>

I told her this; her laughter light
  Is ringing in my ears;
And when I think upon that night
  My eyes are dim with tears.

'She dwelt among the untrodden ways'

She dwelt among the untrodden ways
  Beside the springs of Dove,
A Maid whom there were none to praise
  And very few to love:

A violet by a mossy stone
  Half hidden from the eye!
– Fair as a star, when only one
  Is shining in the sky.

She lived unknown, and few could know
  When Lucy ceased to be;
But she is in her grave, and, oh,
  The difference to me!

'She dwelt' variants in W–STC, Longman, 1800, Tinker, 1802–50

<no title> *W–STC, Tinker–1850*] Song *Longman; SONG. 1800*
<stanzas unnumbered> *Longman, 1800–50* <numbered 1–5> *W–STC*
<Before stanza 1, *W–STC* has:>
  My hope was one, from cities far,
    Nursed on a lonesome heath;
  Her lips were red as roses are,
    Her hair a woodbine wreath.
1 dwelt *Longman–1850*] lived *W–STC* the *W-STC, 1815–50*] th' *Longman, 1800–5*
3 Maid *1800–50*] maid *W–STC*; <'M' may be lower case> *Longman* praise‸ *Longman, 1800, 1832–50*] praise, *W–STC, Tinker–1827*
4 And *W–STC–1800, 1805–50*] A *1802* love: *1832–50*] love; *W–STC*; love. *Longman, 1800, 1805–27*; love‸ *1802*
5 violet *W–STC, 1836–50*] Violet *Longman, 1800–32*
6 Half‸hidden *1832–50*] Half-hidden *W–STC, Longman, 1800–27* eye *W–STC, 1805–50*] Eye *Longman, 1800–2*
7 – Fair as a star, *Tinker–1850*] ‸Fair as a star‸ *W–STC*; – Fair, as a star‸ *Longman, 1800*
8 sky. *1802–50*] sky! *W–STC, Longman, 1800, Tinker*
<Before stanza 3, *W–STC* has:>
  And she was graceful as the broom
    That flowers by Carron's side;
  But slow distemper checked her bloom,
    And on the Heath she died.

9–10 <*W–STC* has:> Long time before her head lay low / Dead to the world was she:

9 lived *1805–50*] *liv'd Longman, 1800, Tinker* <starred, with a note, 'not in italics'>; liv'd *1802* and *W–STC, 1800–50*] & *Longman*

10 ceased *1805–50*] ceas'd *Longman, 1800–2*

11 she is *Longman–1850*] now she's *W–STC* grave *W–STC, 1836–50*] Grave *Longman, 1800–32* and, *1815–50*] and‸ *W–STC, Longman, 1800–5* oh, *1815–50*] Oh! *W–STC, 1800–2*; oh! *Longman, 1805*

12 me! *W–STC, 1815–50*] me. *Longman, 1800–5*

'I travelled among unknown men'

I travelled among unknown men,
  In lands beyond the sea;
Nor, England! did I know till then
  What love I bore to thee.

'Tis past, that melancholy dream!
  Nor will I quit thy shore
A second time; for still I seem
  To love thee more and more.

Among thy mountains did I feel
  The joy of my desire;
And she I cherished turned her wheel
  Beside an English fire.

Thy mornings showed, thy nights concealed
  The bowers where Lucy played;
And thine too is the last green field
  That Lucy's eyes surveyed.

'I travelled' variants in 1807–50

1 travelled *1827–50*] travell'd *1807–20*   men *1836–50*] Men *1807–32*
2 lands *1836–50*] Lands *1807–32*   sea *1836–50*] Sea *1807–32*
3 Nor, *1815–50*] Nor‸ *1807*
11 she *1832–50*] She *1807–27*   cherished *1815–50*] cherish'd *1807*   turned *1815–50*] turn'd *1807*
13 showed, *1832–50*] shew'd – *1807*; shewed, *1815–27*   concealed *1815–50*] conceal'd *1807*
14 played *1815–50*] play'd *1807*
15 too is *1836–50*] is, too, *1807*; is‸ too‸ *1815–32*
16 That *1815–50*] Which *1807*   surveyed. *1815–50*] survey'd! *1807*

'Three years she grew in sun and shower'

Three years she grew in sun and shower,
Then Nature said, 'A lovelier flower
On earth was never sown;
This Child I to myself will take;
She shall be mine, and I will make
A Lady of my own.

Myself will to my darling be
Both law and impulse: and with me
The Girl, in rock and plain,
In earth and heaven, in glade and bower,
Shall feel an overseeing power
To kindle or restrain.

She shall be sportive as the fawn
That wild with glee across the lawn
Or up the mountain springs;
And hers shall be the breathing balm,
And hers the silence and the calm
Of mute insensate things.

The floating clouds their state shall lend
To her; for her the willow bend;
Nor shall she fail to see
Even in the motions of the Storm
Grace that shall mould the Maiden's form
By silent sympathy.

The stars of midnight shall be dear
To her; and she shall lean her ear
In many a secret place
Where rivulets dance their wayward round,
And beauty born of murmuring sound
Shall pass into her face.

And vital feelings of delight
Shall rear her form to stately height,
Her virgin bosom swell;
Such thoughts to Lucy I will give
While she and I together live
Here in this happy dell.'

Thus Nature spake – The work was done –
How soon my Lucy's race was run!
She died, and left to me
This heath, this calm, and quiet scene;
The memory of what has been,
And never more will be.

'Three years' variants in Longman, Tinker, 1800–50

<*Longman* uniformly uses '&' for 'and' except in initial position.>
4 take; *Tinker, 1802–50*] take, *Longman, 1800*
7, 13, 19, 25, 31 <no open quote> *Longman, 1800–2, 1820–50*] <open quote> *1805–15*
7–8 Myself will to my darling be / Both law and impulse *Longman, 1800, 1805–50*] Her teacher I myself will be, / She is my darling; – *Tinker, 1802*
8 impulse: and *1815–50*] impulse, and *Longman, 1800*; impulse; and *1805*
9 Girl, *Tinker, 1802–50*] girl‸ *Longman*; Girl‸ *1800*
13 fawn *Longman, 1800, 1836–50*] Fawn *Tinker, 1802–32*
15 springs; *Tinker, 1802–50*] springs, *Longman, 1800*
16 balm, *1800–50*] balm‸ *Longman*
16, 17 hers *Longman, Tinker, 1800–27*] her's *1832–50*
19 clouds *Longman, 1800, 1836–50*] Clouds *Tinker, 1802–32*
20 her; *Tinker, 1802–50*] her, *Longman, 1800* bend; *Tinker, 1802–50*] bend, *Longman, 1800*
22 Storm *Tinker, 1802–50*] storm *Longman, 1800*
23 Grace that shall mould the Maiden's *Tinker, 1802–50*] A beauty that shall mould her *Longman, 1800*
25 stars *Longman, 1800, 1836–50*] Stars *Tinker, 1802–32*
26 her; *Tinker, 1802–50*] her, *Longman, 1800*
28 rivulets *Longman, 1800, 1836–50*] Rivulets *Tinker–1832*
33 swell; *Tinker, 1802–50*] swell, *Longman, 1800*
36 dell.' *1836–50*] dell.‸ *Longman, 1800*; Dell.' *Tinker, 1802–32*
39 died, *1805–50*] died‸ *Longman, 1800–2*
40 this *Longman, 1800, 1805–50*] at his *1802* <not in *Tinker*> calm, *1815–50*] calm‸ *Longman–1805* scene; *1800–50*] scene, *Longman*
42 be. *1800–50*] be. – *Longman*

'A slumber did my spirit seal'

A slumber did my spirit seal;
  I had no human fears:
She seemed a thing that could not feel
  The touch of earthly years.

No motion has she now, no force;
  She neither hears nor sees;
Rolled round in earth's diurnal course,
  With rocks, and stones, and trees.

'A slumber' variants in STC, Longman, 1800–50

<no title> *1800–50*] Epitaph *STC*

1 slumber *Longman, 1800–50*] Slumber *STC*   seal; *1802–50*] seal, *STC, Longman, 1800*

3 seemed *1805–50*] seem'd *STC, Longman, 1800–2*   thing *Longman, 1800–50*] Thing, *STC*

5 force; *STC, 1802–50*] force‸ *Longman, 1800*

6 sees; *1836–50*] sees‸ *Longman, 1800*; sees, *STC, 1802–32*

7 Rolled *1805–50*] Mov'd *STC*; Roll'd *Longman, 1800–2*   earth's *Longman, 1800–50*] Earth's *STC*   course, *1836–50*] course‸ *STC, Longman, 1800–32*

8 rocks, and stones, and trees. *1836–50*] rocks, & stones, and trees! *STC*; rocks and stones and trees! *Longman, 1800–27*; rocks, and stones, and trees! *1832*

Notes

Preface

1 For brevity's sake I shall hereafter call each poem by its first two words: 'Strange fits,' 'She dwelt,' and so on. The Appendix contains texts.
2 As chapter 2 makes clear, my study is indebted to Hugh Sykes Davies' incisive history of the 'Lucy' grouping, which has been largely neglected.
3 As is well known, Wordsworth argues that one function of the writer is to make readers more 'capable of being excited without ... stimulants' (Owen 73). For provocation models of romantic poetry, especially Wordsworth's, see L.J. Swingle, 'On Reading Romantic Poetry'; David Simpson, *Irony and Authority*, especially 17–30, 46, 56, 62–3, 81, 95, 104, 150, 166, 198, 208n7; Karl Kroeber, *British Romantic Art*, especially chs. 1–3 and 9; Susan Wolfson, *The Questioning Presence*, especially 17–41; Tilottama Rajan, *The Supplement of Reading*, chs. 1 and 5; and Mark Jones, 'Interpretation in Wordsworth and the Provocation Theory of Romantic Literature.'
4 William Galperin notes the critical community's efforts to simplify and disambiguate Wordsworth in *Revision and Authority in Wordsworth* e.g., 7, 22–3, 64–5.
5 Barbara Herrnstein Smith, *Poetic Closure*, passim; see also Wolfson, *The Questioning Presence*, passim; Kroeber *British Romantic Art* 1; and Rajan, *Supplement* ch. 1.
6 I am indebted to Geoffrey Hartman's writings on both issues of closure, 'poetic' and 'interpretive.' On the former, see particularly 'Elation in Hegel and Wordsworth' 186–90. Hartman's comments on Wordsworth's 'unpointed' style or 'simplicity' touch on its capacity to resist or problematize interpretive closure: see especially 'Beyond Formalism' and 'Inscriptions and Romantic Nature Poetry' (1965), both in *Beyond Formalism*, 42–57, 206–30. At the same time, he portrays this quality as invoking reader-participation: for instance, while contrasting Wordworth's 'simpli-

city' with 'sententious' or 'pointed' styles which assume a passive recipient, he also compares it with the epitaphic poems of the Greek Anthology that expressly hail the reader (*Siste Viator*) (*Beyond* 211; see also *WP* ch. 1). It nevertheless remains, as he himself stresses, that openness / closure 'cannot be reduced to a technical feature' (*Unremarkable* 189), and one reason is that the wills and resources of readers differ. It is an illustrative irony in this regard that the poet Hartman uses to exemplify unclosure is so often accused of sententiousness.

Chapter One

1 See Jonathan Culler, *Structuralist Poetics* 118–19, 258–9.
2 Anonymous review of John Wright, *Poetry, Sacred and Profane*, in the *Nottinghamshire Guardian*, 30 Oct. 1851, as quoted by Wright (*The Genius of Wordsworth* 29).
3 Samuel Butler, 'Quis Desiderio ... ?' (1888), 102. See also Wright, *Genius* 28–9.
4 As my textual apparatus shows (see Appendix), 'Strange fits' is literally curtailed, having at one time proceeded to describe the speaker's tears. It is this curtailment that provokes Francis Jeffrey (see ch. 2, below).
5 Though he implies that it is already traditional, Powell is the first I have found to link 'A slumber' with the poems naming Lucy; he is discussed further in chapter 2.
6 Mark Reed's more reliable datings of the poems are as follows: 'A slumber' was 'Probably composed between 6 Oct and Dec 1798, possibly Jan 1799'; 'First versions' of 'She dwelt' and 'Strange fits' were 'probably composed between 6 Oct and possibly 14 Dec probably 21 or 28 Dec, 1798' (the terminus being the date of the Wordsworths' letter to Coleridge [*Letters* 1:235–43]); 'Three years' was 'Probably composed between 23 and 27 Feb 1799' (*CEY* 35); and 'I Travelled' was 'Probably composed c but by 29 Apr 1801' (*CMY* 21). The relevant Cornell editions substantially follow these dates, but James Butler and Karen Green date 'Three years' earlier, as 'probably at Goslar between October 6 and December 28, 1798, but perhaps as late as February 23–27, 1799' (221). Their reconstruction of the earliest surviving manuscript (DC MS. 15) suggests that it included drafts or versions of 'She dwelt,' 'The Two April Mornings,' 'Strange fits,' 'A slumber,' and 'Three years,' in that sequence (19).
7 'Lake Reminiscences' 247, or *Recollections* 188; deleted in the standard edition (see *Recollections* 407n91). Hugh Sykes Davies, 'Another New Poem by Wordsworth,' was first to call attention to the De Quincey passage and give it its proper weight as the seed of the 'Lucy Poems' grouping. I am much indebted to Sykes Davies (who is introduced more fully in chapter 2) for both research and interpretation.

8 There is reason to question De Quincey's motives for ambiguity. This passage, leading to the statement that Wordsworth 'made, what for him turns out, a happy marriage,' suggests that Wordsworth settled for Mary out of disappointment. De Quincey was estranged from the Wordsworths when he wrote this, appears never to have got on well with Mary, and had some reason, in the Wordsworths' disapproval of his own marriage, for casting aspersion on theirs. See Mary Moorman 2:234–7 and 520, and John Jordan, *De Quincey to Wordsworth* 292–8.

9 For examples of the amalgamated version see E. Hallam Moorhouse, ed., *Wordsworth* (1911) and Sir Arthur Quiller-Couch, ed., *Oxford Book of English Verse* (1939). Appendix 2 of my 'Lucy and Her Readers,' recording the various groupings of 'Lucy Poems' in Wordsworth's and later editions, cites several other examples.

10 See Appendix. Robert Gittings and Jo Manton point out that in contemporary usage 'amuse' meant 'interest' (*Dorothy Wordsworth* 91).

11 For the revisions, see Appendix. Though his 1815 arrangement of poems is best known, Wordsworth paid attention to sequence from the beginning (see James Averill, 'The Shape of *Lyrical Ballads*' 387–8). The manuscript sheet containing 'Strange fits,' 'She dwelt,' and 'A slumber' bears a note in Coleridge's hand prescribing their order: if printing had not begun they were to be poems 5, 6, and 7, following 'Ellen Irwin' (to Biggs and Cottle, c. 1 Aug. 1800, in Wordsworth's *Letters* 1:290).

12 Jared Curtis, 'A Note' 198; Mark Reed, *CMY* 168n. See also Butler and Green xxi, 32, 820–1.

13 *Letters* 1:333n. Reed endorses this assumption; see note 6 above.

14 Most important of these is Sykes Davies' essay of 1965; but he was anticipated by Lane Cooper in 1904, by K.D. Sethna in 1958, and by A.P. Rossiter in 1961.

15 Douglass H. Thomson discusses the 'Lucy of "Nutting" ' in DC MS. 16 (in *PW* 2:504–6); Richard Bourke has more recently argued, but neglecting Thomson, that the 'interlocutor in *Nutting* is Lucy ... in disguise' (173).

16 John Danby comments: 'The *Lucy* poems are fragments from the larger complex embraced more adequately, and presented with greater completeness and detachment in "The Fountain" and "The Two April Mornings" ' (88). Even this canny remark illustrates how Wordsworth's arrangement makes one specify one's own 'larger complex.'

17 'The Philosophy of Composition' (1846) (*Essays* 19). I am grateful to Mark Langlet for suggesting the relevance of this passage.

18 Longinus, *On the Sublime*, trans. W.R. Roberts, ch. 22 (Adams 88); Wordsworth, *The Prelude*, 5:230–1; Arnold, 'Wordsworth' (1879) (*Complete Prose* 9:52); Geoffrey Hartman, *Saving the Text* 156.

19 The 'Yarrow Poems' (also grouped by Arnold; see *Poems of Wordsworth* 159–68) are not a comparable case, since they represent a temporal progress and are therefore classed in sequential categories: 'Memorials of a

Tour in Scotland, 1803,' 'Memorials ... 1814,' and 'Yarrow Revisited, and Other Poems ... of 1831' (*PW* 3:83, 106, 262). On the 'Matthew Poems,' see note 32 below.

20 It is surprising how entirely classification has monopolized critical attention. Scoggins notes that 'with the exception of Dowden scholars have focused their attention on the classifications of poems in the collected editions, ignoring almost completely the more useful feature of Wordsworth's system of organization' (55–6). But Scoggins himself focuses on an issue raised by Wordsworth's classification, the distinction between 'Imagination' and 'Fancy,' and subsequent studies follow suit. In 'Wordsworth's Categorization,' the fullest such study, Gene Ruoff considers each class of poems successively and is more concerned with poems' relations to their rubrics than to each other – e.g., with how 'Poems Founded on the Affections' are really about affections. Frances Ferguson anticipates my own view of Wordsworth's classifications as disruptive or parodic (*William Wordsworth* 35–9) but ultimately takes them seriously, arguing that the various 'facultative categories' (41) reflect different rhetorical strategies and views of language. Judith Herman considers 'the re-reading which the classification urges' on the 'Poems of the Imagination' and 'Poems of the Fancy' ('The Poet as Editor' 86). Carl Ketcham's 'Introduction' to the *Shorter Poems* includes a useful and detailed discussion of the ordering's development, also focusing mainly on categorization (19–32). Among more recent and more sympathetic studies of Wordsworth's orderings, see Stuart Curran's 'Multum in Parvo' and Neil Fraistat's *The Poem and the Book* ch. 3, both of which stress the artistry of Wordsworth's orderings and recommend them for readers; and Siskin 108–24, which considers Wordsworth's orderings together with his prefaces as 'extratextual revision.' See also note 23 below.

21 As it turns out, the poem does not explain this name, though it does explain those of Michael's house ('The Evening Star') and of 'The CLIPPING TREE.' 'Poems on the Naming of Places' challenge taxonomy in another way also: in describing idiosyncratic rather than systematic naming, they implicitly reject philosophic language theories and the allied efforts such as Linnaeus' to subordinate naming to taxonomy.

22 As Scoggins notes, there is steady addition of classes from the beginning, from one in 1800 to five in 1807, eight in 1809, fourteen in 1815 (p. 28 and ch. 3, passim). The Wordsworth documents usually cited are the letter to Coleridge, 5 May 1809 (*Letters* 2:331–6), and the Preface of 1815 (*Prose* 3:26–9). Carl Ketcham lists and discusses others, including manuscript materials (*Shorter Poems* 20ff.).

23 For early criticisms of this kind, see the anonymous review of the *Poems* (1815) in *the Monthly Review*, 2nd series, 78 (Nov. 1815), 225–6 (*RR* 734) and John Wilson, 'An Essay on the Theory and the Writings of Words-

worth' (1839) (*Essays* 1:282–3). Coleridge's preference of 'chronological order' over '[a]ll your divisions' of poetical works may glance at Wordsworth (*Table Talk* 1:453 [1 Jan. 1834]). See also Arnold, 'Wordsworth,' (*Complete Prose* 9:42–3). More recently, see James Heffernan 109–10.

24 Typical is the anonymous reviewer's statement: 'he has not suffered his poetry to be the expression merely of his natural and unperverted feelings; but *he has devoted it to the developement and maintenance of a system*' (*British Critic*, 2nd series, 11 [June 1819], 588 [*RR* 167]). The most consistent critic of system is Jeffrey (see *RR*, especially 430, 431, 436, 439), but see also, e.g., *RR* 169, 184, and 734, and Byron's *Don Juan*, 'Dedication,' stanza 4 (Byron 374)

25 See 'Expostulation and Reply,' 'The Tables Turned' (*PW* 4:56–7), and the attack on 'this modern system' of education in *The Prelude* (5:295ff.). The Preface to *The Excursion* declines 'formally to announce a system' (*PW* 5:2).

26 *The Order of Things* 132. In observing that what is excluded is all sense-data except sight, Foucault corroborates the romantic, including Wordsworth's, synechdochic use of the eye to represent reductive rationality.

27 Compare Coleridge's disparagement of taxonomy in his essay 'On Method' (*The Friend* 1:467–9) and in the *Lay Sermons* (59, 77). David Perkins devotes a whole chapter of *Is Literary History Possible?* to 'Literary Classifications' (61–84); his opening observations that 'Classification is fundamental to the discipline of literary history' and that its importance 'to the profession cannot be overstated' (61–2) give some sense of the import of an attack on classification (but see also note 28 below).

28 I make a similar case, but in greater detail, regarding Wordsworth's use of 'pastoral' as a category in 'Double Economics.' I do not claim that Wordsworth is the first to bring such categorization in question; Neil Fraistat cites similar surmises regarding Herbert's and Blake's ordering of their poems (*Poems in Their Place* 10–11). And it may be true that Wordsworth's ramshackle classification is comparable to those of eighteenth-century anthologies or of Hugh Blair's *Lectures on Rhetoric and Belles Lettres* (1783) (see Wellek, *Attack* 34–5), but the implications are different coming from poet than from anthologist or critic. Perkins goes so far as to argue that literary classification is normally 'contingent' and 'irrational,' indeed that 'Literature has no taxonomic system, but only a confused aggregate of overlapping classifications' (*Is Literary History Possible?* 68–9; see 68–74); if so, Wordsworth's system is only business as usual. Yet the complaints of his critics argue otherwise. It strikes me that we can reconcile the outcry against Wordsworth's 'system' with Perkins' description of the 'irrational' disciplinary norm only by considering his system as mischievously exaggerating the irrationality of that norm.

29 In 'an annotated copy of the 1807 *Poems*, vol. I' in the Beinecke at Yale,

containing 'a preliminary draft that Wordsworth made when he was sketching out the 1815 arrangement of the poems (Tinker Collection, item 2335)' (Ruoff, 'Another' 359–60). Elsewhere Ruoff notes that this is 'the only significant difference between Wordsworth's 1813–1814 draft of the arrangement and the published version of 1815' ('Wordsworth's' 20). Ferguson observes that the shifts in class are few (39, 253n7).

30 The sonnets on National Independence and Liberty, Wordsworth tells Lady Beaumont, 'while they each fix the attention upon some important sentiment separately considered, do at the same time collectively make a Poem on the subject of civil Liberty' (21 May 1807, *Letters* 2:147). The 1815 Preface says that the small poems 'might be regarded under a two-fold view; as composing an entire work within themselves, and as adjuncts to the philosophical Poem, "The Recluse"' (*Prose* 3:28). See also *PW* 3:506, 508, and compare Coleridge's representation of *Lyrical Ballads* as 'to a certain degree *one work*, in *kind tho' not in degree*, as an Ode is one work' (Coleridge's *Letters* 1:412). Clifford Siskin explores this ambiguity in Wordsworth's corpus as marking a 'mutually interpretative relationship between parts and wholes' (*Historicity* ch. 5, at 113). I would rather call the ambiguity 'anti-interpretive,' but I think we agree in substance, for Siskin adds that it defers interpretation to 'larger and larger wholes so that it cannot finally be circumscribed' (113).

31 Arguments for winnowing Wordsworth occur earlier too: see the *Eclectic Review*, 2nd series, 12 (July 1819), 74 (*RR* 392), and Wilson, *Essays* 1:295 and 311. Even Arnold was criticized in some quarters for not being selective enough (Charles G.D. Roberts 272–4).

32 I don't examine the 'Matthew Poems' here, but they present an interesting parallel to the Lucy problem and are sometimes considered together with, or used to make explicit what is merely suggested in, the 'Lucy Poems' (e.g., Hodgson 54–62). Even though the 'Matthew Poems' are explicitly linked by the Fenwick notes, their ambiguities resemble those of the 'Lucy Poems' – as the variability of editorial groupings suggests. Hayden presents the most extensive grouping: his notes label each a '"Matthew poem,"' and his index lists under a 'Matthew Poems' heading: 'Address to the Scholars of the Village School,' 'Matthew,' 'The Two April Mornings,' 'The Fountain,' '"Could I the Priest's Consent Have Gained,"' and 'Elegy Written in the Same Place.' In Wordsworth the first of these appears in 'Epitaphs and Elegiac Pieces,' while the second, third and fourth are together in 'Poems of Sentiment and Reflection.' The others were first published from manuscripts by de Selincourt in 1947. Arnold prints only the three Wordsworth placed together. Butler and Green have recently created, 'as an editorial convenience,' a grouping which they call 'Mathew Elegies' (19; see 297–302, 536–43, 807–8).

33 I discovered at a late stage that Wordsworth does use the term 'intention'

in an earlier version of this claim: 'I ... probably ere long may republish the whole arranged in a manner that will make more clear my intentions in writing them' (to John Edwards, 27 March [1811]; *Letters* 2:471). It might be argued that Wordsworth's thinking evolved from 'intentions' to 'purposes' by 1815, when he put his ordering into effect, but so much precision seems unlikely to me; I am not really contending that he recognizes or honours this formal distinction *in terms*, only that his 1815 usage is worth heeding, since the actual intentionality of his works is most precisely explained today in terms of 'purpose.'

34 I more fully discuss Wordsworth's efforts to reduce his own intentionality in 'Recuperating Arnold' 67–77.

35 The distinction is J.L. Austin's (3–7, passim).

36 See *The Prelude*, 5:230–1, 594–5, and the 1842 sonnet, 'A Poet! He hath put his heart to school' – on the theme, 'Thy Art be Nature.' Coleridge's account of the plan for *Lyrical Ballads* describes how 'the sudden charm, which accidents of light and shade, which moon-light or sun-set diffused over a known and familiar landscape,' provided a model for 'the modifying colours of imagination' in poetry (*BL* 2:5). 'Accidents' is a pregnant word in the context.

37 On the ideology of the 'natural,' see Karl Marx, *Selected Writings* 77–8, 98, and 'Introduction to a Critique of Political Economy' (1857) (*The German Ideology* 124–7); Ernst Cassirer, *The Philosophy of the Englightenment* 294–7; and David Simpson, *Wordsworth and the Figurings of the Real* xvii.

38 See Stephen Gill, ed., *William Wordsworth* xxxi; Carl Ketcham, ed., *Shorter Poems* 4–5.

39 Bourke's argument for considering 'Nutting' with the 'Lucy Poems' – that 'In the 1800 edition ... *Nutting* is succeeded by the penultimate lyric of the Lucy cycle' (193) – is typical. 'Nutting' does precede 'Three years' in the 1800 *Lyrical Ballads*, but 'Three years' is not 'penultimate' in this edition, for it is not succeeded by another 'Lucy Poem,' and there is, indeed, no 'Lucy *cycle*' as yet. See also, e.g., Scoggins 40; Durrant, *Wordsworth* 136.

40 In 'The Editorial Problem of Final Authorial Intention,' G. Thomas Tanselle considers this problem extensively from the standpoint of scholarly editing. Jack Stillinger, *Multiple Authorship* 194–202, reflects on the implications for editing of the fact that authorship is virtually never single. I agree with Stillinger's preference for editorial policies that admit different 'versions,' but the fact remains that some 'versions' cannot be justified even as 'multiple authorship.' At least to my mind, the postmortem treatment of the 'Lucy Poems' exemplifies editorial creativity that is quite distinct from 'multiple authorship.' This is not to rule out even bastard versions, so long as the distinctions are appreciated. Supposing one undertook to reprint Arnold's selection of Wordsworth's poems today, this would be highly dubious as a way of representing Words-

worth, but it would still be useful as a representation of Arnold or of nineteenth-century representations of Wordsworth. Strictly speaking, it would not be an edition *of Wordsworth*.

41 William Hazlitt, 'On Mr. Wordsworth's "Excursion"' (1814) (*Complete Works* 4:120–1); John Wilson, 'Essay' (1829) (*Essays* 1:314).

42 *British Critic* 14 (Oct. 1799), 365 (*RR* 128); Francis Jeffrey, review of Southey's *Thalaba*, *Edinburgh Review* 1 (Oct. 1802), 64 (*RR* 416). See also *RR* 8–9, 26, 44, 102, 132, 134, 165, 217, 236, 248, 255, etc., and Preface, note 6, above.

43 Norman Holland, 'Literary Interpretation' 225, 223. Others: 'The so-called 'Lucy Poems'. ... so simple and so barely adorned. ... tell a slight story of passion and of grief for one forever lost' (Pafford 173). 'She dwelt' is 'of no complexity according to Empson's seven types [of ambiguity]' (Burgum 38). F.W. Bateson's facile assumption that line 1 of 'A slumber' 'really means "I was not mentally awake"' may explain his opinion that it is 'much the weakest line in the poem' (*English Poetry* 29).

44 The dispute has especially concerned 'trees'; Alan Grob's fine account of line 8 – it 'subtly passes from barrenness to blossoming' – synthesizes the poles of this dispute (244).

45 Brian Caraher develops the 'my spirit did seal a slumber' reading (44–8); for other precedents see Caraher 45n.

46 Sykes Davies does query this word, though he does not note either of the passages that seem to me most relevant; nor does he attempt a definition (158–9). See also Warren Stevenson, 'Cosmic Irony' 93; A.P Rossiter, *Angel with Horns* 48–9; and J. Hillis Miller, 'Postscript' 115.

47 Though 'seel' was archaic by Wordsworth's time, the *OED* cites a usage by Southey as late as 1814: 'A life-long night / Seel'd his broad eye' (*Roderick* 16:239–40). Compare Wordsworth's 'The Russian Fugitive': 'Sleep sealed her eyes, and stole / Feeling from limbs with travel spent' (lines 46–7; *PW* 4:184).

48 Suzanne Nalbantian considers Wordsworth's use of the bird in *The Symbol of the Soul*.

49 Since Hirsch used them to demonstrate a verification procedure in the essay 'Objective Interpretation' (1960; *Validity* 209–44), the most famous versions of the naturalistic and pantheistic readings have been those of Cleanth Brooks ('Irony') and F.W. Bateson (*English Poetry* 29–30). I am not convinced that a coherent 'election' reading is possible, since 'slumber' must be either subject or object of 'seal.' ('Spirit' poses equal difficulties – generally ignored – for the naturalistic reading.) If this problem could be resolved, a religious reading that dispensed with Lucy might make better sense than usual of the rest of stanza 1. Warren Stevenson compares the other use of 'seal' in Revelation – as in 'the seventh seal' – but I fail to see how this usage would make sense in the poem ('Cosmic Irony' 93).

50 In '"Fields of Sheep,"' Gene Ruoff comments perceptively on how we manage 'not to read a line' that bothers us.

51 Miller subsequently stressed that this supposition was ironic ('Postscript' 116).

52 See, e.g., Paul de Man, 'The Rhetoric of Temporality' 205–6 (or *Blindness* 223–6) and Ward Pafford: 'Here are briefly recalled the days of youthful love as a dream transcending the limitations of waking life' (175).

53 Thus Richard Onorato: 'the poet is not half-mourning, half-envying someone who was very like himself and who may have Life-in-Death, but rather writing numbly about himself as one experiencing Death-in-Life' (198).

54 I am grateful to Karl Kroeber for pointing out this displacement.

55 See de Man, 'Semiology and Rhetoric' and *The Resistance to Theory* 14–7.

56 As Geoffrey Hartman notes (*Beyond* 48n), the conflict of images was first pointed out in Mary Shelley's *The Last Man*. Indeed, Shelley's comments (discussed in chapter 3) directly anticipate Brooks (discussed below) in explaining this contradiction as a contrast between private and public vision. On 'Untrodden ways,' see Bateson, *Wordsworth* 31.

57 Compare D.W. Harding's treatment of this problem as regards symbolism: 'when inexplicit symbolism is used extensively in poetry we face the danger not only of idiosyncratic interpretation on the reader's part but of bogus profundity on the author's. There are too many ways of producing something that looks mysteriously symbolic' (*Experience into Words* 85). It is not clear how Harding distinguishes the 'bogus' from the 'valid obscurity.'

58 In the first extant draft (see Appendix), line 25 reads, '*Strange* are the fancies that will slide,' rather than 'What fond and wayward thoughts will slide.' Wordsworth's revision is apparently designed not to clarify the connection with the '*Strange* fits of passion' but to make it more tenuous (emphases added).

59 See Alfred Cobban, 'Wordsworth and Nationality' 142; Walter Gierasch; and Spencer Hall 174–5.

60 *Wordsworth's Great Period Poems* 8–9. Levinson's introductory polemic is illuminating, but a more persuasive illustration of new-historicist practice is David Simpson's *Wordsworth's Historical Imagination*. See also Jameson, *The Political Unconscious* 60–1.

61 See also Kate Millett, especially 77, and David Sonstroem. I am grateful to my colleague Maggie Berg for sharing with me her paper 'Betrayed by Quotation: Ruskin's "Of Queens' Gardens,"' which shrewdly mediates the Millett-Sonstroem debate. Showing how Ruskin's discursive affirmations of 'women's power' are 'arrest[ed] and contain[ed]' by his quotations, Berg finds his use of 'Three years' his most 'inappropriate quotation' and dwells specifically on his omission of Lucy's death. Curiously,

Hartman cites Ruskin's discussion not only as an example to show that 'close reading' used to be a 'condescending, didactic exercise,' but also as a 'beautiful exposition' (*Criticism* 175).

62 An American reviewer quotes only stanzas 1–5 (*North American Review* 9 [1824], 368); in 1848 Charles Kingsley quotes only from stanzas 4 and 5 (183); in 1878 George H. Calvert writes, 'Never was the active, purifying influence of nature more lovingly exemplified than in the growth of this sweet Lucy,' and quotes only stanzas 4–5 (87–8); in 1897 W.T. Webb quotes only stanzas 4–5 (xlii); in 1898 Ethel Wheeler, writing on 'Great Men's Visions of Womanhood,' notes the 'exquisite happiness' of Lucy and quotes only from stanzas 3, 5, and 6 (270); in 1903 Walter Raleigh quotes only stanza 5 (139); in 1905 George Edward Woodberry quotes only stanzas 1–6 (174–5); in 1923 Hugh I'Anson Fausset quotes only stanza 5 (216). In a study first published in 1922, Arthur Beatty does not quote the poem at all, yet even in stressing that Wordsworth's nature was not always benevolent, he says, 'In contrast [to 'Ruth'] stands the little lyric, *Three Years She Grew*, an ideal picture of what normal human development might be, in which both the law and the impulse, the kindling and restraining power of nature lead to the perfect development of beauty and grace' (213; see also 107). In a study published shortly after Garrod's, H.N. Fairchild quotes only stanzas 2–6 and glosses them: 'If the mind of a human being is the sum of the sensory stimuli that have reached it, one need only catch him young enough and place him amidst the goodness and majesty of nature in order to have him develop like Lucy in *Three Years* ... ' (104). The very few who do admit Lucy's death before Garrod are special cases or actually downplay the admission. For instance, in 1884 Henry N. Hudson does see Nature as "withdrawing [Lucy] from life," but he still quotes only stanzas 1, 3, 4, and 5 (168–9). In 1815 a reviewer of *The Excursion* quotes stanzas 5 and 7 without comment, as a sample of *Lyrical Ballads* (*British Review* 6 [Aug. 1815], 55 [*RR* 229]); a Victorian textbook of 1845 prints the poem entire and glosses every stanza except the seventh (Joseph Payne 109–10); and W.H. Hudson (in 1914) and C.T. Winchester (in 1916) both reprint the poem entire, but these are textbooks rather than critical essays, quoting all poems *in toto* with running commentaries. Aubrey de Vere quotes the whole poem in his 1880 review of Arnold's 1879 selection (*Essays* 1:150–1); this is odd, since he also calls the poem 'a description of youthful maidenhood' and generally out-Arnolds Arnold in his acceptance of Wordsworthian nature's beneficence.

63 Geoffrey Durrant, who believes the poem's repeated use of antithesis implies an antithesis between stanza 7 and the rest of the poem, makes the strongest argument for the 'but' reading (*Wordsworth* 157–66).

64 Jonathan Culler comments on the rise of the ironic reading of romanti-

cism (*On Deconstruction* 248&n), citing Paul de Man and Cynthia Chase in particular. But for the ironic reading of Wordsworth, one does better to recall Brooks's essay 'Irony' and David Simpson's *Irony and Authority*. David Ferry's *The Limits of Mortality* and Hartman's *Wordsworth's Poetry* are essential to the modern revisionism regarding Wordsworthian nature. These developments are treated more fully in chapter 5.

65 'Anecdote for Fathers' and 'Michael' can be read as critiques of governance; more obvious is the critique of teachers (*Prelude* 5:347–63).

66 Simon Stuart compares 'Tintern Abbey' (*New Phoenix Wings* 116–7).

67 See Grob 203 and 245, and Susan Eilenberg 125–32. My elegiac reading resembles Grob's in many respects, but not in seeing the poem as 'bitter.'

68 Wordsworth personifies nature also in the Grand Chartreuse passage of *The Prelude* (6:414–36) and in 'The Tuft of Primroses.' In both cases it is explicable as the effect of emotion. In 'Primroses' the speaking Nature is introduced: 'Yes, I was moved and to this hour am moved,' and closes with the explanation: 'I heard or seemed to hear' (lines 528, 546; *PW* 5:360–1).

69 Spencer Hall suggests an even more tenuous religious – or rather, Death-of-God – reading of 'Strange fits,' seeing the apostrophe 'O mercy!' as an abortive and unanswered prayer (165–6).

70 Hall states (in 1971) that 'they have almost never been meaningfully considered as an intradependent group' (162) – only a slight exaggeration. See (chronologically): Margaret Oliphant, 'A Century' 316–17; Catherine MacDonald MacLean 49–58; Drabble; Durrant; James Taaffe; Hall; Ferguson; Robert Marchant 33–45; Patricia Ball, *The Heart's Events* 9–19; and Richard Matlack, 'Wordsworth's Lucy Poems.'

71 Comparable but not identical cases can be cited in the romantic period, e.g., Coleridge's 'Conversation Poems,' Keats's odes, and Wordsworth's own 'Matthew Poems.'

Chapter Two

1 The works I have found most helpful on literary historiography are H.R. Jauss, 'Literary History as a Challenge to Literary Theory,' and René Wellek's reply, 'The Fall of Literary History' (*Attack* 64–77), which assents to Jauss's diagnosis but rejects his cure (my citations are to Wellek 34–5, and Jauss 3). See also Wellek's 'Introduction to Volumes 5 and 6: Method and Scope' (1986) (*A History of Modern Criticism* 5:xv–xxiv); Robert Weimann, 'Past Significance and Present Meaning in Literary History' (1970) (*Structure and Society* 18–56); Geoffrey Hartman, 'Toward Literary History' (*Beyond Formalism* 356–86); Paul de Man, 'Literary History and Literary Modernity' (1969) (*Blindness and Insight* 142–65); David Perkins, ed.,

Theoretical Issues in Literary History (1991); and David Perkins, *Is Literary History Possible?* (1992). The latter volume's opening chapter (1–27) gives a useful overview of 'The Present State of the Discussion' along with further references.

2 As de Man makes clear, once a crisis is felt in literary history it is easily perceived as the crisis of historiography *per se*: thus 'literary history could in fact be paradigmatic for history in general' (*Blindness* 165).

3 The scant earlier comments by William and Dorothy appear in a letter (14 or 21 Dec. 1798) transmitting 'Strange fits' and 'She dwelt' to Coleridge (*Letters* 1: 236–8).

4 Coleridge's text is reproduced in the textual apparatus, Appendix. On its questionable authority, see Hugh Sykes Davies 139–42.

5 But Gene Ruoff suggests that 'A slumber' was at one time slated for 'Epitaphs and Elegiac Pieces' ('Another' 359–60).

6 John Rea compares Coleridge's poem ('Hartley Coleridge' 120–3). Donald Reiman discusses the relation between Coleridge's comment, 'A slumber,' and 'She dwelt' ('Poetry of Familiarity' 156). See also Ernest de Selincourt (*PW* 2:472).

7 The objections to the argument of Bateson's *Wordsworth: A Re-Interpretation* (1954) tend to be distaste for his view of William and Dorothy and his want of hard evidence: e.g., Helen Darbishire, *TLS*, 19 Nov. 1954, and Edith J. Morley, *MLR* 50 (1955), 333–5. But Richard Matlack's claim that 'Bateson's incest theory has always been' unpopular is overstated (51); several reviews were quite positive.

8 *The Political Unconscious* 75–7, citing Hans-Georg Gadamer, *Truth and Method* 216–20 and 267–74.

9 For studies bearing on the institution, see Richard Ohmann, *English in America*; Hohendahl, *The Institution of Criticism* (on Germany); Edward Said, 'Opponents, Audiences, Constituencies, and Community'; Terry Eagleton, 'The Rise of English' and 'Conclusion: Political Criticism,' both in *Literary Theory*, and *The Function of Criticism*; Karl Kroeber, 'The Evolution of Literary Study, 1883–1983'; Paul Bové, *Intellectuals in Power*; René Wellek, *History* 5:23–5 and 6:59–61; and Gerald Graff, *Professing Literature*. In using Eagleton and Said to argue against a *solely* institutional horizon, I do not mean to denigrate these studies, most of which are superb. On their role of correcting criticism's apolitical postures, see Eagleton, *Literary* 194–7, and Said 7–9 and 18–19.

10 For Said's remarks on Eagleton, see 22.

11 Stanley Fish, 'Profession Despise Thyself: Fear and Self-Loathing in Literary Studies' (*Doing What Comes Naturally* 202); see also 'Anti-Professionalism' (*Doing* 215–46). Fish argues 'that a practice cannot (or should not) be criticized *because* it is professional' (242), true because professionalism is not a practice's *only* horizon.

12 See also Richard Altick, *The English Common Reader*; Lawrence Stone, 'Literacy and Education in England, 1640–1900'; Olivia Smith, *The Politics of Language* 155–62; and Eagleton, *Function* 45–67. Jon Klancher's *The Making of English Reading Audiences, 1790–1832*, addresses both the rise of multi-class readership and its institutional management, not least through the Coleridgean 'clerisy.' A dramatically clear instance of the passage from anxiety to theory qua indoctrination, albeit in a later period, is I.A. Richards' *Practical Criticism* (1929), which begins with 'a piece of fieldwork in comparative ideology' (6) and ends proposing methods to control difference (see 313–24, calling for 'theory'). On Richards' program as indoctrination, see Bové ch. 2, especially pp. 68–74.

13 *Le Beau Monde* 2 (Oct. 1807), 140 (*RR* 42).

14 *Augustan Review* 1 (Aug. 1815), 345 (*RR* 27).

15 Letter of 14 or 21 Dec. 1798 (*Letters* 1:237). Dorothy's journals (which do not cover the Goslar period) mention none of the 'Lucy Poems,' but Susan Levin and Robert Ready show how some of them influence her own poetry.

16 As discourse theory argues, constraint is built into the institutional mode of discourse, though it is by definition not analysable from within that discourse. As Eagleton puts it, 'You can think or believe what you want, as long as you speak this particular language. Nobody is especially concerned about what you say, with what extreme, moderate, radical or conservative positions you adopt, provided that they are compatible with, and can be articulated within, a specific form of discourse. It is just that certain meanings and positions will not be articulable within it' (*Literary* 201). See also Michel Foucault, 'The Discourse on Language' and 'What is an Author?'

17 In general, partisanship was no simple matter of Tory reviewers damning Whig publications; as Hayden points out, Francis Jeffrey attacked the early Wordsworth for 'splenetic and idle discontent with the existing institutions of society,' though he himself had 'interest in social reforms,' and the *Edinburgh Review* was a Whig organ (*Romantic Reviewers* 80) (compare Eagleton, *Function* 37).

18 The individualism of 'She dwelt' is most fully explored by Edwin Burgum, 'The Cult of the Complex in Poetry' 37–41. On the others, see chapter 1 above.

19 John Wilson proclaims that Wordsworth effected 'a *revolution* in Poetry; and a revolution can no more be brought about in Poetry than in the Constitution, without destruction of many excellent and time-hallowed establishments' ('Vindication' 73). Hazlitt declares that Wordsworth had a 'levelling' muse (11:87). Barron Field writes that 'Wordsworth's poetry is essentially democratic, qualify it as he may by some few political pieces' (25). See also Nathaniel Teich, 'Evaluating Wordsworth's Revolution.' Carl

Woodring unfolds the political implications of Wordsworth's humanitarianism not just in obvious poems such as 'The Old Cumberland Beggar,' but also in such as 'Tintern Abbey' and the flower poems of 1802 (*Politics* 85–101) – an exercise that has become widespread with the new historicism.

20 See Francis Jeffrey, *Edinburgh Review* 11 (Oct. 1807), 214–31 (esp. 214–18), the *Satirist* 1 (Nov. 1807), 188–91; Lucy Aikin, *Annual Review* 6 (1808), 521–9 (esp. 521–4); the *Poetical Register for 1806–07* (1811), 540–1; and James Montgomery, *Eclectic Review* 4 (Jan. 1808), 35–43. All these are reproduced in facsimile in *RR*.

21 See Robert Mayo, 'The Contemporaneity of the *Lyrical Ballads*'; Charles Ryskamp, 'Wordsworth's *Lyrical Ballads* in Their Time'; John Jordan, *Why the* 'Lyrical Ballads'?; and Mary Jacobus, *Tradition and Experiment*.

22 'Criticism and Crisis' (1967) (*Blindness* 8–9).

23 On the rise of a specifically romantic self-consciousness, whether as crisis or otherwise, see: Geoffrey Hartman, 'Romanticism and Antiself-consciousness' (*Beyond* 298–310); Earl Wasserman, 'The English Romantics: The Grounds of Knowledge'; A.D. Nuttall, *A Common Sky*; David Simpson, *Irony and Authority* and *Wordsworth and the Figurings of the Real*; and Jon Klancher, *The Making of English Reading Audiences*. Hartman, Wasserman, and Nuttall give more philosophical accounts, Klancher a more historical and sociological account of how audiences became aware of themselves as such; Simpson's accounts combine philosophical and material-historical explanation.

24 My working definition of literary 'theory' as the project of minimizing subjectivity in reading derives from the discussions in W.J.T. Mitchell, ed., *Against Theory*, and especially from Stanley Fish's definition of theory (110). See pp. 147–51, below.

25 These responses correspond to the two 'interpretations of interpretation' sketched by Jacques Derrida in *Writing and Difference* (67–8, 292–3) and *Of Grammatology* (178–9).

26 'Creative criticism' is often associated today with the playfulness of Derrida and Geoffrey Hartman: see Hartman, 'Literary Commentary as Literature' and 'Centaur: On the Psychology of the Critic' (*Criticism in the Wilderness* 189–225). Making a virtue of necessity is a common strategy in romantic responses to subjectivism: see Simpson, *Irony and Authority*, 45, 108, 112, 115, 119.

27 Wellek specifically attacks 'the fallacy of "creative" criticism' in Schlegel (*History* 2:10–11).

28 See Wilson, 'Observations,' 'Vindication,' and 'Letter.'

29 See George Saintsbury, *A History of English Criticism* 426; Alan Lang Strout, 'John Wilson, "Champion" of Wordsworth' and 'William Wordsworth and John Wilson'; and Reiman, *RR* 55–6.

30 Aside from three responses by R.F. Storch, Jonathan Wordsworth, and Gene Ruoff in *Essays in Criticism*, all of which are dismissive and beside the main point, I can think of only two critics who discuss Sykes Davies, and both are dismissive: M.H. Abrams, 'Construing and Deconstructing,' and Brian Caraher, *Wordsworth's 'Slumber'* (27–37). Susan Eilenberg cites and to a large degree heeds Sykes Davies (*Strange Power of Speech* 111–12, 119–20, 244n7). His argument appears to be influenced by A.P. Rossiter, *Angel with Horns*, which discusses 'ambivalence' in 'A slumber' and attacks the grouping as a 'superfluous fiction[] generated by editors' (48).

31 *Recollections* 188; Sykes Davies 147. De Quincey is discussed in chapter 1 above.

32 Palgrave's titles, which had no textual authority, have not been very influential. But the 'Education of Nature' is occasionally used, and Robert Fleissner has argued that 'The Lost Love' influenced Robert Frost's 'The Road Not Taken.' Arnold's selection was probably influenced by Palgrave's; his preface mentions 'Mr. Palgrave's fine and skilfully chosen specimens of Wordsworth' (vii).

33 The grouping was not, of course, accepted by all instantly. In 1887 James Sutherland quotes from 'I travelled' and lists 'Three years,' 'Strange fits,' and 'She dwelt' among other poems written at Goslar, but never mentions the 'Lucy Poems' (60). In 1889, James Rowley, having read Arnold's preface, nevertheless speaks of 'the three Lucy poems' and then lists '*Education of Nature* and *Lucy Gray*' separately (57).

34 On the role of aesthetic preferences, see James Thorpe, 'The Aesthetics of Textual Criticism.'

35 Bateson comments on the importance of the early 'Wordsworthians,' a 'sort of intimate and enthusiastic audience' that made oral poetry possible for Wordsworth (*Wordsworth* 195). See also John Wilson's description (1829) of a meeting in which the Immortality Ode is discussed with more enthusiasm than understanding (*Essays* 1:267–75; also 261–3, 287, 292–3).

36 Unfortunately, Powell's text corresponds to no edition, but it may be a misquotation of 1800. If so, 'the poems that precede it' would be 'Strange fits' and 'She dwelt.'

37 'She dwelt' was by far the most popular of the 'Lucy Poems' throughout the nineteenth century, 'A slumber' the least or second least. While 'She dwelt' remains popular, 'A slumber' now draws most attention by far. A crude tally I've made of the pre-Arnoldian judgments ranks the poems as follows (counting positives, negatives, and parodies): 'She dwelt' (11–2–4), 'Three years' (6–0–0), 'Strange fits' (3–0–0), 'I travelled' (2–0–0), and 'A slumber' (3–2–0).

38 See especially Frances Ferguson, 'The Lucy Poems'; James Averill, *Wordsworth and the Poetry of Human Suffering* 207–8; Michael Cooke, *Acts of Inclusion* 58–62; and Geoffrey Hartman, 'Elation in Hegel and Wordsworth'

190. Richard Bourke (193–7) adapts to 'Nutting' Ferguson's argument that 'Lucy' has been elided from 'A slumber.'

39 Remarkably, Riding and Graves introduce Lucy without noting that 'A slumber' never mentions her; thus even in attacking anthologies they illustrate their power. Equally ironic is the anthologization of their anti-anthological reading of 'A slumber' in *Understanding Poetry*, ed. Cleanth Brooks and Robert Penn Warren (1938); the editors cite their analysis of the poem's ungrammaticality and add: 'But Riding and Graves conceded that the poem has great beauty and a "supra-logical harmony"' (378). They *concede* no such thing, for it is their main point; they are defending, not attacking the poem.

Among more recent treatments of literary groupings and sequences, Neil Fraistat's books are far more helpful in clarifying purposes and effects than is Rosenthal and Gall's. The latter suggest that the 'sequence' can be considered a hard-and-fast genre which arose only recently (3, 8); Fraistat's concern with the orderings within volumes of poetry demonstrates how mistaken that notion is (see *Poems in Their Place* 3–17).

40 *The Power of Genre* 20, 25. Rosmarin borrows 'expedient error' from Hans Vaihinger.

41 Jameson argues that 'literary production has in modern times ceaselessly and systematically undermined ... generic restrictions,' and that writing *within* genres is now 'subliterary' (*The Political Unconscious* 106–7). The crossings of genres in the 'Lucy Poems,' as in 'lyrical ballad' generally, can only alter whatever genres are crossed and deteriorate their distinctiveness in the long run, thus evincing their conventionality. When it has to be pointed out to us that 'lyrical ballad' is contradictory, or that it was in Wordsworth's day (see pp. 14–15 above), this is in no small part because *Lyrical Ballads* has actually made lyric and ballad compatible – and thus effaced the conditions for appreciating its own originality. See also Rosmarin 35, on the value of breaking genres; Herbert Lindenberger 13–15; and Stuart Curran, especially 182.

42 So far as I know, Geoffrey Hartman was first to dwell on the importance of 'borderers' in Wordsworth (*WP*, esp. 158f, ch. 6, and 224–6). But I am obliged to an anonymous press reader who notes Charles G.D. Roberts' observation of 1892: 'Wordsworth's peculiar province is that border-land wherein Nature and the heart of Man act and react upon each other. His vision is occupied not so much with Nature as with the relations between Nature and his inmost self' (Roberts 274–5).

43 *Jameson, Althusser, Marx* 95; see ch. 5, 'Narrative and Interpretation.' Actually Dowling is not so much arguing this point as explaining a 'notion' he thinks Jameson's *Political Unconscious* assumes. I may seem to trivialize Dowling's hypothesis: as he puts it, to call narrative an 'epistemological category' 'is not to make the conventional claim that we make up stories about the world to understand it, but the much more radical claim that

the world comes to us in the shape of stories' (95). Yet Dowling's second claim is not just 'epistemological' but ontological: it allows the corollary, essential to Jameson's project, that we can understand the world *aright* through (or as) narrative. Whatever Dowling may mean by 'radical,' the more modest claim he represents as 'conventional' seems to me both more credible and more unsettling. At any rate, it is this 'conventional' claim I make here. See also J. Hillis Miller, 'Narrative,' which uses 'A slumber' to illustrate the ubiquity of narrative.

44 Citing 'Hart-Leap Well,' line 97 (*PW* 2:252).

45 *Romantic Narrative Art* 51, 58. Kroeber has recently developed his historical thesis in 'Narrative and De-Narrativized Art,' suggesting that romanticism flirts with de-narratization and ultimately re-embraces narrative: only with modernism is the 'decision *against* narrative' made firm (see especially 215–16). On a romantic retreat from narrative, see also Susan Wolfson, 'Keats's *Isabella*'; and Alan Liu, *Wordsworth* 75–87. In an argument that anticipates my own, Tilottama Rajan views the 'Lucy poems' as 'the lyricisation of the beautiful soul' (88) and Shelley's 'Alastor' as its re-narratization ('The Web of Human Things,' especially 87–8, 104).

46 See Eric Robertson 151; G.M. Harper 129–30; John Jones 72–3. See also p. 10, above.

47 Various orderings in editions and anthologies are listed in appendix 2 to my 'Lucy and Her Readers.' Sykes Davies tabulates the orderings of Palgrave, Arnold, de Vere, and Symington (151).

48 The best examples of psychobiographical criticism are the arguments of Bateson and Matlack (discussed above) and various essays by Geoffrey Hartman, especially 'The Interpreter's Freud' (*Easy Pieces* 137–54). Psychobiography is not, of course, wholly distinct from simple efforts to identify Lucy. Donald Reiman's 'The Poetry of Familiarity,' informative as to William's and Dorothy's relations, lies somewhere between: it invokes Freud and in some ways follows Bateson, but generally rests content with identification rather than dwell on the text's repressive and refractive qualities. 'Strange fits,' Reiman claims, 'certainly refers to Dorothy as Lucy,' and 'the five so-called "Lucy poems" were written about the same imagined death of Dorothy' (156; but see also 157–8).

49 In 1934, Herbert Hartman listed previous identifications for Lucy: Dorothy, Mary, 'Annette Vallon, "Lucy Gray," some ideal maiden, an adopted gipsy child, or the unknown object of a "real experience of youthful love and bewildering grief" – to these has been added "Li'le Hartley" Coleridge' (137–38). Hartman gives sources for most of these.

50 One can make a fair case for this view. I hesitate to mention Coleridge's comment of 1799, since he was speaking solely of 'A slumber' when we don't know that the poems were associated. For a balanced account, see Mary Moorman, 1:423–6. Since Dorothy is important to most psychoana-

lytic approaches to the poems, it is not surprising that Bateson (*Wordsworth* 151–3) and Matlack make strong cases for the identification. The hardest evidence is that Wordsworth uses 'Lucy' (1) in 'Among all lovely things,' and told Coleridge that 'The incident of this Poem took place about seven years ago between Dorothy and me' (letter of 16 April 1802, *Letters* 1:348), and (2) in an early draft of 'Nutting' (DC MS. 16, *PW* 2:504–6), and that 'Other fragments of "Nutting"... demonstrate conclusively that the "Beloved Friend" of the poem is Dorothy' (Bateson 152). Now that Butler and Green have made these fragments available, it is plain that the evidence is hardly 'conclusive.'

For others: Thomas Hutchinson notes that 'Louisa,' 'like several if not all of the poems on Lucy, was inspired in part, if not wholly, by his sister Dorothy' (699). Catherine MacDonald MacLean uncritically assumes the Lucy-Dorothy equivalence (and includes 'Louisa' as well) (49–58). Sir Arthur Quiller-Couch likewise takes it for granted that the poems 'were really intended for Dorothy,' and in depicting Dorothy physically he in fact relies on 'Three years' (*Studies* 87). See also Reiman, 'The Poetry of Familiarity.'

51 For early dismissals of reference, see the discussion of Winchester and Garrod, below. Geoffrey Durrant speaks for many later critics in pronouncing Lucy's identity 'irrelevant' ('Zeno's Arrow' 60). More generally, see Derrida's discussions of the 'transcendental signified,' *Of Grammatology* 6–7, 20, 48–9 (also 154, 158–9, on referentiality); *Positions* 19–20, 29–31, 65; *Speech and Phenomena* passim. For arguments with a more specifically literary bearing, see Michael Riffaterre, 'Interpretation and Descriptive Poetry' especially section 1, 'The Referential Fallacy' (231–7), and 'Intertextual Representation.'

52 Matlack's project is not, however, entirely distinct from identifications. While the identification of Lucy and Dorothy generates psychobiographical readings, it is designed also to 'dispel the mystery of [the poems'] genesis' (46).

53 Both Boris Eichenbaum's apologetical 'The Theory of the "Formal Method"' (105–6) and Victor Erlich's *Russian Formalism* (70–86) discuss the emergence of formalism as a 'rebellion.' The objective biographical approaches to the 'Lucy Poems' are not unlike Erlich's examples of the 'positivism' and 'petty factualism' to which the formalists objected: research into ' "the care of Pushkin's children and property" or the vital question: "Did Pushkin smoke?" ' (54).

54 Formalist literary history is 'dialectical' in that it explains literary development as reaction against 'source' or predecessor forms, but also as their subsumption, as in parody or 'foregrounding.' Geoffrey Hartman's comparative discussion of 'Lucy Poems' by Wordsworth and by Lyttelton ('Beyond Formalism' [1966]) is exemplary. But the majority of source

studies of the 'Lucy Poems' fail to make such use of them: that 'sources' are so often listed in footnotes and appendices, the cul-de-sacs of scholarship, may indicate how little we understand about putting them to use. I myself have compiled a master-list for the curious in appendix 4 to 'Lucy and Her Readers.'

55 Rosmarin's phrase suggests that all classifying is mistake, while her useful comments on wilful errors of classification (21–2, 45) imply that some mistakes are greater – or more 'edifying' – than others. 'What makes a genre "good,"' she argues, 'is its power to make the literary text "good"' (49). Classification, she suggests, is a way of imposing comparisons between dissimilar objects – in Averill's case, between lyrics and narratives.

56 As Mario Praz remarks, 'between 1830 and 1860 English painting, with its emphasis on subject, on the moral to be inculcated, the story to be told, was almost a branch of literature' (*The Hero in Eclipse* 28).

57 As Wellek notes, Poe's theory 'has influenced all subsequent theories of the short story' (*History* 3:161).

58 See especially David Ferry's 'metaphysical' reading of Wordsworth, including the 'Lucy Poems' (discussed in chapter 5). Sacvan Bercovitch argues that 'Lucy embodies the idea of creative *light*, and that the narrator's grief at her loss expresses the poet's fear of losing his creative powers.'

59 Donald G. Marshall's 'Foreword' to Hartman's *The Unremarkable Wordsworth* includes an acute discussion of Hartman's ambivalence and of his aim for values 'beyond formalism' (see especially viii–x and xx). For examples of Hartman's search for grounds of universal human relevance with which to connect the formal aspects of literature, see *Unremarkable* 42, 52, 117, and especially 190.

Chapter Three

1 Quoted by J.H. Alexander (61); see chapter 2 above.

2 I attribute this mode of interpretation to Wordsworth and elaborate it in response to arguments against interpretation in 'Interpretation in Wordsworth.'

3 Alan Liu provides a good overview of the 'subversion/ containment' dynamics while arguing against the prevalent assumption that subversion is always, already contained, in 'Wordsworth and Subversion.' On containment in particular, see Fredric Jameson, *Political Unconscious* 52–3, 70–3, 210–19, 287, and William Dowling ch. 4. Liu's footnotes (esp. 1, 2, and 34) provide other useful references.

4 Robert P. Falk and William Beare 602; George Kitchin xii. Walter Jerrold and R.M. Leonard claim that *Rejected Addresses* (1812) 'revived and estab-

lished the art of parody' (vi). According to John Jump, 'the modern vogue' of parody in England begins in 1701, 'with John Philips' "The Splendid Shilling,"' and matures in 1812, 'with *The Anti-Jacobin* and *Rejected Addresses*' (18–23). George Marshall refers to Tennyson's lifetime as 'the hey-day of parody' (5). Dwight Macdonald, following Kitchin, calls the Victorian period 'a, if not the, great age' of parody (564–5).

5 See note 23, below.

6 Bakhtin's periodization is clearest in *Rabelais and His World* (e.g., 83–8); the impoverishment he refers to is a loss of ambivalence and an increasing accentuation of 'the negative' (83–4). See also *DI* 51–9, 71–82, and *Problems of Dostoevsky's Poetics* 127–8. One must allow, evidently, for the simple bias of specialists toward their own periods. Richmond P. Bond asserts that 'the [neo-] classical period is the golden age of parody' (229), while others press the claims of the moderns and the postmoderns to the title: see especially Richard Poirier's early essay on postmodern fiction, 'The Politics of Self-Parody,' and Linda Hutcheon.

7 See, e.g., 156–8, 167.

8 I refer to Susan Sontag's classic 'Against Interpretation' (1964). Some famous examples of the parody of interpretation are the misadventures of Malvolio (*Twelfth Night* 2:5), of Don Quixote, and of Austen's Emma (especially her readings of word games, chs. 1:5 and 3:9), and perhaps the scholastic gloss added by Coleridge to the 'Rime of the Ancient Mariner' in 1817. For others, see Frederick Crews; Angus Fletcher 8–10; Gilbert Highet 142; and Linda Hutcheon 12, 61. Closely related, of course, is parody of scholarship, as in *Sartor Resartus* and the works of Borges.

9 Paul de Man, 'Criticism and Crisis' (1967), *Blindness* 3–19. De Man's argument is discussed more fully in chapter 2, above.

10 Falk and Beare note that parody 'was originally "a song sung beside," i.e., a comic imitation of a serious poem' (601). See also Hutcheon, 32, 52–3, and Margaret Rose, *Parody* 6–19.

11 Macdonald similarly surveys definitions and complains that they fail to 'distinguish parody from its poor relations,' travesty and burlesque. 'Such definitions tend to run together, which is just what a definition shouldn't do, since *definire* means "to set limits."' He proposes a 'hierarchy' of terms to clarify matters (557). As a recent compendium of parody theory by one of the most prominent specialists, Rose's *Parody* is an important illustration of this tendency. It opens with two chapters on 'Ways of Defining Parody from the Ancients Onwards' and 'Distinguishing Parody from Related Forms,' and makes no mention anywhere of the arguments that parody is indistinguishable or is not a genre; though Rose quotes and paraphrases Bakhtin's views on parody at length (125–70), she takes no notice of the anti-generic aspects even of his account.

12 See also Wolfgang Karrer 13, and Gary Saul Morson 64–5.

13 'Postscript' 116. Miller probably refers to Rousseau: 'Why ... do we not have a vocative mark? ... [A]n equivocation ... would be eliminated. ... The same equivocation is found in irony, when it is not made manifest by accent' (Rousseau 22n).

14 My view of irony is indebted to David Simpson, who views romantic irony as 'the studied avoidance on the artist's part of determinate meanings'(*Irony* 190).

15 'Semiology' 10; compare *Resistance* 14–16. For a more elaborated version of these arguments, see Derrida, *Limited Inc*, e.g., 13–19.

16 On Hone's trials, see the London *Times*, 18, 20, and 22 Dec. 1817, and *TT*. Edgell Rickword provides a good brief account of Hone's life, including the trials (1–32). For others, see Frederick W. Hackwood 132–73; Olivia Smith 154–201; E.P. Thompson 792–3; and Kitchin 261–4.

17 *TT* 3:31; *Times*, 22 Dec. 1817, p. 2, col. 5.

18 Thompson 135. See also *TT* 1:6–14, 29, 36; 2:15–16.

19 The indictment of Byron's parodic 'Vision of Judgement' for libel in December 1822 provides an equally intriguing but less triumphant example of a parody trial in this period; after a far less resourceful defence, Byron's publisher John Hunt (Hone's equivalent) was convicted of libel in 1824 and fined £100 (William H. Marshall 126–33, 205–9). Marshall's account indicates, interestingly, that in this confrontation parody was deployed on both sides – there were parodies both of Byron's 'Vision' (124) and of the indictment of it (129–30).

Annabel Patterson argues that, from the mid-sixteenth century, civil censorship in England forced writers and readers to cultivate 'the indeterminacy inveterate to language' and thus drew the vigilant state into 'the business of textual interpretation' (18, 27). The analogy might help both to historicize the antagonism between parody and interpretation in the early nineteenth century and to illustrate that antagonism's more trans-historical characteristics.

20 I am aware that negative claims are risky, and I speak only of works in English, but I have found no earlier parody anthologies in any language. Richmond Bond (237–453) provides an annotated 'Register of Burlesque Poems' listing 211 works published between 1700 and 1750, but cites no anthology of burlesque; with three possible exceptions, the 37 collective volumes that he lists all appear to intersperse burlesque with serious original poetry, or conform to my definition of 'presentations' above. John Jump calls Browne's 'our earliest collection of parodies of various authors' (19); Brett-Smith suggests likewise (Browne 1). The new *CBEL*, vol. 2, lists anthologies but overlooks even Walter Hamilton's huge anthology, so its failure to note parody anthologies may not be significant. But Hamilton's own extensive 'Bibliography of Parody and Burlesque' (6:323–46) might reasonably be expected to cite predecessor anthologies,

and none occur. See R.C. Whitford, 'Origin,' on the development of what I am calling parody *presentations* from the 1770s.

Brett-Smith's introduction (describing the context of Browne's work) handily illustrates the historical shift in terms from 'imitation' to 'parody': he habitually uses 'parody' to describe works which were called 'imitations' by their writers and contemporary readers (see Browne 8–14). Bond's 'Register of Burlesque Poems' displays the same taxonomic tension. Fewer than half of the 211 works that he cites as 'burlesque' announce such intentions explicitly in their titles or subtitles by using terms such as 'burlesque,' 'parody,' 'satire,' 'travesty,' etc. More commonly the titular labels are non-committal: 'Poem,' 'Imitation,' 'Translation,' 'Version,' 'Epitome,' 'Paraphrase,' and even (no. 181) 'A Parallel.'

21 'Target' is a popular term for the parodied text, but I question its implications of unireferential and violent intent on the part of parody; hence I use 'target' in connection with this conception, but more deliberately vague terms elsewhere.

22 F.B. Doveton, 436–7; rpt. with minor corruptions by Walter Hamilton, 5:95.

23 All subsequent anthologies of parody I know of perform both these services of definition and 'targeting.' Carolyn Wells, Dwight Macdonald, William Zaranka, Simon Brett, and E.O. Parrott all class parodies by the targeted authors, though not by targeted texts; Jerrold and Leonard arrange them under the parodists' names but always indicate the author targeted. As a volume, Zaranka's *Brand-X Anthology* parodies anthologies generally, particularly *The Norton*, and thus makes an interesting cross between the early parody presentation and the parody anthology. Falk and Beare (602) list other anthologies. I'm grateful to Shelley King for advice on this subject.

The anthologists' prefaces frequently make more explicit the trivialization involved in their project. Wells writes that 'The main intent of the vast majority of parodies is simply to amuse; but to amuse intelligently and cleverly' (xix). Brett argues that 'The first duty of parody is to entertain' (17). Macdonald's 'Appendix: Some Notes on Parody' (557–68) is less reductive than most.

24 On 'parody as criticism,' see especially Kitchin ix–xxiii; J.G. Riewald; and Linda Hutcheon passim. Theory's treatment of parody as genre is discussed above (see note 11). Brecht uses 'refunctioning' to describe the appropriation of hegemonic forms for revolutionary purposes, and Margaret Rose adopts the term 'to describe the new functions gained by a text in a new context such as parody' ('Defining Parody' 19n9). In applying the term to criticism's treatment of parody, I am assuming that it is inessential whether the new function is more or less radical than the old. But my main interest in 'refunctioning' is that it includes the notion of

'functioning,' or ascribing purpose in order to interpret what might otherwise escape understanding altogether because of its a-functionality.

25 Karrer is most systematic and insistent in presenting 'parody, travesty, and pastiche as ... communication processes' (3; see 3–5, 13, 14). See also Pierre Gobin.

26 Hutcheon 55. Hutcheon's peculiar use of 'infer' with 'from' is a symptom of her reluctant intentionalism and exemplifies interpretation's blinding of itself to its own inferential activity. She claims to reject the 'Hirschian view of the real author's meaning,' arguing that intentions are 'inferred or "postulated" ' (88). But the repeated claims to infer meanings *from* the text (cf. 84, 97) fail to enact this concession to scepticism. To 'infer' is, of course, to carry something *in*.

27 Hutcheon 11, 7. That parody may admire as well as censure is an old contention: Hone proposes it in 1817, and Isaac D'Israeli argues that parodies need not 'ridicule their originals' (345); see also Rose ('Defining' 8). Dane mediates the pro and con by arguing that parody is abusive in the first instance if not ultimately (147–8).

28 Not all views of 'parody as criticism' recuperate it as communication. Poirier, who states that it 'has always had the function of literary criticism,' is illuminating on this function (323–4).

29 Hamilton 94–5. The attribution to Hartley Coleridge derives from an exchange between 'G.E.' and 'Makrocheir' in *Notes and Queries*, 4th series, vol. 3 (19 June 1869), 580, and vol. 4 (24 July 1869), 85–6.

30 Lines 1–7, 29–49. Catherine M. Fanshawe, *Literary Remains* (London: Pickering, 1876), 69–71. The text is reproduced by Hamilton (101–2), Brett (364–5), and Parrott (59–60) with considerable differences.

31 Arguably, even this broad categorization involves a greater editorial violence than does the specific targeting of Coleridge's poem. Hamilton himself reprints, from Fanshawe's edition, a note claiming that her 'Imitation' was mistaken for Wordsworth's by a 'distinguished friend and admirer of Wordsworth' (Fanshawe 71; Hamilton 102). Gilbert Highet (72) insightfully suggests that a capacity to be taken for 'genuine work of the original author' is a good test of parody, but subsequent readers of Fanshawe, discovering her poem in Hamilton's or another anthology, have been spared the potential embarrassments of this test.

32 Wordsworth's sinking between poems is frequently noted by the hostile reviewers of *Poems, in Two Volumes* (1807); for his sinking within poems, see 'bathos' in M.H. Abrams, *Glossary*. This 'INCONSTANCY of the *style*' is, of course, the first of the 'prominent *defects*' Coleridge enumerates in Wordsworth's poetry in the *Biographia* ch. 22 (2:121–6). The somewhat testy comment of Leigh Hunt on a passage in *Peter Bell* exemplifies the critical result of such instability: 'Is Mr. Wordsworth in earnest or is he not?' *Examiner*, 2 May 1819, p. 283; rpt. *RR*, 2:539.

33 John Speirs (140–1) also comments on lability or parody in the 'Lucy Poems'; see also Richard Gravil. In 'Double Economics,' I have argued for considering the pastoral poems, especially 'Michael,' as parodic.

34 S.T. Coleridge likewise stresses that the 'defect' of sinking 'is only occasional' (*BL* 2:121, 126); in one sense it is so by definition. But even if Wordsworth is only occasionally double-voiced, *in effect* he is always so, since the mere tendency toward lapses must make readers perpetually less than certain which 'voice' they are hearing.

35 These editorial projects are discussed in chapter 2.

36 See R.R. Palmer, *The Age of Democratic Revolution* 1:35–7, 358–70, 2:394–421, and *The World of the French Revolution* 85–6, 170–6, and William Doyle 353–6. Before 1798, as Palmer explains, Switzerland 'consisted of thirteen German-speaking cantons, associated in a loose, defensive league,' plus many subject 'regions of French or Italian language' (*World* 86). He observes, 'as a sign of the complexity of lordships and jurisdictions, that Switzerland until 1798 had a hundred different tariff zones' and 'no uniform coinage, weights, or measures' (*Age* 1:358, 2:397). The French, seeking to unify Switzerland for purposes of control, occupied Bern in March 1798 and at first declared three republics, the Rhone, Helvetic, and Tellgau, then 'a single unitary Helvetic Republic' with a consolidationist constitution imposing 'a legal homogeneity, or equality of rights between town and country and between region and region' (*Age* 2:411–12). Though Bonaparte's Act of Mediation (Feb. 1803) involved the first use of 'Switzerland' in the official sense, the Helvetic Republic of 1798 established the lasting principles of Swiss unity (*Encyclopedia Britannica*, 11th ed., 26:257–8; Palmer, *Age* 2:420–1).

37 On the resistance of the 'rural, upland, "primitive," and "democratic" cantons, of which six were Catholic and two Protestant,' see Palmer, *Age* 2:415–18.

38 Maxwell argues that the sonnet conflates not only the Directory's occupation of February 1798 and Napoleon's of October 1802, but also Wordsworth's attitudes toward Napoleon's actions between 1802 and 1806.

39 See Palmer, *World* 172, and *Age* 2:394, 411–12; Doyle 354; but also *Encyclopedia Britannica*, 11th ed., 26:257. My thinking on this matter is indebted to W.J.T. Mitchell's comparison between the linguistic or pictorial and the political senses of 'representation' ('Representation').

40 S.T. Coleridge provides one example of English complaints about the burden of the Union with Ireland (*Table Talk* 1:246). As in the unification of Switzerland (see note 39, above), there was also a great tension between autonomous and alien efforts to 'unify' Ireland – between the 'United Irishmen' and the 'United Kingdom,' as it were. R.F. Forster emphasizes the complexity of the factions, both religious and political; Thomas Pakenham gives an admirable account of the rebellion, presenting the Union as its 'direct result' (398).

41 I would not deny that one can read the poem as having vast representative pretensions at a level less touched by irony. Wordsworth's is not only the voice 'of the sea' or Britain – the last voice heard by Liberty – but may also be, through his peculiar association with England's most mountainous landscape, the 'voice of the mountains,' and thus, in sum, the 'two voices' in which Liberty consists. 'Two Voices *are* there,' present tense, even though one has been lost, because the lost voice is represented, and contained, by the last voice.

I've discussed elsewhere ('Interpretation' 585–92) the middle position of Wordsworth's speakers or the impossibility of either identifying them with or differentiating them from Wordsworth himself. The best discussions of this problem that I know of are David Simpson's in *Wordsworth's Historical Imagination* (7, 29, 182–3).

42 See Mitchell, 'Representation,' especially 15, and Derrida's reflections on the problems of exemplarism in *Writing and Difference*, 172–4, 282–4.

43 Wordsworth's disapproval of satire appears in his letter to Francis Wrangham (7 Nov. 1806), in the third 'Essay upon Epitaphs,' and in his ranking of poetical kinds in the 1815 Preface (*Prose* 2:80–1, 3:28). Referring to Johnson's 'I put my hat upon my head,' Wordsworth calls parody 'a mode of false criticism' (Preface to *Lyrical Ballads*, Owen 87). See also S.T. Coleridge, *BL* 1:75–6n.

44 It may be relevant that Wordsworth cut or corrected most of the 'defects' of lability pointed out by Coleridge, a practice documented in the footnotes to the Engell–Bate edition (*BL* 2:123–5).

45 A fascinating late case both of Wordsworth's parody and of his resistance to parody is the pompous-sounding sonnet written against the parodies of *Peter Bell*, 'On the Detraction Which Followed the Publication of a Certain Poem' (1820). While castigating the parodists as 'a harpy brood,' it mimics another sonnet, with which it explicitly invites comparison: 'See Milton's Sonnet, beginning, "A Book was writ of late called 'Tetrachordon' " ' (*PW* 3:11).

46 Stein 3. My list of terms comes from Stein's Preface and Introduction (vii–15). Stein quotes John Hollander approvingly: 'echo, allusion, and quotation ... are forms of citation that are clearly related and *clearly distinct*' (Hollander 72; Stein 223n3; my emphasis). The same note approves Carmela Perri's semiotic theory of marked allusion, to which Wall, above, objects. See also Stein's chapter 4, 'The Principles of Wordsworthian Allusiveness,' 113–21.

47 'Discourse in the Novel' (1934–5), in *DI* 259–422; see especially 308–9, 313–14, 363–5, 409–14. Particularly in *Problems*, Bakhtin distinguishes the dialogical novel from 'novels of the monologic type' (8).

48 On these readings, see chapter 1, above.

49 No one to my knowledge has commented on this poem's use of metamorphosis, but Max Byrd (37) notes its importance in 'A slumber.'

50 René Wellek cites some of the 'enormous literature' on such questions (*Attack* 23–5).

51 Brian Aldiss draws attention to these 'portraits' of Percy Shelley, Lord Byron, and Mary Shelley herself; his caveat that 'the resemblances are not always one-to-one' applies as well to his own identification between Verney and Mary Shelley (ix). Anne K. Mellor, noting that '[r]eaders have long recognized that *The Last Man* is a *roman à clef*' (148), bases a biographical reading upon this precedent to the neglect of all disruptive inconsistencies. Robert Lance Snyder lists *roman à clef* interpretations somewhat discontentedly and stresses the novel's 'resist[ance to] interpretation' (436), but the resistant feature on which he focuses is the plague.

52 Verney's tendency to leave others in distress while pretending to sensibility is one mark of his close relation to Frankenstein. Aside from his treatment of Lucy, note his virtual forgetting of his dead son (245ff.) and of Juliet when she has just saved Idris's life (246, 282–3), his riding-to-death of a favourite horse (294), and his habitual abandonment of the children, Clara and Evelyn, even when they constitute half of surviving humanity (315–17).

53 Robinson 1:191; discussed in chapter 2, above.

54 Moore uses *Pierre* to argue that the rumours regarding Wordsworth's private life were extensive around the time of his death, but it is slippery evidence. On Melville's reading knowledge of Wordsworth, see Thomas Heffernan.

55 The trio is important enough that, after Mary's death, it is made up by the unwed mother, Delly Ulver, who is otherwise superfluous. Carl Woodring calls to my attention that 'Isabel' is the name of Wordsworth's Michael's wife.

56 Yasunari Takahashi argues that Lucy is 'the boy Wordsworth' who had to be killed off before the poet could free his imagination.

57 Tilottama Rajan discusses Schelling's and Dilthey's 'expansion' of hermeneutic categories and problems to include the interpretation of being in *The Supplement of Reading*, especially 6, 25–6, 36. Her phrase 'the text of Being' (25) reminds one that this expansion has in recent years been considered chiefly as the 'textualization' of the world or of history, attributed in particular to deconstruction. But it seems to me that the notion of textualization, in privileging the literary text as the paradigmatic object of interpretation, puts the cart before the horse; surely the problematics of interpreting 'being,' or non-linguistic reality, must have precedence, even if hermeneutics first became self-conscious as a discipline only in the study of writing. Chapter 1, above, argues that Wordsworth's version of the hermeneutic expansion is to assimilate the text to the world, not vice versa. I believe *Pierre* puts the ubiquity of interpretation in a similar light.

58 The novelistic allusion splits Wordsworth into the elder Pierre, who like Wordsworth outgrows his illicit affection to become a respectable citizen, and the younger Pierre, whose courtship with Lucy is overwhelmed by the surfacing of his father's past life. Taken as an *à clef* portrait of Wordsworth, the elder Pierre is not flattering, but the novel does not focus on him: it emphasizes the younger Pierre, who is far more heroic and even bumblingly Christ-like in his attempt to make reparation for his father's transgressions.

Chapter Four

1 Letter to Sara Hutchinson, 14 June 1802 (*Letters* 1:367), and 'Simon Lee,' lines 71–2 (*PW* 4:63).
2 Jack Stillinger provides a useful 'abbreviated survey' of these disputes in *Multiple Authorship* 188–94. Stillinger's charge that the intentionalist disputes have side-stepped vast problems connected with multiple authorship and multiple texts is relevant to my concerns in this chapter; see also note 39, below.
3 Hirsch, 'Meaning and Significance' 211, paraphrasing Gadamer's discussion of the 'historicists'; see also Frank Lentricchia on Hirsch's treatment of 'A slumber' (*After the New Criticism* 267).
4 Fish's argument, which extends to 'theory' at large, is expanded in *Doing What Comes Naturally*. The initiatory and titular essay in *Against Theory*, by Steven Knapp and Walter Benn Michaels (11–30), focuses on literary theory specifically, pursuing Fish's own comments in *Is There a Text in This Class?* 370.
5 In particular, in using 'theory' to mean 'method' or 'algorithm,' Fish overlooks the common use of the term to denote a 'model' or 'view' of things – crucial, since his argument 'against theory' is itself theoretical in this latter sense. He also presents theory's rhetorical functions too cynically, overlooking its *self*-persuasive functions. I present these arguments more fully in 'Recuperating Arnold.'
6 The new pragmatists' attack on theoretical non-sequitur is very much in the tradition of Trotsky's retort to formalism: 'The Formalist school seems to try to be objective. ... [But] Having counted the adjectives, and weighed the lines, and measured the rhythms, a Formalist either stops silent ... or throws out an unexpected generalization which contains five percent of Formalism and ninety-five percent of the most uncritical intuition' (171–2).
7 'Determinacy' and 'indeterminacy' are slippery terms, as Gerald Graff warns in the essay 'Determinacy/Indeterminacy.' I therefore explain my own usage. First, I do not assume a binary option; one can 'determine' the meaning of a text without reducing it to a single meaning. If 'A

slumber' permits several grammatical constructions and each of these permits a range of connotative readings, to pretend that it permits two readings is, I think, to determine its meaning. Second, I use 'determination' to refer also to one's persuasion of others to adopt one's own perspective. (Since collapsing perspectives amounts to reducing the number of appearances, these uses of 'determine' differ only in emphasis.) Conversely, I use 'indeterminacy' to describe a relative rather than absolute resistance to determination; a text permitting three readings would be more indeterminate than one permitting only two. Another source of confusion is the ambiguity of both 'determine' and 'determinate' as to legitimacy or force: to 'determine' a meaning may be an act of arbitrary decision or persuasion, yet the term is often used as though it described acts of legitimate demonstration. Does determining the meaning of a text show that *its* meaning is determinate? That depends on the legitimacy of the demonstration. The following analyses show how many such determinations are *not* legitimate.

8 These were initiated by Hirsch's essay, 'Objective Interpretation' (1960), reprinted as appendix 1 to *Validity* (209–44); most cite or explicitly dispute Hirsch's arguments. I list only those discussed here: Don Geiger, *The Dramatic Impulse in Modern Poetics* (1967); Monroe Beardsley, *The Possibility of Criticism* (1970); A.E. Dyson, 'Symbiosis in Wordsworth' (1973); Norman Holland, 'Literary Interpretation and Three Phases of Psychoanalysis' (1976); P.D. Juhl, 'The Appeal to the Text' (1978); Robert Crosman, 'Do Readers Make Meaning?' (1980); James Phelan, *Worlds from Words* (1981); Knapp and Michaels, 'Against Theory' (1985); Graff, 'Determinacy/Indeterminacy' (1990); and Brian Caraher, *Wordsworth's 'Slumber' and the Problematics of Reading* (1991). Especially since many of these essays have provoked responses, I stress that this is a partial listing. Geoffrey Hartman's 'Beyond Formalism' (1966) and the exchange between J. Hillis Miller and M.H. Abrams on the deconstruction of 'A slumber' (Eaves and Fischer 96–182) might also be considered in this series, but are considered instead in chapter 5.

In addition, at least two critics have called attention to the inconsistency of theoretical argument and example in Knapp and Michaels' use of 'A slumber': Peggy Kamuf, 'Floating Authorship' 9–13, and Alan Liu, 'Local Transcendence' 88–9 and 106–9. As Liu says, 'whether Knapp and Michaels's argument about intentionality is correct or useful we will never know from their example' (108n53; see also 108n51, challenging the presentation of 'A slumber' as a '"standard" example'). Others express a more intuitive unease with the use of example in this project: as Frank Kermode remarks, 'On the whole, Juhl is unlucky with his examples' (*The Art of Telling* 208). My point is to explore this inconsistency as a rhetorical strategy, not ineptitude or luck. See also Stillinger 190.

9 I offer a sketchy genealogy of this anxiety, citing statements and 'theory' essays from Pope to Hirsch, in chapter 2 above. On the institutional response to these concerns, see Frank Kermode, 'Institutional Control of Interpretation' (*The Art of Telling* 168–84), and Paul Bové's more ambitious and detailed *Intellectuals in Power*. As Graff shows in *Professing Literature*, claims to scientificity can be explained also as more superficial features of professionalization; for instance, he quotes H.C.G. Brandt's plea at the first meeting of the MLA in 1883: 'a scientific basis dignifies our profession' (68; see ch. 5 generally).

10 A possible exception is Caraher's murder-reading of 'A slumber,' which is achieved by inverting the usual reading of line 1: 'my spirit did seal a slumber' (44–8). But Caraher himself does everything he can to consensualize this reading (see discussion below).

11 K.D. Sethna and Hugh Sykes Davies both read the poem as a description of mystical trance. The latter is discussed at length in chapter 2, above.

12 On interpretation as 'necessary error,' see Jonathan Culler, *The Pursuit of Signs* 14.

13 'For this universality I use the expression *general validity*, which denotes the validity of the reference of a representation, not to the cognitive faculties, but to the feeling of pleasure or displeasure for every Subject' (Kant, *Critique of Judgement* 54).

14 Responding to Knapp and Michaels' criticisms, Hirsch invokes the concessions in his 1967 argument to co-opt their argument; they are all fellow 'anti-theoretical theorists' ('Against Theory?' 48).

15 In 1960, speaking of the 'adjudication' between two interpretations of a text – which he also calls 'verification' (*Validity* 238) – Hirsch explains, 'verification is a process of establishing relative probabilities' (*Validity* 236). In 1967 he has scruples about this terminology: 'to avoid giving the false impression that there is anything permanent about an interpretive validation or the consensus it aims to achieve, I now prefer the term "validation" to the more definitive-sounding word "verification" ' (*Validity* 170–71). But 'validation' is just as liable to sound 'definitive.'

16 Friedrich D.E. Schleiermacher, quoted by Hirsch, *The Aims of Interpretation* 76. See also Schleiermacher, 'Introduction' 84–86. I say 'relatively stable' because even this system could not entirely stabilize constructions of meaning: for instance, changes in our knowledge about an era's usage, or disagreement about which dictionaries to consult, would both bring the lexic 'meaning' in question, and as Schleiermacher himself points out, 'these dictionaries must be constantly emended by interpretation itself' ('Introduction' 84). A post-structuralist might likewise dispute the stability of grammar or its distinction from rhetoric; see Paul de Man, 'Semiology and Rhetoric' 3–19, and *The Resistance to Theory* 14–16.

17 In some respects Hirsch seems to qualify his claims in subsequent state-

ments, but by 1984 he is arguing not to delimit the realm of 'meaning' but on the contrary for 'a more generous and capacious view of what remains the same' ('Meaning' 210).

18 Hirsch's Preface disclaims the theoretical importance of his examples as 'presented en passant and not as substantial parts of the argument' (x), but since he also speaks of his theoretical argument as a tool which should have 'practical implications' (x), his failure to attend to his own theoretical distinctions in practice indicates a liability. My critique of Hirsch focuses chiefly on this discontinuity between theory and practice; for critiques on more consistently theoretical and ideological grounds, see Lentricchia and David Couzens Hoy.

19 Even this super-focused comparison of readings raises more complexities than the single one Hirsch wants to see (for instance, only Bateson assumes that 'she' is 'Lucy'). Caraher notes how much of their readings Hirsch neglects (72n).

20 Hirsch's concept of genre, largely indebted to Husserl's concepts of pre-understanding and the horizon of expectation, is to my mind his book's most valuable contribution. Here it may suffice to say that by 'genre' he means not just a conventional genre, but any expectation one has about the holistic meaning of a work which informs one's interpretation of the parts and is altered and refined by this in turn. On the hermeneutic circle, see also Schleiermacher, 'Introduction' 84–6.

21 Gerald Graff analyses several versions of the fallacious 'argument about political consequences' in 'The Pseudo-Politics of Interpretation.' See also Crosman 159–61.

22 Fish disallows even this degree of consequentiality, arguing that the notion of holding beliefs loosely is incoherent: 'one believes what one believes, and one does so without reservation'; 'If one believes what one believes, then one believes that what one believes is *true*.' Hence 'one cannot be a relativist' (*Is There a Text* 361; see also 'Consequences' 120–2, *Doing* 245–6). The question Fish neglects is *For whom?* Relativism is not, as he pretends, a claim to disbelieve in what one believes, but rather a theory that what one beholds and believes is relative to one's own view-point and circumstances, hence possibly true for oneself but not necessar-ily for others. There may be beliefs that can't be held relativistically, and it seems to be true that one can be relativist on some points and absolutist on others. But on a relativist view of meaning I might be con-vinced that 'A means X' from my own standpoint, and might even wish to find others for whom the same is true, without insisting that A *does* mean X in the sense that it would for all competent readers, or that it should for everyone.

23 An expanded version appears in Juhl's *Interpretation*.

24 Hirsch says: 'I wish ... to focus attention on the criterion of coherence. ... I

shall try to show that verification by the criterion of coherence, and ultimately, therefore, verification in general, implies a reconstruction of relevant aspects in the author's outlook' (*Validity* 236–7). Juhl does not mention this passage and may be unconscious of its influence, but it presents a similar argument. It is important because Hirsch proceeds to raise the problem, which Juhl ignores, that whatever criterion one uses is subjectively decided, a fact that fictionalizes the 'appeal to the author.'

25 As Peggy Kamuf demands regarding Knapp and Michaels' argument, which both criticizes and resembles Juhl's, 'Is anyone keeping count of the number of quotation marks?' (13n). The problem keeps getting worse, of course, but Juhl may be accused of making the most of the confusion. His use of shorthand symbols, I_1 and I_2 to represent Bateson's and Brooks's readings of 'Rolled round,' and *f* to represent 'the fact ... that "rolled round" is qualified by the words "in earth's diurnal course"' (279), makes it hard to follow his arguments and virtually impossible to quote them for disputation. For instance: 'to say that (with respect to *f*) the line is more coherent on I_1 than on I_2 is to say (roughly) that the words "in earth's diurnal course" are a more appropriate means for a purpose in accord with I_1 than for a purpose in accord with I_2; and from this we infer that the function of "rolled round" is more likely to be that specified by I_1 than the function specified by I_2' (279). A few pages of this and most readers will surrender.

26 G. Thomas Tanselle lists several distinctions that critics of the 'intentional fallacy' have found necessary, and suggests that this one (from Michael Hancher, 'Three Kinds of Intention') is most useful ('The Editorial Problem of Final Authorial Intention' 317). 'Programmatic intention' is 'the author's intention to make something or other,' while 'Active intentions characterize the actions that the author, at the time he finishes his text, understands himself to be performing in that text.' In these terms, Hirsch is seeking active intentions, which he argues must be specific and determinate; but what Juhl says we 'appeal to' is merely our unavoidable assumption that the author must have intended something. Similarly, Kamuf faults Knapp and Michaels for their 'refus[al] to make the distinction between a particular, finite (empirical) intention of some speech act and intentionality as an animating principle of language *in general*' (8).

27 Even the criterion of 'coherence' is not inevitable, but is more in the order of a traditional interpretive decision. A remark by Northrop Frye illustrates how such decisions may be unconsciously projected or objectified: '"Every poem must necessarily be a perfect unity," says Blake: this, as the wording implies, is not a statement of fact about all existing poems, but a statement of the hypothesis which every reader adopts in first trying to comprehend even the most chaotic poem ever written' (*Anatomy of Criticism* 77). But in 'every reader,' Frye himself hypostatizes a criterion held

by New Critics but subsequently challenged by various postmodernist theories (which may posit discontinuity or 'rupture' instead). Historical variability is a corollary of the condition that aesthetic criteria are posited by the consumer.

28 The distinction between 'extrinsic' and 'intrinsic' evidence appears in Wimsatt and Beardsley, 'The Intentional Fallacy.'

29 Juhl's reasoning about extrinsic evidence is fallacious. He reasons: textual features indicate meaning by indicating intention; therefore intention is relevant to meaning; therefore extrinsic information indicating intention is equally relevant. This simply overlooks the possibility argued by Wimsatt and Beardsley, that only the intentions indicated by textual features are relevant to textual meaning.

30 Frank Kermode's 'The Single Correct Interpretation' (*The Art of Telling* 201–20) includes a critique of Juhl's argument and an exchange with Juhl. Juhl denies Kermode's charge that he is a 'disciple' of Hirsch (213).

31 Wallace Stevens, 'Extracts from Addresses to the Academy of Fine Ideas' (*Collected Poems* 255).

32 Geiger finds a certain tension or even contradiction between these conceptions of the poem in New Critical theory; the aim of his book as a whole is to reconcile them (see 3–23).

33 Wimsatt and Beardsley 5; Geiger 130. I have corrected Geiger's quotation.

34 See Georg Lukács, 'Art and Objective Truth,' and Raymond Williams, 'Base and Superstructure.'

35 It may be worth recalling that Wordsworth referred to *Lyrical Ballads* as 'experiments' (Owen 65, 69).

36 Derrida attacks the assumption that meaning precedes expression by arguing that meaning is an effect of language (as differance), 'a *function of play,*' not a pre-existing presence to which language refers (*Writing and Difference* 260). See also 10–11; *Of Grammatology* 8, 58, 82, passim; *Speech and Phenomena*, especially chs. 1, 3, and 6; and *Positions* 32–4. On the 'effect' of intention specifically, see Culler, *On Deconstruction* 216–17. V.N. Voloshinov's attack on the expression model from a dialogical standpoint is also relevant, since it stresses that in practice meaning assumes not just a meaner (as Hirsch argues) but also an understander; 'understanding is a response to a sign with signs' (*Marxism and the Philosophy of Language* 11; see especially 84–5).

37 See, for instance, Roman Jakobson, 'What Is Poetry?' (1933–4) (*Language in Literature* 368–78), stressing 'poeticity'; or Boris Eichenbaum, 'The Theory of the "Formal Method"' 107. Geiger's argument may in fact be indebted to Eliot by way of D.W. Harding: 'T.S. Eliot has spoken of the two way traffic between the dramatist and his characters: though in a sense he creates his character he also finds that it draws out of him the potentialities of which he may have known nothing before. In the same way what

the poet writes may far outrun anything that he was capable of intending before he wrote' (Harding, *Experience into Words* 79).

38 Robert Crosman's rebuttal to Hirsch, 'Do Readers Make Meaning?' (1980), includes an ampler version of Geiger's suggestion that 'The very act of writing includes reading' (Crosman 163). (I am essentially agreement with, not to say indebted to, Crosman's discussion; I do not analyse it because its treatment of Hirsch's discussion of 'A slumber' [158–9] is brief and purely negative, an exception to the rule that those 'disputing' Hirsch have really sought to reaffirm his conclusions.) E.H. Gombrich's *Art and Illusion*, which inspired some of Wolfgang Iser's theoretical thinking (Iser 284–6), clarifies the links between artist-as-reader and reader-response theories. Gombrich stresses 'the beholder's share' in minimalist and illusionist art, but he also discusses how some artists 'read' their own random marks such as inkblots before developing them into more distinct forms (see 105–9, 187).

39 It should not pass unnoticed that this is actually an understatement of the problem. Even the text's objective existence, hence identity, can be theoretically challenged by the argument that what we appeal to as a 'text' is always already our interpretation of it; see Fish, *Is There a Text* 167–73, and 'Why No One's Afraid of Wolfgang Iser' (*Doing* 68–86). More empirically, several authorial texts exist for 'A slumber,' and they differ considerably, if only in accidentals (see Appendix). Any argument for the poem's determinate meaning *should* address problems such as 'Is one text authoritative, which, and why?' 'Is it one poem with multiple texts, or are there several poems?' These problems are entirely repressed in the determinacy-dispute ensuing from Hirsch; almost without exception, these theorist-critics cite the final version dating from 1836. On multiple texts, see also Stillinger 69–95, 194–202.

40 Compare Fish's claim: 'I would rather have an acknowledged and controlled subjectivity than an objectivity which is finally an illusion' (*Is There a Text* 49). More recently, Fish has challenged such claims: see 'Critical Self-Consciousness, Or Can We Know What We're Doing?' (*Doing* 436–67); see also *Doing* 331–2, 421–3, 428–30, 348, 394–5, and 584n60. I discuss such claims as strategy and as modern variants of romantic irony in 'Recuperating Arnold.'

41 As Crosman puts it, 'we *make* the author's meaning,' but 'readers generally believe, whatever interpretation they make of a text, that they have discovered the author's intended meaning' (161).

42 Fish supposes an 'informed reader,' 'suppressing, insofar as that is possible, ... what is personal and idiosyncratic and 1970ish in my response' (*Is There a Text* 49); Jonathan Culler supposes a normative 'literary competence' (*Structuralist Poetics* 113–30); Michael Riffaterre supposes a 'superreader' ('Describing Poetic Structures' 37–8). On Fish's 'interpretive communities,' see especially *Is There a Text* 167–73.

43 Oddly enough, Caraher himself offers the basic arguments against inductive claims in rejecting others' 'controlled experiments' in reading: 'the very principles an experiment attempts to establish or verify are already present within the operational procedures' (135–6).

44 Derrida, *Writing and Difference* 282; compare 284. Derrida does not use the phrase 'double gesture' in this passage, though the passage does describe one; see also 194, 274–5, 338n41; *Positions*, 6, 18–19, 35, 41, 65–6, 100n8; and Culler, *On Deconstruction* 149–51.

45 I.A. Richards, *Practical Criticism* 6. The second half of Richards' study (173–329), seeking to control the chaos documented by the reading 'protocols' in the first half, forecasts the 'slumber' project. On this containment, see Bové ch. 2.

Chapter Five

1 A quick illustration is James Phelan's analysis, which begins by observing 'the lack of any *explicit* emotion in the second stanza' of 'A slumber,' then assumes that it evinces 'acceptance' of mortality since 'acceptance is implied in full knowledge' (*Worlds from Words* 95; see ch. 4, above).

2 I cannot do justice here to the Victorian views of Wordsworthian nature, since I wish to focus chiefly on the period since 1960. Though they are undoubtedly more complex than I have implied, I think they are less complex than the modern views – partly because Victorian criticism was less analytical and took isolated statements by Wordsworth as having a general validity in his work, and partly because, as Arnold's 'Memorial Verses' suggest, it needed to read Wordsworth more optimistically. For useful characterizations of the Victorian view, see A.C. Bradley 107–9, 127–9, and Carson Hamilton 159–82.

3 H.W. Garrod, 'Wordsworth's Lucy' 83; see also chapter 1, above.

4 'Ode. The Morning of the Day Appointed for a General Thanksgiving,' lines 278–82 (*Shorter Poems* 188). The line offended some readers, and Wordsworth dropped it after 1832 (see *PW* 3:155, 461–2; also Carl Ketcham's 'Introduction' to the *Shorter Poems*, 15–16).

5 I correct Bradley's quotation in minor details. See also Bradley's note on the Gondo Gorge passage (139–40n).

6 It may be no accident that Bradley skips over the naturalistic, narrative stanzas of 'Lucy Gray' that a contemporary was razoring out to make a new 'Lucy Poem' (see pp. 10 and 77, above).

It is illuminating to consider Bradley's manoeuvre in connection with contemporary attacks on romantic symbolists for flying 'away into the circumambient gas' (T.E. Hulme, 'Romanticism and Classicism' [1913–14] [Adams 729]). Do modernist assaults on romantic idealism touch on the poets, or only on the modernists' own peculiarly transcendental-symbolist reading of them? One point of the present chapter is to reflect on the consequences (such as what Geoffrey Hartman calls 'reader-responsibility') ensuing from the fact that texts are not entirely 'symbolist' or 'realist' in themselves.

7 Paul de Man comments on the Coleridgean symbol: 'Its structure is that of the synecdoche' (*Blindness and Insight* 191). In Coleridge's famous statement, 'a Symbol ... always partakes of the Reality which it renders intelligible; and while it enunciates the whole, abides itself as a living part in that Unity, of which it is the representative' (*Lay Sermons* 30). Schelling is less explicit, but the emphasis on both meaning and being appears in the statement that good 'Art imparts to its work, together with the utmost clearness to the understanding, that unfathomable reality wherein it resembles a work of Nature' (112). David Simpson argues, quoting Shelley: 'there is a very important aspect of Romantic aesthetics which insists on our beholding "at once the sign and the thing signified" ' (*Irony and Authority* 217n6). The romantic topos of inexhaustibility follows from this conception of symbol: 'All high poetry is infinite. ... Veil after veil may be undrawn, and the inmost naked beauty of the meaning never exposed' (Percy Shelley 500; compare John Keats to J.H. Reynolds, 19 Feb. 1818). In contrast, in a transcendental conception of symbol, the symbol is understood and discarded as mere vehicle; hence Ferry's tendency to speak of ' "inner" or "final" or "deeper" meanings' (14). While this conception resembles what Coleridge and Goethe despise as 'allegory,' it differs in that Ferry's symbols are still conceived as natural rather than conventional.

8 Norman Holland, 'Literary Interpretation' 231; Archibald MacLeish, 'Ars Poetica' (1926), lines 23–4. MacLeish's actual phrase is, of course, 'A poem should not mean / But be.' Holland is discussed in chapter 4, above.

9 See *WP* 159; *Saving the Text* 148.

10 David Simpson's notion of a poetics of the 'second look' in Wordsworth is, I think, closely related to this conception (*Wordsworth and the Figurings of the Real* 54–8).

11 The *application* of the ironic reading to the 'Lucy Poems' is also historically dubious. Since 'Tintern Abbey' was written before the 'Lucy Poems,' its meanings seem obviously relevant, but the ironic reading of 'Nature never did betray' derives from contrast with 'Elegiac Stanzas' (1806), which pass judgment on a former 'illusion' (and even here nature is never accused of betrayal). Ernest de Selincourt quotes a letter from the Duke of Argyle, dated 1848, describing a recent performance of 'Tintern Abbey' by Wordsworth in terms that make one wonder if he ever felt nature's 'betrayal' (*PW* 2:517).

12 J. Hillis Miller comments: 'We need ... all the help we can get. One such

help is other "similar" passages in the same writer or in other writers, in a widening field which ... creates as many problems as it solves, especially by way of what is problematic about that "similarity"' ('Postscript 1984' 116).

13 Derrida, *Writing and Difference* 280. Derrida refers to 'the moment' when the loss of the centre (e.g., the death of God) was extended to language itself, that is, when (a) 'in the absence of a center or origin, everything became discourse,' and (b) in the 'absence of the transcendental signified,' language itself was found to be without centre (280).

14 Wallace Stevens, 'Examination of the Hero in a Time of War' (1942), sec. xvi (*Collected Poems* 280). I am grateful to Patricia Rae for both of my epigraphs from Stevens.

15 The 1983 edition of *Blindness and Insight* garbles the text in crucial passages and should be avoided. Since it is in print I cite page numbers for this edition, but I have checked all references against the original publication in *Interpretation: Theory and Practice*, ed. Charles Singleton. Where discrepancies occur, the Singleton page number is given first.

16 See Derrida, 'Differance' (1968), in *Speech and Phenomena*, 129–60; see also 67–9, 88, 99–102. De Man's assertion appears to rest also on a figural understanding of *precedence* as specifically temporal precedence, e.g., in his claim that 'the allegorical sign refer[s] to another sign that precedes it.' It is not clear that one signifier must precede the other temporally rather than logically.

17 'Dejection: An Ode,' line 48; see also 'To William Wordsworth,' lines 18–19. The line cited by de Man is from 'The Eolian Harp' (line 26).

18 The essay by Wasserman to which de Man responds, 'The English Romantics: The Grounds of Knowledge,' gives a good account of this inconsistency.

19 I am anticipated here by Clifford Siskin's analysis of this essay in *The Historicity of Romantic Discourse* (30–4). As he puts it, 'What de Man has done is translate subject/object ... into subject/time' (32).

20 Abrams, 'Structure and Style' 556. De Man quotes different statements from the same passage in Abrams.

21 I set the quotation off as a separate block for ease of comparison with what Wordsworth actually wrote (see below). The interpolation in Wordsworth's quotation is de Man's.

22 The word 'symbol' is not even listed in Markham L. Peacock's compendium of *The Critical Opinions of William Wordsworth* or in the index to the *Prose Works*. Of the twenty-four uses of 'symbol' and its cognates in Lane Cooper's *Concordance*, only one instance even suggests that the symbol has a power of transcending self or temporality. Usually the term refers to conventional signs such as letters and religious or political emblems: the cross (twice), the altar, or the sceptre (four times).

23 De Man's comment that it is 'one of Wordsworth's Lucy Gray poems' (223) is odd, since 'Lucy Gray' is almost never included with the other 'Lucy Poems,' and de Man's reading does not elsewhere assume that 'she' refers to any 'Lucy,' Gray or otherwise.

24 Presumably, de Man is referring to figura, or prefigurative interpretation, according to which the 'thing' in stanza 1 would prefigure the thingness of stanza 2. Figurative interpretation is often associated with allegory, but Erich Auerbach stresses 'the important difference ... between figurism and other similar forms of thinking such as allegorism or symbolism' ('Typological Symbolism' 6). See also Auerbach's ' "Figura" ' (1944), in *Scenes from the Drama of European Literature*, especially 53–8. Since Auerbach stresses the 'historicity' and 'concrete reality' of the 'figura' (' "Figura" ' 54–5), de Man's appeal to its temporally 'prefigurative pattern' as a criterion for allegorism in his new sense (which suspends reference to concrete actuality) seems to me both confused and illicit.

25 Murray Krieger, even in critiquing de Man's discussion of this poem, accepts that the poem is allegorical (*Theory of Criticism* 223). J. Hillis Miller also accepts that 'A slumber' is ' "allegorical" in the technical sense in which that term is used by Walter Benjamin or by Paul de Man' ('On Edge' 104). Jonathan Culler reports that de Man's essay 'identified in the work of major Romantics an allegorical mode of figuration, ... cit[ing] as an example Wordsworth's "A Slumber ..." where the word *thing* helps to produce an allegorical narrative of mystification and demystification' ('Changes in the Study of Lyric' 53).

26 De Man touches on relations between Protestantism and 'allegory' (202–4), but more often simply phrases value judgments in puritanical terms: symbolism 'will never be able to gain an entirely good poetic *conscience*'; 'the term "symbol" had in fact been substituted for that of "allegory" in an act of ontological *bad faith*' (208, 211, my emphases). Lentricchia's trenchant analysis shows that these terms belong also to existentialism ('Paul de Man: The Rhetoric of Authority,' ch. 8 in *After the New Criticism*).

27 Jameson, *The Political Unconscious* 105; Byron, *Manfred* 1.1.10 (Byron 275); Wordsworth, 'Elegiac Stanzas,' lines 57–8 (*PW* 4:260).

28 Don Bialostosky explores such distortions in 'What de Man has Made of Wordsworth,' ch. 6 of *Wordsworth, Dialogics, and the Practice of Criticism*, 152–9; see especially 176–8, on de Man's use of examples or 'substitutions.'

29 Susan Eilenberg's reading of the 'Lucy Poems' ('The Haunted Language of the Lucy Poems,' ch. 5 of *Strange Power of Speech*, 108–35) appeared too late for me to integrate it fully in this discussion, but it closely resembles de Man's, Ferguson's, and Miller's readings in arguing that Lucy is not human (113–14) but 'a creature of words' (131) who 'allegorizes the prob-

lems of allegory' (133). In that it borrows also from Averill and Ball the emphasis on 'occluded narrative' or 'internal' story 'purg[ed of] incident' (111, 109), and from Hall and Grob the perception of nature as rival (121–2), Eilenberg's reading is highly eclectic, and might stand as a compendium of modern disenchantment-readings.

30 'On Edge' 98–9. 'On Edge' appears as part of an exchange with M.H. Abrams (see also Abrams, 'Construing').

31 In 'Questions and Answers,' Miller reaffirms these claims more explicitly: 'I don't agree that my conclusions are predetermined' (Eaves and Fischer 119).

32 Ferguson too argues that the 'Lucy Poems' 'attempt to figure forth a microcosmic English literary history' (179).

33 As de Man puts it, 'Allegories are always allegories of metaphor and, as such, they are always allegories of the impossibility of reading' (*Allegories of Reading* 205).

34 *Spectator* 418 (30 June 1712) (Adams 287). On the popularization of literary theory as containment, see also Lentricchia, especially 103–4.

35 Schleiermacher remarked the ubiquity of interpretation much earlier (c. 1819); see his 'Introduction.' The Derridean version appears in his various denials of 'perception' (e.g., *Speech and Phenomena* 54n and 103).

36 *Writing and Difference* 284. Jeffrey Nealon comments incisively on the 'commodification of deconstruction,' especially through neglect of the 'double gesture' ('The Discipline of Deconstruction').

37 In 'Questions and Answers,' Miller comments, though on a reading of a different poem: 'I think my reading of Yeats's poem is right, that all right-thinking people will come, given enough time, to my reading. When one speaks of undecidability as a feature of deconstructive criticism, one doesn't mean a free-for-all but a very precise identifiable movement back and forth. ... My notion is that a poem has a coercive effect on any reader and on any reading' (Eaves and Fischer, 122).

38 The point of the 'double gesture' is that what is deconstructed is not thus abolished; as Derrida puts it in an interview, 'I do not at all believe in what today is so easily called the death of philosophy (nor, moreover, in the simple death of whatever – the book, man, or god, especially since, as we all know, what is dead wields a very specific power).' In a separate interview he refers to subjectivity and, apparently, to God, as 'effects of *différance*' (*Positions* 6, 28).

39 On Averill's reading of the 'Lucy Poems' as anti-narrative narratives, see chapter 2, above.

40 It may be recalled that Hirsch rules out the possibility of synthesizing Brooks's and Bateson's readings (*Validity* 229); if one accepts this judgment, Hartman's both-and is not so much synthesis as the insistence on two readings.

41 Coleridge, *Lay Sermons* 30; Coleridge's conception builds on the etymology of 'symbol' as a broken token that indicates something (i.e., its other half) by virtue of its physical participation in it. Auerbach's essays on ' "Figura" ' and on 'Typological Symbolism' (see note 24 above) are important statements of the possibility of a mode of signification where the signifier is not lost in its significance. '[B]oth entities in the figurative relationship are equally real and equally concrete; the figurative sense does not destroy the literal, nor does the literal deprive the figured fact of its status as a real historical event' ('Typological' 4). While Auerbach distinguishes this conception from both allegory and symbolism, in which 'at least one of the two elements combined is a pure sign' (6), he also admits that 'figural interpretation is "allegorical" in the widest sense' and that it resembles symbol in its insistence on the actuality of the signifier (' "Figura" ' 54, 56–7) (see also *Mimesis* 195–6). Following Vico in using the term 'symbol' to describe a 'mythical' or 'primitive' mode, Auerbach stresses the magicality of its 'presence' in opposition to the *historical* actuality that figural interpretation attributes to events. But it still seems fair to me to view Coleridgean symbolism, which finds 'the Eternal *through and in* the Temporal' (30, my emphasis), as an effort to resurrect the both-and stance of figural interpretation, and even to preserve the historical event in Auerbach's sense. In the *practice* of symbolic interpretation, nevertheless, the actuality of the symbol may often be forgotten, just as figural interpretation gives way, in Auerbach's account, to more strenuously abstractive modes (' "Figura" ' 54–5). On formalism's repudiation of low symbolism, in which the meaning becomes of greater account than the symbol, see Victor Erlich, *Russian Formalism*, especially ch. 2, 'From the "Forest of Symbols" to the "Self-Valuable Word" ' (32–50). In formalism, Erlich explains, 'Attention was focussed on the outward form or sensory texture of the linguistic symbol rather than on its communicative value, on the sign rather than its object. Indeed, a deliberate attempt was made to ... emancipate the word ... from its "traditional subservience to meaning" ' (45). See also Boris Eichenbaum, 'The Theory of the "Formal Method"' 108–15. On the both-and conception in Marxist dialectics, see Georg Lukács, 'Art and Objective Truth,' especially 34–44. 'The goal for all great art,' Lukács argues, 'is to provide a picture of reality in which the contradiction between appearance and reality, the particular and the general, the immediate and the conceptual, etc., is so resolved that the two converge into a spontaneous integrity. ... The universal appears as a quality of the individual and the particular, reality becomes manifest and can be experienced within appearance, the general principle is exposed as the specific impelling cause for the individual case.' He quotes Engels: 'Each is simultaneously a type and a particular individual, a "this one" (*Dieser*), as old Hegel expressed it, and so it must be' (34–5). At the same

time Lukács is a critic of bourgeois symbolism: see Jameson, *Marxism and Form* 196–8. In every case there appears to be an effort to reassert the tensionality of the signifier in opposition to a poetics or hermeneutics that would reduce it – more specifically, there is an effort to reassert concreteness or actuality against abstraction and transcendence. But it is important to stress that these disputes are not just about poetics, about how texts have been written; they are also about hermeneutics, about how they ought to be read. Hartman's *Wordsworth's Poetry*, inscribed to Auerbach, may be an effort to read Wordsworth through Auerbach's figural stipulation: 'the figurative sense does not destroy the literal.' But see also Atkins 34, 40, on Hartman's reservations about typology as a totalizing mode.

42 Though David Haney's stimulating discussion appeared too late to be considered integrally here, his argument that 'one of Wordsworth's concerns in the Lucy poems is to reset epistemological questions in their ethical contexts' (92) is profoundly relevant to my own. I mainly agree with Haney's view that the poems stress 'the impossibility of an epistemological knowledge' of Lucy and demand 'an ethical rather than epistemological' relation to her (94, 92); but I would add that this is not merely a matter of theme, as he presents it, but also one of mode. That is, what he says of the epistemological and ethical relations of the *speaker* to Lucy applies equally, and even primarily, to the relation of the poetry's *readers* to Lucy and to the poems themselves. Thus a significant tension obtains between Haney's emphasis on the ethics of knowledge-claims *in* the poems, and his conventional hypostatization *of* them as 'the Lucy poems' (including 'A slumber') (96–7), even though a footnote (241n18) declares the grouping to be problematic.

43 My argument for the indeterminacy of double readings assumes that one cannot appreciate both meaning and existence at once. As Lacan says, or as Terry Eagleton paraphrases him, 'I cannot "mean" and "be" simultaneously' (*Literary Theory* 170). Derrida writes: 'what opens meaning and language is writing as the disappearance of natural presence' (*Of Grammatology* 159). In a discussion of Rousseau's theory of the child, which is thus oddly resonant for the 'Lucy Poems,' he adds: '*For Rousseau the concept of the child is always related to the sign. More precisely, childhood is the nonrelation to the sign as such.* But what is a sign as such? There is no sign as such. Either the sign is considered a thing, and it is not a sign. Or it is a reference, and thus not itself. According to Rousseau, the child is the name of that which should not relate in any way to a separated signifier, loved in some way for itself, like a fetish' (204). (Derrida is referring to the child's use of signs, e.g., coins, not primarily to her function *as* a sign.)

44 See, e.g., Eagleton, *Literary Theory* ch. 4, especially 146; Jerome McGann, *The Romantic Ideology*, ch. 5.

45 On the Lucy of 'Nutting,' see DC MS. 16 as printed in *PW* 2:504–6 and in Butler and Green 305–7; see also Douglass H. Thomson, 'Wordsworth's Lucy of "Nutting."'

46 See George Steiner, *Language and Silence*, especially 'Humane Literacy' (3–11) and 'To Civilize Our Gentlemen' (55–67), and *In Bluebeard's Castle.*

Appendix

1 For more extended critiques, see Jack Stillinger, 'Textual Primitivism and the Editing of Wordsworth,' *SiR* 28 (1989), 3–28, since reprinted in *Multiple Authorship*; Mark Jones, 'Interpretation in Wordsworth'; and Zachary Leader, 'Wordsworth, Revision, and Personal Identity.' 'Archaeology' is Stephen Parrish's figure; see 'The Editor as Archaeologist.'

2 Some volumes are devoted to historical collections, and later volumes have turned to later poems – e.g., *The Fourteen Book Prelude*, ed. W.J.B. Owen (1985). I am chiefly concerned here with those that aim to recover 'lost' poems, such as the two-part *Prelude*, 'Home at Grasmere,' and 'Salisbury Plain.'

3 Stephen Gill, ed., *William Wordsworth* 685; Gill, 'Wordsworth's Poems' 189n. While these editions reproduce manuscript gaps (usually in square brackets) and so may be said to indicate the actual state of the texts, they are editorially 'finished' in other respects, as in the addition and emendation of punctuation.

4 Gill, ed., *Salisbury Plain Poems* 23, 51.

5 See Butler and Green, ed., *Lyrical Ballads*, 729–34 for a description of MS. 1800, and 556–9 for representative reproductions.

6 Jared Curtis, ed. *Poems, in Two Volumes* 51.

7 *TLS*, 27 Sept. 1928, quoted by Christopher Ricks, *The Force of Poetry* 89. Alan Helms cites the first and last editions of 'A slumber' in discussing the value of Wordsworth's own punctuation ('The Sense of Punctuation'). Besides the distinction between grammatical and rhetorical or poetic punctuation, one must bear in mind how much rules of punctuation have changed over the past three hundred years, and how much between 1800 and 1850 (see Percy Simpson, *Shakespearian Punctuation* 8–16). Without simply attributing to the printers all developments in Wordsworth's punctuation, Curtis seems to assume, reasonably enough, that these changes were due to the closely related 'pressure of normalization' (*Poems* 55–6).

8 For instance, Dorothy Wordsworth comments: 'his ideas flow faster than he can express them' (*Letters* 1:200).

9 See, e.g., the Fenwick notes to 'Tintern Abbey' and 'Yes it was the Mountain Echo' (Alexander Grosart, ed., *Prose Works* 3:45), and *The Prelude* 4:110–30.

10 Editors who do so (e.g., John Hayden, ed., *William Wordsworth* 1:23) like to invoke Wordsworth's statement: 'you know what importance I attach to following strictly the last Copy of the text of an Author' (Letter of 19 April 1830, *Letters* 5:236). But *his* attitudes to authoritative editions are not really relevant to *our* principles in editing *him*; moreover, they are more complex and less reliable than this statement suggests. Wordsworth says this in concession; in the context he is actually complaining that Dyce's edition of Collins includes an 'unsuitable' though apparently authoritative reading. The same letter broaches a project Wordsworth had suggested to Lamb: 'abridging the plays [of English dramatists] that are not likely to be read as wholes, and telling such parts of the story in brief abstract as were ill managed in the Drama' (235).

Bibliography and Works Cited

This list actually combines two in one, my 'works cited' and a 'Lucy Poems' bibliography. Since there is so much overlap between works specifically on the 'Lucy Poems' and more general works on Wordsworth and/or literary theory, I use asterisks to indicate those that directly concern the poems, whether primarily or in part; but not parody anthologies or texts considered merely as parodies. Where an essay is listed separately from the volume in which it is collected, the asterisk is given to the essay, not the volume.

*Abrams, M.H. 'Construing and Deconstructing.' Eaves and Fischer 127–82.

– *A Glossary of Literary Terms*. 5th ed. Fort Worth: Rinehart, Holt, and Winston, 1988.

– 'Structure and Style in the Greater Romantic Lyric.' Hilles and Bloom 527–60.

Abrams, M.H., et al., eds. *The Norton Anthology of English Literature*. 2 vols. 4th ed. New York: Norton, 1979.

Adams, Hazard, ed. *Critical Theory since Plato*. 2nd ed. New York: Harcourt Brace Jovanovich, 1992.

Aldiss, Brian. 'Introduction' to Mary Shelley, *The Last Man*. i–x.

Alexander, J.H. '*Blackwood's*: Magazine as Romantic Form.' *Wordsworth Circle* 15 (1984), 57–68.

Altick, Richard. *The English Common Reader: A Social History of the Mass Reading Public, 1800–1900*. Chicago: U of Chicago P, 1957.

Anon. *The Three Trials of William Hone*. London: W. Hone, 1818. Rpt. London: W. Dugdale, n.d.

Arac, Jonathan. 'Bounding Lines: *The Prelude* and Critical Revision.' *boundary 2* 7:3 (1979), 31–48.

*Arnold, Matthew, ed. *Poems of Wordsworth*. 1879. 2nd ed., 16th printing. London: Macmillan, 1904.

– *The Complete Prose Works of Matthew Arnold*. Ed. R.H. Super. 11 vols. Ann Arbor: U of Michigan P, 1960–77.

Atkins, Douglas G. *Geoffrey Hartman: Criticism as Answerable Style*. London: Routledge, 1990.
Auden, W.H. *Collected Longer Poems*. New York: Vintage, 1975.
Auerbach, Erich. *Mimesis: The Representation of Reality in Western Literature*. 1946. Princeton: Princeton UP, 1968.
– *Scenes from the Drama of European Literature*. Minneapolis: U of Minnesota P, 1984.
– 'Typological Symbolism in Medieval Literature.' *Yale French Studies* 9 (1952), 3–10.
Austin, J.L. *How to Do Things with Words*. 2nd ed. Cambridge: Harvard UP,1975.
Averill, James. 'The Shape of *Lyrical Ballads* (1798).' *Philological Quarterly* 60 (1981), 387–407.
*– *Wordsworth and the Poetry of Human Suffering*. Ithaca: Cornell UP, 1980.
*Baker, Harry T. 'Wordsworth and Annette.' *North American Review* 207 (1918), 433–9.
Bakhtin, Mikhail M. *The Dialogic Imagination: Four Essays*. Ed. Michael Holquist. Trans. Caryl Emerson and Michael Holquist. Austin: U of Texas P, 1981.
– *Rabelais and His World*. 1965. Trans. Hélène Iswolsky, 1968; Bloomington: Indiana UP, 1984.
*Ball, Patricia. *The Heart's Events: The Victorian Poetry of Relationships*. London: Athlone, 1976.
*Bateson, F.W. *English Poetry: A Critical Introduction*. 1950. 2nd ed. London: Longman's, 1966.
*– *Wordsworth: A Re-Interpretation*. 1954. Revised ed. London: Longmans, Green, and Co., 1956.
Bauer, N.S. 'Early Burlesques and Parodies of Wordsworth.' *Journal of English and Germanic Philology* 84 (1975), 553–69.
– *William Wordsworth: A Reference Guide to British Criticism, 1793–1899*. Boston: G.K. Hall, 1978.
*Beardsley, Monroe C. *The Possibility of Criticism*. Detroit: Wayne State UP, 1970.
*Beatty, Arthur. *William Wordsworth: His Doctrine and Art in Their Historical Relations*. 1922. 3rd ed. Madison: U of Wisconsin P, 1960.
*Beatty, Frederika. *William Wordsworth of Dove Cottage: A Study of the Poet's Most Productive Decade, June 1797–May 1807*. New York: Bookman, 1964.
*Bercovitch, Sacvan. 'Lucy and Light: An Interpretation of Wordsworth's Lucy Poems.' *English* 16 (1966), 11–12.
*Berg, Maggie. 'Betrayed by Quotation: Ruskin's "Of Queens' Gardens." ' Paper read at the ACUTE conference in Montreal, 1985.
Bialostosky, Don. *Wordsworth, Dialogics, and the Practice of Criticism*. Cambridge: Cambridge UP, 1992.

Black, Henry Campbell. *Black's Law Dictionary*. 6th ed. St Paul: West Publishing, 1990.

Blake, William. *The Complete Poetry and Prose of William Blake*. Ed. David V. Erdman. Revised ed. New York: Anchor, 1988.

Bloom, Harold. *The Anxiety of Influence: A Theory of Poetry*. New York: Oxford UP, 1973.

Bond, Richmond P. *English Burlesque Poetry, 1700–1750*. Cambridge: Harvard UP, 1932.

*Boulger, James D. *The Calvinist Temper in English Poetry*. The Hague: Mouton, 1980.

*Bourke, Richard. 'Legitimating Public Pleasure: *Nutting*, Lucy and Propriety.' *Romantic Discourse and Political Modernity: Wordsworth, the Intellectual and Cultural Critique*. New York: Harvester, 1993. 175–97.

Bové, Paul A. *Intellectuals in Power: A Genealogy of Critical Humanism*. New York: Columbia UP, 1986.

Bradley, A.C. *Oxford Lectures on Poetry*. 1909. London: Macmillan, 1959.

Brett, Simon, ed. *The Faber Book of Parodies*. London: Faber, 1984.

*Brooks, Cleanth. 'Irony as a Principle of Structure.' 1949. *Literary Opinion in America: Essays Illustrating the Status, Methods, and Problems of Criticism in the United States in the Twentieth Century*.Ed. M. D. Zabel. 2 vols. 1951. 3rd ed. New York: Harper and Row, 1962. 2:729–41.

*– 'Metaphor, Paradox, and Stereotype.' *British Journal of Aesthetics* 5 (1965), 312–28.

*Brooks, Cleanth, and Robert Penn Warren, ed. *Understanding Poetry*. 1938. 3rd ed. New York: Holt, Rinehart, and Winston, 1960.

Browne, Isaac Hawkins. *A Pipe of Tobacco: In Imitation of Six Several Authors*. 1736. Ed. H.F.B. Brett-Smith. Oxford: Blackwell, 1923.

*Burgum, Edwin Berry. 'The Cult of the Complex in Poetry.' *Science and Society* 15 (1951), 31–48.

Burns, Robert. *Poems and Songs*. Ed. James Kinsley. Oxford: Oxford UP, 1978.

*Burra, Peter. *Wordsworth*. 1936. New York: Macmillan, 1950.

Butler, James, and Karen Green, eds. *'Lyrical Ballads,' and Other Poems, 1797–1800*. Ithaca: Cornell UP, 1992.

*Butler, Samuel. 'Quis Desiderio ... ?' 1888. Rpt. in *The Humour of Homer and Other Essays*, ed. R.A. Streatfeild [sic] (London: A.C. Fifield, 1913), 99–109.

*Byrd, Max. 'Metamorphosis and *Tintern Abbey*: Two Notes.' *Modern Philology* 81 (1983), 24–37.

Byron, George Gordon, Lord. *Byron*. Oxford Authors. Ed. Jerome J. McGann. New York: Oxford UP, 1986.

*Calvert, George H. *Wordsworth: A Biographic Aesthetic Study*. Boston: Lee and Shepard, 1878. Rpt. Folcroft, 1970.

*Caraher, Brian. *Wordsworth's 'Slumber' and the Problematics of Reading*. University Park: Pennsylvania State UP, 1991.

Cassirer, Ernst. *The Philosophy of the Enlightenment*. Trans. Fritz C.A. Koelln and James P. Pettegrove. Princeton: Princeton UP, 1951.

*Christensen, Francis. 'Wordsworth's "Three Years She Grew."' *Explicator* 4:3 (Dec. 1945), note 18.

*Cobban, Alfred. 'Wordsworth and Nationality.' Chapter 5 in *Edmund Burke and the Revolt against the Eighteenth Century: A Study of the Political Thinking of Burke, Wordsworth, Coleridge, and Southey*. London: Allen and Unwin, 1929. 2nd ed. New York: Barnes and Noble, 1960. 133–53.

*Coleridge, Samuel Taylor. *Biographia Literaria; Or Biographical Sketches of My Literary Life and Opinions*. 1817. Ed. James Engell and W. Jackson Bate. 2 vols. Princeton: Princeton/Bollingen, 1983.

*– *Collected Letters of Samuel Taylor Coleridge*. Ed. Earl Leslie Griggs. 6 vols. Oxford: Clarendon, 1956–71.

– *The Friend*. Ed. Barbara E. Rooke. 2 vols. Princeton: Princeton/Bollingen, 1969.

– *Lay Sermons*. Ed. R.J. White. Princeton: Princeton/Bollingen, 1972.

– *Poetical Works*. Ed. Ernest Hartley Coleridge. London: Oxford, 1912. Rpt. 1978.

– *Table Talk*. Ed. Carl Woodring. 2 vols. Princeton: Princeton/Bollingen, 1990.

Conrad, Joseph. *Heart of Darkness*. 1899. Harmondsworth: Penguin, 1973.

*Conran, Anthony. 'The Goslar Lyrics.' *Wordsworth's Mind and Art*. Ed. A.W. Thomson. Edinburgh: Oliver and Boyd, 1969. 157–80.

*Cooke, Michael G. *Acts of Inclusion: Studies Bearing on an Elementary Theory of Romanticism*. New Haven: Yale UP, 1979.

Cooper, Lane. *A Concordance to the Poems of William Wordsworth Edited for the Concordance Society*. 1911. New York: Russell and Russell, 1965.

*– 'Raleigh's "Wordsworth": A Note.' *Athenaeum*, 2 Jan. 1904, pp. 16–17.

*Crawfurd, Oswald, ed. *Lyrical Verse from Elizabeth to Victoria*. London: Chapman and Hall, 1896.

Crews, Frederick. *The Pooh Perplex: A Freshman Casebook*. 1963. New York: Dutton, 1965.

*Crosman, Robert. 'Do Readers Make Meaning?' *The Reader in the Text: Essays on Audience and Interpretation*. Ed. Susan R. Suleiman and Inge Crosman. Princeton, NJ: Princeton UP, 1980. 149–64.

Culler, Jonathan. 'Changes in the Study of Lyric.' *Lyric Poetry: Beyond New Criticism*. Ed. Chaviva Hošek and Patricia Parker. Ithaca: Cornell UP, 1985. 37–54.

– *On Deconstruction*. Ithaca: Cornell UP, 1982.

– *The Pursuit of Signs*. Ithaca: Cornell UP, 1981.

– *Structuralist Poetics: Structuralism, Linguistics, and the Study of Literature*. Ithaca: Cornell UP, 1975.

Curran, Stuart. 'Composite Orders.' *Poetic Form and British Romanticism*. New York: Oxford UP, 1986. 180–203.

– 'Multum in Parvo: Wordsworth's *Poems, in Two Volumes* of 1807.' Fraistat, *Poems* 234–53.

*Curtis, Jared. 'A Note on the Lost Manuscripts of William Wordsworth's "Louisa" and "I travell'd among unknown Men."' *Yale University Library Gazette* 53 (1979), 196–201.

– 'The Wellesley Copy of Wordsworth's *Poetical Works*, 1832.' *Harvard Library Bulletin* 28 (1980), 5–15.

Curtis, Jared, ed. *Poems, in Two Volumes, and Other Poems, 1800–1807, by William Wordsworth*. Ithaca: Cornell UP, 1983.

*Danby, John F. 'Goslar Poems.' Ch. 3 of *The Simple Wordsworth: Studies in the Poems 1797–1807*. 1960. New York: Barnes and Noble, 1961.

Dane, Joseph. 'Parody and Satire: A Theoretical Model.' *Genre* 13 (1980), 145–59.

Darbishire, Helen. Review of Bateson, *Wordsworth*. *TLS*, 19 Nov. 1954.

Darlington, Beth, ed. *The Love Letters of William and Mary Wordsworth*. Ithaca: Cornell UP, 1981.

*Davies, Hugh Sykes. 'Another New Poem by Wordsworth.' *Essays in Criticism* 15 (1965), 135–61.

de Man, Paul. *Allegories of Reading: Figural Language in Rousseau, Nietzsche, Rilke, and Proust*. New Haven: Yale UP, 1979.

– *Blindness and Insight: Essays in the Rhetoric of Contemporary Criticism*. 1971. 2nd Ed., Revised. Minneapolis: U of Minnesota P, 1983.

– *The Resistance to Theory*. Minneapolis: U of Minnesota P, 1986.

– *The Rhetoric of Romanticism*. New York: Columbia UP, 1984.

*– 'The Rhetoric of Temporality.' *Interpretation: Theory and Practice*. Ed. Charles Singleton. Baltimore, MD: Johns Hopkins UP, 1969. 187–228.

– 'Semiology and Rhetoric.' 1973. *Allegories of Reading* 3–19.

*De Quincey, Thomas. 'Lake Reminscences, From 1807 to 1830. By the English Opium-Eater. No. 1 – William Wordsworth.' *Tait's Edinburgh Magazine* n.s. 6 (Jan., Feb., April, 1839), 1–12, 90–102, 246–54. Rpt. as 'William Wordsworth' in *Recollections of the Lakes and the Lake Poets*. Ed. David Wright Baltimore: Penguin, 1970. 119–206.

– 'On Wordsworth's Poetry.' *Tait's Edinburgh Magazine* 12:141 (Sept. 1845), 545–54.

Derrida, Jacques. *Limited Inc*. Evanston: Northwestern UP, 1988.

– *Of Grammatology*. Trans. Gayatri Spivak. Baltimore: Johns Hopkins UP, 1976.

– *Positions*. Trans. Alan Bass. Chicago: U of Chicago P, 1981.

– *Speech and Phenomena, and Other Essays on Husserl's Theory of Signs*.Trans. David B. Allison. Evanston, IL: Northwestern UP, 1973.

– *Writing and Difference*. Trans. Alan Bass. Chicago: U of Chicago P, 1978.

de Selincourt, Ernest, ed. *The Prelude, or Groth of a Poet's Mind, Edited from the Manuscripts*. Oxford: Clarendon, 1926.

*de Vere, Aubrey. *Essays, Chiefly on Poetry*. 2 vols. *vol. 1: Criticisms on Certain Poets*. London: Macmillan, 1887.

*– 'The Genius and Passion of Wordsworth,' Part the Second, *Month* 39 (April–May 1880), 1–30. See 13–15.

*Dilworth, Thomas. 'Wordsworth's "She Dwelt Among Untrodden Ways" ' [sic]. *Explicator* 42:3 (1984), 22–3.

D'Israeli, Isaac. 'Parodies.' ?1817. *Curiosities of Literature*, new ed. London, 1867.

Doveton, F.B. *Sketches in Prose and Verse*. London, 1886.

Dowling, William C. *Jameson, Althusser, Marx: An Introduction to The 'Political Unconscious.'* Ithaca: Cornell UP, 1984.

Doyle, William. *The Oxford History of the French Revolution*. Oxford: Clarendon, 1989.

*Drabble, Margaret. *Wordsworth*. New York: Arco, 1969.

*Dudley, Fred A. 'Wordsworth's "Three Years She Grew in Sun and Shower." ' *Explicator* 2:4 (Feb. 1944), query 19.

*Dunklin, Gilbert T., ed. *Wordsworth: Centenary Essays Presented at Cornell and Princeton Universities*. Princeton: Princeton UP, 1951.

*Durrant, Geoffrey. *Wordsworth and the Great System: A Study of Wordsworth's Poetic Universe*. Cambridge: Cambridge UP, 1970.

*– 'Zeno's Arrow: Time and Motion in Two of Wordsworth's Lucy Poems.' *Mosaic* 2:3 (spring 1969), 10–24.

*Dyson, A.E. 'Symbiosis in Wordsworth.' *Critical Survey* 6:1–3 (1973), 41–3.

Eagleton, Terry. *The Function of Criticism: From 'The Spectator' to Post-Structuralism*. London: Verso, 1984.

– *Literary Theory: An Introduction*. Minneapolis: U of Minnesota P, 1983.

Eaves, Morris, and Michael Fischer, eds. *Romanticism and Contemporary Criticism*. Ithaca: Cornell UP, 1986.

Eichenbaum, Boris. 'The Theory of the "Formal Method." ' 1926. *Russian Formalist Criticism: Four Essays*. Trans. Lee T. Lemon and Marion J. Reis. Lincoln: U of Nebraska P, 1965. 99–139.

*Eilenberg, Susan. *Strange Power of Speech: Wordsworth, Coleridge, and Literary Possession*. New York: Oxford UP, 1992.

*Elwin, Malcolm. *The First Romantics*. New York: Longmans, Green and Co., 1948.

Empson, William. *Seven Types of Ambiguity*. 1930. 3rd ed. New York: New Directions, 1966.

Erlich, Victor. *Russian Formalism: History -- Doctrine*. 3rd ed. New Haven: Yale UP, 1981.

*Fairchild, H.N. *The Romantic Quest*. London, 1931.

Falk, Robert P., and William Beare. 'Parody.' *The Princeton Encyclopedia of Poetry and Poetics*. Enlarged edition. Ed. Alex Preminger et al. Princeton: Princeton UP, 1974. 600–2.

Fanshawe, Catherine. *Literary Remains*. London: Pickering, 1876.
*Fausset, Hugh I'Anson. *Studies in Idealism*. 1923. Rpt. Port Washington, NY: Kennikat, 1965.
*Ferguson, Frances. 'The Lucy Poems: Wordsworth's Quest for a Poetic Object.' *ELH* 40 (1973), 432–48. Rpt. in *William Wordsworth* 173–94.
– *William Wordsworth: Language as Counter-Spirit*. New Haven: Yale UP, 1977.
*Ferry, David. *The Limits of Mortality: An Essay on Wordsworth's Major Poems*. Middletown, CT: Wesleyan UP, 1959.
Field, Barron. *Barron Field's Memoirs of Wordsworth*. Ed. Geoffrey Little. Sidney: Sidney UP, 1975.
Fish, Stanley. 'Consequences.' Mitchell, *Against Theory* 106–31.
– *Doing What Comes Naturally: Change, Rhetoric, and the Practice of Theory in Literary and Legal Studies*. Durham: Duke UP, 1989.
– *Is There a Text in This Class? The Authority of Interpretive Communities*. Cambridge: Harvard UP, 1980.
*Fleissner, Robert F. 'A Road Taken: The Romantically Different *Ruelle*.' *Robert Frost: Studies of the Poetry*. Ed. Kathryn Gibbs Harris. Boston: G.K. Hall, 1979. 117–31.
Fletcher, Angus. *Allegory: The Theory of a Symbolic Mode*. Ithaca: Cornell UP, 1964.
Forster, R.F. *Modern Ireland, 1600–1972*. London: Penguin, 1988.
Foucault, Michel. 'The Discourse on Language.' *The Archaeology of Knowledge*. Trans. A.M. Sheridan Smith. New York: Pantheon, 1972. 215–37.
– 'What is an Author?' *Language, Counter-Memory, Practice: Selected Essays and Interviews*. Ed. Donald F. Bouchard. Ithaca: Cornell UP, 1977. 113–38.
– *The Order of Things: An Archaeology of the Human Sciences*. Translation of *Les Mots et les choses*. No translator. New York: Vintage, 1973.
Fraistat, Neil. *The Poem and the Book: Interpreting Collections of Romantic Poetry*. Chapel Hill: U of North Carolina P, 1985.
Fraistat, Neil, ed. *Poems in Their Place: The Intertextuality and Order of Poetic Collections*. Chapel Hill: U of North Carolina P, 1986.
*Fry, Paul H. *The Poet's Calling in the English Ode*. New Haven: Yale UP, 1980.
Frye, Northrop. *Anatomy of Criticism: Four Essays*. Princeton: Princeton UP, 1957.
Gadamer, Hans-Georg. *Truth and Method*. 1960. No translator. New York: Crossroad, 1985.
Galperin, William H. *Revision and Authority in Wordsworth*. Philadelphia: U of Pennsylvania P, 1989.
*Garber, Frederick. *Wordsworth and the Poetry of Encounter*. Urbana: U of Illinois P, 1971.
*Garrod, H.W. 'Wordsworth's Lucy.' *The Profession of Poetry and Other Lectures*. Oxford: Clarendon, 1929. 78–92.

*Geiger, Don. *The Dramatic Impulse in Modern Poetics.* Baton Rouge: Louisiana State UP, 1967.

*Gierasch, Walter. 'Wordsworth's "I Travelled Among Unknown Men."' *Explicator* 1:8 (June 1943), note 65.

Gill, Stephen, ed. *William Wordsworth.* The Oxford Authors series. Oxford: Oxford, 1984.

– 'Wordsworth's Poems: The Question of Text.' *Review of English Studies* 34 (1983), 172–90.

Gittings, Robert, and Jo Manton. *Dorothy Wordsworth.* Oxford: Clarendon, 1985.

Gobin, Pierre. "Preliminaries: Towards a Study of the *Parodying* Activity." Clive Thomson 36–47.

Gombrich, E.H. *Art and Illusion: A Study in the Psychology of Pictorial Representation.* 1960. Princeton: Princeton/Bollingen, 1984.

*Graff, Gerald. 'Determinacy/Indeterminacy.' Lentricchia and McLaughlin 163–76.

– *Professing Literature: An Institutional History.* Chicago: U of Chicago P, 1987.

– 'The Pseudo-Politics of Interpretation.' Mitchell, *Politics* 145–58.

Gravil, Richard. '*Lyrical Ballads* (1798): Wordsworth as Parodist.' *Critical Quarterly* 24:4 (1982), 39–57.

*Grob, Alan. *The Philosophic Mind: A Study of Wordsworth's Poetry and Thought 1797–1805.* Columbus: Ohio State UP, 1973.

Grosart, Alexander B., ed. *The Prose Works of William Wordsworth.* 3 vols. 1876. New York: AMS, 1967.

Hackwood, Frederick W. *William Hone: His Life and Times.* London: Unwin, 1912.

*Hall, Spencer. 'Wordsworth's 'Lucy' Poems: Context and Meaning.' *Studies in Romanticism* 10 (1971), 159–75.

*Hamilton, Carson C. *Wordsworth's Decline in Poetic Power: Prophet into High Priest.* New York: Exposition Press, 1963.

Hamilton, Walter, ed. *Parody of the Works of English and American Authors.* 6 vols. London: Reeves and Turner, 1888. 5:90–106.

*Hancher, Michael. 'The Science of Interpretation and the Art of Interpretation.' *Modern Language Notes* 85 (1970), 791–802.

– 'Three Kinds of Intention.' *MLN* 87 (1972), 827–51.

*Haney, David P. 'Facing Death in the Lucy Poems.' *William Wordsworth and the Hermeneutics of Incarnation.* University Park: U of Pennsylvania P, 1993. 89–102.

*Harding, D.W. *Experience into Words: Essays on Poetry.* London: Chatto and Windus, 1963.

*Harper, G.M. 'Wordsworth's Love Poetry.' *John Morley and Other Essays.* 1920. Freeport, NY: Books for Libraries, 1968. 125–33.

*Harris, [James] Rendel. 'Wordsworth's Lucy.' *After-Glow Essays*, no. 8. London: U of London P, 1935. 3–24.
*Hartman, Geoffrey. 'Beyond Formalism.' 1966. *Beyond Formalism* 42–57.
– *Beyond Formalism: Literary Essays 1958–1970*. New Haven: Yale UP, 1970.
– 'Blindness and Insight.' *New Republic*, 7 March 1988, pp. 26–31.
– *Criticism in the Wilderness: The Study of Literature Today*. New Haven: Yale UP, 1980.
– *Easy Pieces*. New York: Columbia UP, 1985.
*– 'Elation in Hegel and Wordsworth.' 1987. *Unremarkable* 182–93.
*– 'Evening Star and Evening Land.' 1972. *The Fate of Reading* 147–78.
– *The Fate of Reading, and Other Essays*. Chicago: U of Chicago P, 1975.
*– 'The Interpreter's Freud.' *Easy Pieces* 137–54.
*– 'The Poetics of Prophecy.' 1981. *Unremarkable* 163–81.
*– 'Retrospect 1971.' *Wordsworth's Poetry* xi–xx.
*– *Saving the Text: Literature/Derrida/Philosophy*. Baltimore: Johns Hopkins UP, 1981.
*– 'A Touching Compulsion: Wordsworth and the Problem of Literary Representation.' *Georgia Review* 31 (1977), 345–61. *Unremarkable* 18–30.
– *The Unmediated Vision: An Interpretation of Wordsworth, Hopkins, Rilke, and Valery*. 1954. New York: Harcourt, 1966.
– *The Unremarkable Wordsworth*. Minneapolis: U of Minnesota P, 1987.
*– 'Wordsworth and Goethe in Literary History.' *The Fate of Reading* 179–200.
*– 'Wordsworth, Inscriptions, and Romantic Nature Poetry.' 1965. *Beyond Formalism* 206–30.
*– *Wordsworth's Poetry, 1787–1814*. 1964. Rpt. with 'Retrospect, 1971.' New Haven: Yale UP, 1971.
*Hartman, Herbert. 'Wordsworth's "Lucy" Poems: Notes and *Marginalia*.' *PMLA* 49 (1934), 134–42.
Hayden, John O. *The Romantic Reviewers, 1802–1824*. Chicago: U of Chicago P, 1969.
Hayden, John O., ed. *William Wordsworth: The Poems*. 2 vols. 1977. New Haven: Yale UP, 1981.
Hazlitt, William. *The Complete Works of William Hazlitt*. Ed. P.P. Howe. London: Dent, 1930–4. Rpt. New York: AMS, 1967.
Heffernan, James A.W. 'Mutilated Autobiography: Wordsworth's *Poems* of 1815.' *Wordsworth Circle* 10 (1979), 107–12.
Heffernan, Thomas F. 'Melville and Wordsworth.' *American Literature* 49 (1977), 338–51.
*Helms, Alan. 'The Sense of Punctuation.' *Yale Review* 69 (1980), 177–96.
Herman, Judith. 'The Poet as Editor: Wordsworth's Edition of 1815.' *Wordsworth Circle* 9 (1978), 82–7.
Highet, Gilbert. *The Anatomy of Satire*. Princeton: Princeton UP, 1962.

Hilles, Frederick W., and Harold Bloom, eds. *From Sensibility to Romanticism: Essays Presented to Frederick A. Pottle*. New York: Oxford UP, 1965.

Hirsch, E.D., Jr. 'Against Theory?' Mitchell, *Against Theory* 48–52.

– *The Aims of Interpretation*. Chicago: U of Chicago P, 1976.

– 'Meaning and Significance Reinterpreted.' *Critical Inquiry* 11 (1984), 202–25.

*– 'Objective Interpretation.' *PMLA* 75 (1960), 463–79. Rpt. *Validity* 209–44.

– *Validity in Interpretation*. New Haven: Yale UP, 1967.

*Hodgson, John A. *Wordsworth's Philosophical Poetry, 1797–1814*. Lincoln: U of Nebraska P, 1980.

Hohendahl, Peter Uwe. *The Institution of Criticism*. Ithaca: Cornell UP, 1982.

*Holland, Norman. 'Literary Interpretation and Three Phases of Psychoanalysis.' *Critical Inquiry* 3 (1976), 221–33.

Hollander, John. *The Figure of Echo: A Mode of Allusion in Milton and After*. Berkeley: U of California P, 1981.

Hoy, David Couzens. *The Critical Circle: Literature, History, and Philosophical Hermeneutics*. Berkeley: University of California, 1978.

*Hudson, Henry N. *Studies in Wordsworth*. Boston: Little, Brown, 1884.

*Hudson, William Henry. *Wordsworth and His Poetry*. London: Harrap, 1914. New York: AMS, 1971.

Hutcheon, Linda. *A Theory of Parody: The Teachings of Twentieth-Century Art Forms*. New York: Methuen, 1985.

*Hutchinson, Thomas, ed. *Wordsworth: Poetical Works*. 1904. Revised Ernest de Selincourt, 1936. New York: Oxford UP, 1978.

Huxley, Aldous. 'Wordsworth in the Tropics.' *Do What You Will: Essays*. London: Chatto and Windus, 1929. 123–39.

Iser, Wolfgang. 'The Reading Process: A Phenomenological Approach.' *The Implied Reader: Patterns of Communication in Prose Fiction from Bunyan to Beckett*. Baltimore: Johns Hopkins UP, 1974. 274–94.

*Jack, Augustus Adolphus. *Poetry and Prose; Being Essays on Modern Poetry*. 1911. Port Washington, NY: Kennikat, 1969.

Jack, Ian. *English Literature 1815–1832*. Oxford History of English Literature. New York: Oxford UP, 1963.

*Jackson, Wallace. *The Probable and the Marvelous: Blake, Wordsworth, and the Eighteenth-Century Critical Tradition*. Athens: U of Georgia P, 1978.

Jacobus, Mary. *Tradition and Experiment in Wordsworth's 'Lyrical Ballads' (1798)*. Oxford: Clarendon, 1976.

Jakobson, Roman. 'What Is Poetry?' 1933–4. *Language in Literature*, ed. Krystyna Pomorska and Stephen Rudy. Cambridge: Harvard/Belknap, 1987. 368–78.

*James, G. Ingli, and Howard Mills. 'Wordsworth's Unknown.' *Anglo-Welsh Review* 15 (1966), 67–76.

Jameson, Fredric. *Marxism and Form: Twentieth-Century Dialectical Theories of Literature*. Princeton: Princeton UP, 1971.

– 'Metacommentary.' 1971. *The Ideologies of Theory: Essays 1971–86.* 2 vols. Minneapolis: U of Minnesota P, 1988. 1:3–16.
– *The Political Unconscious: Narrative as a Socially Symbolic Act.* Ithaca: Cornell UP, 1981.
Jauss, Hans Robert. 'Literary History as a Challenge to Literary Theory.' 1970. *Toward an Aesthetic of Reception.* Trans. Timothy Bahti. Brighton, Sussex: Harvester, 1982. 3–45.
*Jeffrey, Francis. Review of *Poems* by George Crabbe. *Edinburgh Review* 12 (April 1808), 131–51.
Jerrold, Walter, and R.M. Leonard, eds. *A Century of Parody and Imitation.* London: Oxford UP, 1913.
Johnson, Samuel. *The Rambler.* Ed. W.J. Bate and Albrecht B. Strauss. Vol. 4 in *The Yale Edition of the Works of Samuel Johnson.* New Haven: Yale UP, 1969.
*Jones, [Henry] John [Franklin]. *The Egotistical Sublime: A History of Wordsworth's Imagination.* 1954. London: Chatto and Windus, 1960.
Jones, Mark. 'Double Economics: Ambivalence in Wordsworth's Pastoral.' *PMLA* 108 (1993), 1098–1113.
– 'Interpretation in Wordsworth and the Provocation Theory of Romantic Literature.' *Studies in Romanticism* 30 (1991), 565–604.
*– 'Lucy and Her Readers: A History of the Criticism of Wordsworth's "Lucy Poems."' Diss. Columbia University, 1988.
– 'Recuperating Arnold: Romanticism and Modern Projects of Disinterestedness.' *boundary 2* 18:2 (summer 1991), 65–103.
Jordan, John E. *De Quincey to Wordsworth: A Biography of a Relationship, with the Letters of Thomas De Quincey to the Wordsworth Family.* Berkeley: U of California P, 1962.
– *Why the 'Lyrical Ballads'? The Background, Writing, and Character of Wordsworth's 1798 'Lyrical Ballads.'* Berkeley: U of California P, 1976.
*Juhl, P.D. 'The Appeal to the Text: What Are We Appealing To?' *Journal of Aesthetics and Art Criticism* 36/7 (1978), 277–87.
– *Interpretation: An Essay in the Philosophy of Literary Criticism.* Princeton: Princeton UP, 1981.
Jump, John D. *Burlesque.* London: Methuen, 1972.
*Kamuf, Peggy. 'Floating Authorship.' *Diacritics* 16:4 (1986), 3–13.
Kant, Immanuel. *The Critique of Judgement.* 1790. Trans. James Creed Meredith. 1928. Oxford: Clarendon, 1988.
Karrer, Wolfgang. *Parodie, Travestie, Pastiche.* 1977. Trans. in part by Anthony Wall. Clive Thomson 1–33.
Keats, John. *Complete Poems.* Ed. Jack Stillinger. Cambridge: Harvard/Belknap, 1982.
– *The Letters of John Keats.* Ed. H.E. Rollins. 2 vols. Cambridge: Harvard UP, 1958.

Kelliher, Hilton. 'Thomas Wilkinson of Yanwath, Friend of Wordsworth and Coleridge.' *British Library Journal* 8 (1982), 147–67.

Kermode, Frank. *The Art of Telling: Essays on Fiction.* Cambridge: Harvard UP, 1983.

– *Romantic Image.* London: Routledge Kegan Paul, 1957.

*Kingsley, Charles ('Parson Lot'). 'The National Gallery. – No. 1.' In *Politics for the People* (6 and 20 May 1848). Rpt. in *Victorians on Literature and Art.* Ed. Robert L. Peters. New York: Appleton–Century Crofts, 1961. 183–5.

Kitchin, George. *Survey of Burlesque and Parody in English.* London: Oliver and Boyd, 1931.

Klancher, Jon P. *The Making of English Reading Audiences, 1790–1832.* Madison: U of Wisconsin P, 1987.

*Knapp, Steven, and Walter Benn Michaels. 'Against Theory.' 1982. Mitchell, *Against Theory* 11–30.

*Krieger, Murray. *Theory of Criticism: A Tradition and Its System.* Baltimore: Johns Hopkins UP, 1976.

*Kroeber, Karl. *The Artifice of Reality: Poetic Style in Wordsworth, Foscolo, Keats, and Leopardi.* Madison: U of Wisconsin P, 1964.

– *British Romantic Art.* Berkeley: U of California P, 1986.

– 'The Evolution of Literary Study, 1883–1983.' *PMLA* 99 (1984), 326–39.

– 'Narrative and De-Narrativized Art.' *The Romantics and Us: Essays on Literature and Culture.* Ed. Gene W. Ruoff. New Brunswick: Rutgers UP, 1990. 215–36.

– *Romantic Narrative Art.* Madison: U of Wisconsin P, 1960.

*Lamb, Charles, and Mary Anne Lamb. *The Letters of Charles and Mary Anne Lamb.* Ed. Edwin W. Marrs, Jr. 3 vols. Ithaca: Cornell UP, 1975–8.

*Landor, Walter Savage. 'Archdeacon Hare and Landor.' 1853. *The Works and Life of Walter Savage Landor.* London: Chapman and Hall, 1876.Vol. 5.

*Langman, F.H. 'Wordsworth's Patriotism.' *Theoria* 18 (1962), 29–37.

*Lawrence, D.H. 'On Human Destiny.' 1924. *Phoenix II: Uncollected, Unpublished, and Other Prose Works by D.H. Lawrence.* Ed. Warren Roberts et al. New York: Viking, 1959. 623–9.

Leader, Zachary. 'Wordsworth, Revision, and Personal Identity.' *ELH* 60 (1993), 651–83.

*Leavis, F.R. '"Thought" and Emotional Quality.' *Scrutiny* 13 (1945/6), 53–71.

Lentricchia, Frank. *After the New Criticism.* Chicago: U of Chicago P, 1980.

Lentricchia, Frank, and Thomas McLaughlin, eds. *Critical Terms for Literary Study.* Chicago: U of Chicago P, 1990.

*Levin, Susan, and Robert Ready. 'Unpublished Poems from Dorothy Wordsworth's Commonplace Book.' *Wordsworth Circle* 9 (1978), 33–5.

Levinson, Marjorie. *Wordsworth's Great Period Poems: Four Essays.* Cambridge: Cambridge UP, 1986.

Lindenberger, Herbert. *On Wordsworth's Prelude*. Princeton: Princeton UP, 1963.

*Liu, Alan. 'Local Transcendence: Cultural Criticism, Postmodernism, and the Romanticism of Detail.' *Representations* 32 (1990), 75–113.

– *Wordsworth: The Sense of History*. Stanford: Stanford UP, 1989.

Lukács, Georg. 'Art and Objective Truth.' 1954. *Writer and Critic, and Other Essays*. Trans. Arthur D. Kahn. New York: Grosset and Dunlap, 1971. 25–60.

Macdonald, Dwight, ed. *Parodies: An Anthology from Chaucer to Beerbohm – and After*. New York: Random House, 1960.

*McGann, Jerome J. *The Romantic Ideology: A Critical Investigation*. Chicago: U of Chicago P, 1983.

*MacLean, Catherine MacDonald. *Dorothy and William Wordsworth*. London: Cambridge, 1927.

McLuhan, Marshall. *From Cliché to Archetype*, with Wilfred Watson. New York: Viking, 1970.

*Marchant, Robert. *Principles of Wordsworth's Poetry*. Swansea: Brynmill, 1974. See 33–45.

*Margoliouth, H[erschel] M[aurice]. *Wordsworth and Coleridge 1795–1834*. London: Oxford UP, 1953.

*Marshall, Donald G. 'Foreword: Wordsworth and Post-Enlightenment Culture.' Hartman, *Unremarkable* vii–xxix.

Marshall, George. *Tennyson in Parody and Jest: An Essay and Selection*. Lincoln: Tennyson Research Centre, 1975.

Marshall, William H. *Byron, Shelley, Hunt, and 'The Liberal.'* Philadelphia: U of Pennsylvania P, 1960.

Marx, Karl. *Selected Writings in Sociology and Social Philosophy*. Ed. T.B. Bottomore and Maximilien Rubel. 1956. Harmondsworth: Penguin, 1986.

Marx, Karl, and Frederick Engels. *The German Ideology, Part One, with Selections from Parts Two and Three, Together with Marx's 'Introduction to a Critique of Political Economy.'* Ed. C.J. Arthur. New York: International, 1970.

*Matlack, Richard. 'Wordsworth's Lucy Poems in Psychobiographical Context.' *PMLA* 93:1 (Jan. 1978), 46–65.

Maxwell, J.C. 'Wordsworth and the Subjugation of Switzerland.' *MLR* 65 (1970), 16–18.

Mayo, Robert. 'The Contemporaneity of the *Lyrical Ballads*.' *PMLA* 69 (1954), 486–522.

Mellor, Anne K. 'Love, Guilt and Reparation: *The Last Man*.' In *Mary Shelley: Her Life, Her Fiction, Her Monsters*. New York: Routledge, 1988. 141–68.

*Melville, Herman. *Pierre; Or, the Ambiguities*. 1852. Rpt. in one volume with other works, compiled by Harrison Hayford. New York: Library of America, 1984.

Miles, Josephine. *Eras and Modes in English Poetry*. 1957. 2nd ed. Berkeley: U of California P, 1964.

*Miller, J. Hillis. 'Narrative.' Lentricchia and McLaughlin 66–79.
*– 'On Edge: The Crossways of Contemporary Criticism.' *Bulletin of the Academy of Arts and Sciences* 32:2 (Jan. 1979), 13–32. Rpt. Eaves and Fischer 96–111.
*– 'Postscript 1984.' Eaves and Fischer 111–26.
*– 'The Still Heart: Poetic Form in Wordsworth.' *New Literary History* 2 (1971), 297–310. See 307–8.
Millett, Kate. 'The Debate over Women: Ruskin versus Mill.' *Victorian Studies* 14 (1970), 63–82.
Milton, John. *The Complete Poetical Works of John Milton*. Ed. H.C. Beeching. Oxford: Oxford UP, 1921.
– *The Prose of John Milton*. Ed. J. Max Patrick New York: Anchor, 1967.
Mitchell, W.J.T. 'Representation.' Lentricchia and McLaughlin 11–22.
Mitchell, W.J.T., ed. *Against Theory: Literary Studies and the New Pragmatism*. Chicago: U of Chicago P, 1985.
– ed. *The Politics of Interpretation*. Chicago: U of Chicago P, 1983.
Moore, Maxine. 'Melville's Pierre and Wordsworth: Intimations of Immorality.' *New Letters* 39:4 (1973), 89–107.
*Moorhouse, E. Hallam, ed. *Wordsworth*. The Regent Library. London: Herbert and Daniel, 1911.
*Moorman, Mary. *William Wordsworth: A Biography*. 2 vols. London: Oxford UP, 1957–65.
Morley, Edith J. Review of Bateson, *MLR* 50 (1955), 333–5.
Morson, Gary Saul. 'Parody, History, and Metaparody.' 1981. *Rethinking Bakhtin: Extensions and Challenges*. Ed. Gary Saul Morson and Caryl Emerson. Evanston, IL: Northwestern UP, 1989. 63–86.
*Myers, F.W.H. *Wordsworth*. New York: Harper, 1881.
Nalbantian, Suzanne. *The Symbol of the Soul from Hölderlin to Yeats: A Study in Metonymy*. New York: Columbia UP, 1977.
Nealon, Jeffrey T. 'The Discipline of Deconstruction.' *PMLA* 107 (1992), 1266–79.
Nietzsche, Friedrich. *The Will to Power*. Trans. Walter Kaufmann and R.J. Hollingsdale. New York: Vintage, 1968.
Norris, Christopher. *Deconstruction: Theory and Practice*. London: Methuen, 1982.
Nuttall, A.D. *A Common Sky: Philosophy and the Literary Imagination*. Berkeley: U of California P, 1974.
Ohmann, Richard. *English in America: A Radical View of the Profession*. New York: Oxford UP, 1976.
*[Oliphant, Margaret]. 'A Century of Great Poets, from 1750 Downwards. No. III. – William Wordsworth.' *Blackwood's Edinburgh Magazine* 110 (Sept. 1871), 299–326. Attribution from N.S. Bauer, *William*.
*Oliphant, Mrs [Margaret]. *The Literary History of England In the End of the*

Eighteenth and Beginning of the Nineteenth Century. 3 vols. London: Macmillan and Co., 1882.

*Olney, Clarke. 'Lucy Revisited.' *Notes and Queries*, n.s. 5 (Dec. 1958), 539.

Ong, Walter J. *Rhetoric, Romance, and Technology: Studies in the Interaction of Expression and Culture.* Ithaca: Cornell UP, 1971.

*Onorato, Richard J. *The Character of the Poet: Wordsworth in The Prelude.* Princeton: Princeton UP, 1971.

Owen, W.J.B., ed. *Wordsworth's Literary Criticism.* London: Routledge, 1974.

*Pafford, Ward. 'Wordsworth's Art of Poetry.' *Emory University Quarterly* 6 (1950), 172–80.

Pakenham, Thomas. *The Year of Liberty: The Bloody Story of the Great Irish Rebellion of 1798.* 1969. London: Panther, 1972.

*Palgrave, Francis Turner, ed. *The Golden Treasury of the Best Songs and Lyrical Poems in the English Language.* 1861. Rpt. 'Together with One Hundred Additional Poems (To the End of the Nineteenth Century).' London: Oxford UP, 1916.

Palmer, R.R. *The Age of Democratic Revolution.* 2 vols. Princeton: Princeton UP, 1959–64.

– *The World of the French Revolution.* New York: Harper, 1971.

Parrish, Stephen. *The Art of the Lyrical Ballads.* Cambridge: Harvard UP, 1973.

– 'The Editor as Archaeologist.' *Kentucky Review* 4 (1983), 3–14.

– 'The Worst of Wordsworth.' *Wordsworth Circle* 7 (1976), 89–91.

Parrott, E.O., ed. *Imitations of Immortality: A Book of Literary Parodies.* Harmondsworth: Viking, 1986.

*Parson, Frank. 'On Wordsworth's "Lucy."' *People's and Howitt's Journal*, n.s. 1 (Nov. 1849), 292–4.

Pater, Walter. 'Wordsworth.' *Fortnightly Review* 21 (1874), 455–65. In *Appreciations, With an Essay on Style.* 1889. London: Macmillan, 1913. 39–64.

Patterson, Annabel. *Censorship and Interpretation: The Conditions of Writing and Reading in Early Modern England.* Madison: U of Wisconsin P, 1984.

*Payne, Joseph, ed. *Studies in English Poetry, With Short Biographical Sketches and Notes, Intended as a Text-book for the Higher Classes in Schools.* London: Relfe and Fletcher, 1845. 8th ed. London: Crosby Lockwood and Co., 1881. See 109–10.

Peacock, Markham L., Jr. *The Critical Opinions of William Wordsworth.* 1950. New York: Octagon, 1969.

*Pennington, Walter. 'The "Lucy" Poems.' *Modern Language Notes* 41 (1926), 314–16.

Percy, Thomas, ed. *Reliques of Ancient English Poetry: Consisting of Old Heroic Ballads, Songs, and Other Pieces of our Earlier Poets; Together with Some Few of Later Date.* 1765. Ed. J.V. Prichard. 2 vols. New York: Crowell and Co., n.d.

Perkins, David. *Is Literary History Possible?* Baltimore: Johns Hopkins UP, 1992.

*– *Wordsworth and the Poetry of Sincerity.* Cambridge: Harvard UP, 1964.

Perkins, David, ed. *Theoretical Issues in Literary History.* Harvard English Studies 16. Cambridge: Harvard UP, 1991.

*Perry, John Oliver, ed. *Approaches to the Poem: Modern Essays in the Analysis and Interpretation of Poetry.* San Francisco: Chandler, 1965.

*Phelan, James. *Worlds from Words: A Theory of Language in Fiction.* Chicago: U of Chicago P, 1981.

*Pipkin, James W. 'The Lucy Poems and Wordsworth's Dream Vision.' *Ariel* 8:4 (1977), 27–41.

Poe, Edgar Allan. *Essays and Reviews.* Selected by G. R. Thompson. New York: Library of America, 1984.

Poirier, Richard. 'The Politics of Self-Parody.' *Partisan Review* 35 (1968), 339–53.

Pope, Alexander. *Poetical Works.* Ed. Herbert Davis. Oxford: Oxford UP, 1978.

*Potts, Abbie Findlay. *The Elegiac Mode: Poetic Form in Wordsworth and Other Elegists.* Ithaca: Cornell UP, 1967.

*– *Wordsworth's Prelude: A Study of Its Literary Form.* 1953. New York: Octagon, 1966.

*Powell, Thomas ('Pierce Pungent'). 'Literary Characters. – No. III. Mr. Wordsworth.' *Fraser's Magazine* 3 (June 1831), 557–66. Attribution from N.S. Bauer, *William.*

*Praz, Mario. *The Hero in Eclipse in Victorian Fiction.* Trans. Angus Davidson. London: Oxford UP, 1956.

*Price, John. 'Wordsworth's *Lucy.*' *American Imago* 31 (1974), 360–77.

*Quiller-Couch, Sir Arthur, ed. *Oxford Book of English Verse.* Oxford: Clarendon, 1939.

*– *Studies in Literature,* 3rd series. Cambridge: Cambridge, 1929.

Rajan, Tilottama. *The Supplement of Reading: Figures of Understanding in Romantic Theory and Practice.* Ithaca: Cornell UP, 1990.

*– 'The Web of Human Things: Narrative and Identity in *Alastor.*' *The New Shelley: Later Twentieth-Century Views.* Ed. G. Kim Blank. London: Macmillan, 1991. 85–107.

*Raleigh, Walter. *Wordsworth.* London: Edward Arnold, 1903.

*Rea, J.D. 'Hartley Coleridge and Wordsworth's Lucy.' *Studies in Philology* 28 (1931), 118–35.

*Read, Herbert. *Wordsworth.* The Clark Lectures, 1929–1930. 1930. London: Faber, 1968.

Reed, Mark L. *Wordsworth: The Chronology of the Early Years, 1770–1799.* Cambridge: Harvard UP, 1967.

– *Wordsworth: The Chronology of the Middle Years, 1800–1815.* Cambridge: Harvard UP, 1975.

*Regueiro, Helen. *The Limits of Imagination: Wordsworth, Yeats, and Stevens.* Ithaca: Cornell UP, 1976.

*Reiman, Donald. 'The Poetry of Familiarity: Wordsworth, Dorothy, and Mary Hutchinson.' *The Evidence of the Imagination: Studies of Interactions between Life and Art in English Romantic Literature.* Ed. Reiman et al. New York: New York UP, 1978. 142–77.

Reiman, Donald, compiler. *The Romantics Reviewed: Contemporary Reviews of British Romantic Writers, Part A: The Lake Poets.* 2 vols., continuously paginated. New York: Garland, 1972.

Richards, I.A. *Practical Criticism.* 1929. New York: Harcourt, n.d.

– *Principles of Literary Criticism.* 1925. New York: Harcourt, n.d.

Ricks, Christopher. *The Force of Poetry.* Oxford: Clarendon, 1984.

Rickword, Edgell, ed. *Radical Squibs and Loyal Ripostes: Satirical Pamphlets of the Regency Period, 1819–1821.* London: Adams and Dart, 1971.

*Riding, Laura, and Robert Graves. *A Pamphlet against Anthologies.* Garden City, NY: Doubleday, 1928.

Riewald, J.G. 'Parody as Criticism.' *Neophilologus* 50:1 (1966), 125–48.

Riffaterre, Michael. 'Describing Poetic Structures: Two Approaches to Baudelaire's "Les Chats." ' 1966. Tompkins 26–40.

– 'Interpretation and Descriptive Poetry: A Reading of Wordsworth's "Yew Trees." ' *NLH* 4 (1973), 229–56.

– 'Intertextual Representation: On Mimesis as Interpretive Discourse.' *CI* 11 (1984), 141–62.

– *Semiotics of Poetry.* Bloomington: Indiana UP, 1978.

Roberts, Charles G.D. 'Wordsworth's Poetry.' 1892. *Selected Poetry and Critical Prose,* ed. W.J. Keith. Toronto: U of Toronto P, 1974. 271–5.

*Robertson, Eric. *Wordsworthshire: Wordsworth and the English Lake Country: An Introduction to a Poet's Country.* New York: Appleton, 1911.

*Robinson, Henry Crabb. *Henry Crabb Robinson on Books and Their Writers* Ed. Edith J. Morley. 2 vols. London: Dent, 1938.

*Rollins, Hyder Edward, ed. *The Keats Circle: Letters and Papers 1816–1878.* 2 vols. Cambridge: Harvard UP, 1948.

Rose, Margaret. 'Defining Parody.' *Southern Review* [Adelaide] 13 (1980), 5–20.

– *Parody: Ancient, Modern, and Post-Modern.* Cambridge: Cambridge UP, 1993.

Rosenthal, M.L., and Sally Gall. *The Modern Poetic Sequence.* New York: Oxford UP, 1982.

Rosmarin, Adena. *The Power of Genre.* Minneapolis: U of Minnesota P, 1985.

Ross, Donald, Jr. 'Poems Bound "Each to Each" in the 1815 Edition of Wordsworth.' *Wordsworth Circle* 12 (1981), 133–40.

*Rossiter, A.P. *Angel with Horns and Other Shakespeare Lectures.* New York: Theatre Arts, 1961.

Rousseau, Jean-Jacques. 'Essay on the Origin of Languages, which treats of Melody and Musical Imitation.' c. 1755. *On the Origin of Language: Two Essays.* Trans. John H. Moran and Alexander Gode. 1966. Chicago: U of Chicago P, 1986.

*Rowley, James. 'Wordsworth' [Lectures given 1889]. In *Wordsworth and Other Essays*. Bristol: J.W. Arrowsmith, 1927.

*Ruoff, Gene. 'Another New Poem by Wordsworth.' *Essays in Criticism* 16 (1966), 359–60. Reply to Sykes Davies.

– 'Critical Implications of Wordsworth's 1815 Categorization, with Some Animadversions on Binaristic Commentary.' *Wordsworth Circle* 9 (1978), 75–82.

– ' "Fields of Sheep": The Obscurities of the Ode.' *TWC* 12 (1981), 45–51.

– 'Wordsworth's Categorization and Arrangement of His Shorter Poems.' Diss. University of Wisconsin, 1970.

*Ruskin, John. 'Lecture II. – Lilies: Of Queens' Gardens.' In *Sesame and Lilies: Two Lectures Delivered at Manchester in 1864: 1. Of Kings' Treasuries, 2. of Queens' Gardens*. 1865. New York: Dutton, 1909.

Ryskamp, Charles. 'Wordsworth's *Lyrical Ballads* in Their Time.' Hilles and Bloom 357–72.

Said, Edward. 'Opponents, Audiences, Constituencies, and Community.' Mitchell, *Politics* 7–32.

Saintsbury, George. *A History of English Criticism, being the English Chapters of A History of Criticism and Literary Taste in Europe*. 1900–4. New York: Dodd, Mead, 1911.

*Schapiro, Barbara A. *The Romantic Mother: Narcissistic Patterns in Romantic Poetry*. Baltimore: Johns Hopkins UP, 1983.

Schelling, Friedrich Wilhelm von. 'On the Relation of the Plastic Arts to Nature.' Trans. J.E. Cabot. *The German Classics of the Nineteenth and Twentieth Centuries*. 20 vols. New York: German Publications Society, 1913. 5:106–36.

Schlegel, Friedrich. *Dialogue on Poetry and Literary Aphorisms*. Trans. Ernst Behler and Roman Struc. University Park: Pennsylvania State UP, 1968.

Schleiermacher, Friedrich D.E. 'Introduction' to the *Compendium of 1819*. Trans. J. Duke and J. Forstman. *The Hermeneutics Reader*. Ed. Kurt Mueller-Vollmer. New York: Continuum, 1988. 72–97.

Scoggins, James. *Imagination and Fancy: Complementary Modes in the Poetry of Wordsworth*. Lincoln: U of Nebraska P, 1966.

*Sethna, K.D. 'Sri Aurobindo and a Famous Wordsworth Lyric.' *Mother India* 10 (Aug. 1958), 26–41.

Shaftesbury, Anthony, Earl of. *Characteristics of Men, Manners, Opinions, Times*. 1711. Ed. John M. Robertson. 2 vols. in 1. Indianapolis: Bobbs-Merrill, 1964.

Shakespeare, William. *The Complete Works*. General ed. Alfred Harbage. Rev. ed. Baltimore: Penguin, 1969.

Shelley, Mary. *The Last Man*. 1826. Ed. Hugh J. Luke, Jr. 1965. London: Hogarth, 1985.

Shelley, Percy Bysshe. *Shelley's Poetry and Prose*. Ed. Donald H. Reiman and Sharon B. Powers. New York: Norton, 1977.

Shlonsky, Tuvia. 'Literary Parody: Remarks on Its Method and Function.' *Proceedings of the IVth Congress of the International Comparative Literature Association*. The Hague: Mouton, 1966. 2:797–801.
Simpson, David. *Irony and Authority in Romantic Poetry*. London: Macmillan, 1979.
– 'Public Virtues, Private Vices: Reading between the Lines of Wordsworth's "Anecdote for Fathers."' *Subject to History: Ideology, Class, Gender*. Ed. Simpson. Ithaca: Cornell UP, 1991.
– *Wordsworth and the Figurings of the Real*. Atlantic Highlands, NJ: Humanities Press, 1982.
– *Wordsworth's Historical Imagination*. London: Methuen, 1987.
Simpson, Percy. *Shakespearian Punctuation*. Oxford: Clarendon, 1911.
Siskin, Clifford. *The Historicity of Romantic Discourse*. New York: Oxford UP, 1988.
Smith, Barbara Herrnstein. *Poetic Closure: A Study of How Poems End*. Chicago: U of Chicago P, 1969.
Smith, Horace, and James Smith. *Rejected Addresses; Or, The New Theatrum Poetarum*. 1812. Jerrold and Leonard 1–80, 393–9.
Smith, Olivia. *The Politics of Language, 1791–1819*. Oxford: Clarendon, 1984.
Snyder, Robert Lance. 'Apocalypse and Indeterminacy in Mary Shelley's *The Last Man*.' *Studies in Romanticism* 17 (1978), 435–52.
Sonstroem, David. 'Millett versus Ruskin: A Defense of Ruskin's "Of Queens' Gardens."' *Victorian Studies* 20 (1976), 283–97.
Sontag, Susan. *A Susan Sontag Reader*. New York: Vintage Books, 1982.
Speirs, John. *Poetry towards Novel*. London: Faber, 1971.
Spivak, Gayatri Chakravorty. 'Displacement and the Discourse of Women.' *Displacement: Derrida and After*. Ed. Mark Krupnick. Bloomington: Indiana UP, 1987. 169–95.
Stein, Edwin. *Wordsworth's Art of Allusion*. University Park: Pennsylvania State UP, 1988.
*Steiner, George. *In Bluebeard's Castle: Some Notes toward the Redefinition of Culture*. New Haven: Yale UP, 1971.
– *Language and Silence: Essays on Language, Literature and the Inhuman*. 1970. New York: Atheneum, 1977.
S[tephen], J[ames] K[enneth]. *Lapsus Calami*. New ed. Cambridge: Macmillan, 1891.
Stevens, Wallace. *The Collected Poems*. New York: Knopf, 1961.
*Stevenson, Warren. 'Cosmic Irony in Wordsworth's 'A Slumber Did My Spirit Seal.' *TWC* 7 (1976), 92–4.
Stillinger, Jack. *Multiple Authorship and the Myth of Solitary Genius*. New York: Oxford UP, 1991.
Stoddard, Eve Walsh. 'The Spots of Time: Wordsworth's Semiology of the Self.' *Romanticism Past and Present* 9:2 (1985), 1–24.

*Stoddart, John. Review of *Lyrical Ballads*. *British Critic* 17 (Feb. 1801), 130–31. *RR* 134.

Stone, Lawrence. 'Literacy and Education in England, 1640–1900.' *Past and Present* 42 (1969), 69–139.

*Storch, R.F. 'Another New Poem by Wordsworth.' *Essays in Criticism* 15 (1965), 473–4. Reply to Sykes Davies.

Strout, Alan Lang. 'John Wilson, "Champion" of Wordsworth.' *MP* 31 (1934), 383–94.

– 'William Wordsworth and John Wilson: A Review of Their Relations between 1802 and 1817.' *PMLA* 49 (1934), 143–83.

*Stuart, Simon. *New Phoenix Wings: Reparation in Literature*. London: Routledge, 1979.

*Sutherland, James Middleton. *William Wordsworth: The Story of His Life, with Critical Remarks on His Writings*. London: Elliot Stock, 1887.

*Swinburne, Algernon Charles. 'Wordsworth and Byron.' *Nineteenth Century* 15 (1884), 583–609, 764–90. See 776.

*Swingle, L.J. 'On Reading Romantic Poetry.' *PMLA* 86 (1971), 974–81.

*Sykes Davies, Hugh. See Davies, Hugh Sykes.

*Symington, Andrew James. *William Wordsworth: A Biographical Sketch, with Selections*. 2 vols. London: Blackie, 1881.

*Taaffe, James G. 'Poet and Lover in Wordsworth's 'Lucy' Poems.' *Modern Language Review* 61 (1966), 175–9.

*Takahashi, Yasunari. 'Who Is Lucy? – On the Structure of the Wordsworthian Imagination.' *English Criticism in Japan*. Ed. Earl R. Miner. Tokyo: U of Tokyo P, 1972. 170–86.

*Tandon, B.G. 'Imagery in Wordsworth's Lucy Poems.' *Studies in Nineteenth Century Literature, 5th Series*. Ed. James Hogg. Salzburg: Institut für Anglistik und Amerikanistik, 1982. 23–34.

Tanselle, G. Thomas. 'The Editorial Problem of Final Authorial Intention.' *Studies in Bibliography* 29 (1976), 167–229. Rpt. *Selected Studies in Bibliography*. Charlottesville: U of Virginia P, 1979. 309–353.

Teich, Nathaniel. 'Evaluating Wordsworth's Revolution: Romantic Reviewers and Changing Taste.' *Papers on Language and Literature* 11 (1975), 206–23.

Thomson, Clive, ed. *Essays on Parody*. Monographs of the Toronto Semiotic Circle. Toronto: Victoria UP, 1986.

*Thomson, Douglass H. 'Wordsworth's Lucy of "Nutting."' *Studies in Romanticism* 18 (1979), 287–98.

Thompson, E.P. *The Making of the English Working Class*. 1963. Harmondsworth: Pelican, 1986.

Thorpe, James. 'The Aesthetics of Textual Criticism.' 1965. *Bibliography and Textual Criticism, English and American Literature, 1700 to the Present*. Ed. O M Brack, Jr, and Warner Barnes. Chicago: U of Chicago P, 1969. 102–38.

Tompkins, Jane P., ed. *Reader-Response Criticism: From Formalism to Post-Structuralism*. Baltimore: Johns Hopkins UP, 1980.

Trilling, Lionel. *The Liberal Imagination: Essays on Literature and Society*. New York: Anchor, 1953.

Trotsky, Leon. 'The Formalist School of Poetry and Marxism.' 1924. *Literature and Revolution*. Trans. Rose Strunsky. Ann Arbor: U of Michigan P, 1971. 162–83.

Voloshinov, V.N. *Marxism and the Philosophy of Language*. 1929. Trans. Ladislav Matejka and I.R. Titunik. Cambridge: Harvard UP, 1986.

Wall, Anthony. 'Parody without Markers: Baudelaire's *Le Mauvais Vitrier*.' Clive Thomson 60–75.

Wasserman, Earl. 'The English Romantics: The Grounds of Knowledge.' *Studies in Romanticism* 4 (1964), 17–34.

*Watson, J.R. 'Lucy and the Earth-Mother.' *Essays in Criticism* 27 (1977), 187–202.

*Webb, W.T., ed. *Selections from Wordsworth*. London: Macmillan, 1897.

Weimann, Robert. *Structure and Society in Literary History: Studies in the History and Theory of Historical Criticism*. 1976. Expanded ed. Baltimore: Johns Hopkins UP, 1984.

Wellek, René. *A History of Modern Criticism, 1750–1950*. 7 vols. New Haven: Yale UP, 1955–91.

– *The Attack on Literature, and Other Essays*. Chapel Hill: U of North Carolina P, 1982.

Wellek, René, and Austin Warren. *Theory of Literature*. 1942. 3rd ed. New York: Harcourt, 1977.

Wells, Carolyn, ed. *A Parody Anthology*. 1904. New York: Dover, 1967.

*Wheeler, Ethel. 'Great Men's Visions of Womanhood: Wordsworth's Vision.' *Great Thoughts* (London), 4th series, 1 (22 Jan. 1898), 270.

White, W. Hale. *A Description of the Wordsworth and Coleridge Manuscripts in the Possession of Mr T. Norton Longman*. London: Longmans, 1897.

*Whitford, Robert C. 'Another Lucy.' *Journal of English and Germanic Philology* 18 (1919), 369–71.

– 'On the Origin of *Probationary Odes for the Laureateship*.' *MLN* 35 (1920), 81–4.

Will, George F. 'Literary Politics.' *Newsweek*, 22 April 1991, p. 72.

Williams, Raymond. 'Base and Superstructure in Marxist Cultural Theory.' *Problems in Materialism and Culture*. London: Verso, 1980. 31–49.

*Wilson, John. *Critical and Miscellaneous Essays. By Christopher North (Professor Wilson.)* 3 vols. Philadelphia: Carey and Hart, 1842.

– 'Letter Occasioned by N.'s Vindication of Mr Wordsworth in Last Number.' *Blackwood's Edinburgh Magazine* 2 (Nov. 1817), 201–4.

– 'Observations on Mr Wordsworth's Letter Relative to a New Edition of Burns' Works.' *Blackwood's Edinburgh Magazine* 1 (June 1817), 261–6. Rpt. *RR* 56–61.

– 'Vindication of Mr Wordsworth's Letter to Mr Gray, on a New Edition of Burns.' *Blackwood's Edinburgh Magazine* 2 (Oct. 1817), 65–73.

Wimsatt, W.K., Jr. *The Verbal Icon*. Lexington: U of Kentucky P, 1954.
Wimsatt, W.K., Jr, and Monroe C. Beardsley. 'The Intentional Fallacy.' *Sewanee Review* 54 (1946), 468–88. Wimsatt 3–18.
*Winchester, C.T. *William Wordsworth: How to Know Him*. Indianapolis: Bobbs-Merrill, 1916.
Wolfson, Susan. 'Keats's *Isabella* and the "Digressions" of "Romance."' *Criticism* 27 (1985), 247–61.
– *The Questioning Presence: Wordsworth, Keats, and the Interrogative Mode in Romantic Poetry*. Ithaca: Cornell UP, 1986.
*Woodberry, George Edward. 'Wordsworth.' In *The Torch: Eight Lectures on Race Power in Literature Delivered Before the Lowell Institute of Boston MCMIII*. 1905. Freeport, NY: Books for Libraries, 1969. 174–6.
Woodring, Carl. *Politics in English Romantic Poetry*. Cambridge: Harvard UP, 1970.
*– *Wordsworth*. 2nd ed. Cambridge: Harvard UP, 1968.
Wordsworth, Dorothy. *Journals of Dorothy Wordsworth*. 2nd ed. Ed. Mary Moorman. London: Oxford UP, 1971.
Wordsworth, John. *The Letters of John Wordsworth*. Ed. Carl H. Ketcham. Ithaca: Cornell UP, 1969.
Wordsworth, Jonathan. *The Music of Humanity: A Critical Study of Wordsworth's 'Ruined Cottage.'* New York: Harper, 1969.
*– 'A New Poem by Wordsworth?' *Essays in Criticism* 16 (1966), 122-3.
Wordsworth, William. *The Fourteen-Book Prelude*. Ed. W.J.B. Owen. Ithaca: Cornell UP, 1985.
– *The Poetical Works of William Wordsworth*. Ed. Ernest de Selincourt and Helen Darbishire. 5 vols. Oxford: Clarendon, 1940–9. Revised ed. 1952–9.
– *The Prelude 1799, 1805, 1850*. Ed. Jonathan Wordsworth, M.H. Abrams, and Stephen Gill. New York: Norton, 1979.
– *The Prose Works of William Wordsworth*. Ed. W.J.B. Owen and Jane Worthington Smyser. 3 vols. Oxford: Clarendon, 1974.
– *The Salisbury Plain Poems of William Wordsworth*. Ed. Stephen Gill. Ithaca: Cornell UP, 1975.
– *Shorter Poems, 1807–1820*. Ed. Carl H. Ketcham. Ithaca: Cornell UP, 1989.
*Wordsworth, William and Dorothy. *The Letters of William and Dorothy Wordsworth*. 2nd ed., rev. by Chester Shaver et al. 7 vols. Oxford: Clarendon, 1967–88.
*Wright, John. *The Genius of Wordsworth Harmonized with the Wisdom and Integrity of his Reviewers*. London: Longman's, 1853.
*– *Poetry, Sacred and Profane*. London: Longman's, 1851.
Zaranka, William, ed. *The Brand-X Anthology of Poetry*. Cambridge: Applewood, 1981.

Index